AF505703

IN/SECURITY IN COLOMBIA

Manchester University Press

New Approaches to
Conflict Analysis

Series editor: Peter Lawler, Senior Lecturer in International Relations, Department of Government, University of Manchester

Until recently, the study of conflict and conflict resolution remained comparatively immune to broad developments in social and political theory. When the changing nature and locus of large-scale conflict in the post-Cold War era is also taken into account, the case for a reconsideration of the fundamentals of conflict analysis and conflict resolution becomes all the more stark.

New Approaches to Conflict Analysis promotes the development of new theoretical insights and their application to concrete cases of large-scale conflict, broadly defined. The series intends not to ignore established approaches to conflict analysis and conflict resolution, but to contribute to the reconstruction of the field through a dialogue between orthodoxy and its contemporary critics. Equally, the series reflects the contemporary porosity of intellectual borderlines rather than simply perpetuating rigid boundaries around the study of conflict and peace. *New Approaches to Conflict Analysis* seeks to uphold the normative commitment of the field's founders yet also recognises that the moral impulse to research is properly part of its subject matter. To these ends, the series is comprised of the highest quality work of scholars drawn from throughout the international academic community, and from a wide range of disciplines within the social sciences.

PUBLISHED

Christine Agius
*Neutrality, sovereignty and identity:
the social construction of
Swedish neutrality*

Eşref Aksu
*The United Nations, intra-state
peacekeeping and normative change*

M. Anne Brown
*Human rights and the borders of
suffering: the promotion of human rights
in international politics*

Anthony Burke and Matt McDonald (eds)
Critical security in the Asia-Pacific

Lorraine Elliott and Grame Cheeseman (eds)
*Forces for good:
Cosmopolitan militaries
in the twenty-first century*

Greg Fry and Tarcisius Kabutaulaka (eds)
*Intervention and state-building
in the Pacific: the legitimacy
of 'cooperative intervention'*

Richard Jackson
*Writing the war on terrorism:
language, politics
and counter-terrorism*

Tami Amanda Jacoby and Brent Sasley (eds)
Redefining security in the Middle East

Jan Koehler and Christoph Zürcher (eds)
Potentials of disorder

David Bruce MacDonald
*Balkan holocausts?
Serbian and Croatian victim-centred
propaganda and the war in Yugoslavia*

Adrian Millar
*Socio-ideological fantasy and the
Northern Ireland conflict: the other side*

Jennifer Milliken
The social construction of the Korean War

Ami Pedahzur
*The Israeli response to Jewish
extremism and violence:
defending democracy*

Maria Stern
*Naming insecurity – constructing identity:
'Mayan-women' in Guatemala
on the eve of 'peace'*

Virginia Tilley
*The one state solution: a breakthrough
for peace in the Israeli–Palestinian deadlock*

In/security in Colombia

Writing political identities
in the Democratic Security Policy

JOSEFINA ECHAVARRIA A.

Manchester University Press

MANCHESTER AND NEW YORK

distributed exclusively in the USA
by Palgrave

Copyright © Josefina Echavarria A. 2010

The right of Josefina Echavarria A. to be identified as the author of this work has been asserted by her in accordance with the Copyright, Designs and Patents Act 1988.

Published by Manchester University Press
Oxford Road, Manchester M13 9NR, UK
and Room 400, 175 Fifth Avenue, New York, NY 10010, USA
www.manchesteruniversitypress.co.uk

Distributed exclusively in the USA by
Palgrave Macmillan, 175 Fifth Avenue, New York,
NY 10010, USA

Distributed exclusively in Canada by
UBC Press, University of British Columbia, 2029 West Mall,
Vancouver, BC, Canada V6T 1Z2

British Library Cataloguing-in-Publication Data
A catalogue record for this book is available from the British Library

Library of Congress Cataloging-in-Publication Data applied for

ISBN   978 0 7190 7985 6   *hardback*

First published 2010

The publisher has no responsibility for the persistance or accuracy of URLs for any external or third-party internet websites referred to in this book, and does not guarantee that any content on such websites is, or will remain, accurate or appropriate.

Typeset in the UK
by Helen Skelton, Brighton
Printed in the UK
by the MPG Books Group

For Norbert

Contents

Preface

This book offers a political reading of how the in/security discourse of the Colombian government, named the Democratic Security Policy (DSP), *does* the identities of 'state', 'nationals' and 'others'. I investigate how, by naming the danger of narco-terrorism as posing a vital threat to the 'state' and 'its people', the DSP creates ideal identity categories. Subjects are hailed as constituents of these categories via multiple practices that summon them to occupy the positions of a 'strong sovereign state', 'good nationals united in the front against narco-terrorism' and 'terrorists', respectively. This book examines the Colombian case study by referring to critical security insights that ask 'unauthorised questions' (Dillon, 1996) about the violence prompted when ambiguous, fluid and changing identities are forced to fit neat pictures of seemingly coherent and unproblematic referent objects and subjects of in/security discourses (Stern, 2005).

Following Stuart Hall (1996a), I understand the process of identification as an imperfect articulation, which requires that subjects perform their identities. Looking for different ways in which disparate subjects reinforce, contest or resist the logic of in/security, I analyse the responses and provocations that are expressed in the discourses of the guerrillas known as the FARC-EP, the nonviolent plan of the Province of Antioquia and the nonviolent movement of the indigenous group Paeces del Cauca. My intention is to underscore the multiple ways in which 'others', the 'state' itself and 'nationals' react to, reinforce or contest the logic of in/security that the DSP inscribes. By looking at these diverse responses, I intend to underscore how the grammars of harm of discourses on safety/danger (Stern, 2005) can be reproduced or disrupted in marginal settings.

My contention is that by producing fixed, coherent and 'secure' identities, state and non-state political violence is legitimised. In the name of in/security, spaces and times for 'many peaces' (Dietrich and Sützl, 2006) and politics are closed down, since encountering and connecting with 'others' can bring about unknown possibilities for becoming something/somebody different from the fixed subjects of the DSP. In this way, I attempt to show that the writing of in/security implies the writing of peace and war and attendant notions of identity. Ultimately, writing in/security is about political imaginaries (Campbell, 1998).

The concrete forms in which these concepts and practices inform each other in the Colombian conflict offer insights into the often-violent relations that render the pursuit of both peace and security so very problematic. Hence, in the last section, I venture into presenting a collection of international relations (IR), politics and peace studies readings that embrace the impossibility of 'securing' subjectivities by accepting fragility and vulnerability. These readings call for the opening of possibilities for becoming, rather than being (Hall, 1996a), and for recognising uncertainty as fundamental to experiencing more peaceful ways of relating to each other. In short, this final section considers calls for imagining otherwise (Butler, 2004).

The fact that Alvaro Uribe, the 'brains' of the DSP in power since 2002, gained the highest number of votes in the history of Colombia when running for (irregular) re-election in 2006, can only be understood if one approaches the in/security promise as a governmental discourse. The DSP informs people's identities, their fears, their loves and their ways of conceptualising themselves and relating to each other. Once the DSP postulates are built-in to the daily behaviour of citizens and shape their imaginings about peace and war, the oppressive and repressive violence of the state is no longer indispensable. 'We' have become our most feared security forces.

There is no war front, nor is there a home front. This is a war waged everywhere – from shopping malls to telecommunications – and everyone is suspect. This in/security discourse tells 'us' who and where 'we are' by telling us 'who we are not' (Walker, 1993; Campbell, 1998). In order not to be labelled 'terrorist' or 'terrorist-sympathiser', 'we' have to constantly monitor 'ourselves', for the membership in the 'good nation' requires permanent and visible reconfirmation. Consequently, who 'the others' are becomes a blurred concept. According to the government, 'we' can recognise 'them' because they do not 'act in solidarity' with the security effort. 'They' are critics of state policies, dissenters from joining the 'army of good people', those who do not place their affiliation to the nation over any other political and personal affinity 'they' might have. The 'others' are among 'us'. 'I' might even be 'one of them'.

While I view this research project on the DSP as a product of critical security and peace studies and not as my own personal life story, this project did, of course, also give rise to personal reflection and – at the same time – shape me. This research emerged from a sense of disturbing puzzlement: the fact that in the name of 'democratic security' we (all good Colombians) have to fight in the 'army of good people' against the 'narco-terrorist threat'. The state draws on 'us' to kill and die in the name of security, to close ranks against 'them' and to inform public and private security forces about 'any suspicious person', meaning anyone who does not behave in a depoliticised way. We have become the eyes and ears of the military.

In May 2002, when I learned that the elected government in Colombia promised 'security' by erecting a state based on the principle of authority and waging a united war against terrorism, I was at a loss. I thought we had always been in and at war. As far back as I could remember, there has been war in Colombia. I was born and raised in Medellín, frequently classified as the most violent city in the world. While I attended high school during the decade of the 1990s, a 'war against drugs and terrorism' had been declared by the state against the drug cartels. Systematic violence was exercised by state and non-state forces, paramilitary groups were created, the practice of kidnapping became a commonly used method of warfare and targeted killings of political figures were complemented by indiscriminate attacks against the population.

The first massacre I remember took place a few blocks from my house. It was the last weekend of June 1990. The gang 'Security and Control' entered a bar called Oporto around midnight and killed nineteen members of a party of young people. A few of the victims studied at my school. I was thirteen years old. I incorporated certain codes of behaviour in order to live in a 'country in war', such as not joining large concentrations of people at concerts, soccer games or shopping malls. However, the recommended measures to be taken in order to 'be safe' became impossible to follow. The war made it as dangerous to stay at home as to go to the supermarket or to school. With the passing of years, I witnessed and experienced violence.

Although this visible, personal and direct violence shaped me profoundly, my study and professional choices were marked more by concerns with structural and cultural violence (Galtung, 1996). By being aware that I belonged to the economically privileged in an unequal country and world, I became closely involved with human rights issues while studying international relations. In my first job, I worked with development projects that aimed at 'modernising' the systems of potable water and sanitation in urban and rural areas of Colombia. Soon I realised that my 'intentions' to 'develop' the less fortunate (i.e. peoples and communities who were poor, with little or no formal education and who were mostly non-white), were actually doing more harm than good. Their knowledge, ways of living and worldviews clearly contradicted the 'modernisation' programmes I was running for the World Bank and the UNDP. Crudely put, under the 'standards' set by these institutions, they were 'underdeveloped' and, therefore, in need of 'fixing' (Gronemeyer, 1992). Thus, in the name of 'development and modernisation', they were 'fixed', their ways of living marginalised and their knowledge subjugated. Many instances of my 'development aid' experience made me realise the epistemic violence of idealism.

I found myself disbelieving and disappointed, and, paradoxically, decided to enrol in a Master's degree in peace and development studies in Spain. Due to a cooperation agreement, I graduated from the University of Innsbruck (Austria) and later earned a PhD in the field. I was fortunate to be in a critical academic environment, where I had the chance to meet people from around the world who were eager to encounter and to learn with and from difference. Crucially, they were more interested in asking questions than in finding answers. Both students and professors were like a breath of fresh air that shocked my well-grounded beliefs. In our conversations, I came to understand that they regarded violence as 'extra-ordinary'. Certainly, for many of them, violence was not uncommon, but it was not an accepted way of being, relating to others or living. These insights have been reinforced during the last six years while teaching peace, security and Latin American studies at different times and in different places, mainly in Austria.

My experiences in Austria have been highly rewarding and, at the same time, troubling. On the one hand, I have had the opportunity to reread the meanings of my childhood, the professional and personal journeys I have made in different fields, and I have had the time and space to teach and to undertake research. I have also encountered my life partner (in the widest sense of this expression) and some of the most loving and caring human beings who play crucial roles in my life. Most of them are Austrians, a powerful label that haunts me permanently because – although I can 'integrate' – the notion of *ius sanguinis* nationality deters me from becoming 'one of them'. I have experienced the difficulties of being a foreigner in a country whose legal and political system does not want foreigners to come, and, if already here, does its best to make them leave. Strict immigration laws are some of the salient expressions of a larger process of nation-building that can be recognised in multiple cultural, political and economic arrangements.

In these different moments and circumstances, I have positioned (and still do position) myself differently. While living in Colombia and during my visits, I am aware of the socio-economic privilege I embody and experience being a member of a large and loving family. In repeated academic activities, I am regarded as a 'third-world woman', which is a burdensome combination made of two powerful yet indefinable labels. These labels allow me to 'speak with authority' (Roof and Wiegman, 1995) of and about Latin American issues, while, at other times, I am a foreigner living in a territory that does not want me. On the phone, I am a daughter, a sister, and a friend. I am a lover. I am a professor. I am also Colombian.

All these different and often contradictory locations change in their prioritisation, sometimes instantly, depending upon the setting. Certainly, not all these senses of belonging and affiliations can be rearranged with the same facility. There are some that I have come to feel, think of and embody as more entrenched than others. However, I could draw a list of almost endless positions where 'I am' and do occupy, and it could never fully account for 'myself'. No matter how long this list might be, it could never represent 'who' and 'where' I am, or who I have been or might become (Edkins and Pin-Fat, 1999). These and many more markers and locations make up my 'identity constellation' (Stern, 2005).

When naming the danger of narco-terrorism as vital for the survival of state and nationals, national identity is called to become the overriding category. It should determine political (in)actions, behaviour and interests, it should take precedence over any other identity affiliation and affinity one can have, whether loves (Dillon, 1996) or fears (Campbell, 1998). This national identity feature should dominate the whole spectrum of identity constellation and reduce it to a 'knowable' and 'certain' being: Colombian. Likewise, by naming danger, the in/security discourse informs practices that regulate the population's circulation and connection (Dillon, 2005). It should make us soldiers of the nation, undifferentiated bodies who make up a sacrificial mass in a war fought for the highest value of in/security. It so seeks to define 'who' and 'where' one is and who one might become.

This in/security discourse and the practices it informs are precisely what I attempt to address in this book. The writing of this particular war makes peace appear to be the result of security, absorbing any possible alternative meaning of it by making peace synonymous with the absence of war and the presence of a promised security. Yet, I believe that peace cannot be known in advance. I conceive of peace in the plural, and, like politics and subjectivities, it includes open-ended and uncertain possibilities that can only acquire a concrete shape within a particular context. Thus, as I elaborate further in the text, I also hope that this particular reading of the DSP contributes to discussions about possible ways to rethink peaces and political imaginaries that question violence, and, in so doing, reduce harm and suffering.

This exercise of 'self-reflexivity' (Ackerly et al., 2006) sheds some light on the intersubjective grain of this book, and on how my own self as researcher is in a dynamic relationship to the case study presented in this work. Moreover, in this same line of making the implicit explicit and reflecting upon it, I also consider it important to point to the context in which this work was produced. I wrote the original text in 2006 as my dissertation at the programme in Peace, Conflict and Democracy at the Universitat Jaumé I in Castelló, Spain. This book is the direct result of my doctoral research.

Most of the chapters that make up this book were written before or shortly after the thesis. Each in turn has been substantially altered to become part of this book. The second chapter is in part informed by my earlier article 'Rethinking (in)security from a critical perspective' in *Asteriskos Journal of International and Peace Studies* (volume 1/2, 2006, 61–82). Early drafts of Chapters 3 and 4 were presented at the International Studies Association (ISA) conference in Chicago (2007) and at A-Cost 24 'The Social Construction of Threats' meetings at the International Peace Research Institute in Oslo (PRIO, 2006) and Tallinn University (2007). The fourth and fifth chapters were carefully revised after presenting a paper at the 'Peace Building and Trauma Recovery' Conference at the Conflict Resolution Institute, University of Denver, in February 2007. I thank the organisers of those events for inviting me to present my work, as well as the participants for their comments and questions.

When revising the manuscript for publication two years later, I tried to make it accessible to a wider readership; however, the traces of 'a dissertation' are still present. These traces unravel a particular way of academic argumentation characterised by detailed accounts of theoretical contributions and reading of a large base of empirical material. In both spaces there has been substantial development in recent years, and I have integrated some of the most relevant and pertinent happenings into the book.

This book could well be described as a *work in progress*. Throughout the process of researching and writing, I have been transformed. I hope I can make myself as clear as possible while still being true to my efforts of embarking on a journey, in the best academic sense of the word.

Acknowledgements

Throughout the process of researching and writing this book, I have been fortunate to count on supportive and helpful individuals and institutions. Firstly, I sincerely thank my doctoral advisers, Vicent Martínez and Sonia París at the Universitat Jaumé I in Castelló, Spain. They patiently read the initial manuscript of the dissertation, provided me with insightful feedback, and gave me their time and energy, which were invaluable in shaping the original thesis.

The team of European doctorate advisers, consisting of Peter Waldmann from the University of Augsburg (Germany), Maria Stern from Gothenburg University (Sweden) and Wolfgang Dietrich at the University of Innsbruck (Austria), was also of immense help and support. Since I met Peter Waldmann in 2002, I continue to find constant new insights in his writings. His readiness to answer my questions has been accompanied by a generous sharing of his profound knowledge of Colombia. Maria Stern has gone beyond any formal expectation of mentoring. She listened patiently to my very first ideas concerning this research, and guided and supported my passion for in/security and identity issues. Later on, Maria read the dissertation text and commented in such detail that her notes have contributed immensely to improving the typescript for this book. Her writings on in/security and identity are spread throughout this text.

Wolfgang Dietrich deserves my sincerest thanks. He has supported me over the years and has accompanied me on such manifold academic and personal journeys that I can only name his contributions incompletely. His insightful perceptions on what is at stake when thinking, imagining and experiencing peaces continue to challenge me in every possible way. Wolfgang's extensive knowledge and curiosity keep making me question anew what I take for granted. His gestures of confidence and trust in my abilities, together with a good sense of humour and kindness, have been a wonderful stroke of luck in my life. His outstanding dedication to research and his enthusiasm for teaching and didactical skills continue to guide me as examples of excellence.

Although not officially on the list of academic advisers, Martina Kaller-Dietrich's sage advice has also been priceless. She has been present at difficult stages of writing this book, offering me great support and invaluable insights in those moments when I needed inspiration. Martina's own commitment to systematic and exigent methodological considerations, combined with loving and sharp critique, has continuously challenged and encouraged me. Her trust in my abilities and her constant backing has allowed me to take on risky teaching and research projects. Through such experiences, I have had the opportunity to be theoretically imaginative both inside and outside the classroom.

In the past few years, I have had the opportunity to present different theses contained in this book to students and colleagues. At the University of Vienna and at the Latin American Institute, the students of the MA in Latin American Studies were my first sounding board for many of the ideas contained in this book. My teaching partner and co-coordinator during the winter term 2006, Wolfgang Sützl, was an excellent colleague and source of inspiration for thinking about the philosophical and political implications of cultural practices of in/security. I benefited enormously from our conversations. Furthermore, the students' questions in the course on 'Security Policies in Latin America' made me explain in more concrete and explicit ways my own assumptions about the topics of in/security and identity in Colombia, clarifying several aspects that were crucial to making this a better text. In the same vein, the students at the MA in Peace, Conflict and Development at the Universitat Jaumé I, who attended my course on 'Identity, Security and Possibilities for Peace', gave me fresh ideas for thinking about the issues dealt with in this book. At the UNESCO Chair for Peace Studies and MA Program for Peace Studies at the University of Innsbruck, where I have been working since 2007, I have found in the students and faculty a large pool of inspiration, good resonance and enthusiasm for continued work on these topics. My sincere thanks go to Daniela Ingruber, whose kindness and intelligence never cease to amaze me.

I am also grateful to the team at Manchester University Press for their work in preparing the manuscript for publication. I am especially thankful to the Series Editor, Peter Lawler, who kindly encouraged me to pursue this book project. Luis Lobo-Guerrero was the first reviewer of the text and his helpful feedback and recommendations were crucial to improving the manuscript. I also thank an anonymous reviewer for incisive advice when I was revising this book. Lastly, I am very grateful to Anthony Mason, Commissioning Editor, for his trust in this project and readiness to answer my many queries.

To all of you, my sincerest thanks.

There is an additional source of inspiration for this book that cannot be classified under any traditional heading of 'acknowledgements'. Throughout difficult moments of doing this research and during the process of writing and revising this text, I have found in a particular story both sadness and strength. It is the true story of the kidnapping and later assassination of the three brothers Luis Guillermo, Camilo and Oscar Restrepo Mejía. Their bodies were found in a common grave two months after 'demobilised' paramilitary groups in Valle kidnapped and tortured them in January 2005. This crime has not been investigated and their sister and close family friend, Luz María, still tries to come to terms with her loss. Their story has encouraged me to believe that writing about in/security and identity in Colombia is worthwhile. I want this book to help others to remember you.

This book is also the result of the support of a beautiful group of loving friends and family members. They have believed in me throughout the years and guided me in moments of disorientation, accompanied by more *mudanzas* than I care to recall. To my mom, my dad and Vira, my sister, and her family, Anny, my family-in-law, and my friends in Colombia and spread all over the globe, but always close to my heart and mind, to all of you, thank you very much.

I dedicate this book to my life partner, Norbert Koppensteiner, thanks to whom I started, pursued and finished this project. Nobs, thanks so much for putting things in perspective, for your words of encouragement, and for your unconditional support, invaluable insights and opportune cups of coffee. You have given me all these things and so many more, and they have made me think differently and have informed this book.

List of abbreviations

ACIN	Association of Indigenous Councils of Northern Cauca (Asociación de Cabildos del Norte del Cauca)
AFP	Associated France Press
AI	Amnesty International
ANUC	National Association of Peasant Smallholders (Asociación Nacional Usarios Campesinos)
AUC	United Self-defence Groups of Colombia (Autodefensas Unidas de Colombia)
CIA	Central Intelligence Agency
DEA	United States Drug Enforcement Administration
DMZ	Demilitarized Zone
DSP	Democratic Security Policy
ELN	National Liberation Army (Ejército de Liberación Nacional)
EPL	Popular Liberation Army (Ejército Popular de Liberación)
EU	European Union
FARC-EP	Revolutionary Armed Forces of Colombia – People's Army (Fuerzas Armadas Revolucionarias de Colombia – Ejército del Pueblo)
FTO	Foreign Terrorist Organizations
GEOS	Psychological Operations Special Group (Grupo Especial de Operaciones Sicológicas)
IHL	International Humanitarian Law
IR	International Relations
ICRC	International Committee of the Red Cross
MIQL	Indigenous Movement Quintín Lame (Movimiento Indigenista Quintín Lame)
NGO	Non-Governmental Organisation
OAS	Organisation of American States

ONIC	National Indigenous Council of Colombia (Organización Nacional Indígena de Colombia)
PCP	Congruent Peace Plan (Plan Congruente de Paz)
PPR	Peace and Reconciliation Programme: model of intervention for returning to legality (Programa de Paz y Reconciliación: modelo de intervención de regreso a la legalidad)
PRT	Revolutionary Worker's Party (Partido Revolucionario de los Trabajadores)
TMO	Theatres of Military Operations
UN	United Nations
UNDP	United Nations Development Program
US	United States of America

List of tables

xx

Introduction

I**N FEBRARY** 2005, eight people were killed in a massacre in the peace community of San José de Apartadó (Urabá). The victims included a two-year-old boy whose head was bashed in with a cudgel. Even though the Inter-American Court of Human Rights had previously obliged the state to implement special protective measures in this community, the government did not react. It did not even issue a declaration condemning the massacre afterwards (Yarce, 2005a: 8A). Three weeks later, President Uribe responded by saying that the peace experiment in San José had to end. According to Uribe, the community was defying state sovereignty and the state had the right to exercise its military power in the whole of the national territory. Thus, the army was to be sent in for the first time in eight years to recover the authority of the state (Yarce, 2005b: 10A).

For decades, San José de Apartadó has suffered violence from different armed actors, including guerrillas, paramilitaries and the army. In March 1997, after an intense political discussion, more than five hundred people decided to create a neutral territory in which none of the armed groups, including the army, would be allowed to enter or receive any collaboration. They decided to constitute an actively neutral territory for peace, where their lives and personal integrity would be respected. The peace community had been born. Regardless of attacks by armed groups, it had been able to keep up civil resistance activities that had been awarded several international peace prizes (Yarce, 2005a: 8A). Besides advocating a nonviolent position towards the war, the community had established an alternative development programme for the region as well as a self-government model in which disputes were regulated internally. Amnesty International, Peace Brigades International, the Fellowship of Reconciliation and the Inter-American Commission on Human Rights, among other international institutions, have supported and encouraged the community's activities (Yarce 2005a, 2005b).

This recognised experience of nonviolent resistance and communitarian organisation presented a challenge for President Uribe. According to his point of view, the people of San José did not have the right to reject the armed forces. He accused some of the leaders, supporters and sponsors of the community of helping the FARC-EP and of protecting this terrorist organisation (Gómez and Vélez, 2005: 2D). The leaders of the community explained to the president that they had never rejected the state, that for years they had been asking for the presence of doctors, infrastructure engineers and of a representative of the attorney general without a positive response. This is corroborated by the fact that despite more than 160 murders committed since 1997, there has been little investigation and only two suspects have been arrested (Rodríguez, 2005). Likewise, the community warned the president that the armed forces had been involved in the February massacre and that their renewed presence would put the community in danger again. In this case, they would be forced to leave their houses and to seek refuge in other territories (Yarce, 2005c: 10A).

By the time the armed forces entered the town centre of San José de Apartadó, only ten families remained there. The military transported more than two thousand people in buses to the urban centre and orchestrated an amusement show with clowns for the children. After the circus ended, the people were driven back to their rural homes in the army buses. At dawn, the town was left almost entirely empty, except for the ten families who stayed. The rest of the population had fled to other municipalities and to a newly constructed communitarian centre called *La Holandita*, located in the rural area resembling a bunker that the community thought might protect it from possible attacks (Mogollón, 2005: 6A).

Multiple questions emerge from the occurrences in San José. First, why did the government claim that a peace community that asked for a non-military state presence was defying state sovereignty? Why are the inhabitants of the peace community not valid political subjects? Why do they lack the authority to hold political conversations about the situation with state representatives? Why is the dissent of this community stigmatised by the state as collaboration with terrorists? Why is a peace community on the list of security threats to the nation-state? What possibilities for expressing dissent are being foreclosed when the government sends in troops to a neutral peace community after pointing at its leaders as collaborators with terrorist organisations? Who is being silenced with this action? Which options are being silenced with this action? Why is the ability to criticise war banned from the public sphere?

The peace community argued that their neutral territory for peace ought to be respected by the army, yet this possibility of living differently, of excluding themselves from armed confrontations, exceeded the limits of what the government understood to be its sovereign right to occupy the national territory. At the same time, sending troops to the peace community, after its leaders had explicitly stated that the army was directly involved in the massacres, excluded from public discussions their dissent and debate of state policies. Furthermore, by branding the critics as terrorist-sympathisers and terrorist-collaborators, the state destroyed their personal credibility and censored their participation in the public sphere (Butler, 2004).

Critics are thus silenced by the sending of troops. They then no longer speak up or voice their dissent, in part because of the fear of being branded as terrorists. In this way, the state produces the limits of what can and cannot be spoken, who counts as a viable political subject and who does not, and thus determines what is a reasonable opinion in the public domain (ibid.: xix).

Guiding questions

The particular case of San José in February 2005 allows entrance into the discussion of the Colombian case from the critical security and peace studies perspective offered in this book: political identities and imaginaries being shaped by a state security discourse that underwrites the meaning of peace. My main concern in writing this book has been the violent spiral of war that is created by the security programme of the Colombian state, which produces and reproduces the very violence it promises to halt. My thesis is that the state security discourse contributes to shaping political identities in such a way that the writing of war is intermingled with the writing of peace, ultimately involving the moulding of political imaginaries in Colombia. Such imaginaries are written according to security concerns, legitimising state and non-state violent actions that propel the very political violence the state promises to eliminate. The state in/security discourse produces – it does not prevent – more violence.

Since the launching of the US-led global war on terror, the prolonged violent conflict in Colombia, which now has persisted for over five decades, has gained global attention as an example of the pervasiveness of globalised terrorism as well as of the danger of 'failed states'. In addition to serving as a vaguely defined example of the evils of terrorism, the situation of violence has been analysed from several perspectives that define it in multiple ways: armed groups struggling to take over power, a democratic nation-state under the threat of narco-terrorism, and a low intensity armed conflict are amongst the most common interpretations. Perhaps most famously, Mary Kaldor's use of Colombia as a quintessential 'new war' has gained widespread appeal among both policy elites and academics.

Most of these security discussions take place in limited circles of security experts who, in turn, design national security policies analysed and studied by (an even more limited number of) students and professionals of international relations. These kinds of debates are generally located in a group of professionals who take for granted what security is about, what the state is and what needs to be secured. The list of threats might change, but not the modes of exclusion and its rationale (Campbell, 1998). They are discussions on texts and policies that take place among like-minded people who have already agreed upon the fundamental grounds that inform their conversations. Hugh Gusterson (1999: 236) points to how these discourse communities enforce agreement or conformity by thriving on debate and controversy in the so-called incitement to discourse. This incitement channels criticisms and disagreements into frameworks that unthinkingly reproduce the obvious and self-evident categories that make disagreement possible. Therefore, the questions that arise and the answers normally derived from these discussions are not directed toward the founding grounds of security, but rather towards its modes of (re)production (Dillon, 1996).

Consequently, thus far, political analysts and academics, as well as politicians, have not considered the role that security policies play in the continuation and legitimation of state and non-state violence, nor have they paid attention to what security practices do to identity in the Colombian context. This book offers this much-needed perspective. This research interrogates the self-evident goodness of security. It is directed at rethinking the way the problems are posed in the first term. It is a way not of asking what has to be secured to secure security. Instead, I ask what has to be foreclosed, expelled from the public sphere, erased and taken for granted to offer the promise of security (ibid,). This is the reason why the term 'security' appears as 'in/security' throughout the text.

Michael Dillon's work on *The Politics of Security* precisely points to the agonal relationship between security and insecurity: because we can never think security without insecurity, both terms contour each other (ibid.: 120). Contrary to the conventional mode in which security and insecurity are portrayed in official accounts, they are not opposites, but rather are two terms that dynamically define one another. Any discourse about security necessitates insecurity, dangers, the uncanny, the strange and the unknown. Without insecurity, there is no security. Hence, insecurity is security's very possibility for existence. Furthermore, when any security discourse names the dangers that 'threaten us' (Campbell, 1998), it in turn also proscribes, sanctions and propels actions and measures to secure whichever object or subject is said to be at risk (Dillon, 1996: 121). Therefore, any discourse on security is, at the same time, a discourse of insecurity. The term 'in/security' thus precisely aims to make visible the inherent contradiction that the word bears within itself.

My focus of attention is the Democratic Security Policy (DSP), officially launched in 2003[1] with the promise of recovering state authority, of bringing back security to all Colombians waiting for the birth of peace. I present this case study on the DSP as an example of how security discourses constitute political identities. I claim that the current Colombian security policy delimits politics, the political, and the conditions of possibility for identity formation. This research shows that the promise of in/security written into the DSP ultimately feeds the violence it pledges to halt.

Because the DSP aims to control the political and physical lives of the population, its primary state aim has been disseminated among members of society in such a way that 'everybody's responsibility' is to achieve security. The DSP is an in/security discourse that makes complementary the *dispositif* of biopolitical and geopolitical security (Dillon, 2007). The effects of the DSP have extended beyond conventional warfare strategies to combat narco-terrorism and have entered the political realm of institutional and informal politics, washing away dissent, debate and criticism of violence and state policies. This has been achieved, in part, by producing subject categories for a new type of 'good Colombian'.

In this war against terror, 'good Colombians' are part of the army of 'good people' who fight the 'terrorists'. Citizens offer the transparency of their apolitical ways of life (Vattimo, 1992) to the government and the army, share their data and communicate constantly among themselves through networks of informants. Those in rural areas and from lower socio-economic classes are sent to the barricades to bolster the national army. As is common, the poorer sacrifice their lives for the continuation of the nation. The realm of state actions performed in the name of national security is enlarged and so the state enjoys less public scrutiny (Jabri, 2006). Its actions are sheltered in secrecy under the label 'security issues' (Wæver, 1995), and democratic debate about state actions is suspended. Society turns transparent and the government more opaque (Vattimo, 1992).

Any discourse draws boundaries around it and excommunicates certain statements, which turn into subjugated knowledge (Gusterson, 1999: 326). What is foreclosed and excluded from the political realm by the DSP comprises alternative, uncertain and possibly peaceful interpretations of 'us' in the world, thereby excluding other ways of relating to society by making those interpretations seem unreasonable or threatening (Jackson, 2005: 18). In this sense, I suggest thinking about in/security discourses from an angle that questions their primary and basic foundations and that is committed to introducing ethical concerns about their consequences for peaceful relations within and among communities.

From the particular perspective offered in this book, *security* – and especially the conception of a *secure peace* as the idea of securing populations, places and spaces – can be twisted (*verwunden*) toward reconciling insecurity and peace. Some authors have ventured into the risky enterprise of twisting security and peace away from certain grounds and opening possibilities for constantly reconstituting the subject as possibly free (Dietrich, 2006; Dillon, 1996; Connolly, 1991). I underline the notion of possibility here because possibilities are an open window for resignification. Although every individual and collective subject is positioned differently along hierarchical axes of identity categories, and therefore enjoys more or less authority to speak and act (Roof and Wiegman, 1995), there is no way in which the reaction of the subject to a particular discursive provocation can be known in advance (Butler, 1999; Dillon, 1996).

In other words, peace needs insecurity. Peace needs uncertainty, and it requires not knowing in advance what an encounter with 'others' might produce (Arendt, 1998; Haraway, 1991). This requires first an encounter, meaning a space and place to connect, that can bring about risky situations and perhaps instances, experiences and moments of peace. To rethink peace as *insecure* entails deepening our awareness of human fragility and vulnerability and opening public and private spaces for the expression of political dissent in the face of official (and/or hegemonic) state security policies (Martínez, 2001a). In this direction, peace ought to be contextual. It cannot be exported or reproduced (Dietrich, 2006; Dietrich and Sützl, 2006) because it only takes place in 'present moments' of intersubjective encounters (Stern, D., 2004). This implies that possibilities to resist the logic of in/security without reproducing its same rationale of exclusion, marginalisation and violence (Stern, 2005) necessitate spaces and places for democratic negotiations (Connolly, 1991) where the possibility for 'insecure peace' arises (Martínez, 2001a).

Following this call for insecure peace, I focus on how the DSP is brought to life by the government and how it informs state and non-state actions, establishing the foundations that authorise certain subjects and their ways of interacting politically, and, at the same time, de-authorises others. My primary concern is the violence generated and legitimised by the identity categories that the DSP constructs for the state itself, 'nationals' and 'others' which, just like all identity categories, are not 'merely descriptive, but always normative, and as such, exclusionary' (Butler, 1995a: 50).

Hence, at the heart of this particular interrogation about the state in/security discourse in Colombia, the question of identity is paramount. The way threats are recognised, labelled as such, and represented in discourse, and their consequences for the very ways in which politics and the political are enacted, has been well researched in IR and security studies (Campbell, 1998; Dillon, 1996; Edkins, 2003; Stern, 2005; Walker, 1993). These different studies underline how naming threats and dangers is a specific sort of boundary-producing performance, as David Campbell (1998) argues, since, by naming what to fear, security discourses construct one's problems and dangers, contributing to the representations of the 'other'. Following William Connolly (1991: 64), any identity can only be recognised by what it is not, through difference. Henceforth, the 'other' becomes a key element of what the 'self' is, and, more importantly for the purposes of this book, of what the 'self' might become. As a result, simultaneously, by telling 'us' what 'we are not' (Campbell, 1998), such 'other' coconstitutes the contours of the 'self' (Said, 2003a).

The critique of the DSP here offered is directed at drawing attention to the kinds of assumptions and unchallenged ways of thinking upon which our accepted security practices rest. As David Campbell (1998: 191) notes in recalling the words of Michel Foucault, criticism is an exercise in which the obvious and self-evident is no longer treated as such. To criticise leads us to making the seemingly simple more difficult, problematising and questioning our own sedimented beliefs. The present book questions that security signifies a state or a process that is 'right, good and beautiful' (Wæver, 1995; 2004). On the contrary, this examination is driven by the distrust in the balm that legitimises the violence security brings about for freezing possibilities of becoming subjects that exceed the fixed positions informed by security concerns.

By exploring the resistance discourses of the FARC-EP guerrillas, the peace programme of the Province of Antioquia and the indigenous group Paeces del Cauca, this book also reflects discourses that have been provoked by the state security policy. This last move shows how the constitution of political identities, as they are written in the Colombian security policy, is a much-negotiated process in which the very definition of peace and security is contested.

In sum, this book offers a contribution to the discussion on identity and security by using these theoretical questions as lenses to read the concrete security landscape in Colombia. Concerning the particular case study of the DSP, I survey a large empirical base of security discourses in order to read how the writing of security implies attendant notions of identity and, ultimately, political imaginaries that shape the ways in which peace is talked, thought about, lived and experienced.

I approached this investigation by first contextualising the DSP, and by asking which type of armed conflict has been taking place in Colombia. The official definition of violence, as a narco-terrorist war between a democratically elected government and its 'good' people fighting against 'evil terrorists', enables the qualification of this confrontation within the larger framework of the global war against terror. The latter is understood as a large enterprise waged by 'liberal regimes' against an enemy who has no citizens or nation to defend, which implies that those engaged in waging war (the so-called liberal regimes) 'have now committed to a war without end, temporally, spatially, and politically' (Reid, 2006: 3). The official definition of the war in Colombia as another stage of the global war on terror allows the government to disregard any political claim that potentially endangers 'Colombia' as a terrorist threat.

By looking at how the threats named, mainly narco-terrorism, pose a vital danger to the continuation of the imagined political national community (Anderson, 1991), I pursue how the danger of narco-terrorism contributes to the creation of attributes of both 'self' and 'other'. This particular danger has become a marker that allows distinguishing 'us' from 'them' as a bridge that separates 'us'. By telling 'us' what *we are not* (dangerous terrorists), the DSP also draws on which type of people *we are* (law-abiding citizens who actively collaborate with the security forces). Yet, just like the project of state security, the constitution of 'us' as 'good nationals' is also never-ending, it is a constant undertaking that needs to be acted upon again and again. One has to prove one's belonging constantly. It is not enough to have participated in the war effort once. This is a never-ending battle and therefore calls for never-ending security duties from 'the good ones'.

In order to develop this thesis as coherently as possible, this book first identifies the discursive formations that the DSP creates for political categories: 'state', 'nationals' and 'others'. In this section, I look for the ways in which these subjects are represented, how they ought to be recognised, which interests inform their behaviours and the ways in which they interact with one another. Since the DSP is a state security discourse that mobilises manifold resources, from political and symbolic imaginaries to large amounts of money, arms and bodies, the ideal categories devised in the DSP have clear material effects in the form of specific state and non-state actions. Among these, we find the creation of peasant soldiers' battalions, the establishment of large networks of informants and the demobilisation of former paramilitary groups. This materiality hails subjects into place; it summons people to adopt the necessary gestures and expressions that allow distinguishing 'who belongs' or does not belong to the 'good nationals'.

Furthermore, identity seems to be a constant process of negotiation of several (and often contradictory) subject positions that defy a perfectly articulated subject (Edkins and Pin-Fat, 1999; Hall, 1996a; Stern, 2005). In a permanent negotiation, the subject never finds a proper fit into the ideal categories of identity she is supposed to occupy. Whether the issue is nationality, gender, class or ethnicity, the subject strives for an impossible completion and full representation of herself in the identity pictures depicted in discourse (Stern, 2005). Nonetheless, subjectivity seems to spill over, there is always too much or too little (Edkins and Pin-Fat, 1999). Thus the process of identification becomes an imperfect articulation between, on the one hand, the discourses that speak (to) 'us' and, on the other, the investment or resistance of the subject to occupy the positions designed for her in discourse (Hall, 1996a; Stern, 2005).

This imperfection or improper fit does not only comprise the failed attempts of the subject to fit in, but is also the result of the very provocations that discourses on security/identity produce (Edkins and Pin-Fat, 2004). Each discourse creates its own resistance and provocations. Some resistance can be channelled into perfecting even more the lacunae present in the text (co-option), while other types of resistance can take the form of a resignification of the identity category in question. Furthermore, such provocations can also be branded as dangers to the very identity categories constructed, and are, henceforth, subject to rationalisation, exclusion and normalisation (Butler, 1999; Campbell, 1998).

According to this line of thinking, the mere production of identity categories does not necessarily imply that the subjects in question enact such constructions without hesitation. Therefore, it becomes necessary to explore some responses that contest the official definitions of their subjectivities. The resistance discourses of the FARC-EP guerrillas, the nonviolent programme of the Province of Antioquia and the discourse of the indigenous group Paeces del Cauca offer a spectrum of diverse and contradictory reactions to the DSP. Though this interrogation cannot provide a complete picture of the process of identification borne out of the DSP, it sheds some light on the workings that legitimise sacrificing lives and political liberties in Colombia today for a promise of a bright and secure future when the terrorist threat is mastered.

As I argue in further sections, however, security has to continue being a future promise that remains unfulfilled. Only because security is promised in the future, the present holds such a powerful political capital for sacrificing political voices of dissent. If the promise of security were fulfilled, the state would lose its main political ground of legitimation, that of promising security to its citizens, and would wither away (Campbell, 1998). Therefore, in order to exist, the state depends upon its own production of dangers. The state requires insecurity that keeps citizens in awe, as Thomas Hobbes (1651) prescribed in his *Leviathan*. Only by inciting fear of the 'other within and among us', upon its subjects, can the government rule.

In the face of such an impossibility of achieving security, a call is made for the acceptance of uncertainty, insecurity, vulnerability and fragility. Only by recognising that it is precisely insecurity and uncertainty which make us free, to paraphrase Hannah Arendt (Arendt, 1998; Dillon, 1996), can I imagine a way of becoming insecure, of dealing with differences without attempting to turn 'them' into 'one of us' (Dietrich and Sützl, 2006), without exercising violence to counterbalance violence. Accepting the impossibility to know in advance 'who' 'we' might become allows 'us' too to be something different than 'nationals' who fulfil their security duties, who shut up in the face of violence and conform to security measures that legitimise violence against the traces of the strangers in 'us' and try to erase the traces of our connectedness to 'others'. In short, I argue that opening up the possibilities to become something/somebody different necessarily implies living insecurely and, hopefully, it implies enjoying the possibility for imagining political options that stop the political violence that the DSP reinforces.

Methodological considerations

The very domains of this research inform its methodological approach. As mentioned earlier, this work is a critique of the assumptions upon which the DSP rests, and it questions the different identity categories that this discourse constructs and produces to reproduce more political violence. This idea is the beginning of the methodological question, which necessarily involved 'an act of delimitation by which something is cut out of a great mass of material, separated from the mass, and made to stand for, as well as be, a starting point, a beginning' (Said, 2003a: 16). In this case, the particular beginning is the DSP as a problematic group of state discourses that have given rise to the present analysis on security and its effects on the process of identification.

I understand discourses as more than mere linguistic formations, for they do have material effects. They mobilise resources, structure power relations, inform state and non-state actions and have powerful effects on politics and the life of the citizenry (Weldes et al., 1999). The underlying idea is that discourses are not just ways of describing 'reality as it is', but that discourses are ways in which we make meaning, which help us to make sense of and to interpret reality in prescriptive and normative manners (Butler, 1995a). Because one of the main aims of this thesis is to bring into question the DSP as a discursive construction that describes and prescribes the Colombian society as a 'nation' divided between 'good' and 'terrorists/bad' citizens, I analyse this text as a particular construction of the world.

My principal methodology has been first to contextualise discourses, positioning them in specific political and social circumstances. Since the DSP is a state discourse, I have focused on delineating the context in which the Colombian state has transformed its subjectivity since the decade of the 1970s, precisely through its own discourses on danger. For this contextualisation, I use a great number of sources from national and international academic and governmental perspectives about the representation of the Colombian conflict (Angarita, 2001; Bejarano et al., 1997; Comisión de Estudios sobre la Violencia, 1995; Deas and Gaitán, 1995; IEPRI, 2006; Nasi and Rettberg, 2005, 2006; Piazza, 2008; Pizarro, 1990, 1991; Rangel, 2005; Uribe de H. and López, 2006). Authors like Mary Kaldor (1999), Paul Collier (2000, 2001), Alvaro Camacho (2002), Maria Teresa Uribe (2001, 2004), Elsa Blair (1999, 2005), Liliana Franco (2002), Eric Lair (2003, 2005) and William Ramírez (2002) are among the most renowned political academicians whose works have influenced the contemporary scholarly discussion on the Colombian armed conflict.

Also of high relevance is the representation of the conflict according to different governmental definitions. The research conducted by Jaime Nieto and Luis Robledo (2001) presents an impressive compilation of the state treatment of the internal armed conflict since the 1970s. In the same vein, the official documents of the Colombian government are directly consulted (DSP, 2003; Uribe, 2002d, 2004a, 2005a). Likewise, I research diverse official sources on the governmental positions in regards to the Colombian conflict, such as those of the European Union (EU, 2002, 2007) and the United States government (Rice, 2005; US Department of State, 2004, 2005). The representations of leading human rights organisations are also taken into account, such as the United Nations Development Program (UNDP, 2003), Amnesty International (AI 2002a, 2005) and the International Committee of the Red Cross (Arboleda, 2005).

The influence of the security discourse on the construction of identity categories is analysed jointly with the DSP, for both the subjectivities of the state and the citizenry emerge in an intertwined manner. Security discourses are then, first, set in context and analysed as they simultaneously produce, reproduce and transform identity categories. The theoretical framework, which informs this analysis of the intimate relationship between security and identity, is the result of bibliographical research on critical security. The work of a leading international relations researcher, Barry Buzan (1991), offers a clear and concise perspective of security discourses as they have been drawn in IR. The conceptual voids left by mainstream security studies are confronted by critical perspectives mainly espoused by a group of scholars from different academic fields who problematise neo-realist accounts of the world and question the natural essence of state sovereignty.

For the close relationship between individual and state subjectivity, the work of R. B. J. Walker (1993, 1999) and Jenny Edkins and Véronique Pin-Fat (1999) delineates the framework for analysis. These authors point to the mutually constructed character of modern state and free individual in Western thought. Edward Said (2003a, 2003b), Jutta Weldes, Mark Laffey, Hugh Gusterson and Raymond Duvall (Weldes et al., 1999) grasp the importance of discourses and the cultural modes of representation. They highlight how each mode of representation entails the legitimation of a set of political arrangements (while rendering others unfeasible) and is always embedded in a matrix of power relations.

Security discourses make use of certain images, tropes and argumentations, which constitute the state with deliberate interests. 'Us' and 'them' are thus addressed in specific forms producing these identity categories. For the drawing out of these identities, I mainly refer to Judith Butler's (1993, 1995a, 1995b, 1999) insights on performativity and to those works which are also based on this approach, such as David Campbell's (1998, 1999) and Stuart Hall's (1996a, 1996b). These make possible the analysis of security discourses as an ensemble of relationships that works to include and exclude certain features of the citizenry. It is present in institutions, like the Congress and the army, and is translated into governmental actions, such as laws and the treatment of the citizenry. Similarly, Paul Chilton (1996) provides an in-depth analysis of the metaphors used by Thomas Hobbes (1651) in terms of conceptualising *state and man*, which I merge with the writings of Michael Dillon (1996). Dillon, concerning the effects that security has on politics, capitalises on Hannah Arendt's (1998) impressive elaboration of the value of a contingent political life.

Considering the discursive formation of identification, I suggest focusing on connecting the DSP with the identity categories it creates by asking the following questions: How is the subjectivity of the state, its interests and character, created in the DSP? How does the DSP depict the sovereign people, the nation? What is the mode of representation that the DSP produces in terms of the Colombian situation? In other words, what does Colombia look like according to the DSP? What types of issues are securitised and who is said to be endangering the nation? How does the state articulate itself regarding the protection of the citizenry from the dangers it names?

Furthermore, according to the representations of danger, which are the ideal types of identity categories that the DSP constructs for 'us' and for 'them'? Within the DSP discursive realms, which other interpretations of the conflict situation are foreclosed, not considered or seem unintelligible? What has to be suppressed politically to make the call for in/security binding? How is the promise of in/security articulated and what and who is sacrificed for this promise?

To comprehend how dominant and resistance discourses relate to each other, I have resorted to examining the insights of several authors. Mainly, the fourth chapter is informed by Jenny Edkins and Véronique Pin-Fat's (2004) writings, as well as by Judith Butler's (1995a, 1995b). They elaborate on this subject using Michel Foucault's proposals on power and resistance. Their inputs are interconnected with the works of peace researchers like Vicent Martínez (2001a, 2001b, 2002, 2005), Wolfgang Dietrich (2006, 2008) and Maria Stern (1998, 2004, 2005). Other authors shed light on the paradoxical character of discourses that try to contest the logic of in/security. Among them, we find the texts of Ana María Alonso (1992), Diana Saco (1999), Karena Shaw (2004) and R. B. J. Walker (2004). I have made this collection in order to draw an interpretative grid for the analysis of resistance discourses from the particular peace studies perspective offered in this book.

Consequently, when asking how some subjects have resisted the DSP, I analyse whom and what is identified in resistance discourses as sources of danger or insecurity. This implies reading theoretical insights about the Colombian case by asking the following questions: What do these denominations of dangers tell about the political identity of 'self' and 'other'? How do resistance discourses articulate the collective identities of 'self' through the inscription of foreignness? How do resistance discourses deal with fear? What alternative means and ends do they elaborate to contest the logic of in/security? How far away are their means from the ends they portray? Which concepts of peace and security do they name?

The analysis of resistance discourses to the DSP is carried out in the fifth chapter by carefully reading these discourses as emanating from situated, particular and contextual circumstances. Bearing in mind the contextualisation of the national situation studied in the first chapter, with all its multiplicity and varied representations, each resistance discourse is introduced by a historical outline and then the exteriority of the texts is analysed.

It is in the above-mentioned senses that I analyse the *exteriority* of the texts, their modes of representing different subjects constructed and produced by them: 'state', 'nationals' and 'others'. My interest does not lie in uncovering dark intentions behind the spoken words, or in trying to figure out what remains hidden in 'the doer behind the deed' (Butler, 1999; Campbell, 1998). On the contrary, I am interested in what the text actually exteriorises, its *mode of representation*, its aims as stated, and the actions and relationships explicitly expressed in the discourses. This analysis attempts to make visible the violence embedded in producing, reproducing and transforming those identity categories and their markers. The border that separates 'us' from 'them', which tries to erase the connectedness between them and then to erase the traces of this process of exclusion (Campbell, 1998), which defines who is an insider and who an outsider (Stern, 2005; Walker, 1993), is thus invested with violence.

The above considerations are framed with ethical concerns, for which an important methodological aspect of this research is interdisciplinarity. If the community of scholars committed to analysing security thinking only come from international relations and security studies, it is very likely that certain assumptions are taken for granted and that some ethical questions are excluded from discussion. Therefore, I bring in the insights of a peace studies perspective that calls for plural peaces. I do so not to attempt to solve the puzzles of security, but rather to pose questions that are not yet authorised in IR and security studies communities.[2]

Peace studies concerns are spread throughout this book and inform the very questions posed about security discourses. How much violence is produced by security thinking? How can we rethink the political in order to accept and cherish our vulnerability, our fragility and the intimate relationship and responsibility we have with others? Where does our freedom lie when we participate in a society created according to security concerns? How can we promote sharing spaces for relating to others? How can we rethink security discourses towards more peaceful relations?

These questions point to an analytical gap between predominant discourses of security and peace studies which I attempt to fill as best I can, without pretending to exhaust the subject or to render definite my own conclusions. This might be the most relevant methodological aspect of this research because the field of peace studies is the academic and ethical point of departure for the present critique. The works of Vicent Martínez – 'Towards an Insecure Peace' (2001a), *Filosofía para hacer las Paces* (2001b) and *Podemos hacer las paces* (2005) – Wolfgang Dietrich and Wolfgang Sützl's 'A call for Many Peaces' (2006) and Dietrich's trans-rational peaces (2006, 2008), in addition to Maria Stern's *Naming Security – Constructing Identity* (2005), serve as the pillars that inform my own perspective regarding security discourses.

As may be evident in the last paragraph, I have maintained most of the original writings in the language of publication in an attempt to keep the coherence of authors' thoughts and discursive constructions. Because this research focuses on the DSP in Colombia, there are several direct quotations in

Spanish. They are accompanied by discussion in English with the hope that the coherence of the argumentation still holds also for those not familiar with the language. For the very few citations in German, on the other hand, I give the English translation in parentheses immediately after the text.

I would like to finish this methodological section by underscoring the non-closure-driven character of this research. Even though this book presents the discursive formations of the DSP, how it hails subjects into place and how some of them have resisted the DSP, it is not my intention to give the appearance of complete coherence or perfect match. The methodological division into these three different levels of analysis corresponds to the working definition of identity that supports the book (Hall, 1996a). Furthermore, this division serves to make coherent the academic text. However, this is not the same as asserting that identities can be apprehended as a whole.

As pointed out in the last section, this particular reflection of the in/security discourse in Colombia and the different alternatives (op)posed to it are committed to a particular peace studies perspective that calls for the many ways of conceptualising peace, the so-called Many Peaces (Dietrich and Sützl, 2006). Precisely because I believe that fixing identities serves to legitimise more political violence (Stern, 2005), I show how the writing of in/security implies the writing of peace (and war) and attendant notions of political imaginaries. I argue that offering a clear-cut solution to this problem is a contradiction in and of itself. Hence, once the DSP is understood in light of analysing how these concepts and practices inform each other and by offering insights into the often-violent relations that render the pursuit of both peace and security so very problematic, I put forward possibilities that could be translated into lessening harm and suffering. I point to how in/security can be twisted towards many and in/secure peaces. In so doing, I try to break away from reproducing the search for in/security within peace and political frames. I hope I can contribute to this coherent principle throughout this work.

Overview of the chapters

In order to develop my ideas about how the DSP contributes to constituting political identities that (re)produce political violence, this book starts by contextualising the DSP in Colombia. Chapter 1, 'An overview of the Colombian context', serves to open the stage to the different modes in which violence in the country has been represented. My aim is to situate the in/security discourse of the Colombian government in this particular context. Depending on the source, Colombia can be represented as a new war (Kaldor, 1999), as a situation of violence fed by criminals in search for profit (Collier, 2000), as a society at war (Blair, 1999), as a fragile state (Piazza, 2008), or as an internal armed conflict (Franco, 2002).

These different names and definitions participate actively in giving shape to the war itself. My interest is to underscore the multiple consequences produced by each of those naming. Thus, after considering the different depictions of the situation by academics, governments and the international community, I analyse the political consequences of adopting the current governmental definition of Colombia as a democratic nation-state under the threat of narco-terrorism (Uribe, 2005a). This perspective on the Colombian conflict is simultaneously derived from the global war on terror in which the US and the Colombian governments project themselves as democracies under the threat of a non-political and illegitimate violence. If the enemy and its violence lack rationality, then a (normalised) state of exception is justified in order to face such threat (Butler, 2004; Jabri, 2006).

Chapter 2, 'Theorising security discourses', considers the theoretical framework needed to approach the DSP. I first outline the conventional understanding of security policies according to mainstream views in IR, identifying the main pillars that give them grounding in this logic. The analytical vacuum left by such perspectives is deeply questioned by a heterogeneous group of critical security scholars who propose a different set of interrogations in regards to security policies, challenging the received view in IR and offering a different interpretation of what in/security practices actually do.

This second chapter begins to question the natural character of the state (Dillon, 1999; Walker, 1999), the intertwined relationship between sovereignty and subjectivity (Edkins and Pin-Fat, 1999; Stern, 2005), the production of dangers by in/security discourses and what these do to identity (Campbell, 1998), the effects on politics when in/security is embraced as its founding ground (Dillon, 1996), and the dynamic of in/security inscribed within security itself (ibid.; Stern, 2005). These different points of entry into the analysis of in/security discourses underscore the combination of geopolitical and biopolitical strategies and practices (Dillon, 2007, 2008) present in the DSP.

Although the second chapter provides an overview of the literature on the dominant perspectives in traditional and more critical security studies, it also adds a new dimension to these more familiar discussions: namely, it sets the stage for reading security discourses in a postcolonial context. The methodology it constructs allows for making clear how the Colombian in/security discourse – within the global war against terror – constitutes and produces the identity categories of 'state', 'nationals' and 'others' in the Colombian case.

Following this theoretical framework, the main body of the book is to be found in the third and fourth chapters. Chapter 3, 'The end of peace and the beginning of in/security', starts by examining in detail through a close discursive reading of the DSP how the promise of security turned into a hegemonic discourse. The end of the peace talks between the government and the FARC-EP in February 2002 signalled the foreclosed possibility of a peaceful transformation of the armed conflict. The DSP was then issued as the state discourse that institutes the promise of in/security.

In Chapter 4, 'Identity categories constructed and produced by the Democratic Security Policy', I outline the discursive effects that the DSP has on the construction and production of political identities. I explore, on the one hand, the discursive formations which characterise 'state', 'nationals' and 'others', and, on the other hand, the material practices that hail collective subjects to adopt those specific subject positions (Hall, 1996a). In this sense, some of the most important governmental and non-governmental actions are also examined in relation to their effects on identity constitution. In line with Dillon's arguments (2007, 2008), I examine how geopolitical and biopolitical micro-practices of in/security summon peoples and bodies to assume the identity categories defined in the DSP.

Chapter 5, 'Resistance and peaces', concerns the analyses of discourses that have emerged in resistance to the DSP. After constructing a framework to interpret resistance discourses, three such discourses are examined. First, by examining the FARC-EP discourse, the book explicitly argues that armed discourses of resistance do not challenge the logic of violence and exclusion of the DSP. Subsequently, two other types of resistance discourses are considered: the institutional Peace Programme in Antioquia and the nonviolent discourse of the Paeces del Cauca. This chapter shows how looking at resistance discourses reveal the heterogeneity of reactions to the DSP and some alternative peaceful responses to it.

As a final point, I present a collection of proposals originating from different currents of thought and by authors who seem to find a common ground in a call for agonistic and democratic politics (Arendt, 1998; Butler, 2004; Connolly, 1991; Dillon, 1996; Haraway, 1991; Maalouf, 2000; Mouffe, 1992; Said, 2003a). These proposals embrace insecurity, tension and uncertainty, not just as inevitable components of life, but also as the very elements necessary to frame politics and to disrupt the global in/security discourse. The book concludes with a call for a continued exploration of possible routes that have been opened through the present critique to the Colombian in/security discourse, a task that I hold to be of the highest possible relevance to the political and academic agendas.

NOTES

1 As detailed in Chapters 3 and 4, candidate Alvaro Uribe first used the DSP as his political platform for the 2002 presidential elections. 'Democratic security' became Uribe's main thesis in the Political Manifesto, his candidacy programme. After Uribe was elected president in May 2002, in August of the same year the DSP was adopted as the government's plan and was officially released in June 2003 by the presidency and ministry of defence. Hence, although the references made allude to the year 2003, the DSP has been in place since 2001 as political proposal.

2 Regarding interdisciplinary questions, as John Mowitt (1999: 350–1) argues, they 'are crucial because they highlight precisely what reigning disciplinary paradigms render unintelligible'. As such, I hope that the very unruliness of this interdisciplinary book prompts us 'to gather at ... shared boundaries [of affected disciplines] in order to participate in the labor of collective self-examination' (ibid.).

1

An overview of the Colombian context

T HE PRESENT BOOK IS BASED UPON the assumption that discourses are *living texts*, which simultaneously describe and prescribe realities (Jackson, 2005; Weldes et al., 1999). In this sense, discourses are not just 'mere linguistic artefacts' but rather have material effects, constructing and producing identity categories (Hall, 1996a). At the same time, discourses come into being within contexts, positioned, constituted and constitutive of power relations (Said, 2003a). This is the reason why in this section concerning the DSP, I first set the Colombian context. I have tried to outline it as briefly but as completely as necessary to articulate the different modes in which the Colombian situation has been represented.

Trying to contextualise, *grosso modo*, the Colombian context is a major task. The great number of texts that deal with it evidences the difficulties of grasping the Colombian reality. The abundant literature about war and violence in Colombia also echoes the interrogations of peace researchers (Illich, 1988: 167; Muñoz, 2001) in the sense that Colombian history has been made a history of war. Especially in a country that has attested to high levels of violence for decades, the compilation of information and the great multiplicity of texts, from journalism to political programmes and academic publications, allows for a large assortment of versions or different modes of representation of the Colombian context. Depending upon the source, 'Colombia' can be represented as a new war (Kaldor, 1999), as a situation of violence fed by criminals in search for profit (Collier, 2000, 2001), as a society at war (Blair, 1999), as a fragile State (Piazza, 2008), or as an internal armed conflict (Franco, 2002). These different names and definitions actively shape the war itself.

My interest is in underscoring the multiple consequences that each of these naming practices produces. Thus, after considering the different depictions of the situation by academics, governments and the international community, I analyse the political consequences of adopting the current governmental definition of Colombia as a democratic nation-state under the threat of narco-terrorism (DSP,

2003; Uribe, 2005a). This perspective on the Colombian conflict also derives from the global war on terror in which the US and the Colombian governments project themselves as democracies under threat of non-political and illegitimate violence. If the enemy and its violence lack rationality, then a state of exception is justified in order to face such a threat (Butler, 2004; Jabri, 2006).

Naming the Colombian conflict

The first question that arises when dealing with the Colombian context is its definition. Various authors, schools of thought, governmental officials and international institutions categorise the high levels of violence characteristic of the country differently. This results in a plurality of definitions. What is important and usually forgotten is that definitions are powerful tools to qualify the actors involved, the character of their struggle and the ways of dealing with the situation (Jackson, 2005). In this sense, definitions are not just the result of objective tabulations, but are already embedded in the power to name, to qualify certain aspects as relevant and to disqualify others as such, and to value specific dynamics in a particular way. 'Language has a reality-making effect; it is a way of constructing reality and not merely reflecting it' (ibid.: 23). In other words, definitions are constituted by and constitute power relations. Moreover, in the case of an armed conflict, the way in which violence is represented (actors, dynamics, causes, among others) bears important consequences for the options considered to deal with the situation, ranging from an open military confrontation to annihilate the enemy to political solutions involving peace negotiations (Edkins, 2003; Jackson, 2005; Nasi and Rettberg, 2006).

Academic perspectives

In academic realms, there seems to be no consensus about the representation of the armed conflict. Some Colombian academicians have focused their attention on the causes for the war, privileging political and social explanations that mainly address injustice and inequality issues, as well as the inability of the state to accomplish its functions (Angarita, 2001; Comisión de Estudios sobre la Violencia, 1995).

Other academic currents have centred their attention on the characteristics of the armed struggle, first classifying the armed actors and, from there, inferring conclusions about the character of the conflict (Franco, 2002; Pizarro, 1990; 1991; Rangel, 2005). The financing of the guerrillas and paramilitary groups with drug money has marked economic analyses by denying much of the political character to the armed conflict (Deas and Gaitán, 1995). Several academics have tried to trace the development, evolution or transformation of the armed groups in the past four decades and to assign to each period a different characterisation (Nieto and Robledo, 2001). Finally, there are a considerable number of academics who comprehend the history of the conflict within a wider spectrum. They trace the causes of the current armed conflict to the day of independence in the nineteenth century as a way of highlighting it as a long and violent process of nation-building (Ramírez, 2002; Uribe de H. and López, 2006).

Since there is no specific typology of war concretely developed for the Colombian conflict (Nasi and Rettberg, 2006: 66), the discussion about it has made use of international armed conflict classifications and war studies developments. Three influential contemporary trends in scholarship currently inform many of the analyses of the Colombian conflict: new wars (Kaldor, 1999), rebel groups in search for profit (Collier, 2000, 2001; Collier and Hoeffler, 2001; de Soysa, 2000) and failed states (Lambach et al., 2003; Piazza, 2008). These three theses, as explained in more detail below, have changed the language of the Colombian armed conflict and are present in most of the academic understandings of the war, whether as criticisms of them or as their reconstitution.

The main thesis of Colombia as a new war finds its inspiration in Mary Kaldor's work *New and Old Wars: Organized Violence in a Global Era* (1999), which has provided a prevalent framework of analysis for the Colombian context.[1] Kaldor's main idea is that during the 1980s and 1990s, a new type of organised violence developed due to its occurrence in a globalised era, one characterised by the blurring of distinctions between war, organised crime and large-scale violations of human rights (ibid.: 1–5). The new wars are localised in a myriad of transnational connections, which obfuscate the limits between aggression and repression, and between local and global. This makes the new wars a typical globalised phenomenon understood as the intensification of global interconnectedness in the context of the erosion of the autonomy of the state (ibid.: 2–6). As if echoing the Colombian security policy, Kaldor proposes that the key to resolving new wars' confrontations is to restore the legitimacy of the state and to reconstitute 'the control of organized violence by public authorities' (ibid.: 10). She points out how this 'is both a political process – the rebuilding of trust in and support for public authorities – and a legal process – the re-establishment of a rule of law within which public authorities operate' (ibid.).

Kaldor's arguments have been echoed in Colombia, for her characterisation has proven especially useful for some analysts to describe the eroded role of the state and the blurred divisions between terrorist actions by the guerrillas and 'traditional' political violence. The conclusions to which Kaldor's analyses have led in Colombia include that the war is not fought on ideological grounds (anymore). The armed actors and, above all, the guerrillas are denied political ideals. Their involvement in the drug business and organised crime further support this argument.

A second contemporary current of thought that has greatly influenced the analysis of the Colombian situation is the one portrayed by Paul Collier (2000,

2001). Collier sustains that, from an economic viewpoint, armed groups are all criminal organisations whose motives are not the same as those exposed in their discourses for obtaining popular support. Whether a government or a guerrilla, for Collier, each armed group needs to feed their warriors and the general population with ideas that legitimise fighting and dying for a cause. Injustice, oppression and grievances are mere parts of the discourse, and only serve to veil the real character of organised criminal activities. From this angle, rebel groups invest in public relations to maintain the support of the warriors and of international financial sources. The grievance they portray is largely a consequence of their own need for legitimation rather than the real cause for their struggle. From this point of view, the question 'is there a just cause for the war?' has no practical importance. If there were no grievance, the armed group would eventually dissolve. Therein lays the motivation for continuing to feed the grievance (Collier, 2001: 30).

This economic theory of conflict suggests that there will be an armed conflict as long as the armed organisation is financially viable. Since there might be social injustice everywhere around the world, Collier's (2000, 2001) explanatory argument for the eruption of an armed conflict in a specific country and not everywhere, is that only in countries where the armed organisation can finance itself will war arise and continue. The author also identifies a short list of characteristics that make a country more prone to war, such as dependence on primary export goods, a small rate of economic growth and ethnic rivalries (Collier, 2001). To find a solution to an armed conflict, Collier (ibid.: 34–50) proposes reducing these potential risks factors – especially dependency from primary goods – which feed predation. In sum, whether social injustices are real or perceived, whether criminals want to access power for legitimate reasons or only to fill their personal pockets with money, is unimportant. Whether grievance or greed is the underlying motive has no significance (ibid.).

A third and quite influential thesis in the analysis of the Colombian situation underscores the inability of the state to exercise its functions as the cause for the emergence of armed groups. As James A. Piazza (2008) notes, recent literature about failed states has accentuated the connection between weak state functions of security and the emergence and continuance of transnational terrorism (Crocker, 2003; Fukuyama, 2004; Rotberg, 2003). Taking into consideration Max Weber's definition of the modern nation-state as 'that human community which (successfully) lays claim to the monopoly of legitimate violence within a certain territory' (Weber, 1994: 310–11), Piazza (2008) argues that studies of failed states and political violence try to establish a relationship between state failure and transnational terrorism along the following lines:

> Failed and failing states are states that due to severe challenges cannot monopolize the use of force vis-à-vis other non-state actors in society and are therefore incapable of fully projecting power within their national boundaries. ... As a consequence, failed

states ... continually face the threat of secession, civil war, and large-scale violent internal struggles for control between the government and one or more non-state actors. (Rotberg quoted in Piazza, 2008: 470)

As Piazza (ibid.) observes, theses about failed states' policy proposals to address violence include 'robust multi- or unilateral intervention to prevent state failure and proscribe a range of policy courses, such as building stable democratic institutions, increasing economic assistance, multilateral military intervention, and the creation of an American empire' (ibid.).

In the particular case of Colombia, the thesis of state weakness is presented in a direct relationship to the emergence of guerrilla and paramilitary groups. First, the state is seen as a weak entity insofar as, in large parts of the national territory, non-state actors challenge the state's monopoly on the use of force. 'Colombia is showing signs of state failure (or state weakness) since the mid-1980s and this situation has been deteriorating since the mid-1990s' (Lambach et al., 2003). Consequently, in those areas where the state has repeatedly failed, guerrillas and paramilitary groups have emerged to replace the state. They substitute for the state's role regarding the control of territory and the monopoly on violence. Hence, these illegal armed groups function as alternative centres of authority. 'In the vacuum left behind by the shrinking monopoly of violence still exercised by the state, a culture of violence, insecurity and disorder has emerged' (ibid.). Since a main contributing factor to the continuance of war is precisely the inability of the state to exercise its authority in the whole of the national territory, a renewed call for sovereign power is made as a counterweight against the power of guerrillas and paramilitary groups.

In the following section, I have selected a few of the most diverse representations of the Colombian war made by Colombian political scientists to explain the violence in the country. I have done this to contextualise the DSP, since providing a comprehensive bibliographical review of the analyses of the Colombian conflict exceed the objectives of this section. As will become evident by reading the pages that follow, most of the analyses merge several explanations (new wars, search for profit and failed states), and do not affirm one and only one cause or characterisation of violence.

Is there a civil war in Colombia?

The debate about whether or not the violent conflict in Colombia is a civil war has been the focus of heated academic discussion, especially since the middle of the 1990s. These arguments have coincided with the end of the Cold War, multiple demobilisations of guerrilla groups, the killing of the leaders in charge of the main drug cartels of Medellín and Cali, high levels of political violence and the continuance of the FARC-EP and National Liberation Army (ELN) as powerful guerrilla groups (IEPRI, 2006). Partly because the government insists upon defining the situation as a narco-terrorist struggle, since 2003 an important group of scholars has engaged in discussion of whether or not violence in Colombia can be classified as civil war, or whether the armed conflict could be better understood and handled as a society at war (Nasi et al., 2003a, 2003b).

For instance, in a vein similar to the thesis of state failure (Piazza, 2008), the lack of a social contract in Colombia is the investigative perspective adopted by the political scientist William Ramírez (2002). Ramírez portrays the national situation in the following terms:

> *La historia de nuestro país es la de un contractualismo coactivo nunca resuelto y, en consecuencia, caracterizado por el hecho de que desde varios ángulos del poder social dominante se han impulsado contradictorias alternativas de hegemonía nacional sin que desde ninguna de ellas se logre el monopolio legítimo de una fuerza que permita articular el inconexo tejido de la Nación.* (Ibid.: 154)

As Ramírez points out, the history of the country is commonly divided into three periods of violence: the civil wars of the nineteenth century, 'The Violence' around the 1950s and the violence occurring from the last decades of the twentieth century through the present day. It has been argued that the violence of the civil wars of the nineteenth century was the form of doing politics *par excellence*. Political leaders, transformed into elites after independence from the Spanish Crown, manipulated their political quotes and armed peasants as their soldiers to guard their own particular economic interests. For Ramírez, it was the politico-economic elites who did not have a real will to overcome the obstacles to conform a social contract as a symbolic referent for state power which also constituted a primary cause of 'The Violence' in the middle of the twentieth century:

> *La incapacidad y resistencia de las capas dirigentes alojadas en el Estado para contener la descomposición campesina dentro de límites controlables y cohonestar, en consecuencia, la acelerada acumulación de factores de enfrentamiento dentro de un lenguaje y una práctica de liquidación física, social o política del adversario que se fue apropiando de mayores y nuevos recursos de guerra, incorporando cada vez más sectores de población y dificultando de modo creciente el desmonte de la beligerancia y la resolución de conflictos.* (Ibid.: 156)

Therefore, the current situation cannot be classified under the same typology of the civil wars of the nineteenth century, nor of the violent period in the 1950s. In the 1960s, Colombian guerrillas were seen as an armed group of peasants excluded from the political pact of the National Front, which was founded between the liberal and the conservative parties in order to rotate the office of the Presidency of the Republic (Bushnell, 1994: 305–37). Under the influence of the logic of the Cold War, they were portrayed by the Colombian government as communist guerrillas, subject to the logic of the Doctrine of National Security (Leal, 1999). The successive governments exchanged the violence between liberal and conservative followers for a war against a social armed group providing their resistance with certain dignity and legitimacy (Ramírez, 2002: 157).

Between 1964 and 1982, the objectives of the guerrillas both elevated their strategic peasant struggle and intensified the official repression against them. By 1982, Ramírez (ibid.: 158) frames the Colombian war as a mass violent conflict, two or more fighting forces (at least one of them serving the state), and a minimally centralised belligerent organisation and combatants. Ramírez also refers to Kaldor's (1999) arguments that the Colombian conflict represents a new type of civil war. Since 1982, the Colombian conflict – especially the war against drugs – has had vast transnational repercussions widened by globalised interconnections. The line between political struggle, organised crime and large-scale violations of human rights has been thoroughly blurred. Ramírez (2002) also recognises how the high financial viability of the rebel groups due to drug business enabled recognition of the Colombian conflict within the framework espoused by authors like Paul Collier (2000, 2001).

Nevertheless, Ramírez (ibid.: 163) emphasises that the violent conflict in Colombia is not reduced to left-wing guerrillas fighting right-wing self-defence groups and state forces; it is also a war in which the citizens fight each other and often support one or another of the armed groups. Ramírez calls attention to the fact that the Colombian armed conflict should not be understood as a civil war, but rather as a larger social conflict in which there is support for the groups in combat, including the state. This is why Ramírez pleads for a socio-political solution to the situation, which encourages peace negotiations, and why he distances himself from those who call for the annihilation of the adversary.

A SOCIETY AT WAR

The last remarks of Ramírez bring us to another dimension of the representation of violence in Colombia, one that goes beyond the reasons for illegal armed groups to perpetrate constant acts of violence against the institutionalised political power, and that opens spaces for analysing why the population at large has resorted to public and private violence (Lair, 2003; Pécaut, 2001). This type of research finds elements that serve as tools of study to comprehend the generalisation of violence in the construction of national identity.

In her reflection on symbols, Elsa Blair (1999: 13) examines violence as a problem of imageries that influence social practices through significant and affective mobilisations. Blair investigates cultural values that inform the violent situation in Colombia: cultural referents and the way they intervene in the practices of different actors. According to Blair, the normative background of Colombians had been characterised by the power of the Catholic Church. The church had been the structuring factor of the *mestizo* society: as a religious meta-narrative, Catholicism provided a sense of order to the colonial world and to most of the Republican Era. It imposed itself as the main moral, normative and political order; it marked and named places and territories with symbols and institutions. Recalling Maria Teresa Uribe de H., she argues that Catholicism provided the religious worldview to structure cognitive and normative principles, subordinating both laws and the state itself (ibid.: 22).

A disrupted process of secularisation began when the different processes of modernisation were first undertaken. Modernisation included both economic processes of industrialisation and the opening of society to international currents of thought. The traditional referents were eroded and society has not yet identified new ones. In this direction, Blair characterises the Colombian crisis with three concrete problems: legitimacy, secularisation and anomie. The absence of a normative and symbolic order to regulate the citizenry creates

> *formas alternas de referencia, que construyen sus propias legitimidades: la guerrilla aduce la estrechez del régimen político; los militares, la defensa de la institucionalidad; los paramilitares, la inoperancia del Estado en su lucha contra la guerrilla; los sicarios, su derecho a 'ganarse la vida'; las milicias populares, la defensa de las comunidades amenazadas por el sicariato. Éste es entonces un proceso de atomización de los intereses colectivos. Un proceso de individualización de valores o propósitos particulares típico de sociedades en estado de anomia.* (Ibid.: 19–20)

This analysis of violence addresses two aspects: its dimension as a collective practice and its subjective dimension. The underlying assumption is the belief in the ability of social actors to construct society according to their cultural orientations, their social, political and organisational relations. In this sense, social actors would not be merely passive subjects acting according to their status in society, nor would they be understood as simple spectators of objective and structural situations (Comisión de Estudios sobre la Violencia, 1995). This reflection leads to placing the emphasis of the analysis on the social actor as *producer* of social reality and binding it to the situation in an interactive manner (Blair, 1999: 44).

In Blair's perspective, it is in the construction of identity that social actors recognise their own collectivity (the 'us') and the 'other' ('them'). For her, the generalised resorting to violence by the Colombian population involves an underlying image of an enemy, framed in the constitution of the 'other' and carried out by its exclusion. The collective imaginary is characterised by warrior features: the symbolism of the construction of the identity of the *other-enemy* serves to make cohesive the 'us'. The new unit is based on the identification of solidarity bounds in defensive and aggressive activities.

The influence of the drug business

One recurrent point of agreement among the scholars who study the Colombian armed conflict is that the drug-dealing era affected and changed the Colombian war abruptly. The decade of the 1980s, with the boom of the drug business and the self-defence groups, set the scene for this critical change. Most of the analyses focusing on the influence of the drug business in the conflict emphasise that drug money substantially altered the character of the armed struggle, somehow corrupting the ideological motives of the guerrillas (Bejarano and others, 1997; Gutiérrez, 2003; Nasi and Rettberg, 2005; Richani, 2002).

Regarding this point, Alvaro Camacho (2002: 137) suggests that there are actually two literary trends in the current academic debate. First, for those who support an ideological current, the founding elements for civil wars are political beliefs, sentiments of pain, and perceptions of injustice and the need to invert social and political conditions. For the supporters of the economic political trend, on the other hand, the ability and capacity of the rebels to access economic resources determine their possibilities to organise and to survive. In the first view, altruism would dominate; in the latter, what really counts is greed.

Camacho identifies Paul Collier's writings as enjoying the greatest influence on the representation of the Colombian conflict as greed-driven (ibid.: 139). As briefly examined at the beginning of this section, according to Collier, many societies go through intense political conflicts for long periods without reverting to wars. In his view, political conflict is omnipresent, whereas war is scarce. Camacho, following Collier, argues that this trend views financial viability or lack thereof as the cause for violent rebellion. In conclusion, the war produces the intense political conflict, and not vice versa.

Colombian researchers (Richani, 2002; Rubio, 1999; Salazar and Castillo, 2001) have followed this latest trend, abandoning traditional explanations about social injustice and economic and political exclusion and embracing the desire of the rebels, especially guerrillas, to profit as a main reason to continue their struggle:

> *No puede desconocerse, por supuesto, que el fenómeno de la exclusión política, generado por el Frente Nacional, explica el surgimiento y proliferación de las organizaciones armadas revolucionarias activas en las décadas del setenta y del ochenta. Pero la dimensión política y revolucionaria de esas organizaciones actúa en el contexto más amplio de una organización social en la que la depredación sistemática, el ejercicio de la violencia y la búsqueda de ventajas económicas prevalecen.* (Salazar and Castillo, 2001 quoted in Camacho, ibid.: 140)

Guerrilla movements reject this approach outright and uniformly. According to several press releases and communications from the FARC-EP and ELN collected by Camacho himself, their founding and current task is to answer the political, economic, social and armed aggression of the political oligarchic regime of the liberal and conservative parties. The mistreatment of the peasants, the unequal distribution of economic resources and the lack of state ability to provide justice and to satisfy the needs of the population are cited by the guerrillas as the immediate and just causes for rebellion.

For Camacho, the Colombian armed conflict combines the ideological and economic perspectives. He analyses both in a careful and specific manner with the following conclusions: first, Colombian guerrillas have emerged and developed based on their perception of injustice and grief yet, second, there is a tendency –

at least in some sectors of these organisations – to distort their ideology of social transformation in search for profit. However, says Camacho, one of the most perverse effects of the Colombian armed conflict has been that it has facilitated and encouraged the greed of those who profit from the war (ibid.: 149–50). Camacho so fuses the insights of Collier without extending the economic predation logic to the whole of the armed groups, in this case, the guerrillas.

PARAMILITARY OR SELF-DEFENCE GROUPS?

However, the Colombian war also contains other vital armed actors, primarily the paramilitary groups (Duncan, 2005; International Crisis Group, 2003; Rangel, 2005; Romero, 2003). The paramilitary groups call themselves self-defence organisations (Autodefensas Unidas de Colombia – AUC) and claim that their main function is to defend the segments of the population who are being attacked by guerrillas and who do not receive proper protection from state forces (Aranguren, 2001).

Liliana Franco (2002: 68–70) dedicates part of her research activities to the analysis of paramilitarism in Colombia. She highlights that the approach to this phenomenon has been mainly state-centred, from which two interpretative complementary propositions have been derived. First, that paramilitarism only exists because of the insurgency and that therefore, if the latter disappears, the paramilitaries would as well. The second proposition is that the paramilitaries are part of a state policy, so their form and capacity are determined by the ability of the state to maintain a monopoly on violence and justice.

However, for Franco the presence of guerrillas is only a necessary condition for the paramilitary forces to exist. In her view, this does not constitute a sufficient condition to explain their expansion and significant power in Colombia. Franco contends that the paramilitary forces are a form of privatisation of the functions of defence and security of the state, viewed as an irregular corporative military unit, a decentralised state force. As long as the paramilitaries in Colombia do not question the establishment, but serve as its protector and guarantor, these illegal armed groups reinforce the arbitrary power of the state in defined spaces of the national territory (ibid.: 70).[3]

AN IRREGULAR WAR

Tied to this last point, according to several academic perspectives, we find the involvement of civilians to be one of the most prominent characteristics of the Colombian armed conflict (Lair, 2003). After overcoming the traditional understanding of an armed conflict between regular and irregular armies, we encounter a more problematic issue: an irregular war that actively involves the civilian population, increasing the levels of violence in the community as a whole (Pécaut, 2001).

Eric Lair (2003, 2005) analyses the differences between a regular and an irregular war in order to highlight the consequences that the involvement of the civilian population has on the conflict. For Lair (2003), the irregular war in Colombia is mainly characterised by decentralised violence that supersedes the military theatre of armed combats. Thereby, the population is increasingly affected. The notion of combat acquires a passing character, meaning, the attacks are not necessarily directed at armed forces but rather at infrastructure. This disrupts the normality of society and the institutional mechanisms of social functioning (Lair, 2005). Attacks are mainly carried out in an indirect manner, in which the illegal armed actors avoid frontal battles.

Prolongation is a primary feature of the conflict that Lair conceptualises as a strategy of the illegal armed forces to weaken the military and the pauses in combat are used to rearm and strengthen recruitment, financial resources, weapons and land holdings (ibid.). According to Lair, the main consequence that this prolonged war has had on civilians is that violence has permeated and shaped the representations and the collective memory of Colombians, the primary victims of the war. People generally create continuity between the current war and former war situations as if the violence was unbroken and society will continue to be trapped in an endless conflict. Simultaneously, for the illegal armed groups, the war has turned into a way of life, which offers *career* possibilities for ascension in the hierarchy.

Hand in hand with the transformation of warfare methods and finances, the role of the civilian population has been transformed since the 1960s. For Lair (2003: 4–6), civilians are ever more involved in the war. They give moral and political support, offer logistic and material help, make up the labour market for the war economy, participate in, or are accused of participating in, the war and play a military role as recruits and human shields. The spaces for neutrality are reduced and the lack of trust among the population increases (ibid.: 6).

In Lair's view, the involvement of civilians in the war is mainly due to coercive strategies, since there does not seem to be real popular support for the armed actors (ibid.: 11–12). In the case of the guerrillas, the revolution of the masses has not worked out continuously, so civilians are forced to cooperate mainly through intimidation. Lair suggests the reason the populace chose the military option for ending the conflict, embodied by Alvaro Uribe in May 2002, to be the fact that the general population is the primary victim of the war. People are tired of the violence and do not necessarily identify with the illegal armed groups.

Governmental definitions

While academics acknowledge the inability of the state to accomplish its functions as an important factor in explaining the high levels of violence in Colombia, governmental definitions work under a slightly different logic. The Colombian government's definitions of the armed conflict have to be placed in an

American context, under the direct influence of the United States as the primary economic, cultural and political power in the region. Different national administrations have transformed the representation of the conflict hand in hand with perceived threats to the US: communism, drugs and terrorism are now the three banners under which the conflict has been represented, each worthy of further examination within historical context.

Communist guerrillas and political violence

During the late 1970s, the government of President Turbay Ayala (1978–1982) put into practice an authoritarian state system of political repression (Reyes, 1991). Turbay implemented the Security Statute, which was used to 'fight the subversive armed threat that the guerrillas and their sympathisers pose to the country' (ibid.: 42–3). The government's anti-subversive fight rested upon the assumption that the conflict in Colombia was due to the armed character of communist guerrillas trying to impose their 'socialist' views on state affairs. The effects of the Statute were highly problematic. It instituted state repression in a systematic way, and political and military violence silenced popular leaders and social protesters or made them disappear (Leal, 2002a; Reyes, 1991). These circumstances invested the guerrillas with some legitimacy and general sympathy, if not direct support (Nieto and Robledo, 2001).

Still portraying the Colombian armed conflict as an ideological fight in which the state was confronting communist guerrillas, President Belisario Betancur (1982–1986) designed and implemented a strategy opposite that of Turbay's (ibid.). Betancur created a peace programme and opened institutional channels for the guerrillas to re-enter society (Bejarano, 1995; Pizarro, 1996). The peace strategy of the government was based on the assumption that 'the crisis of violence in the country was a combined product of objective and subjective internal conditions' and was not simply due to the influence of the East–West ideological confrontation (Echandía, 2003; Nieto and Robledo, 2001: 51). The thesis of 'objective and subjective conditions' is based on the assumption that there are political, social and economic structural realities that affect large segments of the population and put their very existence at risk. Among the structural conditions, political exclusion, poverty, unfair land distribution and profound income and wealth inequalities configure the objective causes for the eruption and perpetuation of violence (Echandía, 2003).

Therefore, 'economic underdevelopment' became the obstacle to be overcome if violence was to be reduced or eliminated. Betancur's government represented the internal armed conflict as the reaction to poverty and socio-political marginalisation of large segments of the population. His administration further attributed it to the exclusion of political tendencies different from the two traditional liberal and conservative parties (Nieto and Robledo, 2001). This understanding of the war led the government and some guerrillas like the

Movimiento Revolucionario 19 de Abril (Revolutionary Movement 19 April, M-19), to initiate peace processes. Even though the results of the process were not completely satisfactory (Bejarano, 1995), the administration of Betancur acknowledged and even emphasised the political character of the armed conflict. It pointed to the legitimacy of some of the guerrillas claims, like the narrowness of the political system, even if their methods were not legal or justified (Nieto and Robledo, 2001).

The following administration of President Virgilio Barco (1986–1990) changed this representation of the Colombian conflict dramatically. Barco's government had to face the heightening and strengthening of two additional armed actors, the drug dealers – *capos* – and the paramilitary groups. These circumstances marked the end of the government's primary characterisation of the Colombian armed conflict as a political struggle, and the start of what until today has prevailed in state discourses: the representation of violence in Colombia as primarily a fight of a legitimately constituted government against narco-terrorism.

THE WAR ON DRUGS

At the end of the 1980s, the government tried to separate the subversive political struggle from the anti-drug strategy. This dividing line became blurred ten years later. The process through which the anti-subversive fight, the war on drugs and the war against terrorism have been merged is long and gloomy. During the late 1980s, the murder of political and social leaders, massacres against peasants accused by the paramilitary of sympathising with the subversive guerrillas, the alliances between the military and the paramilitary, and the systematic terrorist attacks of the drug *capos* against the population indicated a major change in the government's strategy (Salazar, 2001).

The Barco administration tried to reach a peace agreement with some of the guerrilla groups, recognising their political character to negotiate. The M-19 was the only group that accepted the governmental proposal and consolidated their own demobilisation (Zuluaga, 1999). The M-19 was able to channel political reforms in the Colombian government and specifically within Congress, joining the traditional political parties in drafting a new constitution. With the signature of the peace agreement in May 1990, the definite conversion of the M-19 from an armed and illegal guerrilla movement into a legal political movement was effected (Nieto and Robledo, 2001: 62–5).

At the same time, the government of Virgilio Barco was unable to deal with the violence posed by the drug dealers in their war against the state. In anticipation of the presidential elections of 1990, three candidates had been murdered, Luis Carlos Galán, Bernardo Jaramillo and Carlos Pizarro. Massacres and selective murders took place almost daily. Within this context, a new president was elected. César Gaviria (1990–1994) continued to offer the guerrillas the possibility for re-entering society through peace agreements (Bejarano, 1995; Zuluaga, 1999), and he succeeded with the demobilisation of most of the members of the Ejército Popular de Liberación (EPL), Partido Revolucionario de los Trabajadores (PRT), and Movimiento Indigenista Quintín Lame (MIQL) (Alape, 1996; Nieto and Robledo, 2001; Palacios, 1995; Peñaranda, 1999; Villarraga and Plazas, 1994).

The fall of the Berlin Wall in 1989 and the demobilisation of these guerrilla groups had important effects on the representation of the conflict. First, some guerrilla groups started losing the initial legitimacy previously recognised in their struggle. The FARC-EP and ELN did not participate in the peace processes, but rather were excluded from the National Assembly for reforming the constitution. They further lost the ideological role model of the Soviet Union (Bejarano, 1995; Leal, 2002a). This situation was aggravated by President Gaviria's declaration of an integral war. Additionally, the war against drugs launched by the US government reached Colombia at a moment in which the terrorist actions of the drug dealers held the state in a stalemate (Salazar, 2001).

The relationship between 'the drug threat' in the US and the production of drugs in Colombia has marked the bilateral relations since the middle of the 1980s (Bagley and Tokatlian, 1992). The administrations of Presidents Ford, Nixon, Reagan, Bush and Clinton all identified drugs as a threat to national security. 'In April 1986, Reagan signed a secret directive that authorized the development of policies to attack the drug supply at its source (meaning the use of military in Central and South America), and equated the problem with terrorism' (Campbell, 1998: 172–3). In the words of US officer Rangel:

> Our national security and future as a stable government are at stake. ... Our survival and strength as the democratic stronghold on this part of the world is delicately intertwined with that of our neighbours to the south. ... If Colombia falls, the other, smaller, less stable nations in the region could become targets. It is conceivable that we could one day find ourselves an island of democracy in a sea of narco-politico rule, a prospect as bad as being surrounded by communist regimes. (Officer Rangel quoted in Campbell, 1998: 185)

In the same vein, the Executive Summary of the US Senate in 1989 issued a report on Narcotics, which read:

> The Colombian drug cartels which control the cocaine industry constitute an unprecedented threat, in a non-traditional sense, to the national security of the United States. Well-armed and operating from secure foreign havens, the cartels are responsible for thousands of murders and drug-related deaths in the United States each year. They exact enormous costs in terms of violence, lower economic productivity, and misery across the nation. (US Senate Report on Narcotics quoted in Campbell, 1998: 186)

In July 1992, President Gaviria was facing the shameful escape of the *capo* Pablo

Escobar from a security prison in Medellín when the US government declared an ultimatum to Colombia. The drug threat was affecting the national interests of the US and, therefore, its treatment had to be shared by the two governments (Leal, 2002a). In this way, the US exported its priorities, military logic and men to Colombia. Gaviria's administration received them with great enthusiasm. The term 'narco-terrorism' started being used to describe the dangers in Colombia. The subversive fight and the drug dealing business were thus named with a single new label (Nieto and Robledo, 2001).

The war on drugs gradually began to take over the whole spectrum of violence and the representation of the armed conflict. At the beginning of the administration of Ernesto Samper (1994–1998), the government tried to approach the FARC-EP, the Jaime Batemán Cayón group and ELN to initiate peace talks, acknowledging that the armed conflict should be resolved in a political manner (Bejarano, 1995). However, peace attempts ultimately failed, in large part due to the problems of legitimacy of President Samper. These problems included the alleged infiltration of drug money into his campaign, the US government's reaction of rejecting his government and the fear of losing the support of the armed forces, necessary to stay in power (Nieto and Robledo, 2001: 79–81). The government's newly defined strategy then reversed course: Samper called for a national front against violence and declared an open war in order to defeat the guerrillas (ibid.).

Subsequently, the presidency of Andrés Pastrana (1998–2002) was marked by the failed attempt of reaching negotiations with the guerrillas (Pastrana, 2005). The peace process, which Pastrana promised in his presidential campaign, materialised in three-year peace talks that ended with the declaration of the end of peace in February 2002.[4] What is important to note is that until this government failure, the Colombian armed conflict was still mainly depicted by the state as a political struggle with the guerrillas while fighting the drug business in a parallel way. Once the failure of peace was consensually accepted and became the hegemonic discourse of the government, the label narco-terrorism erased the political character of the armed groups.

THE WAR AGAINST TERRORISM

It is important to keep in mind the harmonisation of the US government and the Colombian government's definitions of the conflict. Following the attacks against the United States on 11 September 2001, the US launched a global war on terror, and not only in Afghanistan and Iraq. The workings of this global 'matrix of war' (Jabri, 2006) not only encompass the 'securitisation' (Wæver, 1995) of terrorism as one of its main characteristics but, following Vivienne Jabri (ibid.), they also make these practices 'normal', non-exceptional and common in liberal states, thereby erasing any distinction between peace and security politics. For the Colombian government, the global war against terror has provided a framework in which to fit easily the current administration's definition of the Colombian war situation.

Since taking office in 2002, President Alvaro Uribe (2005a: 4), has defined the Colombian situation as a terrorist struggle. For the government, there is no internal armed conflict; Colombia appears to be a democratic state that is facing a terrorist threat. President Uribe has sustained that in the 1960s the guerrillas were armed groups ideologically aligned with communism, who have lost their ideological aims in recent decades. Today they are drug-dealing organisations whose mercenaries only serve criminal activities. According to Uribe (ibid.), previous administrations confused civility with weakness. He concludes that the lack of authority of the state is responsible for the perpetuation of violence in the country.

The government consistently portrays Colombia as a democratic nation-state, where democracy can only be exercised based on the principle of state authority (DSP, 2003). This viewpoint has been expressed in several national and international forums (Uribe, 2002d; 2004a; 2005a), and enables the Colombian government to define any armed action against the state as a terrorist threat. In this sense, the government argues that, because of their methods, the guerrillas are terrorists. Poverty, exclusion, ecological degradation, political margin-alisation, violence, humanitarian crises and 'underdevelopment' are seen as effects of terrorism rather than as conditions for its emergence (Gaviria, 2005). The government, by fighting against terrorism, fights for development and for democracy (Uribe, 2004a).[5] The reactions that contest this particular representation of the Colombian situation are mainly voiced by political analysts and international human rights organisations.

INTERNATIONAL COMMUNITY

Contrary to the government's current understanding, international human rights organisations working in Colombia tend to emphasise the political character of the conflict. This should not lead one to conclude that the nexus between the drug dealing business and the guerrillas and paramilitary forces does not exist. On the contrary, this link is highlighted by those organisations as causing most of the violence in the country.

INTERNATIONAL ORGANISATIONS

The International Committee of the Red Cross (ICRC) argues that, according to the Geneva Convention, the situation in Colombia is an internal armed conflict characterised by its low intensity. According to Juan Pedro Schaerer, representative of the ICRC to Colombia, the Colombian situation is marked by hostilities between the legitimate armed forces of the state and armed groups which have a responsible leadership, with a minimum of organisation and whose actions have a collective character (Schaerer quoted in Arboleda, 2005: 12A). For this organisation, the acknowledgment of an internal armed conflict does not amount to recognising a political or juridical international character in the armed groups nor does it undermine the legitimacy of the state (ibid.). In this sense, for the Red Cross it is clear that both the state armed forces and the armed groups have to observe the norms of International Humanitarian Law (IHL), independently from finding political solutions for transforming the conflict.

In the 2003 Human Development National Report, the United Nations Development Program (UNDP) traces the roots of the current Colombian conflict to the marginalisation of the peasantry in the past century. The UNDP (2003: 5) underscores how most of the war has taken place in the countryside, while the guerrillas try to access the urban centres as part of their political programme. In this way, the UNDP explicitly states that the insurgence remains in the periphery because there is democracy in the cities, whereas the state failure to cope with the internal armed conflict is explained by recalling its weakness and the lack of political will of the elites (ibid.).

The UNDP (ibid.: 4–6) depicts the Colombian armed conflict as a result of the difficult geographical conditions of the country, the weakness of the state, the political exclusion of alternative tendencies from the political legal system and the fragmentation of the ruling class and popular movements. The UNDP then acknowledges the political project of the armed groups and recognises the efforts of the state to cope with this danger (ibid.: 7–9).

However, the UNDP calls attention to the dirty war that has been taking place since the 1980s, as a result of the incursion of the paramilitary groups and the military treatment that the state has given to the armed conflict (ibid.: 6). Echoing the conclusions of the current government, for the UNDP violence is the cause for the 'underdevelopment' of the country and not its consequence. In this sense, the UNDP (ibid.: 11) stresses the importance for Colombia to end violence as a way to reach higher levels of 'development'.[6]

To ameliorate the high levels of violence, the UNDP proposes strategies for humanising the conflict. Among them are observation of human rights norms, protection of the civilian population and the citizenry from being recruited to war parties and compensation for the victims. From this representation of the conflict, the UNDP concludes that the internal political armed conflict cannot be equated to the drug problem, since the latter influences the former but does not fully explain it. Nor does it provide sufficient conditions for the armed conflict to persist (ibid.: 27–38).

Following the same line of argument, Amnesty International (AI, 2005: 2) warns of the violations of human rights that are perceived as justified on the road to winning the war against narco-terrorism. For AI, the Colombian situation is 'an internal armed conflict' which 'continues to lead to the systematic violation of human rights and international humanitarian law by the warring parties' (ibid.: 8). AI (ibid.: 18) defines the guerrillas as 'armed opposition groups'. From this it can be deduced that AI recognises a political project in them, which does not deter this organisation from constantly denouncing the violations of humanitarian law norms by all of the armed groups, including both the state forces and the army-backed paramilitary (ibid.: 18–19).

THE EUROPEAN UNION

In the international arena, other organisations have also articulated their own understanding of the national situation. The European Union (EU, 2002) depicts the Colombian conflict as being rooted in political infighting between political parties and deprived farmers opposed to the agricultural policies of the government. Yet, the EU acknowledges that marginality, inequality, social exclusion and extreme poverty are problems common to many Latin American countries and that what makes the Colombian conflict 'unique' is the 'extreme weakness of the state: Colombia has never succeeded in completing the construction of a strong modern State' (ibid.: 21). For the EU, precisely such state weakness created the conditions for an endemic armed conflict, and additionally encouraged illegal business and the development of a widespread 'non-governmental' culture (EU, 2007: 10).

In the words of Benita Ferrero-Waldner (2004), commissioner for external relations, the EU believes that 'there will be no purely military solution to this conflict. As a consequence it is important to try to find the means of advancing towards a peaceful settlement with all illegal armed groups who are willing to work towards a peaceful solution' (ibid.). The EU favours the thesis of the anomie of the state, acknowledging the state's inability to accomplish its functions as one of the main causes for the conflict.

However, the 'position of the EU' cannot be considered a homogeneous response from a single coherent actor. The different nation-state members of the EU have expressed divergent opinions regarding the situation in Colombia. For our concerns, there are clear disagreements among the various member states regarding the definition and naming of the conflict and the qualification of the armed actors (Vranckx, 2004).

The inclusion of the guerrillas and the paramilitary groups in the EU's list of terrorist organisations has been one of the most difficult issues between Colombia and the EU. The paramilitary AUC was included on the EU's list of terrorist organisations since December 2001. In June 2002, after a massacre in Bojayá and a subsequent meeting between President Pastrana and the Swedish government, the FARC-EP was included on the list of terrorist organisations (ibid.). The consequences of being on this list included freezing and confiscating property and capital in Europe as well as revoking the prerogatives which FARC-EP spokespeople enjoyed (visa, refugee status). Such penalties cause FARC to lose what it had built up in more than a decade of "diplomatic activity"' (ibid.: 15). The government of Belgium, for example, had voiced its concerns in terms of erasing the possibilities for a peace agreement with the ELN by naming them 'terrorists'. 'In Colombia, the non-inclusion of the ELN on the European terrorist list, is taken for an indication that Europe does not cooperate sufficiently well in the "war against terrorism". In the light of widespread European acquiescence to U.S. practices, such non-cooperation is something many in Europe are proudly criticised for' (ibid.: 17).

Until 2005, the ELN had been kept off the European terrorist list, in stark contrast to the American terrorist list. The Foreign Terrorist Organizations (FTO) list registers thirty-nine terrorist organisations catalogued by the US Department of State. The three main Colombian armed groups: FARC-EP, ELN and AUC have been included from the beginning (US Department of State, 2004: 1).

The United States Government

In contrast to the mixed reactions in the EU, the US government has demonstrated few hesitations regarding the naming, defining and characterising of the Colombian conflict. 'Plan Colombia' may be the clearest expression of the US government's official understanding of the Colombian situation as a democratic state fighting narco-terrorism. Envisaged in 2000 under the Presidency of Pastrana and approved at that time by the US Congress, Plan Colombia has enunciated the US vision for handling the narco-terrorist threat.

Even though Plan Colombia was initially conceived as part of the anti-subversive fight, during the visit of President Pastrana to the United States in 2002, President George W. Bush explained how Plan Colombia's focus from combating drug trafficking could be changed to counter-terrorism activities. In President Bush's words: 'We [President Bush and President Pastrana] had a good discussion … about how to change the focus of our strategy from counter-narcotics to include counter-terrorism. I explained to him [Pastrana] that a supplemental I sent up to the United States Congress would do just that' (Bush, 2002: 1). To which President Pastrana (ibid.) gladly replied by saying: 'We have full support of President Bush and the government, … in trying to … change of authorities the use of the military equipment sent by the United States to Colombia to be used against also narco terrorism, not only against narco trafficking.'

At that moment, President Bush presented the characterisation of the Colombian armed actors according to the US government:

> these aren't 'so-called' terrorists, these are terrorists, in Colombia. And the reason they're terrorists is because they're using murder to try to achieve political ends. … They've captured people. … And so my message is that we will work with you [President Pastrana] to root out terror. We've put FARC, AUC, on our terrorist list. We've called them for what they are. These are killers, who use killing and intimidation to foster political means. And we want to join, with Plan Colombia's billions of dollars, to not only fight the – and by fighting narco trafficking, by the way,

> we're fighting the funding source for these political terrorists. And sometimes they're interchangeable. (Ibid.: 2–3)

As is clear from the statements above, fighting drug trafficking and fighting terrorism become *interchangeable*, transposable ways for defending a democratic country which, according to President Bush (ibid.: 3), 'has got a fantastic tradition, a noble tradition of democracy'.

This approach to understanding the Colombian situation has not changed in recent years. Since President Uribe assumed office in August 2002, the US government has continued to support the fight against narco-terrorism. As the 2004 US Report on Terrorism read, 'Colombia remained a steadfast ally of the United States in the fight against narcoterrorism' and 'through bilateral, multilateral, military, and economic activities, [the Colombian government] continued to assist US government counterterrorism efforts and to disrupt terrorist acts, block terrorist finances, and extradite terrorists to face justice in the United States' (US Department of State, 2005: 79).

In 2005, facing the established end of Plan Colombia and having transferred three billion dollars in military aid since 2000, Condoleezza Rice, the secretary of state, reconfirmed the US government's direct aid to the country during her visit to Colombia:

> We are really gratified that we have had an opportunity to contribute to President Uribe's very successful programs and we are committed to continuing our support for Colombia, a trusted friend and ally. In 2005 we will provide more than $600 million to combat terrorism and drug trafficking, to improve the security of Colombian citizens and to promote democracy and human rights. Our meeting today reaffirmed the strength of these values and of the U.S.-Colombian partnership. (Rice, 2005: 2)

The declarations of Condoleezza Rice summarise how the US government perceives the current Colombian administration: as an ally, a partner with whom it shares the same basic understanding of the situation of violence.

As seen in this last section, international organizations, as well as academics, do not agree about what is happening in the country, nor have they arrived at a consensus on how to deal with it exactly. Nevertheless, there is a tendency to progressively depict and treat the conflict as a terrorist struggle, privileging economic reasoning over socio-political analyses.

Representing the context

My intention to present diverse representations of the Colombian conflict is intended to point out the kind of assumptions upon which they rest. In this chapter, different definitions, explanations and interpretations constructed by academics, governments and international organisations concerned with the

Colombian conflict have been presented for discussion. As mentioned at the beginning of this section, each of the later modes of representation is already positioned and constituted by power relations, and in this way, it participates actively in giving shape to the situation itself. Therefore, the consequences for adopting one definition are also significant, for each privileges some factors over others, authorises and legitimises certain actors and actions while rendering inaccurate or false other perspectives. Each mode of representation is based, simultaneously, on some possibilities that are considered, and on some others that are erased and foreclosed from the beginning. That set of foreclosed alternatives is then precluded from the interpretation of the Colombian situation, leaving those possibilities outside the ground for exploration and contestation.

Now we have a clear picture of how the national administration portrays the situation in Colombia. The unanimity between the United States and the Colombian governments in the way they depict the situation should arouse suspicion. They are identical, there is no difference as to what the problem is about (narco-terrorism), how they both qualify the armed actors (terrorists), and with which strategies (plans of war) narco-terrorism should be fought (more violence). If there is an acceptance of how the situation is depicted, then the methods to deal with it are a matter of detail.

> [A] frame for understanding violence emerges in tandem with the experience, and that the frame works both to preclude certain kinds of questions, certain kinds of historical inquiries, and to function as a moral justification for retaliation. It seems crucial to attend to this frame, since it decides, in a forceful way, *what we can hear*, whether a view will be taken as explanation or as exoneration, whether we can hear the difference, and abide by it. (Butler, 2004: 4–5)

To perfectly fit the situation of violence(s) in Colombia into a frame of the war against narco-terrorism is to preclude explanations about social and political conditions, which play an important role in articulating the violent national context. Trying to explain the situation by emphasising other socio-political factors does not necessarily mean a sympathetic identification with guerrillas or terrorist organisations. Recognising those conditions is not equivalent to constructing a justificatory framework for them. In the case of poverty and exclusion, for example, to make a cause-effect relation by claiming that the terrorist-guerrillas are the sole responsible actors for sixty per cent of the population living under the poverty line is a sophism (Garay, 2002).

Another aspect that this mode of representation fails to appreciate is the problem of collective and individual violence. To assume, as does the Colombian government, that killing terrorists, whether by bombing or starving guerrilleros and the civilian population along the way, is the method to root out violence in the country is to believe that these expressions of violence are symptoms of individual pathology or evil. This assumption forecloses the question of how those expressions of violence are embedded in a wider collective phenomenon that gives rise to them. As Butler posits, 'How is it that radical violence becomes an option, comes to appear as the only viable option for some, under some [local and] global conditions?' (Butler, 2004: 16). She offers the following reflection to begin to explain this radical choice:

> If we believe that to think radically about the formation of the current situation is to exculpate those who committed acts of violence, we will freeze our thinking in the name of a questionable morality. But if we paralyze our thinking in this way, we will fail morality in a different way. We will fail to take collective responsibility for a thorough understanding of the history which brings us to this juncture. We will, as a result, deprive ourselves of the very critical and historical resources we need to imagine and practice another future, one which will move beyond the current cycle of revenge. (Ibid.: 10)

Considering the social and political conditions of violence in Colombia is not to build a causal frame, but rather opens the possibilities for a critical conversation about what should change politically. This is different from perpetuating a cycle of violence as a self-defeating method to eradicate violence.

We find another political obstacle when confronted with the representation of the Colombian context as a narco-terrorist struggle. The discursive construction of the government, holding that there is democracy in Colombia and that its historical failure is only due to a deficiency in the principle of authority, silences dissenting voices. The censorship of criticism and questioning is set into place when the situation is depicted as a terrorist threat to a democratic state. How not to be labelled as terrorist when challenging the government and its policies? How not to be equated to a terrorist when calling for the socio-political conditions as important factors to consider when analysing the situation of violence in Colombia?

The DSP is the favoured 'weapon' of the Colombian government to fight the narco-terrorist threat. This is a focal point. Because the government understands the conflict as a terrorist threat that the narco-terrorist guerrillas pose to a democracy sustained by the principle of authority, the DSP was designed and has been implemented. In this sense, the discourse on narco-terrorism informs the DSP and, at the same time, the DSP informs the context to resemble a narco-terrorist struggle ever more. Because of this particular interpretation of what happens in the country and how to deal with the danger of narco-terrorism, the DSP has been made the hegemonic discourse about the Colombian context.

In the introduction to this research, the case of San José de Apartadó was briefly mentioned; now we have additional tools of analysis to comprehend the reaction of the government, which is not to legitimise it. When applied to the case of the peace community of San José de Apartadó outlined earlier, the government's reaction of excluding possibilities for scrutiny and dissent becomes apparent. The discursive formation of the DSP, informed and informing the national context as a narco-terrorist struggle, is precisely what gives rise to the violent measures taken against the peace community. Only when the government understands nonviolent resistance as a daring challenge to state sovereignty can such a military incursion be 'justified'. When the ethical borders of the good nationals are built upon the distinction between 'patriots' and 'terrorists', the spaces for criticism, for resistance, for living out a different form of life are closed. The peace community was subsumed under the label of danger for the state and this incorporation made it into raw material for exemplary measures of sanction, correction, normalisation and discipline.

Nevertheless, the DSP, just as any other discourse, when made official and hegemonic, creates its own resistance, and produces its own provocations.

> [C]ultures are composed of multiple discourses or codes of intelligibility, and ... the world therefore can be and is represented in different, and often competing, ways, ha[ving] significant implications. In particular, it means that any representation can potentially be contested and so must actively reproduced. Meanings are not given, static, or final; rather, they are always in process and always provisional. ... Discourses are themselves not perfectly coherent but always entail internal contradictions and lacunae. These contradictions make possible both resistance to a dominant discourse and the transformation of discourses. (Weldes and others, 1999: 16)

We could argue that the present book is one of those provocations, for it is born out of the construction and production of insecurities and identity categories that this particular representation of 'Colombia as a democratic state under the threat of narco-terrorism' depicts. In this sense, let us remember why this research is a critique, for in the upcoming chapters we question what security means, what thoughts inform this particular way of representing the situation, which other possibilities are foreclosed and how the security discourses constitute, reconstitute and transform identities. I want to engage in questioning these assumptions about the self-evident character of Colombia as a democratic nation under the threat of narco-terrorism and the accepted view of the benevolence of security, as if it were a coherent and rational expression of a sovereign state in order to deal with threats.

Conclusion

In this chapter, a first approximation of the context in which the Democratic Security Policy (2003) is articulated was outlined. Several modes of representing the Colombian situation were considered, since political, social and economic circumstances shape and are shaped by discourses. Without adopting a sole definition as accurate, diverse perspectives on the situation of violence in Colombia were studied.

In terms of defining the Colombian conflict, we first considered the importance of adopting one definition over others. The power to name, to qualify the actors involved, the character of their struggle and the ways of dealing with the situation are all factors that in each representation have a different connotation. In this sense, definitions are not just the result of objective tabulations, but are already embedded in the power to name, to qualify certain aspects as relevant and disqualify others as such, and to value specific dynamics in a particular way.

Considering these insights, three different and diverse sources of definitions were analysed: perspectives elaborated by academics, by the government, and by the international community. Regarding academic perspectives, there is a multiplicity of representations of the situation that result in a plurality of definitions: new war, criminal activities fed by greed, state weakness as cause for the war, a civil war, and society at war, a counter-insurgent struggle, a war against drugs, and an irregular war. This plurality reflects the different foci of attention on the causes of the war, the characteristics of the armed struggle, and the development, evolution or transformation of the armed groups over the past four decades.

In terms of the Colombian government's definitions of the armed conflict, its interlinked relationship to the US government definition was considered. Colombian administrations have transformed the representation of the conflict from a communist struggle to a war against narco-terrorism, hand in hand with US foreign policy priorities. The ideological war between the state and communist guerrillas has been absorbed by a governmental understanding that the war on drugs and the war against terrorism obliterate the comprehension of the situation of violence in the country. Some other perspectives on the Colombian context were also taken into account, including those of international organisations that emphasise the political character of the conflict.

In the second part of this chapter, an analysis of the definition of the conflict as 'a democratic nation under the threat of narco-terrorism' was pursued. This particular articulation of the situation of violence has eliminated other considerations regarding social and political factors that, although not necessarily in the form of a causal determination, still do condition the situation of collective violence in Colombia. The illegal armed groups are depicted as terrorist organisations without ideological ideals that fight a terrorist war against a democratic nation-state.

This mode of representation has given rise to the DSP. However, what is the importance of this in/security policy for understanding identities in the Colombian case? This question guides the reflections of the second chapter, in which the theoretical framework for comprehending the intimate relationship between in/security and identity will be explored. The contributions of several critical scholars who question the ontological basis of conventional security studies will inform our interpretation of the subsequent theoretical framework. By problematising neo-realist accounts of the world and its in/securities, these outline some crucial implications that in/security discourses have on the construction of identities and allow us to grasp the DSP as a geopolitical and biopolitical strategy that draws territorial boundaries and also manages the lives of the population. These reflections advance the particular reading of the DSP in this book, which identifies the danger and impossibility of embracing in/security as the founding ground for politics, leading to the suppression of freedoms, scrutiny and dissent. In short, the following framework becomes necessary to underline the political violence that the DSP reproduces.

Notes

1 Although Mary Kaldor (1999) is recognised for having coined the terms 'new wars', the changing nature of civil wars and the inability for clearly recognising internal armed conflicts according to conventional standards have been a well researched international subject since the 1980s. In German-speaking areas, Herfried Münkler (2002) has shaped the limits of mainstream discussions with his pioneer work on 'new wars' by focusing on the privatisation of security and the figure of the mercenary as propelling the war industry. Likewise, Ulrich Beck (2005) has entered this debate with a reconstitution of 'new wars' as postnational wars in which 'war is peace'. For Beck, postnational wars pose new challenges to the comprehension of cosmopolitanism as a paradoxical prohibition of intervention by nation-states while claiming universal defence of human rights (ibid.: 24). Concretely regarding the Colombian case, the writings of Peter Waldmann (Waldmann, 2007; Waldmann and Reinares, 1999) shed light on this new type of warfare mainly driven by political terrorism and waged by non-conventional actors like warlords. In the same vein, the recently published work of Heidrun Zinecker (2007) offers a critical engagement with the thesis of 'new wars' in the Colombian and Salvadorian cases and points at the fragility of comprehending the Colombian war as a non-political armed confrontation mainly based on the search for profit. Marshal and Messiant (2004) also criticise international literature on the paradigm of 'new wars', particularly Mary Kaldor's theses, and argue that these are no different from the 'old wars'. Their main criticism of the 'new wars' literature is that it suffers from profound theoretical and empirical weaknesses and that it legitimises the adoption of 'just war' premises to deal with the threat of terrorism (ibid.: 30–4). For a more in-depth overview and sociological analysis of the different authors and currents of thoughts, and especially the fallouts and weaknesses of the 'new wars' paradigm, see Malešević (2008).

2 Carlo Nasi and Angelika Rettberg (Nasi and Rettberg, 2006) have compiled a concise bibliographical review of the latest publications concerning the definition of the Colombian war. Likewise, the edited volume *Nuestra Guerra sin Nombre* (IEPRI, 2006) precisely points to the problematic use of adopting a single definition of the Colombian war. In the latter, a comprehensive and profound account of the different types of violence, the diversity of the actors involved in the armed confrontations and the main changes in warfare since the mid-1990s can be found. Especially interesting is the thesis of the introductory chapter of the volume, written by Francisco Gutiérrez and Gonzálo Sánchez, which characterises the Colombian war as a Hobbesian trinity of insurgents, paramilitaries and drug dealers in their violent and changing relationship to the Colombian state. In the thirteen chapters that compose the IEPRI edited volume, some of the most influential contemporary political scientists discuss their own interpretations of why (or not) the Colombian case is a *sui generis* armed conflict or can be defined as a civil war. A common point of agreement among the contributors seems to be that, although it enjoys the

characteristics of an attractive war economy, the war in Colombia has not completely lost political meaning.

3 The role and the very nature of paramilitarism in Colombia is a subject that has been researched by many scholars, such as Duncan (2005), Rangel (2005) and, most recently, Romero (2003). The demobilisation of paramilitary groups in Colombia has been taking place since 2003 under the government of President Uribe (see also International Crisis Group, 2003). As discussed in the fourth chapter, I argue that this demobilisation is part of the DSP material effects that summon people to adopt the necessary positions in order to engross the ranks of the army of 'good people' against the 'narco-terrorist threat'.

4 Since this specific context conditions the promise of in/security, I detail it further in the corresponding third chapter 'The end of peace and the beginning of in/security'.

5 José Obdulio Gaviria (2005), political advisor to the president, by developing this thesis in more detail has arrived at the following conclusions. First, there is no armed conflict in the country because Colombia is a legitimate democracy and not a dictatorship nor an oppressive regime. Therefore, there is no justification for a violent group to commit armed actions. Second, after the fall of the Berlin Wall, Colombian guerrillas do not fight for a political ideal, but are mafias linked to the drug-dealing business. Finally, since the primary victims of the guerrillas are civilians, they ought to be qualified as terrorists (Gaviria quoted in Pizarro, 2005).

6 The relationship between 'underdevelopment' and 'insecurity' is a changing and complex matrix of power/knowledge in Colombia, depending upon the moment in history and sources researched. Both the UNDP (2003) and the Colombian government (DSP, 2003; Uribe, 2004a) depict 'underdevelopment' as mainly understood in terms of political and economic marginalisation, as the consequence of high levels of insecurity in the country. In this light, 'development' will be the future result of a secure country. In other words, first security ought to be installed and then, and only then, will this type of preconceived 'development' materialise. This cause-effect relationship contradicts former theses on the 'objective conditions of violence', as the well-accepted structuralist discourse of the 1970s in Latin America read: poverty, exclusion and discrimination cause violence. It was the violence of wars that presented an obstacle to development. In Mark Duffield's well-known terms, underdevelopment was a security issue; 'underdevelopment' was destabilising and a source of danger (Duffield, 2001). Yet, in the concrete discussion of the DSP in Colombia, this reinterpretation of in/security and its relationship to (under)development is portrayed as the opposite. In order to grasp the depth and consequences of development discourse in Colombia, Arturo Escobar's work is of crucial relevance to comprehend the power of thinking, acting, talking and – ultimately – imagining along the lines of 'development' and 'underdevelopment' (Escobar, 1995, 2004). For a thorough discussion on the pervasiveness and plasticity (Pörksen, 1995) of the terms 'development' and 'underdevelopment' see Wolfgang Sachs' *Development Dictionary* (1992).

2

Theorising security discourses

T HE FIRST QUESTION THAT ARISES when addressing security discourses is the meaning of security itself. Any specific concept of security entails certain implications. Even though security is regarded today as a basic need, what passes under the label 'security' is actually quite wide.[1] Conceptions of security range from traditional understandings in military terms, that is, the classical idea of national security, to contemporary conceptions of comprehensive and human security incorporating virtually every aspect of the political, social, environmental and cultural dimensions.

Answering the question of what constitutes security is inextricably linked to insecurity, or to what security is not. Attempts to solve this paradox have been at the centre of attention of a large group of scholars whose explanations produce a great multiplicity of answers. This evidences the variety of questions posed in relation to security and the wide range of concerns that inform scholars' work on this matter. It is then pertinent to trace some of the different meanings of security in order to outline the notion of security and its implications, especially as these concepts are then used to evaluate the DSP in Colombia.

These tasks delineate the content of the present chapter. First, I focus on the meaning that security has been traditionally given in IR and its understanding of world politics. Secondly, I explore critical security studies, beginning with the conceptual voids left by this view. Critical security studies interpret security and security policies as intertwined with the constitution of political identities. The present chapter identifies the theoretical framework necessary to analyse the DSP in Colombia and its significant effects on identity.

Conventional security in international relations

Security discourses traditionally emanate mainly from the state, which has been the privileged focus of attention in the field of IR. Therefore, most works treating the concept of security as such, and those about security policies, are carried out in this field of study. A very well-known work in IR about the theory of security is Barry Buzan's *People, States and Fear: An Agenda for International Security Studies in the Post-Cold War Era* (1991) to which I turn in this chapter to outline the primary security discourses. Barry Buzan himself is recognised as one of the most influential authors on alternative views on security. This is partly due to this particular publication in which he changed the focus of attention in IR, stopped conceiving of security purely in military terms, and expanded it to be understood as a confluence of contradictions among sectors and levels. The state remains central in this account. It is important to refer to the main arguments of Buzan in order to comprehend how the discussion in the field has changed in recent decades, meshing the different concepts of *security, state* and *identity*.

Besides providing a traditional ontological reading of security, Buzan's text is helpful in tracing a genealogy of the notion of security and the ways in which it has been reconstituted and debated in IR. For this purpose, I focus on the following points to highlight the main pillars of security discussions in IR: 1) defining the concept of security, 2) the anarchical international system, 3) the state of nature, 4) the sovereign state and 5) threats and vulnerabilities.

My main argument is that conventional and alternative security studies remain trapped in interrogations about 'how to achieve security' and 'whom to secure', respectively. Yet, the ontological basis of these discussions leaves aside 'what security does'. In other words, conventional and alternative views on security treat security as a '*thing*, or a determined condition that could be applied to different objects and procured by different agents – as long as its definition is wide or deep enough to be inclusive' (Stern, 2005: 21). Hence, these accounts suffer from serious limitations in analysis when trying to conceptualise what security does to identities.

My contention is that conventional and alternative readings of security do not question 'security' as a process, as a practice that enters in the process of identification of political subjects by 'doing' in/security (Dillon, 1996). This understanding of in/security is necessary in order to address the concerns raised in the present book. Such concerns question the political violence that the DSP produces and legitimises in terms of identity construction and production. In the second section of this chapter, I examine how critical security studies rethink the very same pillars of security discussions in a different light, one that enables comprehension of how security is pivotal for grasping processes of identification.

Defining the concept of security

Since the end of World War II, two classical notions of security in IR have contoured scholarly discussions about this term: realist and idealist-inspired security ideas. The realist school used to 'see security as a derivative of power: an actor with enough power to reach a dominating position would acquire security as a result' (Buzan, 1991: 2). By contrast, the idealist school 'tended to see security as a consequence of peace: a lasting peace would provide security for all' (ibid.). The inability to agree upon a general definition of security (ibid.: 16) is made evident when one looks at how conventional security analyses in IR have defined this tricky term and informed both academic work and political discussions about global politics.

Following Buzan, an extended list of security definitions has developed. Some of these definitions are extremely useful for this book, since they demonstrate the multiplicity of meanings that the concept of security has been invested with in IR. They also illustrate the types of questions that arise when security is treated as a 'thing' or a condition to be achieved, leaving entrenched assumptions unquestioned.

Among the definitions presented in Buzan's work (ibid.: 16–17) we find a group that understands security as the absence of war, very similar to the notion of negative peace (Galtung, 1996). Here, for example, security is defined as 'a relative freedom from war, coupled with a relatively high expectation that defeat will not be a consequence of any war that should occur' (Bellany quoted in Buzan, 1991: 16). Analogously, in this negative-peace group of security definitions, we find the concept of a secure nation 'to the extent to which it is not in danger of having to sacrifice core values if it wishes to avoid war, and is able, if challenged, to maintain them by victory in such war' (Lippman quoted in ibid.: 17). Another example is the definition of national security 'as the ability to withstand aggression from abroad' (Luciani quoted in ibid.).

A second set of definitions combine the notion of national security with issues of identity. For example, national security is defined as the 'preservation of a way of life acceptable to the people and compatible with the needs and legitimate aspirations of others' (National Defence College of Canada quoted in ibid.: 16). Similarly, some definitions merge national interests and values with security, like national security defined as 'the ability of a nation to pursue successfully its national interests, as it sees them, in any place in the world' (Hartland-Thunberg quoted in ibid.: 17). Extending beyond national security, i.e. traditional defence policy, national security can also be understood as 'the non-military actions of a state to ensure its total capacity to survive as a political entity in order to exert influence and to carry out its internal and international objectives' (Loww quoted in ibid.).

However, these notions of security fall short when confronted with the criticisms of the centrality of the nation-state as the primary locus and focus of sovereign political authority (Walker, 1999). Therefore, in later definitions, security was extended beyond national considerations to systemic ones. During the 1980s, the influence of the interdependence school in IR and the political world situation served to broaden the concept of security beyond the spectrum of national power politics 'to add economic, political, societal and environmental issues' (Buzan, 1991: 12). The traditional conception of security no longer sufficed for groups on both sides of the political spectrum. It could not satisfy advocates of isolationism, like small-is-beautiful or unilateral disarmament, nor globalist peace scholars, like defenders of a world government:

> The Brandt Commission called for a new concept of security that would transcend the narrow notions of military defence and look more towards the logic of a broader interdependence. The common theme underlying these voices was that a notion of security bound to the level of individual states and military issues is inherently inadequate. At best, such a notion produced the dangerously ambiguous symbol ...., which 'while appearing to offer guidance and a basis for broad consensus ... may be permitting everyone to label whatever policy he favours with an attractive and possibly deceptive name.' At worst, it drives the security dilemma to such a pitch of intensity that it begins to resemble the model of those who see international relations as an unending struggle for power. (Ibid.: 6)

The idea of common security was and still is subject to a wide-ranging debate. Since the 1994 publication of the *Human Development Report* by the United Nations (UNDP, 1994), the notion of human security has been in vogue once again. Human security was defined as the freedom from want and fear, understood as universal, interdependent, easier to ensure through early prevention and people-centred (ibid.: 23–4). As such, human security focuses on the notion of existential threats like hunger, epidemics and oppression, situations of insecurity that people face in their daily lives as humans, i.e. as 'individuals' as opposed to as citizens of nation-states.[2] Additionally, the new European strategy on security, with the expression comprehensive security, reworks the same underlying assumptions (EU, 2003). Its main tenet is that comprehensive security ought to be widened by human security concerns. In other words, security is no longer to be understood as a purely military enterprise, but also taking into consideration its social, politic, economic and cultural dimensions.

These three approaches – common security, human security and comprehensive security – emphasise the interdependency of international relations and try to prioritise the individual over state, or national, security. However, they do not provoke a change in the very idea of security, but rather serve to expand the agenda of security issues to the environmental, health, economic and political spheres, among others. As Buzan (ibid.: 13) argued a few decades ago about common security, this 'peace and development' perspective does not challenge the assumptions on which realist and neorealist security scholars base their claims. On the contrary, it seems as if the so-called idealist scholars found a new name for making their agenda converge with the realists' programme and allowed themselves to continue using security as their 'preferred conceptual tool', but now face an extended range of issues to be securitised.

These last comments echo the critique of 'securitisation' and the call for 'de-securitisation' (Wæver, 1995) made during the 1980s and early 1990s. The work and insights of Ole Wæver (ibid.) and the so-called 'Copenhagen School' have been especially acknowledged, for they began 'to explore the concept of security in terms of its historical, philosophical and politico-linguistic aspects' (Buzan, 1991: 13).[3] Most famously, Ole Wæver's notion of 'securitisation' made a huge impact on security discussions. Wæver (1995) recognised security as having two different sets of meanings, one related to the everyday use of the word, and a second one resulting from 'the international discussion on national security, security policy, and the like' (ibid.: 49–50). Security, in this latter field of discourses and practices, entails a *speech act* in which a 'state representative moves a particular development into a specific area, and thereby claims a special right to use whatever means are necessary to block it' (ibid.: 55). As Wæver points out, securitisation has, as its main consequence, the suspension on the critical and public scrutiny over governmental actions. Therefore, he called for the desecuritisation of issues as an important strategy for desecuritising politics, as opposed to securitising problems (ibid.: 57).

It is precisely the securitisation of problems which led Buzan (1991: 18) to underscore how all security definitions do a disservice 'by giving the concept an appearance of firmness which it does not merit' because 'the word itself implies an absolute condition – something is either secure or insecure – and does not lend itself to the idea of a graded spectrum'. In this line of thinking, argues Buzan, the best way to conceptualise security is to define it as 'the pursuit of freedom from threat' (ibid.: 19) by a series of attributes that lend themselves to be contextualised in a concrete situation. First, security is depicted as 'the ability of states and societies to maintain their independent identity and their functional integrity'. Second, security is primarily about 'the fate of human collectivities, and only secondarily about the personal security of individual human beings', which means that 'in the contemporary international system, the standard unit of security is thus the sovereign territorial state'. In addition, even though the ideal type of the state – 'where ethnic and cultural boundaries line up with political ones' – does not speak for most of the nations that do not fit neatly inside the borders of constituted states, Buzan insists upon conceiving of the nation-state as the main referent of security.

In other words, the nation-state is the main *object* to be secured. It is, at the same time, the main *provider* of security. Being both the referent and provider of security in the international anarchical system, it is natural that the focus of security concerns the units that form the system. Thus, 'since states are the dominant units, "national security" is the central issue, both in its normal, but ambiguous, reference to the state and in its more direct application to ethno-cultural units' (ibid.).

The security of human collectivities – as individuals and societies – is still circumscribed by the imaginary of nation-states within an international security environment characterised by anarchy.

International anarchy

In conventional IR theories, the conceptualisation of security has been based upon the assumption that there is an international anarchical system characterised by its lack of an *orderer*. That is to say, there is no world government that enjoys and can exercise higher power over sovereign nation-states (Weber, 2005: 14). Therefore, all nation-states are obliged to look after their own security needs in order to secure their survival. Since all nation-states 'behave' according to the same reasoning, they try to increase their power constantly in order to defend themselves from external threats.

This produces a 'security dilemma', an expression coined by John Herz in his 1951 book *Political Realism and Political Idealism*. This 'dilemma' suggests that constant war is explained by the anarchical nature of the international 'system of units without any higher authority offering protection from interference with their existence and independence. Thus there was a need to provide oneself with the means of protection, causing suspicion and fears, armament races, and war' (Herz, 2003: 412).

Hence, the 'security dilemma' is characterised by its 'tragedy'; since nation-states fear, they are insecured by the actions of other nation-states in their accumulation of power, and might even wage war against one another, without ever desiring it (Roe, 1999). In other words, war can arise at any moment without a nation-state even intending to engage in it, but rather purely 'defensively' engaging out of the fear of having its sovereignty challenged by other nation-states' power. It is this defensive posture within the international system that turns into one of the main 'permissive causes of war' (Waltz, 2001) and contours the meaning of security as it is conceived in conventional understandings of the term.[4]

If the myth of the anarchical international system is accepted, as one could argue has been the case in conventional security discussions (Weber, 2005), then this environment imposes three conditions on the concept of security. First, 'states are the principal referent object of security because they are both the framework of order and the highest source of governing authority' (Buzan, 1991: 22). Second, national security is relational and interdependent with the security of other states: 'domestic insecurities may or may not dominate the national security agenda, but external threats will almost always comprise a major element of the national security problem' (ibid.). Thirdly, 'under anarchy, security can only be relative, never absolute' (ibid.: 23).

The incomplete project of state security finds its explanation beyond the 'security dilemma' mentioned above, and directly involves the security relationship between the nation-state and its citizen members. Starting from another assumption about the nature and behaviour of 'men', this incompleteness finds its explanation in the limits that individuals pose to the security-seeking activities of the state and to each others' security (ibid.: 35). This opens the door to analysing the following pillar of security as it has been conventionally conceived: the state of nature as a 'true' image of the behaviour and interests of 'men', who constantly threaten each other and challenge each other's survival, making both the project of state security and individual security an always unfinished and interrelated process.

The state of nature

As it has been conceived of in mainstream security discussions, the primordial dilemma regarding individual security is exemplified by the Hobbesian state of nature (Hobbes, 1651). In mainstream IR, readings of Thomas Hobbes' *Leviathan* have made the image of the state of nature a powerful explanation for the impossibility of total security.

According to Hobbes (ibid.: 40), all 'mankind'[5] has the general inclination to 'a perpetual and restless desire for power after power, a desire that ceases only in death'. Since 'man' is not content with enjoying power moderately, but rather constantly is assuring it for 'himself', 'the competition for riches, honour, command, or any other power tends to produce quarrelling, enmity, and war' (ibid.). 'Because one competitor's path to the achievement of his desire is to kill, subdue, outwit, or repel the other competitor', in the face of fear of violent death and of wounds, 'men' are disposed to obey a common power (state) in exchange for protection.

Following Hobbes, when 'men' live without a common power that keeps them 'all in awe', they find themselves in the condition of war (ibid.: 52). For Hobbes, war is not only circumscribed by acts of fighting, but rather war is recognised as 'a period of time during which it is well enough known that people are willing to join in battle' (ibid.). Such an inclination, full of 'man's' desire for power and without any assurance to the contrary, makes of 'every man the enemy of every man' (ibid.). In this time of war 'men live with no security except what their own strength and ingenuity provide them with' (ibid.: 53). It is in the very passions of 'men' that such a spiral of violence is to be found. Therefore, by themselves, 'men' would not restrain themselves from waging war, but rather quarrel continuously while trying to achieve and enhance their power.

Only because 'men' in the state of war suffer from a 'continual fear and danger of violent death, and the life of man [is] solitary, poor, nasty, brutish, and short' (ibid.: 52), do they agree upon natural laws that procure safety in order to secure their own preservation and lead a more contented life. The natural laws Hobbes refers to concern fairness, justice, gratitude and mercy, among others, and are, consequently, laws contrary to 'man's' passions and desires in the state of nature/war (ibid.: 54–68). Precisely because laws are contrary to 'our passions' does the commonwealth or state need to be a visible power that keeps all men in awe 'and tie them by fear of punishment to keep their covenants and to obey the laws of nature' (ibid.: 71). According to Hobbesian logic, only the fear of a higher authority can create peace and security.[6]

This traditional story about what 'man' is and how the state is born provides a foundational narrative about the competing claims between a free individual and national security in conventional IR (Walker, 2004). Since there is a primary anarchy, in which the living conditions for the individuals involved are marked by unacceptably high levels of societal threats, unbearable chaos becomes the motive for sacrificing some freedoms in order to improve levels of security. In this process, both government and the state are born (Buzan, 1991: 38). 'States of all types benefit from the widespread feeling among individuals that anything is better than reversion to the state of nature. So long as the state performs its Hobbesian tasks of keeping chaos at bay, this service will be seen by many to offset the costs of other state purposes, whatever they may be' (ibid.: 43).

The above reflection gives the state an irreversible character. 'There is no real option of going back, and therefore the security of individuals is inseparably entangled with that of the state' (ibid.: 39). Thus, according to this view, once the foundations for the modern state are put into place, a balance is found between state security and individual security. The paradox dissolves when the state seems to threaten individuals with its actions, for the nation-state 'sacrifices the interests of some [individuals] for what is seen to be a higher collective interest' (ibid.: 45). Hence, the conclusions in terms of security can be structured as follows: (1) individual security is subordinated to national and international security, (2) individual security is affected positively and negatively by the state, and (3) individual pursuit of security might undermine a state's internal coherence and order (ibid.: 54–5).

At this point in the discussion, an entrenched problem arises in questioning national security. The security of the individual depends upon the survival and security of the state itself. If the state disappeared, individuals would face unbearable levels of societal threats and war. Therefore, if ever the competing claims of individual security challenge or put at risk the security of the nation-state, the latter ought to be given prevalence because, in this storyline, without the state, individuals would wage war against each other. This argument thus not only justifies the rise of the modern state, but also identifies the perpetual threat if people do not comply with security policies, measures or restrictions.

In short, the image of the state of nature, its violence and the fear it inflicts is a frequent metaphor that supports the sacrifices made by individuals and legitimises state violence (Connolly, 1991). Only by having assumed an anarchical previous stage for human collectivities can the state be seen as the *necessary evil* that gives prevalence to sovereign power and, as is relevant to this discussion, the primacy of protecting national security as the most important concern for the welfare of civil society. However, if the state of nature was pictured as peaceful, and/or if the state was seriously questioned as an entity that brings about peace, then there will be no need to sacrifice individuals for the higher good of protection supposedly received for obeying sovereign authority. Once this image of violence/security is questioned, then there is a wider range of possibilities open for political organisation that would not necessarily lead to the erection of a powerful state that keeps 'men at awe' (Hobbes, 1651).

The sovereign state

According to conventional security discussions in IR, it is a state's sovereignty that allows it to perform security tasks. The nation-state is an entity different from all others because it can govern itself, which 'requires denial of any higher political authority, and the claiming by the state of supreme decision-making authority both within its territory and over its citizens' (Buzan, 1991: 66). As Kenneth Waltz (2001) explains, sovereignty speaks of a quality that exists when 'a state decides for itself how it will cope with its internal and external problems, including whether or not to seek assistance from others and in doing so to limit its freedom by making commitments to them'. However, the sovereignty of the state, as its ability to govern itself, rests on a higher assumption, that of the state itself:

> The state exists, or has its essence, primarily on the socio-political rather than on the physical plane. In some important senses, the state is more an idea held in common by a group of people, than it is a physical organism. To be sure, the state depends on a physical base, and past a certain point cannot exist without it. ... If the heart of the state resides in the idea of it held in the minds of the population, then that idea itself becomes a major object of national security. (Buzan, 1991: 63–4)

In this sense, the state is an *idea held in common* by the population, which has to sustain itself permanently in a realm of discussion where other ideas about the organisation of political communities and their security defy it. 'Ideas [are] a vital component of the state, essential to its coherence and purpose, and provid[e] a mechanism for persuading citizens to subordinate themselves to the state's authority' (ibid.: 83). When the state is seen as mainly an idea, the primary security task of the state must be securing this idea in itself. In this sense, the state as a natural entity, born out of an anarchical international system, begins to lose validity, and turns into a *fabrication*:

> It seems fair to note that institutions can substitute more for ideas than the other way around. An extreme institutional model of the state – rule by pure coercion – has some empirical credibility, whereas a pure idea model – government without institutions – appears not to exist outside the fantasies of a few anarchists. Against this, however, has to be set the strong disposition of governments to create unifying ideas, either by cultivating an ideological orthodoxy, or by embarking on the state-nation process. (Ibid.: 85)

The previous naturalised sovereign state turns out to be *the idea of the sovereign state*, for which the institutional power of the state itself has to invest resources so that the individuals under its authority do not defy it. This is the reason why, as Buzan points out, the process of nation-building is one of the most important tasks of the state.

A key question arises from this line of thought: if the state is the guardian of the idea of the state and has to invest constantly in this idea so that it continues to be held in the minds of the population, then why is the state regarded as the natural actor of an international anarchical system? If this argument were coherent, the *idea held in common* of the sovereign state would be born *naturally* out the state of nature. In other words, the idea of the state would not have to be defended constantly if *naturally* conflictive human beings, driven by the passions of competition, diffidence and glory-seeking (Hobbes, 1651), decided to found and to obey the sovereign authority of the state. In the face of the fear of 'men's' lives as solitary, poor, nasty, brutish and short (ibid.), the very idea of the state ought to be the natural result of 'men's' survival needs and rational self-interest. The fact that the main national security concern is to secure the idea of the state itself seems to contradict the reifying and neat picture of this political process.

In traditional security studies, this lacuna is mostly ignored. For a field of study that deals mainly with *the state*, questioning it seems to threaten the object of study. It is 'as if conventional analyses of security are incapable of discussing security without taking the state for granted' (Chilton, 1996: 23). In this sense, and as exemplified above, the state is not privy to being questioned, even though it seems that it is the temporary result of its own questioning.

Threats and vulnerabilities

Only by accepting the state as an entity taken for granted can predominant views in IR conceptualise threats and vulnerabilities as objective factors that are measured by the state in order to react against them and seek security. In the words of Buzan (1991: 112), 'only when one has a reasonable idea of both the nature of threats, and the vulnerabilities of the objects towards which they are directed, can one begin to make sense of national security as a policy problem'.

This reading leaves on the margins the problematisation of the state as an *idea* in need of constant reinforcement and considers the state to be a *natural* entity, with a *body* that clearly separates its inside and outside. As portrayed in this account, the state – as a coherent rational entity – evaluates the threats on the dangerous outside and has the ability to implement measures to reduce its vulnerabilities on the inside. The task of analysing security threats and vulnerabilities thus becomes never-ending, since

> The question of when a threat becomes a national security issue depends not just on what type of threat it is, and how the recipient state perceives it, but also on the

> intensity with which the threat operates. The main factors affecting the intensity of a threat are the specificity of its identity, its nearness in space and time, the probability of its occurring, the weight of its consequences and whether or not perceptions of the threat are amplified by historical circumstances. ... The problem, of course, is that not all of these variables can be measured, or even estimated, accurately, and that they frequently occur in complex mixtures which make overall weighting on the spectrum of intensity a highly problematic exercise. (Ibid.: 134)

The measurement of threats has to be carried out by *experts*, who are able to evaluate 'a host of complex factors' in the international arena (ibid.: 140). The art of national security policy 'requires constant monitoring and assessment, and the development of criteria for deciding when threats become of sufficient intensity to warrant action' (ibid.: 141). At the same time, such constant monitoring of threats and vulnerabilities is a necessary function for (not of) the state since 'one might even argue that states need to be threatened. If no threats existed, part of the state's basic Hobbesian function would disappear. Given the mutually constituting character of states and the international system, this logic points either to an anarchical utopia, or to the collapse of government and the rise of civil disorder' (ibid.).

Exactly at this point, the self-referential logic of conventional understandings of security closes itself and the point at which we arrive is the same point of departure. The image of fear and violence of 'men' in the state of nature constitute mutually the anarchical international system of nation-states, serving as a point of entry for this particular understanding of security. At the same time, the state of nature and its mutually constitutive international anarchical system of nation-states serves as metaphysical justification for the same state of nature and international anarchical system.

The state of nature is arguably the *raison de être* of the state. It is treated as the foundation of the modern nation-state; the state is the lesser evil for which individuals sacrifice their freedoms in order to feel safe. The state is, then, this particular idea, this notion of a superior order, which can provide security within its territory and protect it from the dangerous world outside (Walker, 1993). To perform this security task, governmental officials have to measure both threats and vulnerabilities, beyond and within its borders, respectively. If state security enters into a contradiction with individual security, the state solves the dilemma by gearing its decisions and actions towards defending the higher good, meaning, towards prioritising national security over individual security. To accomplish this function, security experts (generally state officials) have to be alert in identifying dangers, for if dangers take over the state, civil disorder will reign and the modern state will end.

This terrifying and chaotic image of what we are told is the violent nature of 'men' reappears again as the legitimising principle of state security discourses. If there were no threats, there would be no justification for state security. If there were no threats, neither would there be justification for the sacrifice of individuals in the name of survival of the modern state. Therefore, we are faced with a contradiction that Buzan timidly identifies: without threats there is no security, insecurity is the condition for the state to be born and, contrary to the common explanation of security policies, it is insecurity, threats and vulnerabilities that form the constituting element of security itself. Without insecurity, security cannot exist. Security, therefore, has to remain a promise. In Buzan's words 'total security is not possible', not because threats are endless but, quite on the contrary, because achieving security would imply the termination of the modern Hobbesian state and the shattering of the political power to obey state security policies.

Conventional stories of state security in IR

In examining conventional readings of state security, I have used Buzan and others' work to draw attention to the main assumptions and lines of argument that sustain them. The first pillar analysed was the conception of an anarchical international system, which is *naturally* divided into units called nation-states. Second, the state is assumed to be a pre-arranged entity, whose constitution is taken for granted as the result of fear and consensus born from the *state of nature*. Third, the state is portrayed as a sovereign actor, which resembles a coherent body whose main attribute is its self-government. Fourth, security policies are born out of the categorisation and classification of threats and vulnerabilities by security experts according to the measurement of objective dangers. Fifth, the problem of security is a matter of not having achieved greater levels of it in order to provide human collectivities with safety.

The self-referential logic of security is thus made evident in this account. The foundational principle and the ultimate justification are the seemingly 'secure' identities of 'men' and the 'state'. This storyline is based upon the assumption that what these identities are is, if not known, at least knowable. They appear as coherent subjects, pre-existing the discursive realm of security. There are 'men' and there exists a 'state', previous identities whose interests, rationalities and behaviour are clearly demarcated by a worldview that sees them mainly as conflictual and prone to war. Then, so we are told, enters security to administer the relationships between these identities in a way that the 'higher good' of the sovereign state's security can be protected inside and outside (Walker, 1993). Inside a state's borders, sovereignty appears as the condition of obedience from citizen-subjects to the state, who gain protection in return. External sovereignty, on the other hand, implies territory outside state boundaries. Sovereignty operates as the double condition that keeps dangers at bay by protecting the state borders (and the citizens inside them) from the threatening international system of anarchy (ibid.).

In this account, the referent objects of security are static. Insecurity appears as a policy problem founded on the inability or failure of not having adequately measured threats and vulnerabilities. Security so becomes a paradigm through which reality is shaped (Lobo-Guerrero, 2007: 332). Yet, this account of security and the identities security administers (Campbell, 1998) fall short in engaging with the security discourse of the Colombian government and how it shapes the very political identities of 'state', 'nationals' and 'others'. My argument is precisely that, by naming dangers and threats, the DSP constructs ideal identity categories for these subjects (including the state itself). It furthermore deploys a plethora of practices so that subjects adopt the positions designed in the same security discourse. Hence, this interrogation of how 'security' *does* identity exceeds the limits of what needs to be pre-assumed in the conventional paradigm of security discourses.

In the subsequent section, I discuss other interpretations that enable questioning of the referent objects of security. By pointing out how reality is constantly being made (Lobo-Guerrero, 2007), rather than pre-discursively given, these interpretations both offer an alternative to traditional discourse and pay special attention to the importance of in/security for delineating both the territorial and ethical contours of political identities (Stern, 2005).

Security from critical perspectives

The conceptual voids posed by the self-referential logic of conventional views of security discussions, the recognition of constantly changing realities and the awareness of identities in flux, have been studied in depth by critical IR schools.[7] I distinguish such 'critical views' by their questioning of the ontology of conventional security discussions. I understand 'ontology' as that which speaks for 'a view of being and the nature of things' (Edkins, 2003: 14). Specifically in IR, ontology refers to that which constitutes relevant units of analysis, such as individuals and states, 'and whether the world and these units are constant or dynamic and able to be changed' (Ackerly et al., 2006: 6). As argued above, conventional readings of security discourses take for granted what 'men', 'state' and 'security' are. They therefore do not explain how these security subjects are (performatively) produced by discourses about danger.

By excluding the historical situatedness and ambiguities that mark the processes of constitution and constant reproduction of these security 'subjects' (Walker, 1993), conventional understandings of security fall short when trying to grasp the importance of the DSP in the constitution and in the production of political identities in Colombia. They are also insufficient for understanding the political violence that is legitimised by the security discourse itself. In analysing the tragic attempts at 'securing' the uncertainties and ambiguities of the political identities that are said to be its foundation, I argue that the DSP produces the very identities that are said to found it. Consequently, the DSP shapes, moulds and changes politics such that political violence is reproduced by the very promise of halting it.

To comprehend the articulations of security and identity in this particular case study, it is necessary to adopt a theoretical framework that does not freeze the identities in question. Such a framework rather accepts that identities are multiple, that subjectivity is plural and that it defies any complete closure (Edkins, 2003; Jabri, 1999; Stern, 2005). In order to interrogate the political violence prompted by the DSP, it becomes crucial to investigate how the founding and continuation of the sovereign state authority over a political community is marked by violence (Edkins, 2003).

The DSP aims to clearly separate 'us' from 'them' in a violent movement of inclusion/exclusion of political bodies and behaviour. It is therefore all the more vital to look for viewpoints that recognise how 'plural selves' are formed in a responsive manner to constitutive others (Jabri, 1999). Only by accepting that security and identity are mutually contingent upon each other can the certain violence of the promise of security be made visible. And only after this violence has been made visible can it be contested. Hopefully, alternative possibilities for rethinking the harmful grammars of in/security can then be imagined (Butler, 2004; Stern, 2005).

The critical security perspectives selected in this section question the foundations of conventional readings of security and embrace its ambiguities. From its beginnings in the state of nature and the sovereign state, these alternative readings illustrate the mutually constituted character of in/security and identity. After presenting different interpretations of what security does, I will concentrate on how security and insecurity are mutually constitutive and how the idea of the state is created in the process of naming dangers. This leads to questioning the self-evidence of the meaning of security as the economy of identity/difference (Connolly, 1991). We will try to follow the pillars of conventional views on security, sketched in the first section of this chapter, and review them from these different and challenging perspectives.

According to conventional (neo)realist views in IR, the foundational principle of the international security system is its primary anarchical character, which *naturally* gives birth to nation-states (Buzan, 1991). The state is assumed to be a pre-arranged entity, whose constitution is taken for granted as the result of fear and consensus born out of the *state of nature* (Hobbes, 1651). In this storyline of security, the state conceals this anarchy by being a sovereign actor, which resembles a coherent body whose main attribute is its self-government (Waltz, 2001).

The structure of knowledge in security studies stereotypically takes the form of positing the existence of certain entities – often but not always states – within an environment in which they experience threat(s). The nature of those entities is assumed to be both given and fixed, at least for all practical purposes, and security is thus understood to mean securing these fixed entities against objective and external threats. ... Security studies, then, treats insecurities as unavoidable facts while problematizing, and consequently focusing its attention on, the acquisition of security for pregiven entities – usually the state. (Weldes et al., 1999: 9–10)

Yet, what if this particular reading of *reality* was challenged? What if the state of nature, as conceptualised by Hobbes (1651), was analysed as including changing and dynamic subjectivities? What if the *world, state* and the *individual* were conceptualised as identities in the process of becoming (Edkins and Pin-Fat, 1999; Hall, 1996a)? What if these *entities* could no longer be clearly separated from each other (Walker, 1993)? What if the processes of constitution of threats and the identities of the modern state and the free individual were mutual (Campbell, 1998; Dillon, 1996; Walker, 1993, 1999)? What if the individual were not a unitary self who would kill and harm others in the absence of a *Leviathan?*

These questions are posed by several scholars who problematise the conventional account of the world and the individual. Their insights offer ways of reading the DSP in Colombia as crucial for comprehending the process of identification. These questions and many others also problematise and make visible how in/security discourses produce the political violence they promise to halt.

State sovereignty

I begin by scrutinising three notions: state sovereignty, free individual and security policies, which, as R. B. J. Walker (1993, 1999) says, cannot be meaningfully separated in contemporary politics. Walker (1993: 165) reminds us that sovereignty has been a historical principle of political modernity conceptualised differently by various theorists and practitioners. Sovereignty, though invoked constantly as the principle that legitimises the obedience of individuals to state security policies, has been marked by an ambiguous relationship with claims about power and authority, state and society (ibid.).

Only by marginalising alternative accounts of sources of authority in national and international politics can state sovereignty be invoked by state officials as an effective discourse to sustain their power and authority over a particular geographical space and the people who inhabit it (ibid.). This is possible due to the marginalisation of other political identities that reside beyond the boundaries of the political community of the modern nation-state. Such boundaries are both spatial and ethical. They distinguish friend from foe, inside from outside, self from other, familiar and safe from outlandish and dangerous (ibid.).

Sovereignty thus acts as a traditional political principle that forges a conventional answer to questions of 'same and different, inside and outside, pluralist and universalist, history and structure, theory/purpose and practice, friend and foe' (ibid.: 73). The usefulness of sovereignty as a principle without question in international politics is the result of a selective interpretation of Hobbes' political writings (ibid.: 110). Hobbes articulated the necessities of the sovereign authority with the 'stunningly simple assertion that the proper subject of politics, and the most basic component of the "state of nature", was the free and equal individual' (Walker, 1999: x). This individual, like the sovereign state, is the new modern subject 'framed in a language of spatial separations, of self and other, self and world', who 'has come to seem entirely natural, inevitable, even as the apogee of all modern desires and possibilities' (ibid.).

In dehistoricising Hobbes' writings, we remove the context in which they were written and the contradictions and nuances to which his writings responded. Reading the Hobbesian state of nature as analogous to an international state of nature provides a legitimising principle for states as being led to war 'because of competition for material possessions, mistrust, fear, and the pursuit of glory, with fear being the prime motive in that it supposedly leads to a concern to secure what we already have' (Walker, 1993: 111). Only by assuming that the state of nature is full of violence and fear can the authority of the state over the individual be legitimised, as occurs in conventional readings of security in IR. This image of unacceptable levels of societal threats haunts individuals and keeps the free subject under the authority of the modern state (Buzan, 1991). This tidy story of ahistorical states, as if they were eternal, devoid from any contextual attachment, a constant, foundational principle without contingencies, makes states into somewhat mystical creatures. This storyline produces states as 'a formal and almost lifeless category, when in fact states are constantly maintained, defended, attacked, reproduced, undermined, and relegitimised on a daily basis' (Walker, 1993: 168).

According to Walker, this explains our conventional story, reconciling the subject with the sovereign authority of the state.

> Stories about the social contract; about nationalism, liberalism, and socialism; about public and private, state and civil society; about rights, representations, and democratizations [are] the ways in which we have managed to reconcile our claims to be both free autonomous individual/collective subjects and yet also subject to the ultimate authority of that sovereign that expresses our true subjectivity. (Walker, 1999: x)

Yet, this reconciliation is not free from dilemmas. Internationalisers and globalisers, among others, have insisted that 'claims of modern sovereignty are insufficient to answer all questions about the character and location of political authority in contemporary circumstances' (Walker, 1999: xii). These claims meet at the fluidity 'of all those boundaries that the early modern taught us to construct as sharp lines between self and other, this state and that state', and they converge 'as a consequence of contemporary reengagements with all those hard questions about who we are and what we can be that Hobbes and his successors thought had been answered once and for all in the twin absolutes of a unitary sovereignty and a unitary individual' (Walker, 1999: xii–iii).

State sovereignty turns into a political principle that demarcates spatial and temporal boundaries both for the modern state as well as for the free and modern individual (Walker, 1993, 1999). Consequently, both state sovereignty and subjectivity are concepts that 'overlap and are intertwined, returning to embrace and include each other' in an 'intensely political relationship' (Edkins and Pin-Fat, 1999: 2). Here lies one of the most difficult tasks for problematising security discourses, as we know them according to conventional IR. 'The particular form of subjectivity [of the modern individual] produces and legitimises the political arrangements of sovereignty. Even more importantly, the residues of this process of writing are erased, giving the appearance of already existing entities or objects and obliterating the production and operation of power' (ibid.). Thought of in this way, subjectivity is 'bound up with the social or symbolic order' and so 'the constitution of the subject and the constitution of social order ... implicate each other' (ibid.: 4).

Therefore, questioning subjectivity implies the questioning of its intertwined relationship with sovereignty, which is the founding stone of the state itself. As Michael Dillon (1999: 117) argues, in western political thought, the concept of sovereignty is 'the apogee of secure self-presence to which this tradition aspired as the secure foundation of its understanding of truth'. Considered in this way, sovereignty has played a chief function in modernity, that of being a master signifier, a 'particular element assuming a "universal" structuring function within a certain discursive field' (Laclau and Mouffe, 2001: xi). As such, this master signifier 'covers the hole or lack in the social symbolic order and provides a nodal point around which meaning is articulated' and thus, within modern politics, the concept of sovereignty has become 'central to discourses of politics and the international' (Edkins and Pin-Fat, 1999: 6).

The notion of the state confirms the right of 'a government over the lives of its citizens in the modern nation-state', and it 'plays a foundational role in discussions of international autonomy' as 'the sovereign state is a bounded unit in the international system' (ibid.). The concept of sovereignty inscribes itself as central to modern politics and co-constitutes the free and modern individual's subjectivity, providing a foundation through the erasure of its artificial imposition. This partially explains why sovereignty is mostly regarded as natural, right, and 'beyond challenge' (ibid.: 10).

When questioning the violence that is prompted by the DSP in Colombia, the above reflections are necessary in order to understand the attractiveness of a security discourse that promises certainty. 'The contemporary form of political community, the state, relies for its existence on the assumption that it can compel its citizens to fight (and die) for its sovereignty. It proffers security in return for obedience. As a political unit, it is produced and defined by organised violence' (Edkins, 2003: 6). The DSP draws spatial, temporal and ethical boundaries (Stern, 2005; Walker, 1993) that give shape to the articulation of political identities. This operation simultaneously constitutes the subjectivities of the sovereign state and the individuals 'inside' (the 'self'). It does this by contouring the borders that allow recognition of the imagined political community of the nation (Anderson, 1991) as different from those who stand 'outside' (Walker, 1993) and who therefore do not belong to 'us' (Campbell, 1998; Connolly, 1991). This discussion then enables serious questioning of how, in the Colombian security discourse, sovereignty and subjectivity 'are constituted as objects of political analysis and action' (Edkins and Pin-Fat, 1999: 10). This traditional discourse ignores the paradoxes of their mutual production (both self and the state), which occurs 'at the traumatic intersection between peace and war, inside and outside' (Edkins, 2003: 10).

Following this line of reasoning, both sovereignty and subjectivity are violently constituted together. Sovereignty, at the centre of modern political thought, is presented as a certain truth beyond challenge, which gives meaning to the rest of the (inter)national system and to the concept of a free individual. This claim takes us to a different dimension of the discussion on security. Contrary to conventional views on sovereignty and subjectivity in IR, which reduce their examination to locating and naming ontologically prior *objects*, we will attempt to illustrate the ways in which sovereignty and subjectivity are *constituted, applied,* and *reinforced.* The questions that critical security scholars pose deal with the assumptions that traditional IR take for granted, disrupting the logic exemplified in (neo)realist security discourses. The premises that sustain this dominant way of thinking about security are put into question. These new insights offer the possibility of transcending the common appreciation in IR about whether sovereignty and subjectivity 'are accurate representations (true)' of the world (Edkins and Pin-Fat, 1999: 12) and lead us to question the representation of the world itself.

Representing the world

If we rethink the relationship between sovereignty and subjectivity by problematising the representations through which they legitimise themselves, we must also question how the world is depicted in security theories and discourses (Weber, 2005). This critical analysis is not directed towards unveiling the *true* representation of what security discourses portray as reality, but rather towards how those representations of the world, the (inter)national system, man, inside and outside (Walker, 1993), are embedded in a matrix of violent and exclusive exercises of power that mobilise and constitute subjectivities.

> [Any] representation is *eo ipso* implicated, intertwined, embedded, interwoven with a great many other things besides the 'truth', which is itself a representation. What this must lead us to methodologically is to view representations (or misrepresentations – the distinction is at best a matter of degree) as inhabiting a common field of play defined for them, not by some inherent common subject matter alone, but by some common history, tradition, universe of discourse. (Said, 2003a: 272–3)

In the realm of critical security studies, the useful and insightful approach of Jutta Weldes et al. (1999) deals with this particular notion of representations of security discourses. They argue that all social insecurities are culturally produced, 'in the sense that they are produced in and out of the "context within which people give meanings to their actions and experiences and make sense of their lives"' (ibid.: 1). Therefore, the *real world* (of the state of nature, for instance) does not exist as such, but rather serves only as a useful representation of a multitude of different meanings and conceptualisations of relations that legitimise a specific type of power relationship.

> On this view, identities (both of self and of others) and insecurities, rather than being given, emerge out of a process of representation through which individuals ... describe to themselves and others the world in which they live. These representations – narratives, collective memories, and the imaginaries that make them possible – define, and so constitute, the world. They populate it with objects and subjects, endow those subjects with interests, and define the relations among those objects and subjects. In so doing, they create insecurities, which ... are threats to the identities, and thus to the interests, of these socially constructed subjects. (Ibid.: 14)

In this interpretation of *the world*, there are no 'subjects' whose identity is independent from the 'objects' with whom they deal. The borders between the inside and the outside begin to blur and the world seems to resemble more what we make out of it than what it *purportedly truly is* according to dominant discourses. Following this logic, the identity of the state, which in traditional accounts of security is the natural result of an anarchical international system and the natural provider of security, is seen in a different light. The state is, just as is any other subject/object, a cultural production. The state is an effect of a set of statist discourses, which 'produce the state, and produce it as a particular kind of subject', as an actor with 'particular kinds of interests' (ibid.: 14–15). Simultaneously, the state produces 'citizens as a particular kind of subject, often as consumers of statist representations of insecurity and danger and as a unified population with shared interests' (ibid.).

These last thoughts propose a different understanding of 'the sovereign state and free and autonomous individuals'. Taking seriously the cultural construction of reality implies embarking on a contest for meaning because, if the entities which serve as the foundation for the traditional view on security are *produced* (which is not to say that they are artificial but that they are manufactured) then any discourse about *what the world* is about faces contestation. 'Contesting discourses, in turn, attempt to rearticulate insecurities in ways that challenge the dominant representations. ... In addition, discourses are themselves not perfectly coherent, but rather always entail internal contradictions and lacunae. These contradictions make possible both resistance to a dominant discourse and the transformation of discourses' (ibid.: 16). By offering a different understanding of the world, its threats, the constitutive elements of the international system, and the modern nation-state and individuals, critical security studies acknowledges the lacunae of (their own) discourses and the impossibility of fully representing identities in language (Edkins, 2003; Stern, 2005).

At this point, it is worth underscoring that discourses also entail material practices. 'After all, discursive articulations, including the construction of insecurities, are always "materialized in concrete practices and rituals and operate through specific state [and other] apparatuses" ... Discourses and their codes of intelligibility have concrete, and significant, material effects. They allocate social capacities and resources and make practices possible' (Weldes et al., 1999: 16–17). In this sense,

> Discourse is not merely spoken words, but a notion of signification which concerns not merely how it is that certain signifiers come to mean what they mean, but how certain discursive forms articulate objects and subjects in their intelligibility. ... Discourse not merely represents or reports on pregiven practices and relations, but it enters into their articulation and is, in that sense, productive. (Butler, 1995b: 138)

In addition, as long as discourses produce meaning and codes of intelligibility, they do not just make practices possible. Perhaps as importantly, through legitimising certain actions they, consequently, delegitimise others (Jackson, 2005: 17–18; Tickner, 2006: 388).

> Implicated in these enabling possibilities is also that which is necessarily excluded in specific articulations ... That is to say, the impossible. Whether implicitly, or explicitly, what is taken to be possible not only implies what shall be taken as impossible, but more importantly, what shall be kept at bay, excluded, as the 'outside'. Indeed, we contend that articulations of the possible are privileged as legitimate but that this can only be adequately understood by paying attention to the role that the impossible plays. (Pin-Fat and Stern, 2005: 28)

For example, a traditional discourse about security pictures the state of nature as dangerous and as an 'uncivilised' past historical episode where violence reigned. Such a belief makes logical the call for state security now, so as to prevent 'us' from falling back again to those times where 'every man was an enemy to every man' (Hobbes, 1651). At the same time, such a call for state security makes less conflictual alternatives for organising political communities seem unintelligible, unreasonable, and even threatening. The realm of the impossible, for example in the DSP in Colombia, confines to absurdity the contingency and impossibility of closure both for the subjectivities of 'the self' and 'others'.

This characteristic of discourses to formulate what might be possible and impossible is what makes a dominant discourse so powerful. It is also the source for generating resistance. Once there is a consensus about the correspondence between a discourse and a certain reality (Weber, 2005), it defines the 'horizon of the taken-for-granted that marks the boundaries of common sense and accepted knowledge' (Weldes et al., 1999: 17). The storyline of conventional security discussions has been installed within the realm of discursive common sense as the negation of insecurity. Furthermore, security has been posited as the pursuit of freedom from threat, as a positive goal in itself, as the primary function of the modern nation-state and as the legitimising promise of political order. However, such a promise of certainty, when articulated through political violence as the solution to political violence, results in the elimination of difference – both within the 'self' and 'others' – commonly understood as threats and dangers.

This particular understanding of security in the DSP initiates practices of exclusion and marginalisation that aim at the impossible overcoming of contingencies of identities. Such interpretations write war and peace as synonymous with controlled and secure living. In short, the DSP is a grammar of war and peace that closes down the spaces for politics and actually inflicts harm.

State discourses on security

Traditional views on security conceptualise national security policies and state discourses about security problems as 'choices about both the objectives of policy (ends), and the techniques, resources, instruments and actions which will be used to implement it (means)' (Buzan, 1991: 330). National security, henceforth,

> can always be criticized as imperfect, because on logical grounds it must be so. It can never serve as a stable resting place, because the factors which define a satisfactory relative level [of security] at any given moment are themselves ephemeral. The structure of the system and its interaction dynamics complete this dilemma by ensuring that any attempt to acquire or even move towards, complete security by any actor will stimulate reactions which raise the level of threat in proportion to the measures taken. (Ibid.: 331)

Nevertheless, when the ontology of security is no longer treated as a stable ground (Lobo-Guerrero, 2007; Stern, 2005; Weldes et al., 1999), state discourses on security can be understood as sites of social power in which the construction and the functions of security discourses and policies can be questioned. The representations of in/security embedded in statist discourses would not emerge out of a rational evaluation of objective threats, but are regarded as representations of state officials who speak for us from the position of an institutional authorising power:

> In their representations of insecurity, for example, state officials can claim access to information produced by the state and denied to most outsiders. They also have privileged access to media ... [and] their representations have constitutional legitimacy, especially in the construction of insecurity. After all, 'national security' is generally understood to be quintessentially the business of the state and the identification of insecurities is thus a task thought rightly to belong to its officials. (Weldes et al., 1999: 17–18)

In this sense, the link between state, security policies, power and the constitution of identity starts to emerge in a clear light, 'because discourses bring with them the power to define and thus to constitute the world, these representations of insecurity are themselves important sources of power' (ibid.: 18). Therefore, what state security policies and discourses *do* is not just to identify threats in the outside and vulnerabilities in the inside as part of an imperfect art of security policy-making, to paraphrase Buzan (1991: 331). The power relations that security policies signify create, recreate and transform the people in whose name they speak (Stern, 2005). Security policies speak to 'us' and speak 'us'. They define what a threat is and what it is not; who is an insider and who is an outsider (Walker, 1993); what actions can be carried out *in the name of the state* and which others *defy* the very idea of the state. In this way, security policies recreate the interests and the attributes of the state itself.

However, although it has primary authority in modern political arrangements, it is not just the state that defines insecurities. Other communities also put forward their own discourses of danger and, in the clash of definitions (Said, 2003b) between 'those different identities ... the politics of difference and otherness, and hence the cultural production of insecurity, is to be found' (Weldes et al., 1999: 19). For instance, the reproduction of in/security can also be found in marginal sites of resistance, even uttered by those who try to procure safety in the face of dangers posed by the modern state (Stern, 2005).

It is then crucial to highlight that the production of meaning, in this case of insecurity, cannot be the result of one actor, even if reified as 'the' legitimate political subject of the state. As Weldes and others (ibid.) suggest, the social construction of insecurities is a creation in concert between several subjects who might not subscribe to state discourses totally, but who, nevertheless, carry on different tasks and comply with state definitions of security.

Since discourses do not simply *reflect* reality but *construct* it, in this process they create identity categories, such as 'us' and 'them', which 'are never merely descriptive, but always normative, and as such, exclusionary' (Butler, 1995a: 50). What makes discourses and practices of security pivotal for the construction of identities is precisely how they shape subjectivity by 'telling us what to fear' (Campbell, 1998) and – simultaneously – what to love (Dillon, 1996), naming dangers as operations that separate 'us' from 'them', fixing where we are and who we are (Campbell, 1998; Stern, 2005; Walker, 1993). Hence, (state) security discourses turn into preferred tools for the delineation of a collective identity as a political subject with clear-cut boundaries.

Yet, the power relations security discourses exercise, necessarily cause their own provocations. As the frequently quoted words of Foucault (1990: 96) indicate, 'where there is power, there is resistance, and yet, or rather consequently, this resistance is never in a position of exteriority in relation to power. ... [Power relationships'] existence depends on a multiplicity of points of resistance: these play the role of adversary, target, support or handle in power relations.'

From state security to in/security and identities

Following this last thought on power and resistance, it is important to note that conventional and hegemonic views on security discourses have provoked a wide range of reactions from the field of IR. For instance, alternative security studies are directed at filling the gaps recognised in the paradox of security, for even if the state is the provider of, it can also threaten individual security. From the perspective of alternative security, the best way to cope with this paradox is to demilitarise the notion of national security and to democratise the subjects of security. This can take the form of a *grand security strategy*, which takes into account that the referent objects of security are individuals, societies and states whose interests enter into conflict in the military, political, social, economic and ecological sectors (Buzan, 1991: 376–7).

Such extension and intensification would make the problem of security a matter of taking into consideration enough factors (sectors and levels) in the calculation. However, if, at some point – likely to happen if one believes in the state of nature and the anarchical international system – securities enter into contradiction with each other, policy decision-makers need to draw a clear hierarchy of whose security is to be given priority. Not surprisingly, this priority is given to the concept of national security as the only one 'able to orient state policy for the international relations of a mature anarchy' (ibid.: 371).

In this way, although alternative security reactions to conventional readings of security might be initially seen as a criticism of state-centric accounts of national security, alternative solutions end up broadening the very same idea of conventional readings of security. They solve security paradoxes by giving priority to the state and by putting it at the top of the hierarchy of political subjects. By discussing the workings of security, i.e. how to make security more secure, alternative accounts of security leave intact the ontology of conventional readings (Stern, 2005). The referent object of security, whether the state or the individual, is still treated as a knowable identity (at least potentially) and the ways of coping with insecurity are then realigned as a problem of not having taken into consideration enough factors in objective calculations of threats and vulnerabilities in a specific sector/level dimension. Yet, the logic of security as being a condition that applies (or not) to certain 'things' remains undisturbed. Alternative securities, by embracing the security of the modern sovereign state as the ultimate solution to people's insecurities, can be read as provocations that support and perfect conventional readings.

Another mode of resistance can be found in David Campbell's book *Writing Security* (1998), in which he reads identity in the foreign policies of the US during the Cold War. For Campbell, in/security discourses are discourses of danger that play an important role in delineating the ethical boundaries of the state, which are as important as the geopolitical boundaries of the political community of the nation-state and together delineate the 'we' inside. When there are questions about who this 'we' is, whether citizens, humans or both, security discourses respond by affirming that 'we have our primary – often overriding – political identity as participants in a particular community' (Walker, 1993: 154).

It is pertinent to make more explicit to which concept of identity we are referring here. Borrowing Aletta Norval's (1999) terminology, in contrast to a *sacred* understanding of cultural identity, this particular reading of security adopts a *profane* view on identity. The first term describes an idea of identity as monolithic, noncontradictory and nonantagonistic; by contrast, a profane understanding of identity accentuates its historicity and insists on the '"madeness" of culture, and, therefore, in the inventedness of every identity' (ibid.: 99–100). As Stuart Hall (1996a) has articulated, this idea of identity is 'not an essentialist, but a strategic and positional one':

> [It] does not signal that stable core of the self, unfolding from beginning to end through all the vicissitudes of history without change; the bit of the self which remains always-ready 'the same', identical to itself across time. ... It accepts that identities are never unified and ... increasingly fragmented and fractured; never singular but multiply constructed across different, often intersecting and antagonistic, discourses, practices and positions. They are subject to a radical historization, and are constantly in the process of change and transformation. (ibid.: 3)

In the same vein as Campbell (1998), Hall (1996a: 3–4) calls for paying attention to the specific historical, linguistic and cultural processes of *becoming rather than being*. He says, 'not "who we are" or "where we came from", as much as what we might become, how we have been represented and how that bears on how we might represent ourselves. Identities are therefore constituted within, not outside representation'. Moreover, the specific representation that security policies construct for identity categories is now the focus of our attention since they have a great share of participation in those discourses that hail subjects into place and enter into the constitution of identity. This way, Stuart Hall (1996a) provides a definition of the process of identification that enables us to understand the importance of the discourses and practices of in/security as they are inscribed in the DSP. Hall argues that identity is the meeting point, the point of suture, between on the one hand the discourses and practices which attempt to 'interpellate', speak to us or hail us into place as the social subjects of particular discourses, and on the other hand, the processes which produce subjectivities, which construct us as subjects which can be 'spoken'. Identities are thus points of temporary attachment to the subject positions which discursive practices construct for us … . They are the result of a successful articulation or "chaining" of the subject into the flow of the discourse … 'an intersection'. (Ibid.: 5–6)

This notion of identification opens possibilities to view the in/security discourse in Colombia as one discursive formation that enters into the constitution of identity yet does not 'command' the formation of identities automatically. As proposed by Hall (ibid.: 6–10), discourses are not sufficient to constitute identity. State discourses can manufacture categories, but subjects do not fit into any one category. They cannot be removed or exchanged like puppets in an unproblematic fashion. Social subjects are hailed into the positions created by discourses, but they necessarily have to *invest* in those positions to articulate their identity. Identity, understood as this particular articulation, needs the subject's *response* or investment to assume certain subject positions, which are never complete. Identity is, then, always a process, a becoming, never a fully exhausted or finished project.

As Jenny Edkins and Véronique Pin-Fat (1999) argue, 'it is not just that the subject has to face a difficult and unsettling choice of a variety of subject-positions', but even more, 'there are no settled identities; the subject never achieves the completion or wholeness toward which it strives' (ibid.: 1). The subject 'remains haunted by that which has to be excluded for subjectivity to be constituted in the first place' (ibid.). This important aspect of identity constitution leaves us with a picture in which 'the subject is always in the process of being constituted; there is no point at which, however briefly, the performance is finished' (ibid.).

The work of Judith Butler (1993, 1999) is vital for grasping identity as performative, 'not as the act by which a subject brings into being what she/he names but rather as that reiterative power of discourse to produce the phenomena that it regulates and constrains' (Butler, 1993: 2). The idealisation that Butler is mainly concerned with is the category of a coherent gender identity, which she conceptualises as performative as far as 'acts, gestures, and desire produce the effect of an internal core or substance' (Butler, 1990: 207). Butler's arguments can also be said to work along similar lines regarding other identity categories, as the process by which 'acts, gestures, enactments, generally construed', perform the very essence of identity as 'a *fabrication* manufactured and sustained through corporeal signs and other discursive means' (ibid.). This shifting emphasis highlights how the interior essence of the (gendered) body 'is a function of a decidedly public and social discourse':

> In other words, acts and gestures articulated and enacted desires create the illusion of an interior and organizing gender core, an illusion discursively maintained for the purposes of the regulation of sexuality within the obligatory frame of reproductive heterosexuality. If the 'cause' of desire, gesture and act can be localized within the 'self' of the actor, then the political regulations and disciplinary practices which produce that ostensibly coherent gender are effectively displayed from view. The displacement of a political and discursive origin of gender identity onto a psychological 'core' precludes an analysis of the political constitution of the gendered subject and its fabricated notions about the ineffable interiority of its sex or of its true identity. (Ibid.: 208)

The performative character of identities is one important tool for analysing the DSP. The state representations of in/security made in the DSP create the ideal of a 'national' in whose name the state operates and it recreates the notion of 'other', otherness and difference when naming threat. While the processes of articulation and striving to create subjectivities are the focus of attention of the third and fourth chapters of this book, for now we attend to Butler's claim (Butler, 1999) and start to trace the political and discursive constitution of identities and the power relations implicated in public security discourses.

Naming danger

If we pay attention to how discourses constitute the 'core of the self' (Butler, 1999) and continue rereading the pillars of conventional security, we resume with the assumption that security policies are born out of the categorisation and classification of threats and vulnerabilities by security experts according to the measurement of objective dangers. In a schematic manner, security discourses mainly consist of a list of threats that state officials claim put a certain population they are supposed to protect in danger. This is generally followed by another list of strategies to cope with those threats. In this way, the linguistic and non-linguistic character of discourse is exemplified: the text names the *people*, describes and prescribes dangers and, accordingly, informs governmental actions.[8]

This particular reading assumes that there are already existing subjects of security (generally states) that face prearranged and already constituted 'threats' from the outside as well as being challenged by 'vulnerabilities' from the inside. The state then displays measures to protect its people. In exchange for protection, these people should obey state regulations (Walker, 1999). This concrete way of assuming the pre-established and unchanging ontology – nature and character – of the subjects, referents and objects of security discourses does not reveal how the DSP creates and produces the security identities of 'state', 'nationals' and 'others'.

Such assumptions of conventional security discussions consequently marginalise the discursive construction of identities (Butler, 1999) and fluid accounts of subjectivity (Edkins and Pin-Fat, 1999; Stern, 2005), reducing the identification of threats and vulnerabilities to an objective enterprise of a pre-discursive, coherent, sovereign subject which is taken-for-granted. Whereas the analysis of the DSP in this book suggests precisely the contrary: the functions of naming dangers (Campbell, 1998), threats and vulnerabilities, are integral to understanding 'who and where we are' (Stern, 2005; Walker, 1993).

One of the most interesting insights that authors like David Campbell (1998) bring to the scene is how in/security discourses first and foremost name dangers. However, security experts do not identify threats and vulnerabilities according to objective and measurable variables, difficult as they are to recognise, as noted by Buzan (1991: 134). On the contrary, Campbell argues, dangers have a non-objective condition.

> Danger is not a thing that exists independently of those to whom it may become a threat ... Danger bears no essential, necessary, or unproblematic relation to the action or event from which it is said to derive. ... [In any society, the amount of dangers that exists is infinite] indeed, there is such an abundance of risk that it is impossible to objectively know all that threatens us. ... [Danger so] results from the calculation of a threat that objectifies events, disciplines relations, and sequesters an ideal of the identity of the people said to be at risk. (Campbell, 1998: 1–3)[9]

As Campbell states, for any in/security policy to describe the dangers that actually *threaten 'us'*, there is a necessary interpretive task involving the subjectivity of those who are said to be threatened. The naming of danger will then be a matter of interpretation. Therefore, there is no other way of understanding or perceiving something or someone as dangerous, but rather only their perception as such within the discursive realm that gives meaning to the person or entity.

The identities of security subjects inform the grid of intelligibility of security discourses which, simultaneously, inform the borders (contours and boundaries) of security subjects. In/security and identity are then entangled in an intense co-constitutive relationship. Furthermore, by naming dangers, security discourses co-constitute the threat in itself. The presumption that security discourses only materialise a danger to society is inaccurate. By naming dangers (ibid.), security discourses recreate danger, and, especially when dealing with official discourses, they inform governmental practices and actions accordingly.

If the first purpose of a security discourse is to represent dangers, then what is achieved through this representation? Which consequences does the securitisation (Wæver, 1995) of an issue, group of people, or any other threat, have on the constitution of identity? In other words, 'what is at stake in the attempt to screen the strange, the unfamiliar, and the threatening associated with the outside from the familiar and safe, which are linked to the inside?' (Campbell, 1998: 36).

Discourses of danger are inextricably related to discourses of the state. They tell us about the uncertainty and ambiguity of the world and about the threats posed to *man*. They also offer the state as the appropriate solution to deal with this uncertainty (Hobbes, 1651; Buzan, 1991). Representations of danger are thus embedded in representations of safety (Stern, 2005). The state presents dangers to the population and, by means of the state's authorising role, it offers itself as the solution to dealing with them.

When state security discourses evoke in both words and images the fear of violence and then offer 'the promise of security to its citizens who, it says, would otherwise face manifold dangers', the state justifies its guarantor role (Campbell, 1998: 50-1). In this way, representations of danger turn into necessary tools of the state to maintain its legitimacy and to justify its own existence. 'The state requires discourses of "danger" to provide a new teleology of truth about who and what "we" are by highlighting who or what "we" are not, and what "we" have to fear' (ibid.: 48–9).

This is one of the reasons why we can consider security discourses an integral part of the state's discourse on the construction of its own identity. 'The state, and the identity of the "man" located in the state, can therefore be regarded as the effects of discourses of danger that more often than not employ strategies of otherness' (ibid.: 51). Security discourses might need to be understood as the state's constant reproduction of danger rather than as the state's response to danger. And here we find again the same image of the *state of nature* as the legitimation for state existence and for its guardian role, though now this view is examined under tighter scrutiny.

> The state of nature is shock therapy. It helps subjects to get their priorities straight by teaching them what life would be like without sovereignty. It domesticates by eliciting the vicarious of fear of violent death in those who have not had to confront it directly. And when one confronts the fear of early and violent death, one becomes willing to regulate oneself and to accept external regulations that will secure life against its dangers. The fear of death pulls the self together. It induces subjects to accept civil society and it becomes an instrumentality of sovereign control in a civil society already installed. (Ibid.: 57–8)

As a result, if representations of danger constitute the identity of the state and of the *people* simultaneously, the settled identities presented in the traditional view of security discussions in IR no longer hold water. Rather, we are grasping a constitution of both *state* and the *people* in a constant mutual process. In this vein, security discourses provide a significant input to construct the *nation*, that imagined community so clearly conceptualised by Benedict Anderson (1991: 6) as 'both inherently limited and sovereign'.

Anderson depicts *imagined* communities as creations that 'are to be distinguished, not by their falsity/genuineness, but by the style in which they are imagined' (ibid). In this *style* or mode of representation, security discourses portray certain dangers as threatening the 'we' inside state borders, telling 'us' what 'we are not', what 'we' have to fear, and what the state should defend 'us' from. In this sense, the process of constitution of both identities, of state and people (Edkins and Pin-Fat, 1999), the inner and outer (Walker, 1993), 'us' and 'them' (Connolly, 1991; Said, 2003a) emerges at the same time (Campbell, 1998: 57).

Remembering the idea of representation here is crucial. These arguments are not geared towards revealing the truth of the identities in question, but rather towards identifying the processes that constitute them and how they appear as 'truths' or myths about origins (Dillon, 1996). The term *representation* implies how events, relations and structures have effects within the discursive realm, conditioning the subject, its limits and modalities and endowing them with meaning (Hall, 1996b). 'How things are represented and the "machineries" and regimes of representation in a culture do play a constitutive, and not merely a reflexive role after the event. This gives questions of culture and ideology, and the scenarios of representation – subjectivity, identity politics – a formative, and not merely an expressive, place in the constitution of social and political life' (ibid.: 91).

This process is, of course, not perfect or without problems. Discourses on danger have their own lacunae, nor does every 'man' fit comfortably into those subject positions reserved for obeying state authority. Thomas Hobbes (1651) recognised this and his metaphor for *accommodating* some 'men' to the rest is therefore articulated as moulding rough stones into plain ones in order to build the edifice of the state.

Paul Chilton (1996) refers to this metaphor of the state-as-edifice as a container concept which was part of Hobbes' demonstration of 'the need for a sovereign power that will be permanent' (ibid.: 85). 'The sovereign state is a container with a building-like structure, a wall-like bounding (and binding) surface, that keeps people in awe, and not only keeps out invaders but casts out its internal threats' (ibid.: 87). In Hobbes' construction of the notion of the sovereign, 'stones and bricks are built into an ordered whole: there is a builder, an architect, an owner, and so forth'. But there are some men who 'simply do not fit in', who 'cannot be easily made plain' and those who 'cannot be corrected' are to 'be left, or cast out of Society, as cumbersome thereunto' (ibid.).

The most powerful implications of representing sovereign states as edifices, says Chilton (1996: 64), are that 'they are presupposed to "cover" a given territory'. The state as edifice implies that this territorial 'boundary is clear-cut, unambiguous, non-overlapping and defined' (ibid.), and that the membership to the sovereign state must be exclusive (Walker, 1993). Additionally, this edifice entails *stability and permanence*. It in/secures the people inside, implying the protection and safety by means of exclusion. In this sense, there is a clear parallel between the state-as-edifice in the discourse of Hobbes and the reconstitution of his arguments in traditional security discussions characterising the sovereign nation-state. The discourse of Hobbes, as basic texts informing realist and neorealist accounts of the world, functions 'to project particular concepts of order, or to legitimate existing concepts, and in some degree have contributed to producing the object they have claimed to represent' (Chilton, 1996: 116).

In this sense, whenever the sovereign state fails to resemble an interior ordered realm, whenever its borders separating the inside from the chaotic and dangerous outside world (Walker, 1993) become porous, the state loses its validity (Campbell, 1998). Without borders, the state cannot function. Borders are the very walls of the edifice that separate the inside from the outside and justify the state's existence. 'The spaces of inside and outside serve to delineate the rational, ordered polity in which good, sane, sober, modest, and civilized "man" resides from the dangerous, chaotic, and anarchical realm in which the evil, mad, drunk, arrogant, and savage people are found' (ibid.: 60).

Such constitution of danger through the identification of threats and vulnerabilities is what makes in/security discourses pivotal in the construction of identities. Among those public and social discourses that create the effect of an interior core or essence (Butler, 1999), in/security discourses are explicitly directed at drawing, shaping and constructing the category of 'otherness'. They tell us what we are not and where we do not reside, to paraphrase Walker (1993). At the same time, in/security discourses of the state, as part of the official culture, provide definitions of patriotism, loyalty, boundaries and belonging. The state 'speaks in the name of the whole. It tries to express the general will, the general ethos and idea which inclusively holds in the official past, the founding fathers and texts, the pantheon of heroes and villains, and so on, and excludes what is foreign or different or undesirable' (Said, 2003b: 335).

When any in/security discourse establishes which events and actors, what and whom we should fear, it necessarily establishes the 'other', the outside and the *to be feared* at the same time that it establishes the domestic, the safe and ordered. Using Campbell's terms (1998: 62), security discourses would be 'a specific sort of *boundary producing political performance*', part of the practices of the state that serve as 'an art of domesticating the meaning of man by constructing his problems, his dangers, his fears' (ibid.). Importantly, in/security discourses, by naming danger and by telling us what to kill for, at the same time tell us what to die for, and so they also construct 'man's' loves:

> All those loves whose affirmative denials, denying the denials upon which we feed, so form and inform the space of our (inter)national politics of security: love of liberty; love of order; love of country; love of church; love of one god; love of the people; love of the leader; love of the party; love of the nation; love of the individual; love of the very cult of the subject. Security always seems to come crenellated in the form of some obligatory, denying and self-denying love masquing the spirit of revenge. (Dillon, 1996: 34)

Within this frame, discourses on in/security simultaneously create idealised pictures of identity to which the *national* and the *foreign* are hailed, because both are constituted in what William Connolly (1991) has named the economy of identity/difference. 'An identity is established in relation to a series of differences that have become socially recognised. These differences are essential to its being. If they did not coexist as differences, it would not exist in its distinctness and solidity' (ibid.: 64). In this sense, the outside co-constitutes the inside (Said, 2003a). For the state to erect its boundaries, what is left outside of them is indispensable. For the 'us' to exist, there has to be a 'them' (Connolly, 1991).

Following Connolly (ibid.), this process of inclusion/exclusion is unavoidable in the construction of any identity category. Echoing Hall, identification 'operates across difference, it entails discursive work, the binding and the marking of symbolic boundaries, the production of frontier-effects. It requires what is left outside, its constitutive outside, to consolidate the process' (Hall, 1996a: 3).

> Above all, and directly contrary to the form in which they are constantly invoked, identities are constructed through, not outside, difference. This entails the radically disturbing recognition that it is only through the relation to the Other, the relation to what it is not, to precisely what it lacks, to what has been called its constitutive outside that the 'positive' meaning of any term – and thus 'identity' – can be constructed ... . Throughout their careers, identities can function as points of identification and attachment only because of their capacity to exclude, to leave out, to render 'outside', abjected. (Ibid.: 4–5)

However, the relation between 'inside' and 'outside' is much more complex than what representations of danger illustrate. For the state to be able to exclude the 'other' from within and to protect the inside from the outside, the traces of their connectedness have to be erased from representation. This erasure gives the 'state, its people and others' an appearance of coherent identities, giving the impression of being independent and separate realms.

> [T]he development and maintenance of every culture requires the existence of another, different and competing alter ego. The construction of identity ... involves the construction of opposites and 'others' whose actuality is always subject to the continuous interpretation and re-interpretation of their differences from Us. Each age and society re-creates its 'Others'. Far from being a static thing then, identity of self or of Other is a much worked-over historical, social, intellectual, and political process that takes place as a contest involving individuals and institutions in all societies. ... In short, the construction of identity is bound up with the disposition of power and powerlessness in each society ... . (Said, 2003a: 331–2)

So, we are faced with the inevitability of difference to constitute identity. Difference does not necessarily entail the condemnation of otherness, inferiority or material in need of perfection or disposal. The relationship between identity and difference might not automatically imply violence against the traces of the 'other' in 'oneself' and against the 'otherness' of the 'other' (Campbell, 1998: 70; Said, 2003a: xxix). This thought will be developed in the fifth chapter of this book when dealing with the subject's investment in the identity categories constructed by the DSP. For the moment, we still have to challenge one last pillar examined in the current review on conventional readings of security discourses in IR: the impossibility of achieving total security, which might better be named the impossibility of in/security.

The impossibility of in/security

According to traditional IR, the problem of security is reduced to a matter of not having adequately considered enough sectors, levels or dimensions in order to provide human collectivities with safety. As argued previously, such notions assume that the ontology of security and the identities it administers are known, if not knowable in principle (Edkins, 2003: 13; Lobo-Guerrero, 2007: 331–2). Yet, in the face of the fluidity and contingency of identities (Edkins and Pin-Fat, 1999; Stern, 2005), these seemingly 'secure' subjects and objects can no longer be treated as such. In/security discourses, as examined in the preceding section, by naming dangers (Campbell, 1998) and by informing state and non-state actions to master insecurities, draw the necessary boundaries that separate inside/outside, self/other and familiar/strange (Walker, 1993). These boundaries appear to be constitutive elements in the production of the very identities of subjects and objects of in/security (Weldes et al., 1999).

Once the certainty of the ontology of conventional readings of security is questioned, the impossibility of 'security' might be twisted towards interrogating what it *does* in the production of in/secure identities and which functions it fulfils by remaining unfulfilled. Furthermore, the impossibility of 'security' raises a fundamental question: can the problem of in/security be that it has to remain a promise since 'achieving total security' would result in the withering of the state (Campbell, 1998; Walker, 1993)? In other words, could in/security's main condition for possibility be its own impossibility? 'If the truth of security compels us to secure security, why, how and where is that grounding compulsion grounded?' (Dillon, 1996: 14)

The insights of Michael Dillon (1996) in the *Politics of Security* on philosophical and political arrangements are crucial to unpacking the ontological functions that the impossibility of in/security have had in western thought. From his own reading of Thomas Hobbes' state of nature and the centrality of security thinking for the conceptualisation of the modern nation-state, Dillon (1996) argues that security has provided modern politics with a new metaphysical truth. For Dillon (ibid.: 14), in modern politics the state and security have been placed as the new 'secure foundation', replacing the lost truth of God and his Church that were central to societies in premodern times. This replacement 'secure foundation' depends upon the assertion that there can be no security without the state, and conversely no state without security (ibid.). As a metaphysical truth, the politics of security become the ultimate stronghold that relieves 'human being of the dilemmas and challenges it faces to discover, in its changing circumstances, what it is to be – to act and live – as human' (ibid.).

Placed as this master signifier, to paraphrase Edkins and Pin-Fat (1999), the project of security has for Dillon (1996) the widest possible ontological sense in modern politics.

> We could not then escape noticing the way security impresses itself upon us as a kind of floating and radically inter-textual signifier which, by constant reference to all other signs of the times, transgresses disciplinary, political, corporeal and geographical boundaries as it courses throughout the defining technologically inspired discourses of Modernity: state security; national security; political security; global security; regional security ... . (Ibid.: 15–16)

Precisely as this master signifier, the impossibility of 'security' is established by Dillon as a tragic and failed attempt to make humans and politics 'secure' and, consequently, unfree. In a similar vein to David Campbell's (1998) notion of representations of danger, Dillon (1996: 18) draws attention to the fact that 'there is never security without insecurity and ... the one always occurs in whatever form with the other'.[10] Dillon (ibid.: 119) develops this argument by first tracing the conflict of security/insecurity to the word 'security' in itself. By looking at the word 'security' , we can see how insecurity is always – and already – folded into security and how it is therefore impossible to have one without the other (ibid.: 78).[11] Security and insecurity are revealed as 'unequal opposites which are rooted and routed together' and hence 'we are dealing here ... with a unified agonal relationship of mutual definition' (ibid: 120).

But it is to the political significance of (in)security that Dillon's etymological contributions call our attention. The word 'security can therefore, only be thought by incorporating the trace of insecurity in the very articulation of security itself ... in short, security and insecurity are unequally co-determined' (ibid.: 127). Hence Dillon's coining of the term (in)security (referred to in this book as in/security) is not just an attempt to be loyal to the etymological roots of the word, but is also a way of making visible the ambivalence of in/security in itself, opening a relatively unquestioned concept for further consideration and contestation.

Second, Dillon shows how security in turn seeks 'to proscribe, sanction, punish, overcome – that is to say, in its turn endangers – that which it says threatens us' (ibid.: 121). Thus, 'security not only means to be free from (danger) but also to constrain' (ibid). In spite of this fact, security insists 'on being the condition which has to be secured so that freedom can be enjoyed' (ibid.: 30). In consequence, for Dillon, security 'does not reflect what a "people" are, and seek to protect it. Rather, it discloses how, in tragic denials of the (in)security of mortal life, people – and a "people" – are actually formed by attempts to extirpate the "foreign, strange, uncanny [and] outlandish" which inevitably constitute their very own free [(in)secure] mortal existence' (ibid.: 35). Such attempts are part of the modern Cartesian subject's striving for certainty, for securing a stable ground for itself. These attempts are doomed to fail, for there is no stable ground that security can disclose. Instead, security betrays 'its own essence as an insistent demand for such a foundation' (ibid.: 78).

Thought of in this way, in/security is the very impossibility of achieving the promise of security. As Arendt (1998: 244) reminds us, since Roman times, the power of making promises has occupied the centre of political thought.

> The unpredictability which the act of making promises at least partially dispels is of a twofold nature: it arises simultaneously out of 'darkness of the human heart', that is, the basic unreliability of men who never can guarantee today who they will be tomorrow and out of the impossibility of foretelling the consequences of an act within a community of equals where everybody has the same capacity to act. Man's inability to rely upon himself or to have complete faith in himself (which is the same thing) is the price human beings pay for freedom; and the impossibility of remaining unique masters of what they do, of knowing its consequences and relying upon the future, is the price they pay for plurality and reality, for the joy of inhabiting together with others a world whose reality is guaranteed for each by the presence of all. (Ibid.)

This twofold function of promising is, 'as such, the only alternative to a mastery which relies on domination of one's self and rule over others; it corresponds exactly to the existence of a freedom which was given under the condition of non-sovereignty' (ibid.). Consequently, such a promise can only be made by non-sovereign subjects. When the promise emanates from a body politic who is *sovereign*, as is the alleged condition of the nation-state, then this twofold function of promising fades away. Sovereignty, as the mastery that relies upon domination of one's self and rule over others, does not leave the unpredictability of human affairs and the unreliability of 'men' as they are.

Quite on the contrary, a promise of a sovereign misuses this twofold faculty 'to cover the whole ground of the future and to map out a path secured in all directions [making the state's promises] lose their binding power and the whole enterprise becomes self-defeating' (ibid.). As Dillon (1996) argues, the place that security occupies in modern political thought is exactly the attempt to overcome this twofold human condition, to supply human freedom. Security's impossibility to deliver is actually what makes the promise of security so attractive. Because it can never be fulfilled, it constantly provides the state with its Hobbesian functions.

In this line of argument, the impossible promise of in/security would not be a paradox, but its own dynamic. In the case of state security discourses, it is then the unfeasibility of in/security and the state's performative identity, which make possible the state's own permanent reproduction as sovereign. 'With no ontological status apart from the many and varied practices that constitute their reality, states are (and have to be) always in the process of becoming' (Campbell, 1998: 12). If the promise of state 'security' would be successful, the state – as we have learned to know it, make it, obey it – in modern politics, would wither away. 'Ironically, then, the inability of the state project of security to succeed is the guarantor of the state's continued success as an impelling identity' (ibid.).

One can argue that the impossibility of in/security therefore, is 'not a threat to a state's identity or existence and, therefore 'while the objects of concern change over time, the techniques and exclusions by which those objects are constituted as dangers persist' (ibid.). In this sense, representations of dangers testify to the incapacity of the 'sovereign' subject to secure its own position and this is why security discourses are constantly updated to newly defined threats, recreating the image of a stable primary state identity that performs its 'sovereign' assigned tasks, as any mainstream reading of Hobbes would suggest. In this light, 'security and subjectivity are intrinsically linked [and, indeed, security] is first and foremost a performative discourse constitutive of political order' (ibid.: 199).

Thus, the politics of in/security merit political attention, for it is the invisibility, erasure and naturalised assumptions about 'security' and the 'state', 'us' and 'them' which, in modern times, are part of the rhetoric of violence and war.

> [C]ountries go to war, not for the purpose of defending their rulers, but for the purpose of defending 'the nation', ensuring the state's security, or upholding the interests and values of the people. ... Security in this formulation is neither just an essential precondition of power nor its goal; security is a specific principle of political method and practice directed explicitly to 'the ensemble of the population'. (ibid.: 201)

The difficulties that arise from critically studying security make visible the legitimation of violence that in/security engenders. This rereading of in/security enables us to discern the extensive and intense violence invested in containing the state's identity, the production, reproduction and transformation of 'nationals' and 'uncanny' identities within their 'natural' borders, and the violence which is authorised by this process in the name of protecting 'the ensemble of the population'. Security discourses constitute political identities and the very notion of political order, as has been the case of the DSP in Colombia.

Biopolitics and geopolitics of in/security

The above reflections on in/security discourses permit a clearer understanding of how the security practices of the DSP in the Colombian case are, simultaneously, directed at managing populations and controlling the political spatial limitation of the state (Dillon, 2007). Before examining the effects that the DSP has on the constitution and production of political identities in Colombia and how it reproduces the political violence it promises to halt, it is necessary to understand its grammars as logics of both sovereign power and biopower.

Sovereign power, as conceptualised by Michel Foucault and as conceived of by critical security and other political theorist scholars, denotes the 'juridical sovereign kind of power that threatens death' (Dillon and Reid, 2001: 41). Geopolitical security problematics concern territoriality and the 'geopolitical mechanisms of war, diplomacy alliances, subjective self-interest, *raison d'état*, and *Macht Politik*', they speak the history of the present in terms of states and nations (Dillon, 2007: 10). In short, geopolitical security problematics refer to the security promised by the modern state that offered physical protection and the preservation of ways of life. In exchange, citizens were supposed to grant states the legitimacy to rule (Dillon, 2005: 3). The geopolitics of security thus involve a contract between individuals and a social body.

This type of sovereign power derived from the modern nation-state is not sufficient to understand the DSP's effect on identity. It could be seen as a governmental programme, driven by the chief concern of national security, state survival and defence of its territory that evokes institutional apparatuses for its enactment. Seen in this light, the DSP would be merely one of those multiple in/security discourses that, precisely because it emanates from a 'weak' state – as can be argued about the Colombian state – can easily be challenged by other in/security discourses. Such a (sovereign) security reading fails to appreciate the powerful role that the DSP plays in the constitution of political identities, to the point of redrawing the imaginaries of peace and war in Colombia.

In order to comprehend how greatly the DSP contributes to the process of articulation of identities, it is necessary to conceptualise, treat and analyse it as a biopolitical strategy. Biopolitics in this framework

> operate as a pervasive, complex and heterogeneous network of practices. Structuring the desires, proprieties and possibilities that shape the operation of life, working on and through subjective freedoms, governmental rationalities typically develop around specific problematics, such as those of ... security ... . These in turn constitute the principles of formation around which populations may be defined and networks developed. (Dillon and Reid, 2001: 48)

On the one hand, the geopolitical problematisation of sovereign security involves 'deeply embedded discourses of danger said to be foundational to individual welfare, social formation and political order' (ibid.: 51). Yet, at the same time these discourses of danger and their allied discourses of fear are 'the very means by which specific programmes of life, individual, welfare, social formation and political order are introduced, circulated, reproduced and enacted' (ibid.). The 'toxic combination' (Dillon, 2007) of geopolitics and biopolitics of security seek 'an additional shift in our analytical focus' (Dillon, 2008: 310), which enable reading the security discourse in Colombia as a combination of power over death and power over life.

This implies that the power of the DSP is not only a repressive state-based power that kills, subdues and crushes difference, but it is also a productive power that makes life, generates specific forms of living, and promotes and secures life 'through the regulation and fructification of its defining transactional properties and capabilities' (ibid.: 315). It does punish disobedient citizens by killing them, but it also moulds the desires, fears, interests and behaviour of the population in order to curtail their potential. It aims to control their modes of communication, their connection and their circulation in complex and open networks (Dillon, 2005). In sum, it dictates the accepted identity of the political community and it also manages the population.

It is precisely because it is not only oppressive that the DSP is a pervasive in/security discourse and practice. It is disseminated within society, embraced by 'the people' in a deadly mixture of fear – of 'themselves' and 'others' – in combination with hope – holding to the promise of certainty that the politics of in/security will bring by taking away their burdensome freedoms, mastering the contingency of political life and delivering a future secure living. The politics of in/security thrive on the condition of emergent possibility 'for a life that is also "free"' (Dillon, 2008: 316).

Hence, when seen this way, the geopolitics and biopolitics of security reinforce each other so that violence is deployed both in the name of sovereign territoriality as well as 'against life on behalf of life' (Dillon, 2007: 12). This means that subjectivities, boundaries, and territory are comprehensively reconfigured and

> become assimilated into the problematics of global circulation in which lifelike processes are bound up, such that subjects, boundaries, and frontiers matter, as also do territorial authorities, but, increasingly, inasmuch as they provide the technologies, surveillance, and self-monitoring devices for the complex governmental regulation of biopolitical global flows of every conceivable lifelike formation. (ibid.: 18)

At this point in the discussion, the problematisation of in/security as geopolitical and biopolitical strategy emerges in the Colombian context. Besides the political distinction of friend/enemy, what makes political bodies threatening is their potential becoming. It is not what a body 'is', but how it could emerge when connected to others through large and open networks (ibid.).

Herein lays the political violence that the DSP produces. It aims to obliterate spaces and times for encounters, for connecting, for having the possibility of becoming-something/somebody else that challenges the reified conceptualisations of secure fixed identities. Hence, in/security discourses and practices target populations that present no symptoms of dangerousness and these same discourses and practices wage a preventive war (ibid.: 26) that legitimises the very political violence 'security' promises to arrest. By 'securing', the DSP actually destroys the political and physical lives it purportedly aims to protect.

Conclusion

The aim of this chapter has been to outline the theoretical framework from which the Democratic Security Policy in Colombia will be studied. The theory of security was first presented according to a conventional view in international relations and was then challenged by other understandings of 'security' developed by key critical security scholars.

While in mainstream IR security is seen as a 'thing' that can be known, measured and controlled within an anarchical international system – *naturally* divided into units that are nation-states –, critical security studies' insights evidence the complex, mutual and intertwining character of the relation between sovereignty and subjectivity. As long as one of the power effects of security discourses is to create the state itself, and since sovereignty and subjectivity are mutually constituted simultaneously, the state recreates the ideal of the people in whose name it operates. In this sense, security discourses can be perceived as part of state representations of an ideal state identity, an ideal national identity and, through the inscription of foreignness, an ideal of the category 'other'.

Once the mutually constitutive character of security and insecurity is traced etymologically and politically, it becomes clear that such co-constitution provides the notion of security with its own dynamic. In other words, insecurity is not a paradox of security, but rather is the very condition of its possibility: in/security is the agonism that allows the promise of security to exist and to provide for the legitimation of the state's defensive and for its protective role (Campbell, 1998; Dillon, 1996).

This last insight explains how the geopolitics and the biopolitics of security work as complementary strategies (Dillon, 2008). On the one hand, the delineation of subjectivities by security discourses is geared towards shaping 'the people' and towards protecting the sovereign territoriality of the state. However, security discourses also make use of the power over life – no longer of the 'citizenry' as such – but of the population (Dillon and Reid, 2001). The managing of the population, the power over life – as species – is combined with traditional state security concerns about the power over death, its boundaries and territory (ibid.; Dillon, 2008; Lobo-Guerrero, 2007). This amalgamation of geo- and biopolitics sheds some light on the discursive construction of the DSP because the identities of 'state', 'nationals' and 'others' are fabricated through and in (micro)practices that reveal the violence embedded in the DSP's promise of safety in Colombia.

In the following chapter, I will consider the particular context in which the DSP emerged. For this analysis, I refer back to the insights and interpretations reviewed in the present section in order to highlight how the DSP was made into the hegemonic discourse to attempt to master, albeit tragically and violently, the uncertainties of freedom.

NOTES

1 Security might be seen as an all-you-can-fit term and even as a 'plastic word' (Pörksen, 1995). For example, in calling for a 'long night of security research' in Austria, thematic foci were announced as the following: 'Fragt man/frau, wo und wann sie sich unsicher fühlen, und wofür sie (auch von der Forschung) Lösungen erwarten, sind das meist ganz grundlegende Bedürfnisse wie Gesundheit, Altern, Einkommenssicherung, Sicherheit am Arbeitsplatz, Ernährung, Datenschutz, Einzug von Technik in den Alltag, Naturkatastrophen, u.v.m' (Call zur langen Nacht der Forschung, 2005) (Ask any man or woman where and when they feel insecure, and which type of solutions they expect (even from research), and they will mostly indicate basic needs like health, age, income security, security in their work places, nutrition, data protection, the introduction of technology in daily life, natural catastrophes, and many others).

2 There is a large debate about human security because the very notion of 'humanity' does not seem to escape the trap of state-centric views of security. Feminist reformulations and critiques of the concept of human security have revealed how the category 'human' does not alleviate the insecurities that large segments of the population face (mostly) because of their identities. Hence, the use of 'human' to qualify security for 'all peoples' does not provide a solution to those who, in the face of insecurity, should also seek protection in the very state or the international state system that puts them in danger. For a discussion of the issue of human security from various angles, see the special issue of Security Dialogue (2004). For a concise collection of feminist critiques on the notion of human security see Stern (2005: 19–21) and Hoogensen and Rottem (2004: 155–71).

3 It is important to take note of the later convergence between Buzan and Wæver in the 1990s, both authors recognised as the main figures of 'The Copenhagen School of Security Studies', where the debate about regional security has been predominant (Buzan and Wæver, 2003; Buzan et al., 1998).

4 There is a crucial difference between John Herz's 'security dilemma' and Kenneth Waltz's writings on the permissive causes of war. As Herz argues (2003) in his critique of Hans Morgenthau, espousing the viewpoint of the nature of 'man' as naturally aggressive, this psychological explanation does not suffice for explaining the constant state of war in international politics. Hence, Hertz distances himself from this 'man's' question and develops his own account of the 'security dilemma' as mainly a defensive yet tragic situation of the international anarchical system. Contrary to Herz, Waltz' *Man, the State and War* (2001), originally published in 1954, looks for the causes of war in the three 'images' or at the three levels that compose the title of his book. In 'man' (literary meaning 'men'), Waltz finds selfishness, misdirected aggressive impulses and stupidity (Waltz, 2001). Yet, this does not sufficiently explain to Waltz the eruption of wars and hence he searches for explanations at the level of the state and society. In this second level of analysis, Waltz finds 'good and bad states', which might (or might not) wage war. Hence, Waltz continues searching for answers at the international level where anarchy prevails. The lack of a supreme authority that deters states from waging war seems to be, for Waltz, the answer to his question of 'why constant war': 'war occurs because there is nothing to prevent it' (Waltz, 2001). Although both Herz and Waltz picture international anarchy as the permissive cause for war, their arguments differ significantly at least as far as the 'nature of man' is concerned.

5 As Ann Tickner (1988) suggests, the constant naming of 'men' both in political theory texts as well as in IR discussions, is a gendered enterprise. This 'man', seemingly an abstract political being, was elevated to the pinnacle of international politics, making masculinity the dominant gender regime. For Tickner, the 'international community' of international

politics was created and perpetuated by political realism as a reunion of states-men, nation-states, and masculine IR theorists (Tickner, 1992). Also criticising (neo)realist works from a gender-critical perspective, Christine Sylvester's *Feminist Theory and International Relations in a Postmodern Era* (1994) points out how 'early debates in the field [of IR], and the pretheoretical discussions about international relations that preceded them, helped to establish IR as a "man's" realm of politics, removing "the people" and traits of "women" from IR theory' (Sylvester, 1994: 5). By paying attention to how gender has been constitutive of international politics all the way from Hobbes to Locke and Morgenthau, Sylvester provides a devastating critique of the founding myths of IR theory (Jabri and O'Gorman, 1999). These authors are part of a broad group of feminist scholars who have made an enormous contribution to security studies in large part because their lines of critique differ so significantly. They offer a wide field of scholarly and political work characterised by its plurality and richness. For a concise overview, see Blanchard (2003: 1289–1313) and Wibben (2004: 97–114).

6 The role of fear in neo-realist IR is pivotal to comprehending how the myth of the anarchical system and 'man's' nature appear to be true (Weber, 2005). For an insightful discussion of this subject see Ashley (1989) and Campbell (1998), and for an excellent account of fear and security see Delumeau (2001).

7 Instead of following a particular path offered by a specific school, I trace different conceptions of security that serve to illuminate contrasting arguments to conventional readings of security in IR. For a categorisation of specific context-bound critical security schools in 'the core' – '(Western) Europe' and 'the US' – and the timid attempts at 'exporting' their contributions to 'the periphery' (a place called 'the third world'), see Wæver (2004).

8 The security policy of the enlarged European Union (EU) serves as a clear example of this simple scheme of security discourses. In 2003, after the EU was expanded to twenty-five nation-states, a new security strategy was launched in Brussels. Called 'A secure Europe in a better world' (EU, 2003), it considers the new challenges and opportunities an enlarged EU poses for the security in/of the region. First, the security strategy creates a new Europe, constituting it as a global actor with global interests: 'As a union of 25 states with over 450 million people producing a quarter of the world's Gross National Product (GNP), the European Union is inevitably a global player ... it should be ready to share in the responsibility for global security and in building a better world' (ibid.: 2). Following this introduction, the text identifies the key threats that Europe faces, such as: 'terrorism committed to maximum violence, the availability of weapons of mass destruction, organized crime, the weakening of the state system, and the privatization of force' (ibid.: 4–6). This list of threats is followed by three strategic objectives the EU pursues: (1) addressing the threats, (2) building security in the neighbourhood, and (3) constructing an international order based on multilateralism (ibid.: 7–15). Finally, the implications for the Policy of Europe are taken into account. This security policy reveals the very naming of 'the self', its ethical and geographical borders, and the dangers it confronts ('others') as well as the security strategies derived from its own discourses on threat, i.e. how it in turn endangers those/that are said to be posing a threat to the self/EU.

9 Although David Campbell (1998) uses the term 'risk' to develop his arguments about the importance of security policies for constructing identities, his focus of attention in this pioneering work is on security as a geopolitical strategy. It is mainly concerned with sovereign subjects – such as the state – and how the naming of dangers to the geographical and ethical borders of the state produce the identities of its 'people' and 'others'. In a complementary view to Campbell's geopolitical reading, Michael Dillon (2008) has argued that security, as biopolitical governance, differs slightly from 'more traditional rationalistic

and geopolitical accounts of security, inasmuch as they [biopolitics of security] revolve around life and its properties rather than sovereign territoriality ... [and so] risk is also a natural corollary of the biopolitics of security' (ibid.: 311). This way, Dillon (ibid.: 316) emphasises how 'risk' and economy provide the 'basic grid of intelligibility for the biopoliticization of politics'. For a more in-depth discussion, see also Dillon (2007) and Dillon and Reid (2001).

10 A different conceptualisation of the relationship between security and insecurity is espoused by Ole Wæver (1995: 56) when arguing that, although security and insecurity do not constitute a binary opposition, '"Security" signifies a situation marked by the presence of a security problem *and* some measure taken in response. Insecurity is a situation with a security problem and *no* response. Both conditions share the security problematique. When there is no security problem, we do not conceptualise our situation in terms of security; instead, security is simply an irrelevant concern. The statement, then, that security is always relative, and one never lives in complete security, has the additional meaning that, if one has such complete security, one does not label it "security." It therefore never appears.'

11 Contrary to the modern usage of 'security' as a thing and a condition – negating it as a process – and as 'being secure'/not insecurity – which denies the complexity of the act of securing and of the inextricable relation between security and insecurity (ibid.: 121–2) – Dillon takes us back to the ancient meanings of security. Both in Greek and Latin, the togetherness and mutual constitution of security and insecurity are evident. The Greek word for security, *asphaleia*, suggested the present relation between security and insecurity, both at once. *Asphaleia* 'is to avoid falling, error, failure, or mistake. It is to be ... assured from danger ... to be furnished with a firm foundation, to be certain ... the word itself simultaneously ... [refers to] their very interdependence; to the very duality of security itself and thereby to the struggle against the false standing – the *pseudos* – with which *sphallo* is intimately associated' (ibid.: 124). This fundamental duality was also present in the Latin word *sine cura*, from where the English word security is derived. '*Sine cura* comprises *sine*, meaning without, and *cura* from *curio* meaning troubling; solicitude; carefulness; attention; pains; anxiety; grief and sorrow; ... Hence sine cure (and sinecure): without solicitude; careless; free from cares, untroubled; quiet; easy. *Securitas* is consequently defined as freedom from concern; unconcern; composure; freedom from danger; safety; security' (ibid.: 125).

3

The end of peace and the beginning of in/security

As has been explored in the first and second chapters, representations are articulated in particular contexts. This fact makes discourses embedded and constitutive of specific historical, political, cultural and social circumstances within a matrix of power relations. The representations of in/security depicted in the Democratic Security Policy have a history in themselves. It is to this historicity of discourse that we now turn our attention.

The present chapter aims to contextualise the release of the DSP in Colombia. When addressing its precedents, one date immediately surfaces: 20 February 2002, the *end* of peace. On 20 February 2002, President Andrés Pastrana (2002d) announced in a televised speech that, due to the latest terrorist attacks perpetrated by the FARC-EP, the peace process between the government and the guerrillas had come to an end. On this date, after President Pastrana announced the breakdown of the peace process, the Catholic Church, business leaders, the media, and national and international public opinion created a consensus about the *failure of peace* in Colombia. The end was not interpreted as the specific failure of one of many negotiations throughout the history of the armed conflict, nor was it simply ignored or dealt with, two of the possibilities frozen and erased on that date. 20 February 2002 was the beginning of *the* end of the possibility of reaching a peaceful agreement to peacefully transform the Colombian armed conflict.

The interpretation of the events on and after this date lays firm ground for the state in/security discourse. By mapping the discursive articulation of the construction of a hegemonic articulation (Laclau and Mouffe, 2001; Said, 2003a) about the end of peace, we observe the way in which an important source of legitimation for the DSP was set in place. In this sense, what happened on 20 February 2002 needs to be examined, questioned, and understood in order to comprehend, which is not to say legitimise, the promise of in/security.

The end of peace took place during the presidential electoral campaign of 2002. The situation was articulated as the country being at a crossroads. On the

85

one side, the option for *peace* was described as attempting another negotiation with the illegal armed groups. On the other side, the option for security was constructed as pursuing a military campaign to win the war. Each of these options was articulated in an exclusive manner, meaning, the country had to decide whether it would take the road to *peace* through peaceful means or whether it would take the road to *security* through violent means. The latter was personified by candidate Alvaro Uribe Vélez, whose programme rendered the call for in/security as unavoidable, imperative and, above all, urgent. Uribe was voted into office in May 2002, and the option of an open war materialised. The DSP was officially released in June 2003 under President Uribe's leadership.

This background, the end of peace and the beginning of in/security, is the centre of attention of the present chapter. Taking into consideration the insights of critical security perspectives analysed in the previous chapter, we will address the historicity of the DSP by identifying the different modes of representation that were articulated in a way that legitimised and made the promise of in/security seem unavoidable. I will focus on how the hegemonic articulation of the end of peace was constructed. This necessarily requires consideration of the consequences that this reading had for interpreting the 'Colombian war reality'. In the following section, I will examine how the options *peace* or *security* were articulated as exclusive and definitive. This process of questioning brings us to underscore other interpretations of the situation that had to be foreclosed for the success of the promise of in/security. This chapter concludes with an assessment of the political consequences of adopting the promise of in/security. It then opens the door for studying the DSP as discursive practice constructing identities, which will be explored in the fourth chapter.

Rereading the end of peace

In the Colombian context, the DSP came into being after the peace talks with the guerrillas FARC-EP failed. February 2002 was then perceived as a moment in which there had to be a qualitative change in the governmental agenda to deal with the illegal armed groups. In this scenario, the dangers were renamed.

During the Pastrana administration (1998–2002) the FARC-EP guerrillas tried desperately to be acknowledged as a belligerent group. Consequently, the FARC-EP, as well as the government, were defining their struggle in political terms, recognising the aim of the guerrillas to take over state power and, in this way, to legitimise political negotiations. The FARC-EP emphasised its belligerent character several times during the talks, and was recognised as hostile by both the national government and by the international community (Pastrana, 2002b).

Once the failure of the peace process was publicly declared by President Pastrana on 20 February 2002, politicians and journalists claimed that an overwhelming feeling of frustration necessitated a redefinition of the official strategy to deal with the internal armed conflict. It is in this peculiar scenario that the popularity of candidate Alvaro Uribe raised in the opinion polls. The Democratic Security Programme presented by Uribe renamed the conflict and the dangers. The situation was no longer defined as an internal political armed struggle between the state and guerrillas; the Colombian conflict became a situation in which a narco-terrorist organisation (without popular support) was fighting a democratic state and civil society in an illegitimate manner.

These changes in definition are of great importance. The renaming of dangers, from a belligerent group to a narco-terrorist organisation, was the source of justification for changing the state in/security strategy. Within the discursive realm, the internal armed struggle ended and a new danger came to overshadow the old one: Colombia was then reinscribed in the *global war on terror*. The transnational dimension of this redefinition should be highlighted. The terrorist attacks on 11 September 2001 in the US and their aftermath in Afghanistan as well as the internal measures adopted (Butler, 2004; Dudziak, 2003), changed the (inter)national dimension of what was then conceived of as terrorism.

In Colombia, the terrorist threat was not 'new'. But this time it had a different connotation. During the 1980s, which were inscribed within an American transnational *war on drugs*, terrorism was at its highest levels, marked by multiple and systematic terrorist attacks throughout the national territory. The years 1982–1993, from Pablo Escobar's rise within the Medellín Cartel until his death, were marked by extreme violence. The terrorist attacks during those years were unprecedented. Likewise, throughout the peace process between the Pastrana administration and the FARC-EP guerrillas, the military campaign to win the war was constant. The renaming of dangers in 2002, as Campbell (1998) notes, was not referred to as an *objective reality* said to be putting the *Colombian nation* at risk. This was a political interpretation within a moment of ambiguity. The peace process did not succeed, and the presidential candidates bet on offering political projects as alternatives to deal with the situation. In May 2002, fifty-three per cent of the voters chose to make candidate Uribe, who used the slogan *democratic security*, into a Colombian president.

Reviewing this process systematically within the historical context is helpful to clarifying how the events of the 20 February 2002 were interpreted and how a hegemonic discourse was constructed. We will briefly evaluate the peace process, and then re-examine how this particular crisis was created in a way that made the in/security discourse in Colombia seem *the only plausible option remaining*.

The peace process with the FARC-EP

In October 1997, more than seven million people voted 'for peace' through the symbolic suffrage *La Séptima Papeleta* (the seventh ballot), an initiative born out of a group of more than 100 non-governmental organisations (NGOs), which consisted of voting *No Más* to violence and war. The presidential elections took place against this backdrop. The two most popular candidates were Horacio Serpa and Andrés Pastrana, representing the liberal and the conservative political tendencies, respectively.

Pastrana's political campaign was directed at the promise and commitment of carrying on a peace process with the guerrillas. It was clear then that his governmental programme intended to reach a peaceful agreement with the subversive armed groups, especially with the FARC-EP, considered the most violent and powerful illegal armed organisation. In June 1998, Andrés Pastrana was voted into office for the four-year period between August 1998 and August 2002.

The peace process was officially inaugurated on 7 January 1999 with the infamous empty chair, which the FARC-EP leader Manuel Marulanda, alias *Tirofijo*, left next to President Pastrana during the inauguration ceremony. From that moment onwards, the government and the FARC-EP guerrillas began negotiations.

> In October 1998 the government of President Pastrana agreed to a FARC demand to establish a demilitarized zone and withdraw the security forces from the area, as a precondition for the guerrilla's participation in peace negotiations. The DMZ [Demilitarized Zone] came into force for an initial 90-day period on 7 November 1998, and was extended further on several occasions until the definitive breakdown of talks on 20 February 2002. (AI, 2002b: 3)

Offensive military attacks from both sides continued for three and a half years without a ceasefire ever being reached. To understand more comprehensively the end of peace in February 2002, it is important to take into account that throughout the so-called peace process, the military actions of war between government and guerrillas persisted. The development of the peace process and the waging of the war intertwine and their dynamics define each other (Nieto and Robledo: 2001, 108).

The government, for its part, increased its military capacity. First, it implemented the Plan Colombia. Under the Plan, the US government channelled millions of dollars each year to the *war on drugs* in Colombia and logistically supported the military. It is estimated that the US government was able to install a group of more than 300 members of the Central Intelligence Agency (CIA), the Drug Enforcement Agency (DEA) and the US armed forces in the country to provide military intelligence and training during the year 2000 alone (ibid.: 137–8).

Second, the president launched an ambitious modernisation strategy for the military forces. Between August 1998 and December 2001, the government increased the number of recruits from 53,000 to 65,000 and of professional soldiers from 22,000 to 55,000. Helicopters and fighter planes were almost doubled in number during the same period. The results increased in terms of the neutralisation of 274 guerrilla attacks during the year 2000, combating the insurgency more than 700 times (ibid.: 139). Official data suggests that during the first year of the peace process, the army killed more than 900 guerrilleros and captured more than 1,000 of them (Pastrana, 2001; Mindefensa, 2001). 'This means that, compared to the year 1999, the number of guerrilleros killed increased twenty-nine per cent and the number of persons captured increased thirty-five per cent' (Pastrana, 2001: 34). According to the Ministry of Defence (Mindefensa, 2001: 4), the data for the year 2001 showed that the military actions against the guerrillas were increasing, with 900 more guerrilleros killed and more than an additional 1,600 captured.

Legal instruments were also created to heighten the military power. On 13 August 2001, the Defence and National Security Law (Law 684/2001) was issued. It created the Theatres of Military Operations (TMO), which were '*de facto* states of emergency applied in geographical areas where there was a possible threat to and alteration of the constitutional order, sovereignty, independence and integrity of the national territory' (AI, 2002b: 4). The Defence and National Security Law also

> granted the military judicial police powers in certain circumstances; restricted the ability of the Office of the Procurator General, *Procuraduría General de la Nación*, to undertake disciplinary investigations against security force personnel for human rights violations committed during military operations; and limited the obligation of the security forces to communicate the detention of suspects during military operations rather than to ensure their immediate transfer to civilian judicial authorities. (Ibid.: 5)

Meanwhile, during the supposed peace process from January 1999 through July 2000, the FARC-EP attacked over 140 towns. Their actions included kidnappings, massacres, creation of military checkpoints and destruction of urban centres. 'During the three-year peace process the FARC continued to mount numerous disproportionate and indiscriminate attacks on military targets outside the DMZ, which frequently cost civilians lives, and to violate IHL [International Humanitarian Law] inside and in the immediate vicinity of the zone' (ibid.: 3).

In May 2000, the FARC-EP imposed Law 002, consisting of a ten per cent tax for persons and industries with a capital over one million dollars. At the same time, the guerrillas continued fighting the paramilitary groups, especially the AUC, within the context of their struggle over the control of coca-plantation zones. The guerrillas also intensified their military actions in the cities, which made the fact that the guerrillas' war was not only a problem for the rural areas even clearer (Nieto and Robledo, 2001: 120–4).

It is palpable that within the framework of the 'peace process' the military offensive attacks between the government and the FARC-EP continued, echoing

President Pastrana's belief that the war and the peace process could run parallel to each other (ibid.: 142).

> The statistics for 2001 are chilling in themselves, with over 300 people 'disappeared', more than 4,000 civilians killed – most by army-backed paramilitaries – tens of thousands of people displaced and over 1,700 people kidnapped, mainly by guerrilla groups. ... According to the UN High Commissioner for Refugees, the number of displaced persons increased by 48 per cent in 2001 from the previous year. (AI, 2002b: 3)

If the above circumstances are taken into account, what then produced the crisis on 20 February 2002? Considering the data mentioned above, the idea that there was a 'peace process' running throughout the period August 1998–February 2002 seems illusory at best. The 'objective' relation between the terrorist attacks of the guerrillas and the presidential declaration of the end of peace is not congruent. It was the decision of President Pastrana in that particular moment and the consensus it created nationally and internationally that corroborate the idea that the end of peace was constructed. This does not imply that it was artificial, but rather that, as it occurred in February 2002, the end of peace could have been declared as such based on any other previous guerrilla attack during the peace process. It was only the particular reading of the events during that day and the apparent unanimity around this interpretation that laid a firm ground for opting for war and security over peace.

Peace and war at the crossroads

Echoing Weldes et al. (1999), I suggest that the end of peace on 20 February 2002 was not an obvious and self-evident crisis, but rather the hegemonic interpretation of the situation articulated on that day. The power of consensus around the end of peace was only one among many possible interpretations. But the fact that there was a consensus around this unique way of perceiving the situation had two important consequences. First, this specific representation rendered all other possible readings unimaginable. Second, only by closing alternatives did the end of peace produce the necessary political space for the promise of in/security portrayed by Alvaro Uribe and his *democratic security* doctrine.

To comprehend the way in which the end of the negotiations with the FARC-EP was interpreted as *the end of peace*, it is necessary to examine the previous reading of the process by many of the actors involved. The representation of the peace process was 'clear-cut'. After more than three years of talks, without reaching a ceasefire or any other significant agreement, the bets were made. The situation between the guerrillas and the government was no longer seen as a process, but was represented as a definitive moment that would determine whether peace or war would follow.

As stated by James Lemoyne (2002), special advisor of the UN Secretary General for the peace process in Colombia, at stake during the peace process was the possibility for peace in absolute terms: '*Es el momento decisivo para el futuro del país y su pueblo. Literalmente en los próximos días definimos si va a haber esperanzas de paz o un camino hacia la guerra sin negociaciones*' (ibid.). This was a common interpretation of the international community: Colombia was facing the last attempt to solve the conflict peacefully and, in the case of failure, war was the only alternative remaining. For the Colombian peace commissioner, Camilo Gómez (2002), the situation was articulated in similar terms: '*Estos tiempos son para definirnos, sin términos medios: O estamos dispuestos a resolver el conflicto colombiano por la vía política o no lo estamos. O estamos dispuestos a construir la paz o no lo estamos*' (ibid.).

Paradoxically, Lemoyne's and Gómez' words clarify the social construction of the crisis itself (Weldes, 1999). When the UN advisor pronounced the words above, he was referring to a crisis during the month of January 2002. This crisis was solved and the peace process continued until more than a month later. The above words of the peace commissioner correspond to three weeks before the end of peace, also in January 2002. However, the articulation of the events of 20 February 2002 was regarded as definite. Clearly the end of peace could have been decided earlier based on other events, like the deadline for the end of the DMZ to which both Lemoyne and Gómez referred on 10 January 2002.

On 19 February 2002, President Pastrana (2002c) corroborated these fatal remarks in his own words:

> *El Proceso [de paz] necesita hechos concretos, palpables y expresos de Paz que reafirmen ante el país la voluntad de Paz expresada en la Mesa de Diálogo y Negociación, y nos eviten a los Colombianos el holocausto de la guerra total. La posición del Gobierno Nacional ante la Mesa Nacional de Diálogos y Negociación y ante el país, es la posición de los Colombianos.* (Ibid.)

One day after this declaration, the FARC-EP hijacked a commercial plane and kidnapped Congressman Gechem, president of the Peace Commission of the Senate. These events were qualified by President Pastrana (2002d) as the final drop that made the glass of indignation spill over, believing all outlets exhausted for reaching a peace agreement.

> *Me la jugué íntegramente por alcanzar la paz. ... Hemos sido todos los colombianos los que nos la hemos jugado por la paz. Hemos sido todos – la gente del común, los líderes, la iglesia, los partidos políticos, los sindicatos, los mismos candidatos – los que hemos aportado nuestra generosidad, nuestra fe, nuestra paciencia, para apoyar este proceso en el que depositamos nuestras esperanzas.* (Ibid.)

At the same time that the peace process ended in the DMZ of El Caguán between the government and the FARC-EP, peace ended for the Colombian people as well. The logical articulation made in Pastrana's speech was the binding thread for comprehending the articulation of peace as a lost option. In 1997, millions of people voted for the peace initiative, and in June 1998 President Pastrana was elected to specifically carry on the Peace Mandate. Pastrana's governmental programme was committed to signing peace agreements with the guerrillas, in order to 'build' peace. During the three years of peace process, the president was carrying out a people's mandate for peace. When the peace process was declared a failure in such final terms, so were the *legitimate peace aspirations of the Colombians.*

Throughout the peace process, the presentation of what was at stake became disproportional. The peace process turned into a decisive moment for the collectivity and was explicitly articulated as a moment of decision-making between the peace path and the war to be waged. These two options were presented to the public as mutually exclusive. However, if one takes into consideration the continued military attacks by legal and illegal armed forces, this argument seems to lose validity. The official version of the peace process, as a relatively calm time during which the president and the guerrillas were fully committed, is inconsistent with the documented increase in overall military budget, concrete actions, and number of soldiers of both parties during the same period.

By announcing the end of the peace process on the 20 February, the president constructed the same 'end of peace' for the people, leaving war as the only feasible response. Only when this correspondence of people-president-peace is understood, can the option for people-president-war be understood as well.

> *A nivel interno, hemos logrado que todo el país, todos y cada uno de los colombianos, se comprometa con la paz. Antes se pensaba que ese era un problema únicamente del Gobierno con la guerrilla. Hoy somos conscientes de que es una guerra que nos han declarado los violentos a la sociedad y que somos todos los que tenemos que trabajar para detenerla. ... los colombianos de bien tenemos que estar unidos, hoy más que nunca, y tenemos que estar listos a colaborar con las autoridades y a denunciar cualquier conducta sospechosa.* (Ibid.)

Pastrana's depictions of collective national identity were transformed through the discourse from a nation seeking peace into the *good Colombians* united more than ever: alert, ready to cooperate with the authorities and denounce any suspicious conduct, person or group. At the beginning of the president's speech, when referring to the peace suffrage and his mandate to sign peace agreements, all Colombians seemed to want peace. However, when that option was no longer available, 'good people' believed they had to be vigilant, because all good citizens collaborate with the authorities by denouncing neighbours and fellow Colombians. This separation is going to be crucial for comprehending the DSP and its effects on the construction of identity: if there is a group of *good Colombians*, there is a group of *bad ones* or *violent ones*. The identification of such a 'we' striving for internal similarity, necessitates an 'other' that provides the necessary material to construct 'us'. This co-constitutive outside (Said, 2003a) is 'who we are not' and 'where we are not', hence the 'other' becomes crucial to know who and where we are (Campbell, 1998; Connolly, 1991; Walker, 1993).

But how to discern who is *good* and who is *bad?* Who is 'one of us' and who 'is one of them'? Collaboration with the armed forces is the border marker; everyone who does not collaborate is excluded from belonging to the 'good ones'. At the end of peace, this division line seemed thin. By the time President Uribe replaced Pastrana and launched the DSP in June 2003, this borderline was clearer and the identity of the 'good' ones, as opposed to the 'bad' ones, was fixed, stable, clear-cut and frozen. But how did the dividing line become a wall? Let us analyse the process inch by inch.

> *Olvidemos las divisiones internas y los conflictos pequeños y cerremos filas contra la violencia. No vamos a dejar, de ninguna manera, que el terrorismo nos divida. ... ¡Un ejército de 40 millones de colombianos es invencible! ¡Nunca podrán derrotarnos!* (Ibid)

In his speeches at that time, Pastrana made clear that unity among 'good Colombians' implied the erasure of differences among them. 'Terrorism cannot divide us' said the president (ibid.). 'Good' people stay together; their divergent opinions on a myriad of subjects must be forgotten to all stand like good soldiers against terrorist violence. The army of good Colombians is born out of losing the figure of the citizen. Only citizens are different from each other; soldiers are all the same. Soldiers' differences do not matter, and they cannot matter because composing an army cannot be, by definition, a heterogeneous enterprise. In this sense, if *peace* had been the expression of the opinions of the citizens, then *war* was the option left for the army of good people. In this way, voicing political differences, 'being' different and having the possibility for 'becoming' something else than a good soldier, turned into a danger on the list of threats to in/security as viewed by the state. As Michael Dillon (1996: 29–30) posits by citing the words of Hamilton, 'the continual effect and alarm attendant on a state of continual danger, will compel nation ... to resort for repose and security to institutions which have a tendency to destroy their civil and political rights. To be more safe, they at length become more willing to run the risk of being less free'.

Identity is the articulation of the economy of identity/difference between 'us' and 'them', as William Connolly (1991) reminds us. It was not just the identity of Colombians that was transformed along its ethical and physical boundaries on 20 February 2002. The identity of the FARC-EP guerrillas was also irrevocably changed. Before that moment, President Pastrana (2002a) had stated that the power of definition of the guerrillas was in their hands. For Pastrana (ibid.), the guerrilla defined itself by their acts, as political subversion, terrorist group or drug dealers (ibid.). During January 2002, the official press release read that the guerrillas were 'valid political interlocutors for the peace process' (Mesa de Negociaciones, 2002). However, on 20 February 2002, President Pastrana (2002d) recalled the changing international landscape after 9/11 and the attacks perpetrated by the FARC. He thereby redefined guerrillas as terrorists, removing the political status the government had recently granted them:

> *Tristemente, hoy son ellas [las FARC] las que han firmado su propia definición y ya nadie puede dudar de que, entre política y terrorismo, las FARC optaron por el terrorismo.* (Ibid.)

The president followed this decision by declaring the end of the DMZ, the cancellation of the political status of the guerrillas, the reactivation of the orders to capture the FARC-EP leaders, and the abolition of the civic police (ibid.).[1] The state sought its own redefinition; it could not be that weak, waiting entity any longer. It had to regain its strength, authority and determination. On that same night, the military bombing campaign began targeting the FARC-EP rural strongholds.

> Three hours after the breakdown of talks, the armed forces reportedly carried out some 200 aerial missions from the Tres Esquinas base in Caquetá Department ... bomb[ing] 87 sites in the DMZ. ... Immediately following the aerial bombardment, the army entered the DMZ. (AI, 2002b: 9 10)

President Pastrana (2002d) insisted that the decision to go to war was still unmade at that point. It was up to Colombians to support their democratic institutions.

The construction of consensus

The consensus around *the end of peace* is a construction that involved more than the president's speech and the institutional armed and legal actions on 20 February 2002 and thereafter. The reactions from the Catholic Church, media, business leaders, and the international community, among others, are part of that hegemonic representation which made other interpretations and responses unfeasible. Public opinion ranged from hard-line to fearful expectations from the outset. The end of peace was an elaborate web of meaning knit from the moment the president issued the declarations until the electoral victory of candidate Alvaro Uribe in May 2002.

The secretary general of the United Nations (UN), Kofi Annan (2002), recognised the 'extraordinary efforts of President Pastrana in the search for peace during the past four years' and insisted that the forty-year-old armed conflict in Colombia 'required a negotiated solution as a respond to its deep social and political causes' (ibid.).

After acknowledging the efforts of the president in offering all the necessary guarantees for the peace process to the FARC-EP, César Gaviria (2002), former president of Colombia and general secretary of the Organisation of American States (OAS), stated that the guerrillas had chosen terrorism over politics. He concluded that this made the president's and Colombian society's peace efforts *not viable*. After mentioning the terrorist attacks committed by the FARC-EP, Gaviria recalled the compromise of the OAS in the war against terrorism after 9/11 and assured its full cooperation with Colombia in 'its fight against terrorism' (ibid.).

Similarly, the European Union (EU) gave its full support to President Pastrana, whose decision to end the peace process was seen as absolutely just and correct. At the same time, the EU stressed the impossibility of peace: '*El presidente Pastrana ha tomado una decisión, desde nuestro punto de vista absolutamente justa y acertada, y se ha cargado suficientemente de razón a lo largo de estos últimos tres años como para que compartamos su idea de que una voluntad de paz no es compatible con seguir matando, seguir vinculados e involucrados con el narcotráfico y con seguir los secuestros*' (Piqué, 2002).

The Rio Group supported the decision of the government in similar terms and also stressed the terrorist character of the FARC-EP actions: '*El Grupo de Río respalda las legítimas decisiones tomadas por el Presidente Andrés Pastrana en defensa de las instituciones democráticas y del orden público .... Por otra parte, formulamos un vehemente y enérgico llamado para que cesen las acciones de terrorismo y violencia en contra de la población civil*' (Grupo de Río, 2002).

The US Department of State speaker, Richard Boucher (2002), backed the declaration of the Colombian government and confirmed US governmental support in the Colombian war against terrorism:

> *El Presidente Pastrana y el Gobierno de Colombia han hecho todos los esfuerzos para negociar la paz con las Farc. Las Farc no respondieron de buena fe a ninguno de los esfuerzos del Presidente Pastrana por alcanzar la paz. El Gobierno de los Estados Unidos entiende y apoya la decisión que ha tomado el Presidente Pastrana. ... Estamos de acuerdo con el Gobierno de Colombia respecto de la necesidad de evitar que otros grupos terroristas, como las Autodefensas Unidas de Colombia (AUC) y el Ejército de Liberación Nacional (ELN) se aprovechen de la actual situación. (Ibid.)*

The national newspaper *El Colombiano* ran the headline '*Farc cerraron las puertas del diálogo*' and recounted facts legitimising the president's decision:

> *Valiéndose por primera vez de un video, en el que mostró las imágenes de los últimos ataques que perpetró la guerrilla de las Farc en el último mes, y del informe de inteligencia que entregaron los altos mandos militares sobre la utilización de la zona de distensión, Pastrana dijo que no es posible firmar acuerdos con una organización que mientras habla de paz, por el otro lado, pone fusiles en la cabeza de los inocentes: '¡Nos cansamos de la hipocresía de la guerrilla!*' (Vélez, 2002: 3A)

According to the national media following Pastrana's speech, it was the terrorist attacks perpetrated by the FARC-EP that caused the end of peace. *El Colombiano* (2002a) collected several international editorials concerning the breakdown of the peace talks in Colombia. For instance, *El Mundo* from Spain recounted the story as follows: '*El presidente de Colombia, Andrés Pastrana, ha puesto fin de las negociaciones de paz que emprendió en 1999 con las Farc, tras el secuestro de un avión comercial por parte de este grupo guerrillero. El Ejército, ha anunciado, entrará en la zona neutral*' (ibid.). In the same tone, *El País* from Spain titled its news '*Pastrana rompe el proceso de paz en Colombia tras el secuestro de un senador*', and explained this crisis as follows: '*el presidente de Colombia, Andrés Pastrana, ha anunciado esta madrugada la ruptura de las negociaciones de paz con las Farc después de que la guerrilla desviara ayer un avión comercial para secuestrar a un senador liberal. Pastrana ha iniciado además la cuenta atrás para que el ejército recupere la zona neutral creada para favorecer el proceso de paz en 1999*' (ibid.).

The Associated Press in France (AFP) related that the Colombian president had called the guerrilleros drug-dealers, terrorists and kidnappers. After directly quoting Pastrana's words, AFP stressed that the FARC-EP had betrayed their commitment: '*El mandatario* [Pastrana] *presentó pruebas ante la teleaudiencia de cómo las Farc han utilizado la zona del despeje de 42.000 km2 para rearmarse, esconder a los secuestrados y traficar con drogas*' (AFP quoted in El Colombiano, 2002a). In a similar vein, the BBC had as a headline 'Colombia: the end of peace' and in South America, *El Comercio*, from Lima (Peru), titled its news article '*El Presidente Pastrana rompe el proceso de paz*' (ibid.).

The president, alleging that the state had privileged information about the DMZ, disclosed these new facts to support his declaration and to use the power at his disposal. Independently from the events that the president listed as causes for the failure of peace, the media supported his interpretation that the end of peace was due to specific terrorist events. However, human rights organisations and victims alike had previously denounced the terrorist activities of the guerrillas in the DMZ multiple times (AI, 2002b: 1–3).

At the national level, the Catholic Church had been a crucial mediator throughout the peace process. Archbishop Alberto Giraldo, President of the Episcopal Conference, had been chosen as witness of honour to participate in all the negotiations between the government and the guerrillas. The Church and the figure of Monsignor Giraldo had been enjoying as much credibility as the Facilitating Commission and 'friendly countries' accompanying the process.[2] On 21 February, Giraldo (2002) made public the position of the Catholic Church as recognising 'this historical fact of extreme importance for Colombia' and supporting the position of President Pastrana: '*Respetamos y apoyamos la decisión del Señor Presidente. En un Estado de Derecho como el nuestro, es necesario cerrar filas para defender nuestras legítimas autoridades y apoyar las instituciones que aseguren la vida y honra de los colombianos*' (ibid.).

Businesses, represented by the Business Association Council (Consejo Gremial, 2002), and speaking 'on behalf of the private sector' supported the government's position. They went so far as to emphasise their commitment to the armed forces and reminded 'good Colombians' of their duty to reject terrorism and help to prevent it by denouncing suspected terrorists.

Both of the traditional political parties in Colombia, Conservative and Liberal, also supported the decision of the president. The director of the Conservative

Party, Carlos Holguín Sardi, declared to the media that it was 'time to show courage and strength, solidarity, and support the institutions having the certitude that the country goes on' (Pérez et al., 2002: 11A). Luis Guillermo Vélez, director of the Liberal Party, declared that even though the decision of the president was the correct one, 'it had been made too late' and he warned that a difficult situation was to come (ibid.).

Prestigious political leaders who had been involved in former peace process, such as Augusto Ramírez Ocampo, also declared their support for the President's decision to withdraw from the negotiation table (ibid.). Rafael Pardo, former peace advisor, qualified the president's decision as 'absolutely unavoidable' (ibid.). The ex-ombudsman Jaime Bernal also supported the president and called upon the guerrillas to assume responsibility and understand that 'the people cannot be attacked in such absurd manners' (ibid.). Antonio Navarro Wolf, former M-19 guerrilla and member of parliament, publicly warned that the FARC-EP had 'smashed the negotiation table and, with it, the attempt of restructuring and redefining the peace process for which the re-design would come through war' (ibid.). Juan Diego Granados, president of the Peace Commission of Antioquia, said to the press that the last attacks left the president 'without any alternative possibility but to end the peace process' (ibid.).

The presidential candidates at that moment supported President Pastrana and offered their own political programmes as responses to the crisis. It is clear that Alvaro Uribe was the candidate who could take the most advantage of this particular crisis, for he had always maintained a hard line in regards to the peace process. On 21 February, Uribe (ibid.) urged the government to design and implement an emergency plan against terrorism. This involved mobilising the armed forces, calling on the reservists and organising the citizenry in support of the public force. Moreover, Uribe called upon Pastrana to 'use the international support that the President has in the democratic nations and ask them for military support, involving their military logistics and intelligence to halt terrorism' (ibid.).

Other presidential candidates were less determined to call for war. According to declarations in national newspapers, Horacio Serpa, former candidate during the elections in 1998 who was running for the presidency for the second time, estimated that the FARC-EP 'had abused the citizenry and the limits of the government' (ibid.). Serpa called for national unity 'to support the institutions, defend democracy and demonstrate that there is a majority of Colombians willing to respect the law' (ibid.). Candidate Noemí Sanín commented that it was the FARC-EP that had 'buried the peace process and proposed to ask the United Nations and the Red Cross to facilitate the liberation of the kidnapped persons' (ibid.). Ingrid Betancourt insisted on the need to keep the bridges open for a future peace process, which was impossible then because of the terrorist actions of the guerrillas (ibid.). The independent candidate Luis Eduardo Garzón was the sole voice of dissent. He openly criticised Pastrana's decision to end the peace process. In Garzón's view, Pastrana and the guerrillas made a mistake when trying to reach an agreement without a ceasefire and told the press that it seemed to be 'one million dead people between now and the next peace process' (ibid.).

As for the illegal armed groups, the self-defence group Autodefensas Unidas de Colombia (AUC) called for Colombian unity 'to face the terrorism of the FARC, which have been left alone against the world' (Castaño and Mancuso, 2002). The second largest guerrilla group, the Ejército de Liberación Nacional (ELN, 2002), which at that moment was conducting its own peace process with the government in a parallel set of negotiations, pointed out that Colombians could not be dragged into a total war which would only favour the privileged classes. Finally, the FARC-EP reacted to the president's declaration stating to the press (*El Colombiano*, 2002b: 4A) that the failure of the peace process was the government's responsibility. According to the guerrillas, the breakdown of the peace talks was because the agreements in the DMZ were starting to produce results in terms of 'the big themes of the national agenda' (ibid.). Hence, in their view, 'President Pastrana ratified his decision of going to war against the interests of the people' (ibid.).

As seen in the reactions from Garzón, the presidential candidate who dissented from Pastrana's decision to end the peace process, the state discourse was challenged. The state discourse did not create a homogeneous response, nor could it ever do so, for any discourse exists in a web of plurality and the power relations it exercises create its own sites for resistance (Edkins and Pin-Fat, 1999; Foucault, 1990; Stern, 2005). While some voices rose to contest this particular interpretation of the events on 20 February 2002, the official interpretation of the situation was widely shared.

In Gramscian terms, it can be argued that the notion of *the end of peace* was turned into a hegemonic and widely consensual discourse in Colombia in response to the crisis of the breakdown of the peace talks (Laclau and Mouffe, 2001).[3] Edward Said (2003a: 6–7) also took the idea of hegemony to denote how 'the influence of ideas, of institutions, and of other persons works not through domination but by ... consent. In any society not totalitarian, ... certain ideas are more influential than others'.

From the illegal armed groups in Colombia to the church and the UN, the acceptance of the failure of the process was reinforced, strengthened and consented to by a multiplicity of institutions and actors. This consensus turned the interpretation of the end of peace into a hegemonic representation of reality believed to be *true* and *accurate* to the world it portrayed. The end of peace was then carefully and powerfully constructed for all: the President, the state and individual as well as collective 'Colombians'.

As it was underscored in the speech of Pastrana (2002d) and in the reactions to *the end of peace*, the constitution of the Colombian subject was transformed on 20 February 2002. If before that date all *Colombians* were supposedly being represented by the sovereign power of the president throughout the three-year peace process with the FARC-EP, when this peace attempt failed, the *Colombian subject* was divided. The collective identity was not one anymore; it was split in two, the 'good' ones and the 'bad' ones. Even though this division seems extremely primary and basic, it was and has been the pillar for the subsequent in/security discourses (texts, policies and practices). It is in this sense that I would like to call attention to the cultural construction of this particular crisis, what it *did* to the Colombian identity and how it shaped the interpretation of the national situation in a way which rendered the call for in/security unavoidable.

Posing insecurities as social constructions, following Weldes et al. (1999: 12), is not to say that there is no terrorist threat posed by guerrillas to the Colombian state, nor that dangers are inexistent. What the social construction of insecurities implies is, first, that the terrorist threat only acquires meaning as such when it is turned and labelled as a security issue (Wæver, 1995). Second, any security discourse is as much aimed at securing the good nationals against those threats as it is aimed towards *securing national identity* as such. What this approach questions and problematises is how the state discourse and the consensus around it turn the differences within the Colombian people into dividing lines, transforming difference into the condemnation of otherness.

Moreover, this process of otherness is built upon the assumption that the whole population is a dangerous mass of suspects until proof of being a good national is offered. It is not my purpose to focus on the 'real danger' of terrorism in Colombia, but rather on the *discursive constitution* of that threat and its meaning when analysing its effects on the construction of identity. The violence invested in safeguarding the boundaries between the good nationals and the violent ones translates into the loss of political and civil rights as well as the regulation of the population's circulation and possibilities for connecting to each other (Dillon, 2005).

Of special importance among these effects on identity is the loss of the possibilities to *become*, for the state discourse does not only secure national identity *as it is* but, since the production of identity needs to be constantly enacted, it also closes down political spaces where identity could take alternative forms. Read this way, the in/security discourse so turns into both a geopolitical and a biopolitical strategy to control the territorial boundaries of state and people – shape the political identities of nationals and others – as well as a managing strategy that regulates the population as bare bodies devoid of history, rights and political voice (Agamben, 1995). Especially important, as will be shown in the fourth chapter, is how such regulation of the population aims to prevent connectedness and circulation (Dillon, 1995).

At the 'end of peace' in February 2002, the production of subjectivities was then enabled by a particular state crisis that, geopolitically speaking, was also translated into a crisis for the national population's identity. Such crises are paramount to understanding abrupt discursive transformations in the political identities of state, nationals and others. Weldes (1999: 57–8) suggests that 'crises are internal to the functioning of states because they are inextricably intertwined with state identity in two complementary ways: first, state identity enables crises; second and conversely, crises enable state identity'. The state is the subject for which the crisis takes place. In other words, the crisis has to affect something or someone, and that is generally the state. The discursive consensual formation articulated about the end of peace had the effect that the crisis of 20 February was not merely directed at the Colombian state, but was expanded to the construction of national subjectivity too.

At the same time, this crisis facilitated 'the internal consolidation of state power' (ibid.: 58). This crisis enabled the state war machinery to operate with great publicity again. It allowed the armed forces to re-enter the DMZ for the first time in three years and it enabled the government to redefine its power relations in regard to the population by creating new markers for insiders and outsiders: the good ones collaborate with the security forces, denounce any suspect person and stay alert and vigilant.

As the crisis of 20 February exemplified, 'state identity is always potentially precarious, it needs constantly to be stabilized or (re)produced. Crises present important opportunities for that reproduction' (ibid.: 59). And since the end of peace, the new discursive elements for the beginning of in/security started being set in place.

In/securing national identity

Let us focus on how state discourses and identity are mutually constituted, for which the transformation of both during the end of peace is to be a relevant example. The representation of the Colombian identity during the peace process was of one nation united seeking peace, represented by a president committed to carrying on the people's peace mandate.

On 10 January 2002, the DMZ had one of its many deadlines, subject to a prolongation if agreements were reached around a national agenda at the negotiation table. The president did not seem to be willing to prolong the DMZ until James Lemoyne, UN peace advisor, intervened and mediated between government and guerrillas. After solving this crisis, Pastrana's words were clear:

> *El país habló claro y como nunca. ... Yo he interpretado a un pueblo que anhela la paz y este pueblo ha dicho la última palabra. El país habló.* (Pastrana, 2002b)

In/security discourses, by naming dangers and safety (Stern, 2005) and informing practices accordingly (Weldes et al., 1999), tend to naturalise and reify identities, as was discussed in the last chapter. State discourses are assumed to emanate from a taken-for-granted entity that faces an anarchical system full of threats, whether external or internal. Therefore, state discourses evoke 'security in this conventional sense thus invoking the discourse of organised political actors, particularly the state' (ibid.: 10).

During the peace process, Pastrana naturalised the idea of a national identity in the quest for peace. According to the discourse of the government (Pastrana, 2002b), during the peace process and because the president was betting on peace, *Colombians* were a people in solidarity with the government, convinced and willing to sacrifice themselves for the cause of peace. So, when Pastrana declared the end of the quest (Pastrana, 2002d), the end of peace was not just portrayed as an institutional one but as the end of peace from and for the people: the people's peace had failed.

IN/SECURING STATE IDENTITY

At the same time, the identity of the state is transformed along with the representations of dangers (Campbell, 1998). From August 1998 until February 2002, the state was presented as an entity *seeking peace*, willing, offering, trying to negotiate with the guerrillas. The state proposed and the guerrilla disposed, to paraphrase Edward Said (2003a). But after the declaration of the end of peace, the economy of identity/difference (Connolly, 1991) shifted.

According to President Pastrana's reading of the situation, the actions of the FARC-EP in February 2002 exposed the Colombian state as a paper tiger. They were disrespectful; they had betrayed the president's good faith. According to Pastrana, the guerrillas had slapped the country's quest for peace, especially Manuel Marulanda (the FARC-EP leader), who had left the president and all Colombians waiting. The state was committed to making peace with the guerrillas, yet after continuous deceptions, such peace never arrived. The president portrayed this crisis as a situation that made necessary and unavoidable a redefinition of state identity. The state could not be *weak* anymore, which, after the peace failure, was equated with passive. The state had to adopt a virile and strong identity; it had to recover its violent initiative and warrior features after a period of perceived passivity.

These identities of state, nationals and others were reshaped through the representation of the end of peace. In the in/security discourse, the identities of the *state* and of the *people*, which it is supposed to represent, were transformed along with the representations and interpretations of the relations between the government and the guerrillas, and the different dangers and labels under which each of them stands. The *people*, firstly depicted as citizens willing to construct peace, making sacrifices for it, betting on it, are transformed into soldiers, figures constituting the masses in the army of good people. The *people* are so drawn to freeze their different opinions until in/security brings them freedom. Politics is substituted by in/security and the state starts assuming its new virile role.

Even though all throughout the peace process there had been combat between guerrillas and public armed forces, and the legal and logistical reinforcement of war resources, as explained at the beginning of this chapter, such combat and the warfare taking place were never publicly scrutinised. The state continuously tried to prove that it was seeking the people's peace per the mandate reached during the presidential elections 1998. Therefore, based on the crisis on 20 February 2002, from the weak image of the awaiting state to the highly publicised bombings that same night, the state had begun its transformation. Its interests changed; it was not constructing peace anymore, but rather was now embarking on the quest for in/security.

In/securing Colombia

These representations constituted another *Colombia*, another world, another reality. If before 20 February 2002, *Colombia* was a country within which there was an internal armed conflict, after the end of peace it was a *democratic nation under the narco-terrorist threat*. The production of this danger emanated not just from the terrorist attacks, for as we have seen at the beginning of this section, the guerrillas continued their military campaign against the armed forces all throughout the three-year process. At the same time, there is no evidence about the weak role of the state either, as the resources of Plan Colombia, the modernisation and reinforcement of the military and their new unconstitutional prerogatives testify. What is important is how the modes of representation during the peace process and after the breakdown of the talks recreated a different situation with material effects.

The discourse following President Pastrana's announcement of the end of peace on national television on that February night, the institutional decision to terminate the DMZ and recover militarily the territory, and the chain of consensus it generated constructed a different reality for the state, as well as for Colombians and guerrillas alike. The breakdown of the peace talks was equated to the end of peace and each of the several distinct discourses, from that of the president to that of the church, identified a new sense of belonging to the nation. The state was invested with new interests. Its subjectivity changed, from a weak to a strong state. Enemies became narco-terrorists. At the same time, these representations produced social facts, redefining the internal conflict as a terrorist struggle, and fitting neatly into the post-9/11 global war on terror.

The beginning of in/security

The crisis of the end of peace turned into an opportunity to assert state identity, heightened by hot electorate debates during the presidential campaign of 2002, in which the main decision for the voters was *peace or in/security*. The 2002 campaign was articulated as a historical moment and as a turning point. This great event was portrayed as a specific situation, which had to lead the state and the nation on a particular path.

After the end of peace, two political possibilities were presented to the public: either peace or war. The voters had to make *a decision*. They were forced to choose whether they would support a candidate who opted for giving the peace talks another try, or vote for another politician who would lead the country deeper into war.

My contention that the DSP is a governmental discourse of in/security necessarily requires comprehending how such a call for war is democratically legitimised. The consensus around the end of peace channelled timid expressions of resistance into an electoral debate already inscribed in the hegemonic understanding that *peace was no longer an option*. In other words, the timid disagreements and reminders of a self-defeating war were absorbed into the discursive framework of the end of peace.

The electoral campaign 2002 could then be pictured as a moment of undecidability arising between two determinate possibilities (Derrida in Kearny and Dooley, 1999: 66). Aletta Norval (2004a) develops undecidability as a contribution to 'our understanding of a specifically democratic form of hegemony and subjectivity'. It is then through this specific contribution about how certain forms of hegemony are constructed that the insights of Norval can provide an interpretative framework for comprehending how the promise of in/security turned into the hegemonic discourse in Colombia. Norval (ibid.) follows Jacques Derrida in his differentiation between undecidability from indeterminacy,

> Undecidability is always a determinate oscillation between possibilities ... These possibilities are themselves highly determined in strictly defined situations ... I say 'undecidability' rather than 'indeterminacy' because I am interested in relations of force, in differences of force, in everything that allows, precisely, determinations in given situations to be stabilised through a decision of writing (in the broad sense I give to this word, which also includes political action and speech). (Ibid.)

Norval (ibid.) calls attention to the power relations at work for the terrain of undecidability to present two options in the first place, for both are the result of having ruled out other interpretations in the past. In this sense, the spectrum for decision is not infinite, but finite. Not all possibilities are taken into account, for they are already articulated within a web of meaning, within the cultural realm, which articulates certain possibilities and leaves others aside, rendering them unfeasible. Therefore, the options presented have been already partially determined and, in this sense, undecidability 'designates a terrain, not of general openness and contestability, but of a regulated tension and of a suspension in the "between"' (ibid.).

> undecidability acquires its force precisely as a consequence of the suspension of decidability. [Derrida often stipulates that undecidability arises between *two* determinate possibilities only.] Thus, undecidability refers to the holding in abeyance of the decision and to the effects of such abeyance. (Ibid.)

This way, the particular discursive context of the elections in 2002 allowed the two options between *peace* and *in/security* to be presented as a moment in which arriving at one decision would necessarily imply having to leave the alternative aside. One would lead to the erasure of the other. This moment is 'premised upon the fullness of two poles [as a between] in which identity is still at stake waiting to be inscribed' (ibid.). This *between* presents the subject with a decision, which does not take place in a vacuum but within a context, in our case *the end of peace*. Within this context, the subject has to arrive at a decision for which he/she should take responsibility. This experience of undecidability is 'thus not a moment of an easy wavering, or simply weighing up different possibilities or directions that may be taken' for Derrida it was a 'terrible and tragic situation' which had to be undergo in order to make a decision. Given this, 'the subject of this experience could *not* escape from it *un*marked' (ibid.: 19).

Precisely this mark left by such experience in the subject is part of the legitimation of the DSP, thus the government was able to establish that the collectivity had made the decision of embracing the promise of in/security by voting in the 2002 Presidential elections. Following William Connolly (1991: 202), we find how electoral campaigns serve to legitimise the state, since it 'appears to be accountable to a democratic electorate that can replace its officials and revise its priorities through competitive elections'.

Thus, we find ourselves analysing the beginning of in/security within the electoral campaign 2002 as, first, already the result of a hegemonic understanding of the end of peace. Second, the electorate campaign was articulated as a moment of undecidability in which a decision had to be made. Third, it was an opportunity for the state's reinforcement of its legitimacy through elections.

Election time

The different presidential candidates offered their political programmes to deal with the crisis of *the end of peace*. The most popular politicians made a choice between *peace or in/security*. Let us analyse how this offer was articulated by revising several of the political programmes registered for elections. We will focus on each of the candidates' proposals regarding the armed conflict without going into detail about other aspects, such as economic and environmental policies. For the sake of our discussion, these issues are left aside and full attention is given to the similarities and differences in the various candidates' platforms relating to security itself.

INGRID BETANCOURT: VERDE OXÍGENO

Ingrid Betancourt was kidnapped by the guerrillas on 25 February 2002, only a few days after the end of the DMZ.[4] Despite having been kidnapped, Betancourt's name was kept on the list for the 2002 presidential elections. Betancourt's programme was based on the conviction that the only way to deal with illegal armed groups was via political negotiation. Therefore, she offered to reinitiate peace talks (Betancourt, 2002).

NOEMÍ SANÍN: SÍ COLOMBIA

Noemí Sanín (2002) proposed to reinitiate peace dialogues according to a gradual agenda, which would lead the government and the guerrillas to a peaceful settlement of the conflict. Her political programme was structured around a peace strategy, which consisted of conducting negotiations under the condition that the guerrillas observed IHL norms. For Sanín, the problem of the war in Colombia was not a military one, but mainly an economic and social one. She therefore proposed to 'win the war with a legitimate State' (ibid.).

LUIS EDUARDO GARZÓN: POLO DEMOCRÁTICO

Garzón was a popular trade unionist who organised an alternative socialist movement as a political party in 2001. As a presidential candidate, Garzón (2002) proposed a political programme based on reconciliation and sustained by the premise that conducting peace talks was the only admissible strategy for dealing with illegal armed groups. Garzón prioritised 'peace over war, life over death' (ibid.), and questioned the state security strategy, claiming that it would only lead to eroding the state's legitimacy even further. For him, the strategy of trying to win the war militarily in order to debilitate the guerrillas to negotiate at a later point was self-defeating. The starting point for Garzón was to create trust between the state and the guerrillas and then and only then to negotiate (ibid.).

HORACIO SERPA: PARTIDO LIBERAL

Serpa had already run for president in 1998, when Andrés Pastrana defeated him. Serpa has been an important figure in national politics since he was the minister of the interior of President Ernesto Samper (1994–1998), who was made world famous for the infiltration of drug money into his campaign. Throughout Samper's administration, Serpa was able to negotiate with diverse national and international political forces to keep the president in place during the length of his mandate. In 2002, Serpa was still marked by the stigma of corruption, but he was nevertheless considered the second most popular candidate for the presidency in 2002.

Serpa's (2002) political programme emphasised that the war against illegal armed groups could only be won by political negotiation. However, given the end of peace, this strategy did not seem plausible at the time. He therefore offered to reinforce the military capacity of the armed forces. In this way, Serpa proposed to first defeat the guerrillas militarily and then to initiate peace negotiations.

ALVARO URIBE VÉLEZ: PRIMERO COLOMBIA

It is helpful to provide a bit of background on Alvaro Uribe to understand the significance of the programme he presented as a presidential candidate. Uribe was born to a prestigious family in Medellín in 1952. He became a public figure at a very young age, working as head of local administrative offices in his city where he first became mayor (1982) and then city counsellor (1984–1986). His political career continued as a senator from 1986–1990 and 1990–1994. But until his election as president, his most prominent position was as governor of the Province of Antioquia (1995–1997). During that time, he constructed his profile as a popular right-wing politician.

The foundation of the *Convivir* associations brought Uribe national recognition. These associations were rural cooperatives of private security and vigilance supported by the governor's administrative decision and by the province's infrastructure to protect the citizenry from kidnappings, blackmailing, assassinations and massacres committed by the guerrillas. Human rights organisations have found evidence to document the fact that these groups started a strong paramilitary movement in Antioquia. They were denounced at the UN General Assembly sessions of March 1997 and have been recognised by the paramilitary leader Carlos Castaño (Aranguren, 2001).

Even though these cooperatives were only supposed to report the presence of criminals and guerrillas to the armed forces, Uribe armed nearly fifty of them. In Urabá, one of the most violent regions in Antioquia, Uribe installed two *Convivir* against the will of local authorities. The regional administration and the armed forces supplied communication equipment and weapons to the citizenry, trained some of the workers on the banana plantations and involved paramilitaries in the job. In the first year of operations of the *Convivir* in Urabá, the rate of assassinations increased from 600 to 1,097. In 1996, the data of the national police showed 1,431 violent deaths. Finally, in 1997, after the Constitutional Court issued a sentence prohibiting these organisations from using heavy weaponry, the rate descended to 1,001 murders. In 1998, after the *Convivir* were declared illegal, the statistics dropped to 420 violent deaths (*Semana*, 2002a).[5]

Uribe's policies in the Province of Antioquia brought him into the national public political arena triumphantly. For the presidential race, Uribe coined the term *democratic security*, explained in the launching speech for his candidacy as a concept 'to effectively protect all citizens' in which 'the President' would be 'the first soldier of Colombia' (Uribe, 2002a: 6). He equated *democratic security* with the military forces of the state enjoying a broadening of their functions, not only in their classical role as guarantors of the defence of the nation but also as guardians of the tranquillity of the good citizens. In this sense, the expansion of the military functions to impregnate civil life was combined with the character of a citizen-warrior who actively cooperates with the armed forces. The president adopted the image of a soldier and encouraged the citizenry to adopt features of combatants. Regarding the concept of authority, which was the pillar of his political speech and key to winning the election, Uribe explained its scope in the following words:

> *Propongo la cooperación masiva de la ciudadanía con la fuerza pública, de manera transparente y sin paramilitarismo. ... Nosotros tenemos el derecho de vivir en paz y la obligación de contribuir a conseguirla. ... Estoy convencido que los violentos no negocian sino con gobiernos firmes dispuestos a derrotarlos.* (Ibid.: 7)

The identity of the citizenry is reinforced by the arrangement of this group of good citizens, as opposed to the violent ones who have to feel the threat of military defeat in order to negotiate with the establishment. It is in this understanding of the primary conditions for negotiations on which Uribe based the strength of the military forces.

Uribe's initial speech concluded with a reference to his vice-president, Francisco Santos. Uribe mentioned that Santos was a victim of kidnapping, who had fled into exile and had heroically returned to 'fight in the trenches for his compatriots' (ibid.: 9). The specific way in which victimisation was portrayed by Uribe channelled the victims' pain in order to feed war and violence. In the words of Iván Orozco (2002: 81), this matching political formula of president and vice-president as victims of violence legitimised revenge. This political match, in its symbolic dimension, represented the marriage of the vindictive, in which victims would find an echo of their desire to retaliate.

For the 2002 election, Uribe structured his political campaign and political programme in the form of a manifesto consisting of 100 points (2002b: 14). Uribe emphasised the obligation of the guerrillas to declare a ceasefire before any peace negotiations could occur. Since peace did not seem a plausible option, Uribe offered the concept of democratic security as the directing principle for his proposal. Reinforcement of the armed forces with a minimum of 1,000 professional soldiers was articulated as a priority. Second, the resources of Plan Colombia, which were officially directed to combat illegal drugs, would be merged with the fight against terrorism. The division between guerrillas, terrorists and drug-dealers was thus completely erased. For the armed forces to win the war against terrorism, the massive cooperation of the citizenry had to be enforced.

Uribe's programme relied upon the belief that only an open war waged by the armed forces and the citizenry could end the terrorist threat (ibid.: 3).

Uribe's (ibid.: 1) interpretation of the Colombian situation was based upon the premise that the state's decades-long lack of authority had produced the high levels of violence against the civilian population. Because civilians were the primary victims of violence, they were also the primary targets of Uribe's security strategy. Only if the people were united with the armed forces in the quest for state authority and only if they actively participated in the military war would the surviving terrorists be willing to surrender (ibid.: 3–4). From the beginning, Uribe proposed a network of one million citizens who would collaborate permanently with the army (ibid.: 20). In the words of Uribe, after the three-year process with the FARC-EP, which resulted in the end of peace, as president he would not try to engage in dialogue with the terrorists directly. For that, a military defeat would be a precondition to negotiate, and the mediation of the international community was presented as indispensable (ibid.: 3).

Since the DSP is the focus of attention of this book, it is pertinent to consider the proposals of candidate Uribe in more depth. Looking at his political campaign carefully, it is possible to understand how the promise of in/security was articulated originally and how significant his democratic triumph was in 2002. Since the inception of the DSP in the form of the Political Manifesto in 2001, the discourse of in/security promised more political violence in order to end the war. The hegemonic articulation of this proposal, in the form of political elections, seems to me crucial to comprehending the implications of how the writings of peace (and war) shape political identities and, ultimately, political imaginaries in such a way that violence is legitimised and reproduced. With these thoughts in mind, we will first evaluate the main proposals of Uribe's political programme, contained in the Political Manifesto. We will then consider one of Uribe's public interventions during his campaign to grasp his thorough disregard for democracy.

THE POLITICAL MANIFESTO

The manifesto structured Uribe's promise of in/security in one hundred points (2002b: 14–19). Of these, we will focus on the issues related to the present research. Uribe introduced the concept of democratic security in a lengthy way, from points twenty-six to forty of the manifesto. Democratic security is derived from Uribe's conviction that peace as it was portrayed by Pastrana was *illusory* and 'made out of peace doves and virtual declarations on TV' (ibid.). This was no longer an option. Instead of this type of peace, Uribe offered 'peace as born out of authority [as a new] concept in Colombia to halt the criminals' (ibid.: 20). Recalling the traditional label of the state as masculine, Uribe equated it to the *pater familias* who must exercise authority over his children (ibid.: 16–17).

Democratic security is composed of the following elements: security for all; reinforcement of the military to dissuade criminals and to guarantee security in

Colombia; strengthening of the armed forces and more than one million peasants helping with surveillance and active collaboration activities. Private security companies also collaborated with the army, expanding their role as protectors of private spaces to the public space. Finally, in order to promote collaboration, citizens were paid for the information they shared with the army. These citizens were qualified by Uribe (ibid.: 14) as 'a million of good people, who love tranquillity and promote living together'. They are not, thus, every citizen, but only those inscribed as 'good' ones.

In point thirty-one of the manifesto, Uribe (ibid.: 17) stated that the democratic security strategy should be partially financed with the economic resources of Plan Colombia. This way, the concept of terrorism subsumed the label of guerrillas, thereby defining terrorism as the main danger to the Colombian nation. Plan Colombia was presented as the solution to terrorism, the war on drugs and the anti-subversive fight, as well as the form in which Uribe sought international cooperation.

> *Pediré la extensión del Plan* [Colombia] *para evitar el terrorismo, el secuestro, las masacres, las tomas de municipios. ... Demandamos la cooperación internacional porque este conflicto se financia con el narcotráfico, negocio criminal internacional, y se apoya en armas fabricadas afuera.* (Ibid.: 17)

Since the presidency of César Gaviria (1990–1994), different administrations had made efforts to be acknowledged by the international community regarding its shared responsibility in the drug business. These diplomatic efforts aimed at making visible the responsibility of 'developed' countries to fight the distribution and consumption segments of the drug business in their own countries. For Uribe (ibid.: 3), the role of the international community and of the United Nations were reduced to military actions in the war against drugs. His programme did not contemplate the possibility for international cooperation in a broader sense, for example as mediator in a peace process (Leal, 2002b: 65). The lack of articulation between the security policy and a nonexistent peace policy was evident, and underscored the fact that for Uribe in/security was synonymous with peace and contradictory to war.

Suggesting that Plan Colombia was the solution to violence in Colombia was an easy yet unviable proposal that aimed to eradicate violence with more violence. As was briefly sketched in the first chapter, the Plan has been controversial since its publication and, although it may fit neatly into the war on terror rhetoric, it was conceived well before 9/11. This makes clear that, although the DSP intertextually and contextually fits into the war on terror, the war against drugs through military means is problematic in itself and has enjoyed a longer tradition in the country. As Francisco Leal (ibid.: 66) points out, the coercive pressure of the US government to impose its conception of the war against drugs on Colombia has been constant and well publicised since the mid-1980s.

For instance, the government of César Gaviria was highly influenced by the US foreign policy on drugs. When Pablo Escobar escaped from his luxurious high-security prison, 'the Cathedral,' in 1992, bilateral relations entered such a crisis that the Colombian government had publicly to share the official handling of the problem of drug production and the drug capos with the US government, both Congress and the military. The government of Ernesto Samper (1994–1998) systematically followed the expectations of the US as far as how to wage the war on drugs. The legitimacy problems of the president due to the financing of his presidential campaign with drug money put his governing years in a constant stalemate. This led him to implement prohibitionist and repressive drug policies.

President Andrés Pastrana (1998–2002) had prioritised recovering the good image of the country in the international arena. He tried to convince the international community to commit to a new Marshall Plan, first named *Fondos para la Paz* and later renamed 'Plan Colombia' (ibid.). The basic idea was to create an international fund for the reconstruction of and peace in Colombia. After visiting the US several times, Pastrana finished the final version of Plan Colombia hand in hand with North American advisors. The US Congress studied the Plan and approved it as international aid in the summer of 2000 (ibid.).

Plan Colombia is then the most concrete result of the conception of fighting the war on drugs in Colombia via coercion. The militarisation of the drug war was evident in directing sixty per cent of US financial aid to the military and fourteen per cent to the police, whose main functions were taken over by the military forces in the coca and poppy growing areas (ibid.). The focus on fumigation of the growing zones for coca and poppy has been proven wrong by the rise of connected health problems, ecological degradation, and the low actual numeric eradication of crops. Nevertheless, the strategy of the war on drugs continues to place emphasis on this harmful and ineffective mechanism.

For the US government, the most prominent threat to the region before 11 September 2001 was the drug problem. After 9/11, terrorism became *the* threat and the US Department of State's list of terrorist organisations included the guerrillas FARC-EP and ELN and the paramilitary group AUC. The claims of President Pastrana to involve the fight against the guerrillas in the war on drugs found its echo in Alvaro Uribe, who in his manifesto broadened the scope of the drug war to include anti-subversive measures and others against terrorism, massacres and kidnappings.

In point thirty-three of the manifesto, Uribe (2002b: 17) proposes an anti-terrorist statute which facilitates detention, arrests and house searches in order to fight terrorism. 'Contrary to my years as a student', said Uribe, 'today political violence and terrorism are identical. Any act of violence for political or ideological reasons is terrorism' (ibid.).

Here the confusion that the ambiguity of the term 'terrorism' projects upon the understanding of in/security is overwhelming. Both concepts are used by

Uribe in a wide and embracing manner. From this moment onward, Uribe interpreted the Colombian situation as a struggle with terrorism, denying the guerrillas any political character whatsoever. It is evident that this representation already had its origins in the reactions to the 'end of peace'. The discursive articulation that Uribe made thus built upon previously articulated images and meanings.

In the words of William Connolly (1991: 207), this 'contemporary distillation of "terrorism" from the [national] sea of war, violence, surveillance, oppression, and torture provides a paradigmatic example' for the salvation role the state is supposed to play.

> The moral isolation of nonstate violence from other modalities of violence produces multiple effects: it invests nonstate violence with unique causality and danger; it implicitly endows state violence with special sanctity; it conceals holes and cracks in the international economy of states that might otherwise be disclosed through the response of nonstate peoples; it deflects attention from deficiency in state efficacy with respect to the environment, inequality, and coexistence with third-world peoples [*sic*]. (Ibid.)

Terrorism is then the preferred term for describing the Colombian situation and for qualifying nonstate violence. The power of definition of what or who counts as a terrorist is, in return, used by the state as a threat towards all of those who do not comply with the definition of the category 'good citizen'. Again, it is crucial to remember that when the political manifesto was issued, these dangers did not speak to the post-9/11 global war on terror. Such an understanding of terrorism as the main danger to the nation preceded the global war strategy.

Continuing the analysis of the manifesto, one of the most important postulates for understanding how the DSP constructs and produces political identities is point thirty-eight, which pertains to civilian support for the state security effort (Uribe, 2002b: 18). This support has been actively put into force since Uribe entered office as president. It outlines how membership in the category *good nationals* is measured: by the degree of active cooperation with the army.

> *Todos apoyaremos a la fuerza pública, básicamente con información. Empezaremos con un millón de ciudadanos. ... Redes de vigilantes en carreteras y campos. Todos coordinados por la fuerza pública.* (Ibid.)

Francisco Leal (2002b) points out the ambivalence and danger of this proposed measure against the principle of democratic liberty and the impossibility of putting into practice this army of informants. He not only considers this idea in terms of practical implications, but also in terms of the consequences for a society divided between good citizens who inform the military about 'suspect persons, activities or ideas', and the bad, or violent, citizens. In this case, the dangerous character of the other does not matter, for he/she just needs to fit the profile of what some person in their neighbourhood might consider a suspect (ibid.: 70). This reinforces warrior features of a citizenry that, when it considers itself as belonging to the good nationals, adopts military characteristics. Taking sides becomes an obligation for everybody.

In point thirty-nine, the manifesto explains this collaboration is not based solely on patriotic feeling, but also on the fact that informants will be economically rewarded:

> *Concertar con transportadores y taxistas para vincularlos a la seguridad de calles y carreteras. Cada carretera tendrá un coronel del Ejército o de la Policía responsable de su seguridad. El lunes será el 'Día de la Recompensa' que pagará el Gobierno a los ciudadanos que en la semana anterior hubieran ayudado a la fuerza pública a evitar un acto terrorista y capturar al responsable.* (Uribe, 2002b)

Economic rewards have been used as incentives for many years in Colombia in order to obtain information about criminal acts and their perpetrators. How effective and reliable is this method? When the economic reward is directed toward specific individuals, like the leaders of drug cartels or guerrilla organisations, it is supposed to be an incentive for their henchmen to turn them over to the authorities. However, what is actually rewarded is any kind of information leading to 'contain terrorism and kidnapping' (ibid.). The identification of the threat is left to the informant – the citizen – who is constantly encouraged to reveal the 'real' terrorist character in any action or inaction performed by others.

It can be said that this strategy might not only be difficult to implement successfully, but also that it recreates a society of fear and mistrust where citizens lose their ability to act in concert with others in a plural political scene. Following the proposal of the democratic security programme, the task of implementing this in/security policy is carried out to the detriment of democratic principles. As we have already seen in the insights of Dillon (1996), when in/security installs itself as the impossible founding ground for politics, it is a self-defeating project whose price is human freedom.

Within this frame, in point forty-one of the manifesto, Uribe (2002b: 19) describes his notion of peace as synonymous with illegal armed actors surrendering and re-entering society. The democratic manifesto made clear that Uribe's political programme was directed at incorporating the guerrilleros into the in/security society. This platform erased the possibility of negotiating with illegal armed groups. There would be no negotiation of the political situation as it was or of how politics could be – what actors might yet become. Uribe did not and does not leave room for such political conversations with the illegal armed groups. He only recognised in them terrorist actions and not political aims. The doctrine of democratic security extends this terrorist logic to any other act that challenges the democratic institutions of Colombia (ibid.).

To sum up the most important underlying belief of the manifesto, in the words of Uribe, 'security is the founding ground' (ibid.: 26). Security is the 'democratic principle which has been lost and has to be recovered in order for the citizenry to exercise their freedoms' (ibid.). From his point of view (ibid.), 'this proposal does not unleash the war, but quite the contrary it contains it [since] all around the world violent actors know that they do not have to negotiate with a weak government'. In contrast, Uribe proposes a strong state, a strong government, and further suggests good people collaborate with the armed forces to 'close ranks against the terrorists' (ibid.). 'This proposal has to be a permanent action for the day has to come in which we bring down the terrorists of simple weariness' (ibid.: 27). This way, military defeat would lead terrorists to incorporate themselves in the security society where democratic politics is no longer an option for dissent and debate.

In the manifesto, candidate Uribe (ibid.) also made clear that peace was to be the result of war. In short, peace was to be postponed for the day in which in/security brings freedom. If we again recall Michael Dillon (1996), since in/security is an impossible enterprise that tries to disclose a certain and 'secure' unfree human being, then we might say that the day in which in/security brings peace, as it is articulated in the manifesto, is a day that will never come. However, such impossibility allows the promise of in/security to reproduce itself. It enables peace to be postponed permanently into future scenarios while sacrifices of freedoms are to be made in the present.

ALVARO URIBE'S OPINION OF THE POLITICAL CONSTITUTION

Uribe's speech about the 1991 political constitution is a key text for evaluating his political campaign and the implications of the hegemonic articulation of the DSP through democratic elections. The candidate often used the proposed reforms to the constitutional framework as crucial founding principles for his future presidency. In a university seminar in July 2001, when commemorating the tenth anniversary of the constitution, Uribe (2001) highlighted what he thought were its most inadequate features. First, he referred to the great number of congressmen as impossible to control and blamed them for creating 'black holes' in the edifice of the state. Second, he criticised the multiplication of public entities, like the General Attorney Office (ibid.: 6). This criticism of the constitution is based upon the conviction that more spaces for democracy increase the lack of authority of the state. This conception of an *excess of democracy* as cause of disorder reveals a philosophical belief in a state based on authority and on the absence of democratic spaces as appropriate mechanisms for containing threats.

Following his articulated disregard for democracy, Uribe (2002b: 16–18) included these ideas in the 2002 manifesto as part of the political reform in points nine and eighteen, which consist in reducing the Congress from two chambers to one. In the manifesto, Uribe reconfirmed his idea that open political spaces, like those offered by the Congress, have been used by terrorists to infiltrate the democratic institutions of the state and to influence its decisions. Democratic spaces, which Uribe identified as threatening gaps, thus had to be closed down in order to protect state authority. 'The Congressmen have to be carefully watched' said Uribe (2001: 6) during the launch of his campaign. 'Citizens have to know how the Congressmen vote, which laws they promote and whose interests they really defend'.

Likewise, in the eleventh point the Political Manifesto (Uribe, 2002b: 16) proposed fusing the provinces of the popularly elected governors. 'One Provincial administration instead of three', as a way of diminishing costs for the national government. According to Uribe, the large quantity of regional governments was another constitutional mistake. In his list of useless institutions, Uribe included the different control entities, such as the Office of the Ombudsman, which is in charge of documenting the accusations of human rights violations (Uribe, 2001: 6).

For Uribe, democratic spaces were listed as dangers and represented unnecessary public institutions, threatening gaps through which the terrorists infiltrate the state. He described them as an excess and as a burden, visually depicting them as the political equivalent of black holes. It seems as if the possibility to express political opinions and to control the government's actions also constituted threats. Only within this viewpoint can the promise of in/security propose to sweep democracy away in a *justified* manner. As pointed out by Dillon (1996) in the past chapter, it is not a contradiction of in/security but the very possibility of its dynamic when the promise of the sovereign is to bring in/security as a precondition for freedom.

The main arguments and logical connections of the political manifesto may be summarised as follows. First, Uribe (2002b: 16–26) attributed the violent situation in Colombia as due to the state's lack of authority, which, because of its weakness, had been unable to protect the citizenry. A two-pronged strategy to overcome this situation was first to arm the citizenry, turning it from victim to victimiser, making the *good people* collaborate with the army, and paying them for the information. Second, the president had to recover state authority. As a traditional authoritarian figure, the president assumed the role of first soldier of the fatherland and promised to recover in/security for the population to start enjoying their freedom, which 'is only possible after order is in place' (ibid.: 26). First in/security, then freedom. Freedom appears as a postponed prerogative that can only be practised after in/security is reached. In the logic of democratic security, Uribe made security equivalent to war (ibid.).

Along these lines, the discourses of Uribe as candidate present us with an accurate picture of the organising principles that have informed his government's practices, including the DSP, since he was elected president in 2002. Returning to the analysis of his electoral campaign, these principles clearly inform the DSP as well as every other law and policy during his tenure.

Opinion polls

Embedded in the context of the end of peace, the different presidential candidates moved in the opinion polls rapidly. As the 'big survey' conducted by Napoleón Franco (*El Tiempo*, 2002) one week before the elections showed, by September 2001 Uribe enjoyed a voters' intent of twenty-three per cent. After the end of the official peace talks in February 2002, the voters' intentions for electing Uribe showed fifty-nine per cent. Although this high percentage later declined, by 19 May 2002, Uribe still counted on forty-nine per cent of the vote. Compared with Uribe's popularity as it was registered in the national survey (ibid), the voters' intent for the remaining presidential candidates increased marginally and Uribe had more than twenty-six per cent of advantage over his closest rival.[6]

Peace versus in/security was the most debated electoral topic during the initial months of 2002. The *end of peace* was qualified as a profound crisis that called for a redefinition of the role of the state. In this sense, the political proposals made by the candidates were mainly evaluated as far as each presented him or herself offering a strategy for dealing with it (ibid.).

VOTING IN/SECURITY INTO OFFICE

On 26 May 2002, fifty-four per cent of Colombians legally entitled to vote did not participate in the elections. Of the forty-six per cent of those who actually voted, fifty-three per cent chose to make candidate Alvaro Uribe into President Uribe. The result of more than fifty per cent of the votes for one candidate made a second round of elections unnecessary. The official results of the 2002 election in Colombia are shown in Table 3.1.

From the fact that the democratic security government reached office through democratic elections and with an absolute majority, one important

Table 3.1   *Official results of the 2002 Colombian presidential election*

Candidate	Votes	%
Alvaro Uribe Vélez	5,862,655	53.05
Horacio Serpa Uribe	3,514,779	31.80
Luis Eduardo Garzón	680,245	6.16
Noemí Sanín	641,884	5.81
Ingrid Betancourt Pulecio	53,922	0.48

Source: Registraduría Nacional del Estado Civil, 2002.

aspect has to be noted: the promise of in/security was made a hegemonic articulation with vast democratic legitimacy. This produced multiple effects. First, it presented the constituency with the impression that the elections punished the failure of the existing governmental peace programme. Second, the voter participation gave them the opportunity to reinscribe themselves as democratic subjects. Both effects need to be taken into account when dealing with the DSP and the way it has continued to produce, reproduce and transform political identities.

DEMOCRATIC ELECTIONS

William Connolly (1991: 208–9) presents us with a relevant proposition regarding democratic elections in the US. His insights are well suited to unpacking how the DSP has been presented as a hegemonic articulation around the failure of peaceful ways of dealing with the Colombian conflict, and as different from the self-portrayed peace process of the former administration of President Pastrana. I reuse Connolly's analysis to explore the legitimacy of changing governmental programmes and offer an alternative interpretation of what happened in the 2002 election.

Following Connolly (ibid.: 208), the consolidation of terrorism as that ambiguous symbol, as the main hazard, and as the threat that violent ones pose to 'us', constructs a pliable and disposable mass of dangers which 'provides the state with a stage upon which to display its power and conceal its inefficacy'. By constituting this internal target of otherness and danger, the state is enabled 'to present itself as an institution of democratic accountability, since electoral constituencies are able to choose in each election between punishing' [in the Colombian case] attempts at peace negotiations and 'reforming state programs' (ibid.), for example of war and in/security one more time. 'Because the newly elected regime can replace the alternative that has most recently failed, the electorate is able to convince itself ', for instance, that the failure of peace 'is the effect of the last option pursued rather than of the set of options legitimately available to the state' (ibid.).

In this sense, the questions of *peace* and *war* served the state in renewing its own legitimacy with the electorate, giving the impression to the people, as Connolly suggests, that the problems regarding peace and security are directly related to the previous administration. However, after we have problematised *the end of peace*, not as a natural and self-evident result of the breakdown of peace talks, but rather as the hegemonic interpretation of the situation in a moment of undecidability, both alternatives are denaturalised. We are then confronted with a different understanding of electorate times. Each election portrays the failure of the last attempt as if both options were obvious and exclusive, and as if they were the only ones still available.

The failure of peace is thus actually *the success of peace as a lost option*, as 'the political project in the construction and disposition of otherness' (ibid.: 209). The fact that the 1998 presidential elections were decided upon the failure of the war and upon the hopes of peace, together with the fact that the 2002 presidential elections were decided upon the failure of peace and upon the hopes of war, corroborate this political pendulum. 'In the case of ... terrorism ... actions taken by the state demonstrate its punitive and disciplinary power, conceal its deficits in efficacy, and translate defects in the established identity into evils against which the collective identity can be reinstated' (ibid.).

For the presidential period 1998–2002, *Colombians* were being hailed to occupy the position of a people seeking peace, within the framework of peace talks. Yet, in the voting results for the presidential period 2002–2006, *Colombians* were being hailed to adopt a contrary position: that of a people seeking in/security, trying to recover the lost authority of the state, pursuing war as the appropriate path to in/security. The electorate results were read as the erasure of the peace option and as the success of the political project of in/security.

UNDEMOCRATIC DEMOCRATS

The democratic elections, which made a new government out of the promise of in/security, produced a second significant effect: they reinscribed Colombians as democratic subjects and legitimised the state regime. The insights of Stuart Hall (1996a) clarify this effect on identity: the process of identification is an intersection or meeting point between discourse and practice, subjects are virtually chained into the flow of discourse.

In this sense, democratic elections construct discursive categories for *democratic subjects*, but this is not enough to articulate the creation of a *democratic subject* as she also needs to invest in that position. In this sense, 'the creation of democratic forms of individuality is a question of identification with democratic values, and this is a complex process that takes place through manifold practices, discourses and language-games' (Mouffe quoted in Norval, 2004b). Therefore, the participation in democratic elections, as part of those democratic practices, allows people to identify as democrats:

> The subject becomes a democratic subject ... because she participates in democratic practices, which retroactively allow her to identify as democratic subject. ... This 'identification-as' is an embodied act, of a subject passionately involved in an activity, which structures her political life and participation in a certain way. ... bodily, materialized inscriptions, are key to this process. (Norval, 2004b: 12–13)

The moment in which millions of people vote within the framework of democratic elections reinscribes the collectivity and the individual in the category of democratic subjects. By participating in that practical activity, regardless of the results for the candidate of choice, the effect it has on the collectivity is an overwhelming legitimisation of the successful political project. Elections are, in this sense, necessary to sustain the identification of the subject as democrat, both individually and collectively. At the same time, state institutions are also legitimised. If we assume that for *democracy* to succeed, the offer of democratic elections has to be met by an active participation of the people identifying as such, then the overall effect is that of *democracy*. Institutions are then reinforced and the identity of the state as democratic is granted with its reinscription. Each election provides the opportunity for the state to enact its role as democratic. This is what happened in the 2002 presidential elections.

Nevertheless, is it not a contradiction democratically to elect a political project that proposes to postpone freedoms, to erase democratic institutions and to lead to war? This was the case in 2002 after peace was presented and accepted as a failed option. The ability to restrain democratic freedoms was legitimised from the beginning of the democratic security government. This is one of the most disturbing aspects of the promise of in/security in Colombia.

However, this legitimacy of the beginning of in/security cannot be made synonymous with silencing dissenting voices. The fact that in/security has been installed democratically does not erase its undemocratic character but can only encourage to inquiry it critically, it should rouse suspicion even more regarding the promise of in/security and spark questioning that plethora of promises, programmes, policies, texts, actions and omissions that reproduce political violence. This task is pursued in the fourth chapter with its exclusive focus on the DSP itself.

Conclusion

The aim of this chapter has been to contextualise the release of the DSP in Colombia. We addressed two important precedents: first, *the end of peace* as the publicly declared interpretation that the road of peace had failed as a result of the breakdown of peace talks on 20 February 2002. Second, we reviewed the options which were articulated to deal with this crisis within the framework of the 2002 presidential elections and then examined the effects of the democratic success of the promise of in/security portrayed by Alvaro Uribe.

Regarding *the end of peace*, contrary to the way it was depicted by the government, the peace process was characterised by constant clashes between both armed parties. Hence, though represented as deriving from particular terrorist attacks, the crisis was consensually construed as the *failure of peace* by national and international opinion leaders. The end of peace was constructed as a deep crisis, which called for extraordinary measures to redefine the identities involved: the state itself, nationals (good and bad ones) and the renaming of dangers. The 20 February 2002 was marked as the turning point in which the Colombian state was invested with new interests. Its subjectivity changed from a weak to a strong state, and the guerrillas were definitively turned into narco-terrorists. At the same time, these representations produced social facts and redefined the internal conflict as a terrorist struggle.

The presidential elections of 2002 were examined as a second precedent to the DSP. The hegemonic understanding of *the end of peace* took place during the electoral campaign in which each presidential candidate offered a means for dealing with the crisis. From the inception of his campaign, Alvaro Uribe's Democratic Security doctrine derived from the conviction that *peace*, as it was portrayed by Pastrana, was *illusory* and 'made out of peace doves and virtual declarations on TV' (Uribe, 2002b: 20), was no longer an option. Instead of this type of peace, Uribe offered 'peace as born out of authority [as a new] concept in Colombia to halt the criminals' (ibid.), making 'security the founding ground' (ibid.: 17). According to this logic, security became a 'democratic principle which has been lost and has to be recovered in order for the citizenry to exercise their freedoms'. So Uribe (ibid.: 27) proposed a strong state, a strong government, and good people collaborating with the armed forces to 'close ranks against the terrorists'. Peace was postponed until the day in which in/security brought freedom.

The electoral victory of Alvaro Uribe in May 2002 changed the discursive articulation of the Colombian subjectivity. From 1998–2002, *Colombians* were being hailed to occupy the position of a people seeking peace, within the framework of peace talks between the government and the guerrillas. Yet, in the electoral results for the presidential period 2002–2006, *Colombians* were being hailed to adopt a contrary position: that of a people seeking in/security, trying to recover the lost authority of the state, and pursuing war as the path to peace. The electoral results were read as the erasure of the peace option and as the success of the political project of in/security. At the same time, the call for security was legitimised as a hegemonic and consensual articulation by being the result of democratic elections, shielding the DSP as a democratic project.

As we have seen throughout this chapter, the precedents for releasing the DSP, both the end of peace and the beginning of in/security, presented the historical and social circumstances which legitimised the in/security discourse in Colombia. Considering this background, in the next chapter we will explore how the DSP is structured, which ideal types of identity categories it creates and how those constructed categories are hailing subjects to adopt the positions designed by this in/security discourse through state and non-state actions. In this way, we will embark upon recognition of the identity categories constructed and produced by the DSP in an effort to continue showing how this particular state discourse shapes political identities, imaginaries on war and peace and, ultimately, reproduces the violence it promises to halt.

NOTES

1 The peace process and the DMZ were initially established by the government in 1998 (Res. 85/98) and successively prolonged in various Presidential Resolutions throughout the three years peace process. In Resolution 31, 20 February 2002 (Res. 31/02), the government terminated the dialogue, negotiation and signature of agreements with the organisation FARC, marking the end of peace. Immediately afterwards, President Pastrana terminated the DMZ (Res. 32/02) and withdrew the political status to the FARC-EP members (Res. 33/02).

2 On 9 March 2001, the National Dialogue and Negotiating Table, consisting of government and FARC negotiators, agreed to establish a Facilitating Commission of ten countries to provide international support to the peace process. The Commission consisted of Canada, Cuba, Spain, France, Italy, Mexico, Norway, Sweden, Switzerland and Venezuela. The 'friendly countries' were, Austria, Belgium, Brazil, Canada, Costa Rica, Chile, Cuba, Denmark, Ecuador, Germany, Finland, France, Italy, Japan, Mexico, Norway, the Netherlands, Panama, Peru, Portugal, Spain, United Kingdom, Sweden, Switzerland, Venezuela and the Vatican, as well as the Special Delegate of the UN Secretary General and the European Commission. (AI, 2002b)

3 Ernesto Laclau and Chantal Mouffe have extensively developed the notion of hegemonic representations articulated as political relations. In their *Hegemony and Socialist Strategy* (Laclau and Mouffe, 2001), first published in 1985, they present a genealogical reading of hegemony from which they derive insights and elaborate implications of hegemonic articulations through the devising of a socialist strategy in the 1980s. This book, when read with its 2001 preface, makes clear that for Laclau and Mouffe the notion of the 'New Left' hegemonic project was not over after the fall of the Berlin Wall in 1989 and the so-called end of 'communism'. Their work so exceeds the limits of what my concerns on the political violence prompted by the DSP are in relation to the constitution of identities in Colombia. Though I recognise and value their contributions enormously in regards to how hegemonic articulations are made politically by politically constituted subjectivities, I understand their notion of antagonism as highly problematic for reading the violence against 'self' and 'others' in the DSP. Antagonism, in their view, implies that subjects that are differently positioned have irreconcilable interests. Laclau and Mouffe (ibid.) draw on the ideal of consensus in the public sphere as a danger to democracy. From my perspective, such irreconcilability cannot be known in advance. Relying on Michael Dillon's (1996) writings on in/security, I believe that the violence prompted by the DSP against plurality resides precisely in the belief that subjects are – if not knowable – at least potentially so. Herein lays, in part, the violence prompted by the DSP as a discourse that presupposes antagonistic interests.

4 Betancourt was kept captive for more than six years and rescued by security forces, together with other fourteen kidnapped persons, on 2 July 2008 in a military operation called 'Jaque', which has been shrouded both in joy about the liberation yet with multiple criticisms regarding the possible illegal use of ICRC emblems. For the official version of the rescue, visit the website of the Ministry of Defence (www.mindefensa.gov.co).

5 In an interview with the newspaper *Espectador* before his extradition to the US, the paramilitary leader Herbert Velosa, alias H. H., confessed that during Alvaro Uribe's government in the Province of Antioquia, in order to reduce the public number of murders the military forces pressured paramilitary groups to implement common graves (*El Espectador*, 2008). The official data of deaths thus decreased dramatically in the Urabá zone, giving the appearance of a concomitant yet false decrease in violence. The fact that it was precisely an initiative of the armed forces to implement common, mass and

anonymous graves to cover the systematic murders committed by paramilitary groups in the Urabá region confirms the actions in concert of both armed organisations.

6   Following the remaining candidates in the opinion polls (*El Tiempo*, 2002), compared with September 2001, in February 2002 candidate Serpa had lost twenty points and by May 2002 stabilised at twenty-three per cent. Sanín lost around eleven points between September 2001 and February 2002, so the voters' intent for Sanín was around five per cent after the end of peace talks and six per cent in May 2002. Garzón, the candidate who challenged the open war as the solution to face the end of negotiations between the government and the FARC-EP, found himself with two per cent of voters' intent in February 2002, which rose to seven per cent by May 2002.

4

Identity categories constructed and produced by the Democratic Security Policy

IN THE PREVIOUS CHAPTERS, we provided an overview of how violence in Colombia has been represented and examined the theoretical framework and the general and specific contextualisation for the emergence of the Democratic Security Policy (DSP). Taking into account the DSP's emergence at an undecidable moment within the hegemonic articulation of the end of peace in 2002, this has illuminated the analytical tools necessary to rethinking the DSP in an active voice.

In this chapter, I want to pursue a detailed analysis of how the DSP constructs and produces political identities in a way that reproduces political violence. This task already assumes that identities can be constructed and produced in in/security discourses. This difference between *construction* and *production* of identities shows precisely how the DSP in/security discourse informs material practices that hail subjects to enact the discursive ideal images of identities present in discourse, such as state, nationals and others. Such production is intimately linked to the articulation of the process of identification (Hall, 1996a) that requires both linguistic and non-linguistic practices.

> Linguistically, discourses are the vehicle for the *construction* of categories (of difference, of identity, of threat, etc.). Through both linguistic and non-linguistic practices, they are the vehicle for the *production* of social facts (such as insecurities). (Weldes et al., 1999: 16–17)

In this way, state and other institutions enforce the identity categories constructed by the DSP through material practices. Discourses produce knowledge about the 'other' and about the self and simultaneously legitimate the deployment of power in both 'self' and 'other' (Williams and Chrisman, 1994: 8). In other words, these idealisations inform actions that influence subjects to adopt specific positions. As Hall (1996a: 3) reminds us, subject positions constructed in discourses do not fully explain the process of identification.

122

> There is always 'too much' or 'too little' – an over-determination or a lack, but never a proper fit, a totality. Like all signifying practices, [identification] is subject to the 'play', of *différance*. It obeys the logic of more-than-one. And since as a process it operates across difference, it entails discursive work, the binding and the marking of symbolic boundaries, the production of 'frontier-effects'. It requires what is left outside, its constitutive outside, to consolidate the process. (Ibid.)

Given this insight, I attempt both to recognise the ideal subject positions that the DSP constructs and to render visible what is left outside, what has to be excluded from one category (its constitutive outside) to produce it as a coherent unity. Subject categories cannot be understood as synonymous with the identity of the subject, because not everybody fits comfortably or unproblematically into any identity category (ibid.: 6). To occupy a category, the subject has to invest in it. The subject must answer to the hailing of discourse and practices. 'An effective suturing of the subject to a subject-position requires, not only that the subject is "hailed", but that the subject invests in the position, means that suturing has to be thought of as an *articulation*, rather than a one-sided process' (ibid.).

Since identity is a process and is never complete, but rather is always in the process of *becoming*, I would like first to recognise the subject categories produced by the in/security discourse in Colombia. These include the state, the sovereign people or nationals (the 'us') and the 'others' (terrorists, i.e. 'them'), as well as the markers that divide the *good nationals* from the *bad/terrorist* ones. The investment of the subject in occupying those subject positions will be treated in more detail in the fifth chapter on *Resistance and Peaces*, which is geared towards highlighting the manifold responses to the subject categories the DSP constructs and produces to articulate differently these political identities. Such a move unpacks the process of articulating identity as a temporary and imperfect point of suture.

In the present chapter and considering the discursive formation of identification, I focus on connecting the DSP with the identity categories it creates, mainly by asking the following questions: How is the subjectivity of the state, its interests and character, created in the DSP? How does the DSP depict the sovereign people, the nation? What is the mode of representation that the DSP produces in terms of the Colombian situation? What does Colombia look like according to the DSP? What types of issues are securitised and who is said to be endangering the nation? How does the state articulate itself in regards to protecting the citizenry from the dangers it names? According to the representations of danger, which are the ideal types of identity categories that the DSP constructs for 'us' and for 'them'? Within the discursive realm that the DSP manufactures, which other interpretations of the national situation are foreclosed? What has to be suppressed politically to make the call for in/security binding? How is the promise of in/security articulated and what and who is sacrificed for this promise?

In order to address these questions, I first outline the main elements of the DSP, taking into account its main characteristics as far as the representations of dangers it depicts and the identity categories it constructs. In the second part of this chapter, I delve into how the state has implemented a series of micro-practices informed by the DSP. These transcend state agencies and are spread throughout society in order to hail subjects to assume the positions designed in the DSP.

The Democratic Security government

The DSP was developed by Alvaro Uribe during his electoral campaign in 2001. After the elections, President Uribe (2002c) stressed that a majority of democratic votes had made him president. As examined before, from the beginning, this link between voters and the election of the promise of in/security has legitimised the DSP discourse as *democratic*.

In his victory speech, it is important to focus on how Uribe depicted *the nation*, for the subjectivity of the state is constructed hand in hand with it. The nation is understood as a people whose heart cannot stand any more bleeding, who yearns for rest and security. The nation does not want to mourn its dead anymore and is agonising about both its losses thus far and those anticipated (ibid.: 2–3). In a related manner, the nation needs a state erected on the principle of authority, for which the help of Saint Francis is needed to make order and authority give birth to peace (ibid.: 4).

In his speech, Uribe (ibid.: 1) invoked Simón Bolívar, *El Libertador*, the military figure symbolising independence from the Spanish Crown and the *birth of the nation* in the nineteenth century. This evocation of Bolívar, who generally serves to legitimise discourses on state order, called attention to the fact that the strength of the public forces protects the nation from weak individuals. Bolívar has historically been portrayed as the hero of the fatherland who had warned the congressmen that corruption is born out of the indulgence of the tribunals. Where there is no force, there is no virtue, and without this, the Republic dies.

During the inauguration of the president three months later (7 August 2002), the FARC-EP guerrillas placed several bombs near the Congressional Hall where the inauguration ceremony was taking place. While President Uribe was issuing his inaugural speech, referring to the relation between security and freedom (Uribe, 2002d), the FARC-EP were literally destroying it. Once more, Simón Bolívar stands out in this speech as the mythical man symbolising war, order and authority. Contrastingly, Francisco de Paula Santander was described as a mythical figure symbolising the obedience of the citizenry to the law.

> The lives of two men, different in attitudes, upbringing and destiny, inspired the beginnings of our Republic. ... These two men, Bolívar and Santander, stand for the essence of our political identity as a nation. Bolívar embodies the idea of order and authority: order, as an unavoidable premise of freedom; and authority, to make

> equality of opportunity possible. Santander represents the realm of law which guarantees our security and freedoms. Order, to gain freedom through the democratic authority of the law. This is the ethical and political combination which sustains the historical continuity of our nation ... . (Ibid.: 1)

In the construction of the subjectivity of the state and the nation, the men are given different weights: Bolívar/order/authority is privileged over Santander/law/peace. Order and authority have to be in place for freedom and law to be exercised. From the beginning of the in/security government, the inferiority and derivative character of peace from security is clear from the following words:

> Bolívar understood order as the principle of unity and social justice. ... the symbol of authority [is] the guarantee of freedom for all. ... let us restore order. Let unity return to the old New Granada [Colombia], today fragmented into de facto republics of violent organizations. Santander conceived peace, and the harmony ... as being under the exclusive sovereignty of the law. ... He honored the law with his obedience to authority. (Ibid.)

The *character* of the state is construed as a subject going through a moment of historical weakness. This weakness has prompted violence in the country and, therefore, recovering state authority is portrayed as indispensable for peace to be born out of in/security. In Uribe's words, 'I call on all the men and women of this country to seek again our common bond of unity, the law, democratic authority, of freedom and social justice, which we have lost in a moment of weakness in our history' (ibid.: 1–2).

Violence is attributed to the weakness of the state. Furthermore, violence causes the destruction of solidarity among the people and mistrust of the state.

> There is a disproportionate desire to serve one's own interest, and indifference to the fate of the community. But this ... is not born of the nature of being a Colombian, which is both civic-minded and humanitarian. The reason for it is the destruction wrought by violence, of political chicanery and of corruption, which combine to cause uncertainty, poverty and inequality. (Ibid.: 2)

This understanding of the situation of violence is the beginning of the DSP. *Colombia* is a nation that cannot mourn any more dead. It needs a strong and authoritarian state that had been weak in the past. State weakness has caused the violence and only by replacing weakness with order and authority will people be able to enjoy freedom. However, *security* is not reduced to a state obligation. Rather, security is a task which has to be undertaken by everybody, the three branches of state power (executive, legislative and judiciary), the citizenry, the army and police forces and the international community (ibid.). *Security* is then proclaimed as an obligation for society in its entirety.

State of exception

On 11 August 2002, after only four days as president, Uribe declared the state of exception (Decree 1837/2002). 'An emergency power written into the constitution, this measure cedes unusually strong powers to the president, and allows the state to carry out arrests, searches, and wiretapping without warrants' (Hagen, 2003: 67). In the name of in/security, the executive reconstituted the power of the sovereign state. This was done by withdrawing laws and creating a textual space in which the decisions of the president and army officials were implemented without observing national and international norms of respect for political and human rights.

As Giorgio Agamben (1995, 2005) argues regarding the notion of sovereign powers and in direct relation to Carl Schmitt's definition of the sovereign as that who suspends the law, we find the figure of the president as 'commander in chief' (or as 'first soldier' in the words of Uribe), who must be granted authority to rule in emergency situations. By rereading Agamben (2005: 22) within the Colombian context, one could assert that President Uribe attempted to produce a situation in which the emergency became the rule and the very distinction between peace and war became impossible. Within this concrete frame, 'sovereignty is reintroduced in the very acts by which state suspends law, or contorts law to its own uses' (Butler, 2004: 54). This suspension of the law in the name of sovereignty was the first clear material effect of the doctrine of democratic security.

Within the state of exception, President Uribe issued Decree 2002/2002 that created the Rehabilitation and Consolidation Zones, in which

> military commanders have certain judicial and police powers, overriding those of elected civilian authorities. Within these zones, the mobility of civilians is limited, individuals without personal identification can be held for twenty-four hours, censuses are conducted to determine where people work and live, and restrictions are placed on the presence of foreigners and journalists. (Hagen, 2003: 67)

The president and the military exercised control over a given population, which they tried to manipulate for *security reasons*. These *security reasons* cannot be foreseen, for they derive from the arbitrary power of managerial officers. Military officers can detain persons for deeming them *dangerous*, and can neglect due process legislation and impede the movement of persons when considered *suspects*.

> The state *produces* through the act of withdrawal, a law that is no law, a court that is no court, a process that is no process. The state of emergency returns the operation of power from a set of laws (juridical) to a set of rules (governmental), and the rules reinstate sovereign power: rules that are not binding by virtue of established law or modes of legitimation, but fully discretionary, even arbitrary, wielded by officials who

interpret them unilaterally and decide the condition and form of their invocation. (Butler, 2004: 61–2)

This deeming dangerous, a prerogative of state officials, can be enhanced by information provided by the citizenry. For this purpose, the president created a network of one million civilians. These informants (Hagen, 2003: 68) were to report any 'dangerous activities [and] suspect persons, [functioning] as the eyes and ears of the police and military. As such, the network of informants is expected to work as a result of its sheer size. President Uribe asserts, "If we have one, two, or ten [informants], sure they'd be killed. But if we have thousands or tens of thousands, then they would stand together and say, They'll have to kill us all"' (ibid.).

The citizenry was thereby called to fulfil its *security duty* by reporting any suspicious activity. The state's rules ordered the population to maintain a 'heightened awareness of suspicious activity' (Butler, 2004: 76). Based on what the informants deemed dangerous and report to the military, suspects were detained and kept incarcerated until a decision was made, which could take several months (Hagen, 2003: 68–9).

According to the Executive Decree 2002/2002, informants were supposed to report 'suspect activities [about persons who] might participate or plan to participate in criminal activities'. The information reported to the military could lead to arrest if suspects were deemed guilty of *planning* a criminal activity without a previous judiciary order (ibid.) and without actually having committed any wrong-doing. 'If it is the person, or the people, who are deemed dangerous, and no dangerous acts need to be proven to establish this as true, then the state constitutes the detained population unilaterally, taking them out of the jurisdiction of the law, depriving them of the legal protections to which subjects under national and international law are entitled' (Butler, 2004: 77).

The information received by citizens' networks was enhanced by the information provided by private security companies. These were supposed to broaden their guard of the private spheres and to report to the military any persons they considered potentially dangerous for public order. 'In the large cities, some of the nation's 180,000 already-armed private security guards will play a special role in the networks. As Uribe has argued, "one thing is arming one million bandits. But it's another thing entirely to arm ordinary citizens, private security groups, and civil defence organizations so they can support the military"' (Hagen, 2003: 70).

In this sense, the network of informants was not only the one million paid citizens, but also increased by almost 200,000 private security guards across the country. This *army of good people*, the ears and eyes of the military, did not have any precise object on which to report. Whatever any of the informants *deemed dangerous* led to *pre-emptively* arresting 'others' without so much as a judiciary order.

In a geopolitical reading of this situation, the power of the modern state ought to be measured according to its effectiveness at controlling the territory. Consequently, in addition to the biopolitical measures adopted concerning the regulation of populations as life species (Dillon, 2007), the executive also used the state of exception to strengthen the military forces in a toxic combination (ibid.) of geo- and biopolitical measures (ibid.). The first one was a tax for war in which the state would collect money to 'preserve the democratic security' (Decree 1838/2002). The second measure was the increase of military personnel through the figure of the peasant soldier:

> In order to quickly and cheaply establish state presence in lawless zones, the government is recruiting 15,000 'peasant soldiers' through the normal military draft to support the regular armed forces by March 2003. After three months of military training, all peasant soldiers will return to their hometowns to act as soldiers during the day and spend nights under their own roofs. (Hagen, 2003: 68)

These 15,000 peasants can be added to the 1,200,000 informants. In this way, the *army of good people* started to be outlined by the president and by the military as informants, but then became collaborators. Human rights organisations, intellectuals and politicians warned the executive power of the consequences that this huge army of 'good people' could bring and of the difficulties surrounding the theory of dangerousness in itself. As Hagen recalls, the UN High Commissioner for Human Rights at the time, Mary Robinson, told the president that to 'recruit civilians was a call for clouding the distinction between soldier and civilian'(ibid.: 70).

This criticism failed to object to the fact that this clouding of the distinction was precisely the aim of state in/security measures. Such blurring was not a derivative consequence, but rather the goal in itself. To train and arm citizens and to order them to report any suspicious activity to the military is to erase the civilian character of the citizenry and to militarise society. When the state wants to arm citizens and incorporate them into the army of good people, soldiers are what is needed. Consequently, objecting that the measures of organising networks of informants blur the military/civilian distinction is to presuppose that such distinction is concomitant to the liberal state, where inside/outside, self/other, familiar/foreign and civilian/military (Kaldor, 1999; Walker, 1993) are valid dividing limits. Furthermore, a criticism outlined this way hides the fact that it is precisely liberal democratic regimes who wage the global on terror in a way that the premises of an indistinct 'enemy' (and a concomitant indistinct 'self') pervade the normality of political processes and become liberal practices of (il)liberal regimes (Jabri, 2006).

My contention is that criticising the DSP because it regulates the population as a mass of suspects is missing the point, because this is exactly the goal of such measures. Far from being 'collateral war damage', it is a constitutive part of the matrix of war (ibid.). Precisely because dangerousness implies 'that the individual must be considered by society at the level of his potentialities and not at the level of the behavioural potentialities they represent' (Foucault quoted in Dillon and Reid, 2001: 57), the Colombian state and non-state DSP practices attempt to prevent such potentialities from being realised. Only once the in/security discourse in Colombia is understood as both geo- and biopolitical strategy (Dillon, 2007), as this chapter demonstrates, will the possibilities to recreate dissent, scrutiny and accountability regain their visibility (Jabri, 2006).

Moreover, since most people are not terrorists but merely conflictive human beings living together, there are large numbers of conflicts that arise among them. When any citizen, turned into 'a soldier of the army of good people', reports *a suspect person*, he or she might be using this new power to settle problems with neighbours.[1] 'People seeking revenge against others for personal reasons may label their enemies as insurgents, criminals, or terrorists in order to see them arrested or even killed' (Hagen, 2003: 69–70). In this manner, the in/security power stops being exercised by a so-called unified and coherent actor (the executive and the military) and starts being a diffused power, marked by a diffuse set of strategies and tactics.

Such production of in/security so starts resembling what Michel Foucault calls governmentality and which Judith Butler (2004: 52) identifies as gaining 'its meaning and purpose from no single source, no unified sovereign subject. Rather, the tactical characteristics of governmentality operate diffusely, to dispose and order populations, and to produce and reproduce subjects, their practices and beliefs, in relation to specific policy aims.'

The executive and the military branches stopped pursuing the aims of recovering the authority of the state and achieving security as the ground for freedom. Instead, these were turned into a social enterprise. This enterprise simultaneously discloses the combination of geopolitical strategies to depoliticise the people and biopolitical strategies to regulate the population. According to Dillon (2007), such a combination then expands the governmental grain of the politics of in/security to constitute identities. Violence becomes a technology of control over the population as a whole, which is kept under surveillance and is corporeally targeted by state and non-state practices (Jabri, 2006). Within this frame, the permanence of the war on terror disrupts normalcy and inscribes the exceptional into daily political processes. This war on terror has 'a defining influence on elements considered to be constitutive of liberal democratic politics, including executive answerability, legislative scrutiny, a public sphere of discourse and interaction, equal citizenship under the law and ... political legitimacy based on free and equal communicative practices underpinning social solidarity' (ibid.: 49–50).

I would argue that the DSP aims for the normalcy of governmental war practices. It pretends to disrupt the so-called traditional liberal politics of democracy and accountability and to make exceptional measures an integral part of politics. By spreading in/security practices throughout society, the DSP discloses how the power of in/security is a force that mobilises and produces. The DSP is not only a repressive and oppressive state discourse. It is also productive, it makes live, it regulates populations and moulds the subjectivities of 'state', 'nationals' and 'others'.

Moreover, the official adoption of the DSP was the institutional arrangement that allowed the Colombian state to introduce the state of exception as the normalcy of in/security. From August through December 2002, the state of exception allowed the president to rule by decree, to send the poorest to the front lines of the war, to assign civilians police duties and to grant the military additional police powers (Hagen, 2003: 70–1).

Yet, the presidential extension of the state of exception was unsuccessful. The Constitutional Court rejected its prolongation in December 2002. Facing this situation, the executive branch incorporated the geo- and biopolitical measures of this in/security discourse in the DSP, issued by the president and the minister of defence in June 2003. The DSP became the instrument that enabled the exceptionality of war to become the normalcy of politics.

The Democratic Security Policy

The structure of the DSP follows the conventional understanding of security documents outlined in earlier chapters. It first produces the effects of a state subjectivity by invoking a primary and stable identity. It then lists a collection of threats that are said to be endangering the nation, and, from these representations of dangers, imparts strategies for coping with them, thereby reproducing its guarantor role as protector of the people/population (Campbell, 1998; Weldes and others, 1999). In this process, the categories of 'state', 'nation', and 'others' are constructed and then produced as social facts according to in/security practices. Likewise, the border that divides and at the same time joins 'us' and 'them' is outlined according to a set of markers which enable the 'good nationals' to be distinguished from the 'terrorist ones'.

The preface of the DSP (2003: 5–10), written by President Uribe and the minister of defence, Marta Lucía Ramírez, and addressed to Colombian society as a whole, states the theme perfectly. Everybody's goal is to achieve in/security: the executive, the legislative and the judiciary branches of the state, the military and the police especially, the civilian population, the industrial sector and the international community come together on this point. To achieve security, all must unite to fight terrorism. The DSP works to constitute a state that grounds freedom in in/security. Once in/security is achieved, freedom will be exercised. This way, the promise of in/security demands the present sacrifice of freedoms in order to feed the continuous search for a stable and secure ground that cannot be disclosed (Dillon, 1996). In this sense, sacrificing freedoms today is made in the name of a certain 'secure' future that will never come.

> Restoring order and security – a basic prerequisite for the strengthening of civil liberties and human rights – is a central concern of this Government. … a clear line must be drawn between the right to disagree and criminal conduct. Only when the State rigorously punishes crime and combats impunity will the space for opposition and criticism be fully guaranteed. (DSP, 2003: 5–6)

From this point onward, it is clear that once in/security is installed, people will enjoy their democratic rights. However, how to achieve security? Since terrorism is identified as the main threat to security, the armed forces are insufficient for fighting this battle. As the president warned, 'we will defeat it with the support of all citizens. The key concept here is solidarity. Solidarity between citizens and solidarity with the security forces' (ibid.: 6). The international community is also needed to defeat terrorism, 'it is a struggle between the sovereignty of democratic nations against the sovereignty of terrorism. A fight of all against terrorism' (ibid.).

In a subtle way, the president started to delineate the markers that will allow distinguishing the *good* from the *bad* people. 'Colombia has always been an example in Latin American of press freedom. It has never occurred to us to restrict this right through the imposition of exceptional or permanent regulations. We only ask that journalists, like all citizens, act responsibly when it comes to disclosing information that may endanger the security of all' (ibid.).

But, how to know what it is for the media to report *responsibly* about the situation of violence? The president called it 'disclosing information that may endanger the security of all' and then elaborated: 'They [armed forces and national police] are not "actors" in a war or conflict and should not be put implicitly on the same level as the terrorist organisations which they confront' (ibid.). This form of censorship about what can and cannot be said, reported, and shown in the media has been exercised more openly by the government since issuing the DSP (Pizarro, 2005). Journalists are not allowed to call the situation of violence *an internal armed conflict* anymore. The media can only report about terrorism. There are no more guerrillas; there are only terrorist organisations (ibid.).

In this fight of *all against terrorism*, the president called for 'an effort of the entire State and of all Colombians. A strong state structure, supported by citizen solidarity' (DSP, 2003: 6). Uribe concluded his preface by warning people of this endless fight, 'we will not rest until we have made Democratic Security a reality for all Colombians' (ibid.: 7).

In this sense, the policy aims were expanded to what, according to the state, have to be the aims of the whole society: defeat terrorism. Citizens, especially journalists, can only regard the situation of violence as a terrorist fight, in which the entire society has to participate to combat terrorism. Security was turned into everybody's problem and everybody's responsibility. The means to achieve security were those delineated by the government, collaboration with the security forces. As the minister of defence, Martha Lucía Ramírez (ibid.: 8) articulated, 'guaranteeing the security of all Colombians is the responsibility not just of the Ministry of Defence, the Armed Forces and the National Police, but also of the entire Colombian State and of all of society'.

In addition to the biopolitical measures that pursue governmental practices to regulate the population, traditional geopolitical strategies aimed at the military control of the territory are integrated in the DSP. Among them, the following are worth highlighting: 'We have created new mobile brigades, high-altitude battalions, *campesino* soldier platoons ... special anti-terrorist units, mobile *carabinero* squads, and we are extending the coverage of the National Police to all municipalities in the country' (ibid.: 9–10).

The construction of the subjectivity of the state is intertwined with the construction of a subjectivity of the *nation*. 'Security is not principally a matter of coercion: it is the constant and effective presence of democratic authority, based on the collective effort of the whole of society' (ibid.: §7).[2] When the Colombian state acts in a warrior way, when it reacts with war to grief and pain, then it establishes a norm by which the Colombian *people* must act. When *security* turns into a duty for everyone, then the *people* have the obligation to accomplish their security duties or to face the consequences of being labelled a suspect, a non-collaborator with the security forces and, therefore, a security threat in him or herself. Let us next examine the DSP's list of explicit threats.

Representations of danger: terrorism

Even though the government lists six threats 'which pose an immediate danger to the stability of the country, its democratic institutions, and the lives of Colombians', in their explanation, they all relate to terrorism (DSP, 2003: §36). The definition of terrorism adopted is the one offered by the United Nations Security Council. It is a method for which 'the only common denominator among different variants of terrorism is the calculated use of deadly violence against civilians for political purposes' (ibid.: §37). This *method* is the main danger to Colombia and feeds the rest of the threats. The DSP constructs the following list of dangers: terrorism, the illegal drugs trade, illicit finance, traffic of arms, ammunition and explosives, kidnapping and extortion and homicide.

Regarding the illegal drugs trade, the government explains that this threat 'has also become the main source of funding for the terrorist activities of the illegal armed groups' (ibid.: §41). In the case of illicit finance, the government again underscores how money laundering from the commercialisation of cocaine and heroin 'contributes directly to terrorism' and 'finance[s] terrorism:

kidnapping, extortion, the theft of hydrocarbons and contraband' (ibid.: §47). 'It is becoming increasingly clear that terrorists use illegal drug money to finance their activities and launder that money through the same channels as the illegal drugs traffickers' (ibid.: §48). In the same vein, the DSP represents the threat of the traffic of arms, ammunition and explosives, closely linked to terrorism and drugs trade. 'Both the AUC and the FARC exchange illegal drugs for weapons on the international market' (ibid.: §49).

Kidnapping and extortion are presented as 'more than just a criminal or police problem. Like illegal drug trafficking, it constitutes a fundamental means of financing the terrorist acts. ... The ransoms paid for these individuals [kidnapped persons], especially for foreigners for whom particularly large sums are demanded, finance terrorism and undermine democracy' (ibid.: §52). This way, the government depicts the kidnapping problem as related to the fact that the ransoms paid finance terrorism (Lobo-Guerrero, 2007). The crimes of kidnapping and extortion are viewed through this lens as a problem of those who pay to buy back the liberty of others. The government so inverts the condemnation of the crimes from the perpetrators to the victims, making them responsible for financing terrorism.[3]

Finally, homicide appears in the representations of danger as an 'indirect effect' of terrorist activities.

> The homicide epidemic of the last two decades, which resulted in some of the highest rates in the world ... is, rather, the result of institutional weakness and a climate of impunity promoted by the illegal armed groups and illegal drugs trafficking. It is not so much their activities but rather the indirect impact of those activities which encourages homicide. (DSP, 2003: §56)

In this way, the government identifies the illegal armed groups and the drug traffickers as responsible for the high rates of homicides, occluding the responsibility of the state to prevent homicide, as well as to investigate and sanction the murderers and to compensate the victims.

Following the logic of in/security of the DSP, all the dangers are incorporated into one major threat: terrorism. Illegal drugs and arms trafficking, money laundering, kidnapping and extortion as well as homicide are seen either to strengthen terrorism or to be an indirect effect of it. This way, the whole spectrum of threats, from their causes to their effects is integrated under the label *terrorism*, which is defined in an ambiguous manner, as a method of violence against civilians (ibid.: §37). The lack of a clear tool for identifying exactly what counts as terrorism and the erasure of notions of political violence or common delinquency favours the implementation of diffused state strategies to cope with this turbid threat.

State and non-state in/security measures

In order to achieve *security* (ibid.: §58), the government will implement the following courses of action: co-ordinating state action, strengthening state institutions, consolidating control of national territory, protecting the rights of all Colombians and the nation's infrastructure, co-operating for the security of all, and communicating state policy and action.

The majority of these measures directly involve the citizenry in order to implement the various strategies, both as part of the security solution and as direct collaborators who actively participate in the implementation of security policies. For example, 'academics, businessmen and members of civil society' are to participate in regional security committees in order 'to advise on public policy, contribute [with their] know-how and participate in the solution of security problems' (ibid.: §60). Likewise, the ministry of defence and the armed forces 'will establish a series of committees through which the private sector may contribute its knowledge to the security effort' (ibid.: §65).

If such sovereign and biopolitical measures enter into contradiction with democratic norms, the Constitutional and legal framework ought to be adapted to 'counter violence and insecurity' (ibid.: §67). 'In order to successfully deal with the terrorist threat the legal framework must be adapted. If necessary, a number of the Articles in the Constitution will be amended' to create an integrated crime policy to 'pursue individuals, such as terrorists and illegal drugs traffickers, who represent the greatest danger to society and democracy' (ibid.). It is clear then that the normalcy of war (Jabri, 2006) necessitates being incorporated into the normalcy of governmental rules. Concomitantly, the rights of suspect enemies who threaten the newly established order will be diminished. 'The reform of the Government's crime policy will include the abolition of early prison release for individuals who have committed crimes which are deemed a threat to the stability of the country' (ibid.: §69). What those crimes might be, however, is not explicitly identified.

In addition to these citizen's practices, the armed forces will be strengthened with more resources, 'intelligence gathering, processing and analysis will be improved' (ibid.: §76) and they will receive more equipment and material. Following the same line of reasoning, the role of the peasant solider 'will be strengthened to enable more soldiers from rural areas to perform their military service in their own regions. This will allow them to retain their links with the community and will strengthen the trust between the population and the security forces (ibid.).

Hand in hand with the increase of military forces, financial and personal resources will also be directed toward strengthening the national police so it can control all Colombian municipalities. Patrols in rural areas will be strengthened with the creation of sixty-two mobile *carabineros* squadrons, with new rural police stations and more highway police officers. The number of police officers will be increased by ten thousand new patrols and by an additional ten thousand regular auxiliaries. The police will also work with local security fronts, which are squads in the neighbourhoods that watch their own streets and movements, reporting any *suspect activities* to the armed forces. Additionally, the police are to 'prevent terrorism by building citizen co-operation networks working more closely with the local community, companies, businesses and other state institutions' (ibid.: §80).

Since the idea of security is invested with a military character, the state plan to 'recover its control over the territory' is pure war action. This is the DSP sovereign strategy, literally, the plan of war:

> The Government will gradually restore state presence and the authority of state institutions, starting in strategically important areas. Once the intelligence services have identified and located a threat the Armed Forces and the National Police will begin the recovery process with an offensive operation. Reinforcements will be provided when necessary. Once the Armed Forces and the National Police have re-established control over an area, units comprising professional soldiers, *campesino* soldiers and National Police *carabineros* will maintain security and protect the civilian population. ... Once a basic level of security has been established, the State will embark upon a policy of territorial consolidation ... so that projects are executed once territorial control has been consolidated and are thus not the threats and extortion of the illegal armed groups. (Ibid.: §88–§90)

This strategy is mainly designed for rural areas. In the cities, the governmental plan is to 'encourage the participation and co-operation of each and every citizen in the achievement and maintenance of security [through] alliances between the authorities and the citizenry [as] the quickest and surest way of restoring security' (ibid.: §93–4). According to the government, protecting people from terrorism has to prioritise focusing on the major cities. 'The objective is to create a simple and effective system, backed by the necessary legislation to assure the protection of citizens.' This system comprises, among other elements, 'active citizen co-operation, based on the common values of respect for the dignity of the people and the rejection of violence' (ibid.: §104).

In this sense, what the government understands as rejection of violence is only non-state violence because violence exercised by the state cannot be questioned. The government rationalises this distinction between legitimate state violence and illegitimate non-state violence via the concept of *solidarity*:

> The *solidarity* of the citizens and their cooperation with the authorities is a key factor, without which it will be impossible to defeat the terrorists. The authorities will develop prevention programmes, extending the links between the Armed Forces and the National Police and the private sector, the private security companies, public businesses, and society in general, in order to establish a warning network which will assure the protection of the population and the country's infrastructure. (Ibid.: §105)

This warning network is one of the key pillars of the DSP. It works through information and paid rewards to citizens who hand in information about *suspicious activities*. The state seeks to strengthen its *preventive capacity against terrorism* by conducting awareness campaigns 'to encourage individuals to: (i) denounce cases of extortion and kidnapping; (ii) report suspicious activities to the authorities; (iii) rely on the support of the State and resist the payment of ransoms' (ibid.). Additionally, the state will promote the voluntary adoption of a code of conduct 'in unions, businesses, schools, universities, families, among others, to facilitate the rapid detection of suspicious actions or situations, which may lead to extortion or kidnapping' (ibid.: §112).

On the roads, citizens will also cooperate *in solidarity* by participating in networks which, 'with the appropriate communications equipment, will exercise their civic duties and express their solidarity by assisting the authorities in the provision of information on any irregularities which occur on the roads' (ibid.: §128). This *patriotic solidarity* is for the government part of the constitutional duties of all good Colombians. In particular, Colombians have to demonstrate their '*solidarity* demanded by the modern social democratic State to help prevent crime and terrorism, by providing information relating to the illegal armed groups. ... If 44 million Colombians support and feel support by the State, terrorism can be defeated' (ibid.: §130).

The cooperation networks function in a parallel but integrated way to the information networks. The cooperators are citizens from both urban and rural areas who, 'in accordance with the principle of solidarity and the duty to contribute to common security, will provide the authorities with information which will help in the prevention of crime and the pursuit of criminals' (ibid.). This army of good people 'will also participate in programmes aimed at promoting a culture of security ... . These volunteers will act as an extra set of eyes for the authorities with whom they will be in constant contact' (ibid.: §131).

Initially, the government established that the cooperators, unlike the informants, would receive no paid rewards, but it also set up an additional programme to pay for collaboration when the information provided 'leads to the prevention of a terrorist attack or the arrest of members of any of the illegal armed groups' (ibid.: §132). As well, 'the Government will also establish a system of incentives and rewards for information about property belonging to organisations or persons with links to terrorism or illegal drugs trafficking' (ibid.). In this way, the government made sure that whenever pure patriotism was not enough to encourage solidarity, money would promote the handing over of information about *suspicious activities and their perpetrators*.

It is clear that in this fight of all against terrorism, the government must actively involve society to pursue this war without enemies, without timeframes or spaces (Jabri, 2006). Therefore, as the president warned in the Preface to the DSP (2003: 6–7), governmental control over what the media is allowed to communicate seems crucial, their participation in shaping the limits of public debate (Butler, 2004) is ever more needed in this war. The DSP journalists were thus informed of their share of responsibility in this solidarity fight:

> The responsible handling of information is not just a task of the Government. The media, too, should fulfil their constitutional duty by being both responsible and prudent when releasing information which endangers lives or jeopardises operations. Fulfilling these constitutional duties is an especially difficult task in a democratic country that faces a terrorist threat, as is the case in Colombia. ... the use of the media by those who attack the civilian population as a sounding board to justify their actions, and the impact of the language that is used when reporting information. (DSP, 2003: §136–7)

The strong message is clear even if the language is vague: the media cannot be a *sounding board* for terrorists and their actions. But, if the democratic nation is under the threat of terrorism, why is the media not allowed to report it? This fine warning is a form of censorship that demands that the media be *prudent* and *responsible, careful* and that it not treat the state as another armed actor in the internal conflict, even though the edifice of international humanitarian norms is constructed from this definition (Pizarro, 2005). The state dictates the limits of what can be spoken and what cannot be spoken about in the media, censoring criticism of state violence in the name of in/security (Butler, 2004). It seems as if *security* has to be achieved first to exercise press freedom, just like other civil freedoms (Dillon, 1996).

Within this framework, *peace* appears to be a *derivative of security*. The state's notion of peace is elaborated as a demobilisation programme in which terrorists lay down their arms and return to 'the nuclear family and abandon a clandestine life' (DSP, 2003: §116). This peace has been put into action by the office of the High Peace Commissioner, which calls this programme *peace policy*.[4]

Constructing identity categories

Since this book criticises the political violence prompted by how the DSP informs state and non-state measures to hail subjects into specific identity positions, it is relevant to clarify what exactly is being pursued with each of the idealisations that the DSP constructs for the identity categories of 'nation', 'state' and 'others'.

Constructing Colombians

As Nira Yuval-Davis (1997: 4) explains, the notion of the nation calls attention to how 'nations are situated in specific historical moments and are constructed by shifting nationalist discourses promoted by different groupings competing for hegemony'. I am concerned with the specific effects that the state discourse on in/security has on constructing *nationals*. There are several aspects of the DSP that call for analysis in regards to the nation. First, the nation's *origins*, second its *current attributes and interests* and, third, the nation's *common destiny*.

In a general analytical framework, the notion of the nation and the feelings of belonging to the nation are effects of nationalist discourses. The well-known definition of Benedict Anderson (1991: 6): a nation 'is an imagined political community – and imagined as both inherently limited and sovereign' informs the following reflections. For Anderson, the nation is an imagined community, but that does not imply that it is false, but rather that it is created: 'communities are to be distinguished, not by their falsity/genuineness, but by the style in which they are imagined' (ibid.).

Based on Anderson's insights, I focus on the *style* in which the Colombian nation is imagined according to the state discourse on in/security. For such stylisation, following Maria Teresa Uribe de H. (2004), I look at the rhetoric and poetic forms in which the DSP publicly presents the ideal of a citizen. The narrative forms and political language function as structures that shape the contexts in which they are proclaimed, producing cultural and political mutations of great significance.

> *No está por demás recordar que el ciudadano no nace, sino que se hace y se configura en espacios socio-históricos concretos a través de la acción política y bélica, así como del discurso y la narración; que es una figura construida voluntaria y racionalmente, pero también imaginada, deseada e inventada. Por esta razón, las palabras públicas tienen siempre una incidencia amplia en las maneras de hacer imaginable esta figura de la modernidad.* (Ibid.: 76–7)

Within this framework, what does the nation look like according to the DSP? What are the interests and characteristics of this collective subject? How does the representation of danger (terrorism) inform the construction of 'us' and 'them'?

COMMON ORIGINS

At the beginning of this section, we examined the discourses of President Alvaro Uribe (2002d: 1) in which he depicted the nation as born out of two symbolic figures, Bolívar and Santander, representing order and authority and law and liberty, respectively. Bolívar took precedence over Santander and freedoms were represented as the results following the achievement of in/security. This founding myth of the Colombian nation is taken for granted. It is generally accepted as the beginning of the nation-state in which the identity *Colombians* has its origins.

The Revolution of Independence has been recognised as the political act and the war action that made possible the founding of the Colombian state (Uribe de H. and López, 2006). According to Maria Teresa Uribe (2004: 77), throughout the nineteenth century, the figure of the citizen was imagined and construed as a 'patriotic republican'. This mainly referred to the language of Republicanism, which highlights the idea of virtues. Based on this patriotic republicanism, the notion of citizenry was founded upon the virtue of an armed citizen who was called upon to participate in the armed defence of the community (Uribe de H. and López, 2006). The armed defence was the necessary proof of belonging to the new independent nation-state. The language of grief, of having suffered usurpation by the colonisers, was turned into the founding myth of the new nation. This myth emphasised the idea of victims and the condition of victimisation for uniting heterogeneous groups of peoples under the rubric of the Republic (ibid.). This way, to the question *who are we?*, the answer was that *we are the victims*, a platform which could include all different types of peoples by filling up the empty space of a common original community with the experience of colonisation (Uribe de H., 2004: 78–83).

> *Son los agravios recibidos los que permiten ... que los ciudadanos se autoperciban y se identifiquen como víctimas de un orden esencialmente injusto, sustancialmente opresivo y radicalmente excluyente contra el cual sólo cabe levantarse en armas, haciendo de la guerra y del uso de la fuerza no sólo una opción entre otras para fundar sus derechos, sino algo necesario, inevitable y sobre todo justo; la única alternativa posible que tendrían las víctimas para instituir sus derechos ciudadanos.* (Ibid.: 83)

Homeland and Republic have been intertwined from the beginning of the narrative of the nation-state in a way that merges territory and blood. Postcolonial elites used the argument that 'each person, each citizen, had an affective relation with the territory in which he had been born, with their natal soil, with the homeland which extended beyond the regional and local borders, and covered the whole territory of the Nueva Granada' (ibid.: 88).

The 1819 war of Independence, symbolised by the blood of the founding heroes, is constantly invoked to unite the notions of citizen and patriot and to make their meaning synonymous. Within the discursive construction of Republicanism, the citizen did not just have rights, but also obligations to the homeland. These went beyond obeying the law and paying taxes and explicitly included rising in arms to defend the fatherland (Uribe de H. and López, 2006). In this sense, the idea of a civic citizen was permeated by a *patriotic citizen* whose warrior features and moral obligations regarding legitimate violence were manufactured in a concomitant way since the nineteenth century (Uribe de H, 2004: 88–9).

It is of high relevance to take into account how this common origin of the political identity based on victimisation is turned into the obligatory virtue of going to war. Just as in the nineteenth century, this connection is also made in the twenty-first century war in the DSP. Echoing Jacques Derrida, David Campbell (1999) calls these founding moments of the violent 'birth of a nation' an interpretive and performative *coup de force*:

> In the event of such a founding of an institution, the properly *performative* act must produce (proclaim) what in the form of a *constative* act it merely claims, declares,

> assures it is describing. The simulacrum or fiction then consists in bringing to daylight, *in giving birth to*, that which one claims to reflect so as to take note of it, as though it were a matter of recording what *will have been there*, the unity of a nation, the founding of a state, while one is in the act of producing that event. (Ibid.: 24)

In those *historical moments*, for example during the inauguration of President Uribe on 7 August 2002, this act of recalling a common origin for the nation performs the very origin in whose name it is proclaimed. 'Indeed, at each self-declared point of origin, at each supposedly secure ground, the discourse of primary and stable identity "comes up against its limit: in itself, in its performative power itself ... Here [at the limit] a silence is walled up in the violent structure of the founding act"' (ibid.: 24–5).

During the inauguration, the president recalled the founding moment of the Colombian nation as independence from the Spanish Crown. Yet, the moment of independence was a terrifying moment 'because of the sufferings, the crimes, the tortures [that accompanied it and because it is in itself, and in its] very violence, uninterpretable or indecipherable' (ibid.). He did not reflect upon the violence and pain inflicted, but only glorified them to legitimise the continuity and virtuosity of the patriotic citizen.

Thus, according to Uribe, this common historical origin should bind all Colombians. The war of Independence and its subsequent civil wars are the *birth* of a collective subject, of a whole *nation* that is addressed by the government today. The representation of this common origin, as a moment of collective and shared historical roots, is invested with specific characteristics that inform the current national project. Just like in the nineteenth century, today's political project privileges authority over freedoms. In this sense, history is regarded as an *event* that justifies current governmental actions. The performative character of this act of common origins makes sense only when history can be used to legitimise current state policies. Paraphrasing Campbell (1999), interpreting history in this particular way 'is a resource in the contemporary struggle' to legitimise state authority and violence today by invoking a historical moment which is interpreted by the government to comply with its interests in today's conflict (ibid.: 31).

In its frequent references to duty, obligation and solidarity, the moral tone of the DSP is based upon the idea of sacrifice for the motherland. Sacrifice is intimately linked to patriotism, which presents the defence (both to kill and to die, in the words of Anderson, 1991) of the *homeland* not just as a transcendental value but also as a moral duty which calls upon compatriots, co-citizens, war-comrades and veterans to defend the republic and its institutions. This way, belonging to the nation-state turns into the first loyalty of the citizen, overriding any other personal or political affiliations (Uribe de H, 2004: 90–2).

The modes in which Independence and the founding heroes are interpreted in the DSP make use of history to justify the sacrifice of civil and political freedoms of today in the name of in/security. This way 'history [is] violently deployed in the present for contemporary political goals' (Campbell, 1999: 31). Legitimised violence constitutes the common origin of the identity of the *good Colombians* in whose names it is deployed.

A COMMON PRESENT

At present, the Colombian nation is depicted as a people who 'cannot mourn their dead anymore, [as a] nation who is agonising' (Uribe, 2002d: 1). From this pain and grief, the state cries out for war to deal with violence. The representations of dangers serve to constitute 'us', and, following the economy of identity/difference (Connolly, 1991), to constitute 'them'. The danger of terrorism informs the nation's loves and hates (Campbell, 1998; Dillon, 1996). In this sense, that the war against terrorism is fought as a national enterprise is a very important matter, because, as the DSP constantly reminds 'us', this specific war has to be fought by the whole society. There is no space for anyone to be indifferent to it or to not collaborate with the security forces.

> The use of the term, 'terrorism' thus works to delegitimate certain forms of violence committed by non-state-centered political entities at the same time that it sanctions a violent response by established states. ... If this violence is terrorism rather than violence, it is conceived as an action with no political ground, or cannot be read politically. It emerges, as they say, from fanatics, extremists, who do not espouse a point of view, but rather exist outside of 'reason', and do not have part in the human community. (Butler, 2004: 88–9)

In the DSP (2003), terrorists lose any political character and the construction of 'us' is based on the depolitisation of non-state violence. In opposition, state violence to counter the terrorist threat is legitimised. 'We' are united by the enemy '*we*' *face* (Campbell, 1998). In this direction, argues Diana Saco (1999), in 'the process of describing "the threats we face" [the state] not only helps to construct those threats; it also brings a particular identity (a "we") into existence, creates interests for that identity, and provides rationales for particular actions' (ibid.: 264).

From the particular representation of danger as *terrorism*, the state in/security discourse develops a collection of attributes for nationals: the good ones act in solidarity with the security forces and report any suspicious activities. This demarcation implies that those who do not belong to 'us' necessarily have to be terrorists. There is no space for non-collaboration or simple indifference regarding the war. 'We all have to fight against terrorism' said the president, emphasising the notion of 'solidarity with the security forces' (DSP, 2003: 6–7).

The call for in/security, based on a national fight against terrorism, reproduces a feeling of nationalism that calls for the suppression of any other affiliations that a citizen might have. Belonging to the nation appears to be the identity feature that has to override any other individual or collective affinities, loyalties, or political preferences and values a *Colombian* has or might have. This particular concept of identity is murderous, says Amin Maalouf (2000), since it 'reduces identity to one single affiliation – encourag[ing] people to adopt an attitude that is partial, sectarian, intolerant, domineering, sometimes suicidal, and frequently even changes them into killers or supporters of killers' (ibid.: 30).

The DSP (2003) so calls for losing individual and particular traits, and for homogenising a mass of citizens by incorporating them into an army of 44 million Colombians. If the citizenry abstains from expressing critical political positions about the discourse of in/security and supports the state when it suspends democratic freedoms in the name of in/security, it is because citizens are soldiers of the nation.[5] Yet, instead of nationalism, the DSP strives for patriotism. What is exactly the difference between these two terms? Umut Özkirimli (2000) argues that there is

> a tendency to equate nationalism with its extreme manifestations, that is with separatist movements that threatened the stability of existing states or with aggressive right-wing politics. Such a view confines nationalism to the periphery, treating it as the property of others, not of 'us' ... 'our' nationalism is not presented as nationalism, which is dangerously irrational, surplus and alien; it is presented as 'patriotism', which is good and beneficial. (Ibid.: 3)

On the other hand, Özkirimli (ibid.: 4) views nationalism as 'a discourse that constantly shapes our consciousness and the way we constitute the meaning of the world. It determines our collective identity by producing and reproducing us as "nationals" [...]. It is a form of seeing and interpreting that conditions our daily speech, behaviours and attitudes'. In this vein, nationalism and patriotism are not that different from each other. They are depictions based on good (patriotism) and bad (nationalism) and only cause a terminological chaos because 'seemingly disparate emotions, beliefs and actions are all manifestations of the same phenomenon' (ibid.: 5).

Colombian citizens are called to fulfil their duties with patriotism in the name of in/security. As nationals, Colombians are expected to fulfil their obligations and to be prepared to die for their country (Yuval-Davis, 1997: 24). Considering the insights of Uribe de H. (2004) regarding the Republican citizenry constructed in the nineteenth century to which the DSP (2003) explicitly refers, it is obvious that this call to fulfil the duty of defending the homeland articulates previous meanings and conceptualisations of the idea of belonging to the category Colombians. Hence, the present common nationality is directly linked to a purportedly common historical past, emphasising the continuity of the nation to produce the effects of feelings of belonging:

> [Nationalism] offers security and a feeling of continuity ... . As a metaphorical *pater familias* nationalism states that the members of the nation are a large family: through

> the national courts it punishes its disobedient children. … nationalism appears as a metaphoric kinship ideology tailored to fit large-scale modern society – it is the ideology of the nation-state. (Eriksen, 1993: 108)

In this vein, the government calls upon the unity of Colombians, satisfying the ideal of a community as a nuclear family whose father is the state. President Uribe (2002b: 16–17) has made use of these tropes, explicitly recalling his father figure and invoking the 'bond to unite the Colombians in the fight against terrorism' (ibid.).

Following Eriksen (1993), reading national ideal categories in the DSP (2003) brings to light how the Colombian government has appropriated certain symbols and markers that (supposedly) characterise good nationals. The features that the government incorporates in its discourse to mobilise the population are moral prerogatives, like duty and loyalty, preying upon the feeling of solidarity. At the same time, these prerogatives are made into an obligation. Since there are no other groups which compete with the government for making a nationalist call, the DSP (ibid.) is able to channel, through linguistic and non-linguistic effects, the concept of national. The consequences of this co-option of moral virtues and of the ideal of 'national' are that critics of the DSP can also be identified as anti-patriotic, as disloyal to the nation-state and, therefore, can by marginalised politically and excluded from public discussions on state policies.

The included community is also represented when the state names the 'us' as if it were a homogeneous group of people with no significant differences in terms of political opinion, ethnicity, gender or religion, among other possibilities. This tendency to view the Colombian population as a white *mestizo* Catholic society has been in place since the foundation of the Republic. However, great efforts were made in the 1991 constitution to acknowledge the diversity of the population and recognise special political, juridical and administrative rights of minorities historically discriminated against. Nevertheless, in the DSP (ibid.) these differences are erased, because the unity that the state tries to impose attempts to erase divergent opinions and individual traits.

In this sense, the nationalist tone of the DSP represents both love and hate for nationals (Campbell, 1998; Dillon, 1996), since nurturing nationalist feelings is a dual process, not just what and who should one hate and kill (Anderson, 1991) – probably dying in the process – but also what and whom should one love for the very condition of being a national. It is in this direction that the nationalism of the DSP not only circumscribes killing and dying for, but also 'living'. This type of nationalism so regulates the national population to make them live in a 'secure' way. As was considered in the chapter theorising about in/security discourses, the policing love of in/security cannot be overlooked (Dillon, 1996: 34).

In the combination of what/whom one is supposed to hate/abhor and fear and what/whom one is supposed to love and obey, lies the conundrum of nationalism's power. Both hate and love are intermeshed in the logic of identity construction: one is a national because of what/whom one is willing to kill for and for whom, and for what one is willing to die. The first constellation of elements, those who name and represent the 'other', is as essential and constitutive of the self as those elements that belong to the second constellation of love, what could be interpreted as what 'we' are made of. *Our enemies* are as important as *our heroes are*. This relationality of 'us-them' in the constitution of national identity is constantly reinforced through public and social discourses.

In the current fight against terrorism, the government calls upon selected attributes that the citizenry is supposed to hold in order to maintain their status of belonging to 'the good ones'. They have to express their solidarity with the government by collaborating with the security forces and reporting any suspicious activities. This way, the state discourse reproduces a new type of 'us': those who want to belong to this collectivity must fight against terrorism. However, not all social and economic groups have the same share in belonging to the nation.

Following the DSP (2003), peasants and inhabitants of rural areas are to enlist in the army of good people by participating as soldiers, literally willing to kill and die to protect the nation from the terrorist threat. On the other hand, those in the cities and those who have a higher income do not have to be in the line of fire. They can collaborate and demonstrate solidarity by reporting information. This latter group is clearly in a different position from the former one. Inhabitants of the major cities do not have to lose their lives, but they do have to turn *transparent* and are to recreate a society of mistrust in which everybody is a suspect (Vattimo, 1992).

In this sense, the DSP recreates a nation united in the fight against terrorism, but in which there is a differentiated participation. For peasants and the poor, military combat is necessary; their bodies are material to sacrifice. For rich and urban citizens, solidarity can be expressed in the loss of political criticism and renouncing civil and political freedoms in the name of in/security. The overall effect is the organisation of a '44 million army of good people' (ibid.) in the countryside as well as in the cities.

A COMMON DESTINY

The promise of in/security plays on future scenarios. This common destiny is 'oriented towards the future, rather than just the past, and can explain more than individual and communal assimilations within particular nations. ... It can explain a subjective sense of commitment of people to collectivities and nations' (Yuval-Davis, 1997: 19). This future appears marked by the fear of in/security, which is simultaneously translated into the hope for a 'secure' future.

As Eric Hobsbawm argues, it is crucial to take into account that the construction of the nation cannot be understood unless it is also analysed from below, 'that is in terms of the assumptions, hopes, needs, longings and interests of ordinary people, which are not necessarily national and still less nationalist' (Hobsbawm quoted in Özkirimli, 2000: 119). This is why playing on the promise of in/security articulates the hopes and aspirations of people who have lived in war all their lives and are promised that security, equated with peace, will be a reality in the future.

'Once security is achieved, people will enjoy their freedoms' and 'security will give birth to peace' promised the president (2002b: 20). It is of vital importance to consider how in this promise the future is the time-space that takes precedence over the present. All the sacrifices are made in the name not just of security, but also of 'achieving security in the future' (ibid.). The above clearly only works within the framework of winning the war against terrorism with legitimised state violence. Once the terrorists are defeated, people will enjoy liberty and will be able to exercise their freedoms.

However, as examined previously, the promise of in/security made by the sovereign is a self-defeating enterprise (Arendt, 1998). Nevertheless, this does not invalidate its political force. On the contrary, it is exactly the impossibility of achieving in/security that provides the state discourse with its own dynamic and attraction (Dillon, 1996). In this way, the fact that security is a promise and can only remain so is what imbues the state with its Hobbesian functions (Campbell, 1998). At the same time, it drives people's hopes and fantasies to strive for security constantly, and invests their violent republican virtuosity with the sacrifice of their biological and political lives.

Constructing the Colombian state

The role of the state in reproducing political identities is vital, especially its role in performatively constituting its own state identity. At the same time, the state plays a significant role in shaping political, economic, social and cultural contexts and circumstances that simultaneously influence the configuration of various forms of belonging. This way, 'states make countless policies or engage in regulatory practices in the social and cultural realms that impact belonging' (Croucher, 2004: 41–2). Particularly in the case of a state discourse on in/security, as is the case with the DSP (2003), the subjectivity of the state is derived from the representations of danger and in an intertwined manner with the construction of the category *nationals*.

The DSP (2003) creates the effects of a state identity in which the threat of terrorism informs the state's interests and character as an authoritarian subject recovering from a historical moment of weakness. According to the DSP (ibid.), the danger of terrorism has partly emerged and has been able to maintain itself and to grow because the state had not been able to implement security in the past. Therefore, the state needs to recover its authority and its use of force to eradicate the illegitimate violence in the country. As a 'father taking care of his women-

and-children' (Uribe, 2002b: 16–17) the state appears to redefine its subjectivity according to order and authority.

Portrayed this way, the identity of the *current* Colombian state is constructed in opposition to the former identity of the *past* Colombian state. The current state cannot be weak, it cannot negotiate and it cannot expose itself as a paper tiger. On the contrary, facing the rejection of this past fragile state identity and the omnipresent threat of terrorism, the Colombian state is defined in the DSP as an 'actor' (a political body that behaves in a certain way according to its 'interests') with a clear strong and resolute character, whose two main features are strength and will. The state is now strong and willing to defend the nation from the danger of terrorism. At the same time, it demands the nation to pay allegiance to the commitment of order and authority. The state presents its new *self* as the *pater familias* looking after his *women-and-children* and wants to win the war with an offensive military strategy playing as a leader.

This new state subjectivity is highly demanding. To demonstrate constant strength and will, as well as force and authority, implies a great investment in keeping up this image in each confrontation, not just against 'terrorists' in the military field, but also in political spaces where the supremacy and legitimacy of state actions can be called into question. This particular construction of the Colombian state is grounded on the ability to reaffirm its credibility in different stages where political and military power are displayed.

Simultaneously, the identity of the state is now invested with a vindictive character. If in the past the state was supposed to be striving for reconciliation and peace, the current subject is striving for revenge. The desire for revenge is fed by mourning the victims of the war, whose pain and suffering *claim for a just war against terrorism*. In this sense, the newly reimagined Colombian state is represented as a clear-cut distinctive subject different from the former administration. It presents itself as a state that has 'transcended the mistakes of past regimes' (Litzinger, 1999: 317).

Of great importance is how the newly reimagined state embraces the nation as a population to which it dictates which values are important and which are not. The state's fight against terrorism is an enterprise of each and every Colombian, so the DSP transforms the insecurity of the state into the insecurity of everyone (Weldes et al., 1999). The war is fought by state and non-state institutions and persons in the name of the whole population and on behalf of everyone's existence (Butler, 1995a; Campbell, 1998).

This new narrative of biopolitical war, as Michael Dillon (2007) argues, so discloses the biopower that is combined with the sovereign power in the DSP. It is then a blending of geo- and biopolitics of in/security in which the Colombian *war of all against terrorism* is constructed in opposition to the former narrative in which *the state and the guerrillas were involved in an armed conflict*. The new narrative has transformed a war of the state into a war fought in the name of the

Colombian population, yet the state preserves its role of security provider and becomes the people's leader and protector. As depicted by President Uribe (2002b: 20), the notion of peace 'born out of peace doves and virtual declarations on television' is outdated. The new state is now embarked in a struggle for authority which will give birth to peace, someday in the future when in/security is achieved.

Constructing 'others'

The frontier effects that the DSP recreates for 'us' have a clear expression in the co-constitutive outside, the 'other'. Eriksen (1993: 1) evokes the thoughts of Gregory Bateson when saying that 'it takes at least two somethings to create a difference ... Clearly each alone is – for the mind and the perception – a non-entity, a non-being. Not different from being, and not different from non-being. An unknowable, a *Ding an sich*, a sound from one hand clapping.' As seen in the second chapter, identities are constructed based on the economy of identity/difference, in William Connolly's (1991) words:

> Identity is relational and collective. My personal identity is defined through the collective constituencies with which I identify or am identified by others ...; it is further specified by comparison to a variety of things I am not. Identity, then, is always connected to a series of differences that help it be what it is. ... Built into the dynamic of identity is a polemical temptation to translate differences through which it is specified into moral failings or abnormalities. (Ibid.: xiv)

In this vein, 'the definition of difference is a requirement built into the logic of identity, and the construction of otherness is a temptation that readily insinuates itself into that logic' (ibid.: 9). It is pertinent to keep in mind this distinction between building identity categories based upon difference and condemning otherness by turning the 'other' into material in need of extirpation and discipline (Campbell, 1998). That identity needs difference to be does not imply that it needs to construct itself in a deadly relation of opposition to the 'other'.

However, it is clear that 'subjects are constituted through exclusion, that is, through the creation of a domain of deauthorised subjects, presubjects, figures of abjection, populations erased from view' (Butler, 1995a: 48). Meaning, 'collectivities are organised around boundaries which divide the world into "'us" and "them"' (Yuval-Davis, 1997: 19). The 'us' is constructed by the denomination of some features that produce the 'cultural similarity of its adherents and, by implication, it draws boundaries vis-à-vis others, who thereby become outsiders' (Eriksen, 1993: 6). Thus, 'group identities must always be defined in relation to that which they are not – in other words, in relation to non-members of the group' (ibid.: 10).

These last remarks bring us back to William Connolly's (1991) insights pertaining to the economy of identity/difference when he insinuates that any identity is based on difference and exclusion. This does not automatically legitimate violence that converts 'otherness' into 'evil'. This is a call both for being aware of the positive value of difference and for paying attention to and making visible how much violence is invested in keeping the boundaries between 'us' and 'them'.

Relating these points to my concern with how the DSP constructs otherness, by reading dangers in this in/security discourse one might initially conclude that the 'other' is made equivalent to *terrorists*. They are represented as enemies of the good people, guerrillas who have lost their ideological ground, who do not want to take over state power anymore and are no longer valid political subjects (Uribe, 2002b). Terrorists are depicted as evil people who only seek to fill their pockets with money from the drug industry as well as from the ransoms paid for kidnappings and extortion (DSP, 2003). Since the 'other' is an enemy, violence is legitimised to contain the immediate threat it poses to 'us', for what is said to be at stake is the very survival of the population (ibid.).

The options that the state offers to the 'other' are whether to *convert to one of us*, abandoning a criminal life and returning to the nuclear family (DSP, 2003: §116) or to be exterminated. In this relationship between 'us' and 'them' there is nothing 'we' can have, think or do which resembles connections to the 'other'. The borderline that divides the two political identities is constructed as a wall that separates 'us' from 'them' in a totalising manner, which prevents recognition of traces of the 'other' in 'us'.

No matter how clear-cut this distinction might initially appear, the government also explicitly and repeatedly points to the obligations of the good ones to actively participate in the security enterprise in the fight against terrorism (ibid.: §105–31). Those who are indifferent and who do not collaborate, whether in active military tasks or with information and cooperation, are also stigmatised as not belonging to 'us' (ibid.).

In this manner, the constitution of identity/difference operates as drawing an inner differentiation, a borderline within the same confinements of 'the people': the nation is divided between two groups, the *good* ones who align themselves with the government and internalise the in/security logic to guide their lives and deaths, and the *bad* ones who are terrorists. There is no space for opposition and there is no space for political ambiguity. Uncertainty and contingency are not options.

BELONGING AND BORDERLINES

So how to recognise who belongs to 'them'? What types of markers allow distinguishing between the members and the non-members of this specific collectivity *terrorists*? Yuval-Davis (1997: 23), following Armstrong, imagines these markers as symbolic border guards which 'are closely linked to specific cultural codes of style of dress and behaviour as well as to more elaborate bodies of customs, religion, literary and artistic modes of production, and, of course, language'. In the case of the DSP, those markers refer to specific political behaviour. The threat of terrorism is depicted as a method (DSP, 2003: §37). It is a way of exercising illegitimate violence, and it can also be a potential method of violence since terrorism is not reduced to an act but is extended to *persons deemed dangerous* and to *possible participation or planning* of terrorist activities (ibid.: §112–31).

For those who do not identify themselves explicitly as guerrilla fighters (terrorists according to the DSP), the DSP creates a peculiar way of dividing *good* from *bad* people and of separating 'us' from 'them': the concept of solidarity (DSP, 2003: 6–7). In this scenario, solidarity is the obligation that 'all Colombians have with the state and its institutions in the fight against terrorism' (ibid.). It cannot remain an implicit quality, but has to be expressed overtly, actively and publicly. Solidarity is turned into the social project of belonging in which the subject has to collaborate with the security forces (ibid.: 9–10). In this way, criticism, indifference and disbelief in the promise of in/security are perceived as threats to the good society. Scrutiny, dissent and accountability (Jabri, 2006) are securitised (Wæver, 1995).

This mode of belonging produces several consequences. The first is that the particular representation of danger as terrorism points to the omnipresent potentiality of the *enemy within*. Therefore, the efforts to locate the 'other' are directed at the inside of the collectivity, reproducing a state of affairs in which everybody is a potential 'other' in a relationship which does not recognise, nor does it respect, differences. If one does not exercise solidarity, one is not *good*, and therefore must constitute part of the bad/terrorist ones.

The second effect is that the only marker which allows dividing 'us' from 'them' is to behave in a depoliticised and securitised way (Edkins, 2003). In other words, to actively belong to 'us' one has to adopt a life-and-death form dictated by the in/security doctrine, and to comply with security regulations and with institutional arrangements which hinder political freedoms. Otherwise, the subject is inscribed within the 'other'.

Now the image of the 'other' and the ways to discern who is an insider and who is an outsider do not seem to be as clear-cut as the government initially presented them, as 'simply' *terrorists and terrorism*. It seems that we are now confronting a puzzle. The enemies are some of 'us'. The enemy can be anywhere, it can also be an equal who does not collaborate with the security forces and, consequently, is turned into a threat to security in him/herself. This makes 'us' fear and exercise control and supervision, ever more seeking the otherness in ourselves in order to unveil and then extirpate it. *The people* are encouraged to reject the 'other' and all responsibility or connections with it. Beyond this, the people have to perform this very same process of exclusion and erasure with their equals and with themselves.

The idealised identity category of 'other' as pictured in the DSP is blurred because the enemy is shady. The ambivalent notion of 'terrorism' as a method of political violence and the endless character of this war that is contoured by an impossible promise of in/security, make dangerousness the criteria for distinguishing between good nationals and terrorists (Butler, 2004; Jabri, 2006). In other words, 'we' are all suspects. Considering the threat of an arbitrary state with normalised exceptional powers and the ears and eyes of the military in all of 'us', the fear of not belonging (Croucher, 2004: 41), of being excluded, is amplified by the fear of in/security.

Hailing subjects into place

By now, the idealisation of the identity categories constructed by the DSP (2003) for nationals, state and others are clear as far as they represent ideal pictures of subjectivities. How do those constructions materialise in state and non-state policies, programmes, actions and measures? In the following pages, the centre of attention is the *production* of those categories (Hall, 1996a; Weldes et al., 1999), which hail subjects to adopt the specific positions created by the DSP in order to summon them into articulating the processes of identification.

There are several realms in which the DSP can be studied as a discourse that informs governance (Dillon and Reid, 2001) and, as far as our research focus is concerned, actively shapes the concept of political identity. The first case to examine is the direct conversion of the concept of democratic security into military actions with and against the civilian population, specifically in the case of massive captures. Second, we will focus on the conversion of citizens into soldiers. We will subsequently examine the case of the Province of Arauca as the paradigmatic example of the implementation of the in/security thinking depicted in the DSP. Finally, the derivative character of peace from security calls attention to the concept of *secure peace* used by the government to legitimate the process of demobilisation with paramilitary groups. The consequences on politics, peaces and identity at the end of this section point to the final considerations of the fifth chapter of this book.

It is important to keep in mind that the production of social facts which hail subjects to adopt the positions of *good nationals* is not exercised purely by state agents. I have chosen the mentioned practices because they disclose in a clear manner both geopolitical strategies of sovereign power and biopolitical measures to regulate the population. These practices hail subjects into place by working together in a toxic combination: as power over life and as power over death (Dillon, 2007). As one of its aims, the DSP seeks to turn the goal of in/security into a social enterprise in which the good people have to be actively involved and cooperate in solidarity. In this sense, the effects of the DSP are spread across and multiplied in society, making them a diffused power that cannot be said to emanate entirely from the state. It rather is turned into governmentality as portrayed earlier (ibid.; Butler, 2004; Jabri, 2006).

Making citizens transparent: information and cooperation networks

Since *solidarity* with the security forces enables a distinguishing of who belongs to the good ones and who belongs to the terrorists, the state has placed special emphasis on organising and actively engaging people in collaboration with informing security forces, which supposedly leads to prevention of terrorist actions and to pre-emptively arresting suspicious persons.

The information and cooperation networks constitute the first component of the army of good people (DSP, 2003: §80, §105, §128, §130–1). The information and cooperation networks were outlined in the DSP as two separate networks; the informants were supposed to report to the security forces any *suspicious activity* and would receive rewards for information that lead to a pre-emptive arrest of terrorists. On the other hand, the network of cooperation was supposed to participate with solidarity in the achievement of the promise of in/security and initially would receive no payment. However, a parallel reward system was also set in place for those whose cooperation led to arrests (Ejército Nacional de Colombia, 2005).

According to data made public in *Semana* (León, 2003b: 56), in the first year of the DSP government, the number of persons detained for being 'suspect of the crime of rebellion' increased 167 per cent when compared with 2003. Most of these *suspect persons* were detained in massive captures due to information provided by citizens' warning networks. According to data collected by human rights organisations (Velásquez, 2004: 37), between September 2002 and December 2003, 4,846 persons have been arrested based on information provided by the networks. From this group of people, 3,750 (seventy-seven per cent) had to be released *after several days* because no charges were made against them. Only 1,096 (twenty-three per cent) have been accused of helping the guerrillas in one way or another. However, none of them has yet reached the phase of trial or sentence (ibid.).

Such proliferation of accusations made by warning networks against the civilian population, which at the same time leads to pre-emptive arrests in massive captures during which democratic rights are suspended, evidences the biopolitical character of the practices of in/security. These are geared towards regulating the circulation and connection (Dillon, 2005) of the population to prevent possible terrorist attacks. Whether or not such prevention is grounded seems irrelevant when dangerousness is the driving principle of the war against narco-terrorism.

The negative implications for democratic accountability of the warning networks have been known since the beginning of the DSP government. As Franciso Leal (2004: 97) argues concerning the detrimental political effects of the networks, the state does not have any capacity to control such practices that incorporate and foster negative features of living together, such as the volatility and fragmentation of civil society referents. Furthermore, the weak 'intelligence' of the public force does not enable a thorough evaluation of the information received by the networks. In short, warning networks widen the arbitrary ruling power of the state.

Such a lack of proper management of information about suspect populations is at the heart of the criticism that assumes that the war against terror merely concerns sovereign powers traditionally aimed at controlling the territory in an exceptional state of war. Yet, what the DSP logic insinuates is precisely that war has become the rule (Jabri, 2006) and that the managing of the population is an integral part of the biopolitics of in/security, in combination with geostrategic in/securities (Dillon, 2007).

Such biopolitical micro-practice (Lobo-Guerrero, 2007) led in August 2003 to 600 members of the military and police to capture 128 suspects in Chalán, Colosó and Sucre (*Semana*, 2003a). The security forces then publicly presented these individuals as being part of the FARC-EP guerrillas and as trophies in the war against terrorism (ibid.). The reason for detention was, literally, having been pointed out by hooded informants who picked *suspect persons* in different towns. The suspects were detained in their homes and work places (ibid.). All of the detainees had to be released *three months later* when the judge decided there was no evidence to sustain the accusations and, therefore, no charges could be raised against any of them. The judge disregarded the information provided by the citizens' networks, which had grounded the massive captures as valid juridical evidence for trial (ibid.).

For the executive branch and for the military, the fact that there were massive captures, which inevitably led to pre-emptively arresting innocent people, was not a problem at all. President Uribe (2003a: 1) argued that 'with the purpose of condemning them [terrorists] to live in warrens eating roots in the mountains, we have to deprive them of the connections that help them kidnap, traffic drugs, and hand over information. This is why we have to capture all those who help terrorists'.

The commander of the armed forces, General Carlos Ospina (2004), argued that massive captures do not erode public trust. Neither do they make the population turn against the state. 'On the contrary', said Ospina (ibid.: 37), 'people know each other and know that the captured persons are bandits; that increases confidence in the state forces ... In general terms, the massive captures have helped dismantling networks of bandits and that has prevented kidnapping and terrorist acts.'

One has to ask then, if there are no charges raised against someone in particular when groups of people are captured by public security forces according to information provided by citizens' networks, then how can the military be sure that this strategy deters *bandits* from kidnapping and from committing acts of terrorism?

The effect that massive captures have on the population is quite different from the one depicted in the DSP and repeated by the president and military officials. The first effect is that economic rewards buy the willingness of informants to collaborate with the security forces for money. Second, since the informant is not responsible for the inaccuracy of the information provided and since there is no need to provide evidence, an innocent person captured cannot make complaints for arbitrary treatment. Third, the networks produce the effect that each and one of 'us' is suspect and, within the in/security logic, can be held in captivity for several days and even months until one has proven his/her own innocence (Zamora, 2005: 24). This mechanism turns upside down one of the most basic principles of law, which is the presumption of innocence. Quite the opposite, the *presumption of terrorism* inhibits people from participating publicly in political matters, especially in expressing dissent or criticising the in/security discourse. This inevitably reproduces an environment of fear and silence where national security subordinates individual security and liberty (Buzan, 1991: 45).

This form of solving the paradox between individual and national security by giving priority to the latter has manifested itself in Colombia in multiple ways. Private communications, for example cellular phone calls, can be monitored and intercepted by companies and by the government. Since September 2002, cellular companies have an agreement with the office of the attorney general in which they 'denounce abnormal situations' in order to 'speed up justice' (*Semana*, 2002b: 41). The ambiguous language of 'denouncement of abnormality' encourages private companies to watch over the cellular bills of their clients and to monitor their behaviour, looking for something *abnormal* without being told exactly for what they should be looking. They then pass on this information to the state, which controls to whom and about what the citizens are allowed to talk. In the same vein, this information is supposed to *speed up justice* in the sense that 'normal' legal procedures to intercept phone calls, as a judicial order issued explicitly for it, are erased from the process of intervention, undermining citizens' liberties and connectivity.

As part of that toxic combination of geo- and biopolitics of security (Dillon, 2007), people are not simply regarded as the legitimate subjects of the political community. They are also a population whose life is regarded as a process, and is 'defined in terms of an open system engaged in transformative, informationally driven, and knowledge sensitive exchange with its environment' (ibid.: 14). Since such connectivity can open possibilities for becoming dangerous, the government and private cellular companies and, ultimately, the users themselves, police their phone calls to appear as though they belong to the good citizenry. To paraphrase Dillon (ibid.), what is at stake here is not the novelty of these strategies, but their extension, amplification and intensification.

I would further argue that the violent element of managing the population via this particular technology is the ever-easier acceptance of security thinking and measures and the ever-decreasing resistance to being governed and ruled this way (Butler, 2000). The ambiguity of these biopolitical measures in the name of in/security is a conscious political decision of the government which allows it to use the call for in/security as a political tool of convenience. 'At an extreme, the need for national security can even be evoked as a reason for not discussing it' (Buzan, 1991: 11). Without the label of 'security issues', these measures would have to be explained to the public and they would be subject to public debate and scrutiny (Jabri, 2006; Wæver, 1995).

In/security discourse contours the limits of what can and cannot be said (Butler, 2004). *Security* is removed from question, it is a higher good for which 'we' have to sacrifice our freedoms and possibilities for connecting and it legitimises the violence inflicted upon 'us' and the 'other'. On the *secure* grounding of in/security, the DSP establishes the limits of the unspeakable and drives criticisms of policy aims and actions as incitements of discourse (Gusterson, 1999) within the very same limits of in/security. Therefore, what is discussed and debated are the ways to achieve in/security, but never its grounding for politics (Dillon, 1996) nor its grounding as biopolitical way of life (Dillon, 2007).

An additional vital element for comprehending how the DSP reproduces and hails subjects into place is the incorporation of private security guards to the army of good people (DSP, 2003: §105). Widening the already extensive and intensive workings of private security guards to public spaces and making these companies collaborate in solidarity with the security forces in reporting suspect persons, furthers the governmentality of in/security.

Private security companies are one of the most salient features of the many wars in Colombia. They are not just an effect of a country that has been at war since the 1950s but, I would argue, are actively engaged in the continuation of violent conflict. In this line of argumentation, Jorge Echavarría (2002) draws an analogy between the drive for in/security in private spaces and its extension to public urban spaces in Medellín. While conducting a study about future housing and habitat conditions, Echavarría realised that the *conditions of security* seemed to be the key factor for the potential buyers. According to the results of his research (ibid.), the most attractive housing option is the one that belongs to a closed area and offers private security guards twenty-four hours, which also seemed to be the primary conditions to add value to the property.

At the same time, open spaces and contact with urban activities are not desirable. Population nuclei appear as enclosed temporal and spatial units, evoking an inside marked by coherence, security and unanimity, separating the nucleus from an outside of insecurity, chaos and dissolution (ibid.: 214). Inside the residential area, now turned into a fortress, residents try to create a zero-risk environment, ignoring the consequences of this logic of capsules, which extends from the house to the neighbourhood and to the city itself. This produces 'zones of the city under surveillance, pacified neighbourhoods, and the panoptical nightmare came true, because if the criminals do not go to the prisons, then the solution is to make the city a prison in itself' (ibid.: 217).

According to Echavarría (ibid.: 216), the transitional trends from a society of work to a risk society (Beck, 1992; Giddens and Hutton, 1990) are made evident in Medellín where today's *plektópoi* swallows fears and monsters and also creates its own fears and uncertainty. On the one hand, never before was the consciousness of the presence of fear so widespread, clear and omnipresent. On the other hand, national borders were never so useless to delimit fears and never before had a scientific technocracy been given so much power to control, or at least to try to control, or to warn of the fears born out of technological advancements. In this prison-logic, private security is grounded on the belief that control and absence of fear can be equated. Private security companies are part of an industry of protection and 'its gadgets for each situation of risk and fear install themselves with glory, nesting in the cities, naive believers in the edification of a fortress as a mechanism to diminish danger' (ibid.: 218–19).

The DSP expands the already existing trend, making private security the vigilantes of the public space, which is thereby made ever emptier and more aseptic. The community hires private security organisations 'for protection', but their role goes beyond *self-defence*. While the identification of threats increases their number and dimension, the way of dealing with those fears appears to be mainly done through increasing armed guards, surveillance cameras and restrictions of circulation by the community itself. The underlying belief is to mistrust 'us' and the 'other', the foreigner and the neighbour, encouraging private security agencies to act in advance, before threats turn into dangers and to exercise social control in a permanent and omnipresent way. Based on the 'orienting principles of the democratic security', this DSP micro-practice seeks to encourage private security companies to guarantee that the exercise of vigilance and private security and the personnel involved 'really contribute to prevent crime, reducing the opportunities for criminal activity, discouraging the action of criminals in collaboration with the authorities of the Republic' (Ejército Nacional de Colombia, 2005: 2).

Since the purpose of the government is to organise millions of *voluntary and patriotic citizens* as vigilantes, it has instructed private guards to actively collaborate in the official protection of 'the citizenry' by informing the military forces to 'act in an opportune way to impede terrorist actions which affect the security of the civil population' (ibid.: 3). By December 2002, the governmental agency in charge of controlling private security companies (Superintendencia de Vigilancia y Seguridad Privada, 2003) reported more than 182,000 persons working for private security agencies in Colombia.[6] This high number of private security guards reinforces the army of good people with trained personnel. Society turns ever more transparent, more technologically advanced in its own regulation, while the government becomes ever less accountable and ever more opaque (Vattimo, 1992).

Consequently, the above-mentioned measures, such as citizens and cooperation networks, collaboration of cellular phone companies and active involvement of private security guards, cannot be said to emanate solely from the state. When in/security is the grounds for politics, it turns into a worldview, a way of living, thinking, acting, feeling and silencing. The policing role of the state is no longer needed when in/security as form-of-life is successfully reproduced by scared and violent citizens who scrutinise each other and monitor themselves constantly.

Turning citizens into warriors: peasant soldiers

The conformation of the army of good people – as it is named by the Colombian government and regulated by warning networks – has its rural component in the figure of the peasant soldier. 'The peasant soldiers are part of anti-guerrilla military units which have turned hybrid and fulfil police functions while protecting the territory' (Leal, 2004: 97). By sending the poorest rural people to the front line to fight and to die, the peasant soldiers' organisation speaks to the still sovereign power over death that the Colombian state enjoys in the war.

According to the minister of defence, Marta Lucía Ramírez, in an interview with *Semana* (2002c), peasant soldiers are responsible for recovering *the sovereignty of the state* in rural areas. They are seen as an indispensable element that would incline the balance in favour of the state in the irregular war against the narco-terrorist guerrillas. Besides costing the state one-third of what training and keeping regular soldiers cost, peasant soldiers are part of the civilian population that they look after. The government hopes this will dissuade their families and communities from collaborating with the guerrillas, since their own children are part of the army (ibid.: 28–30).

In the same vein, the government supports this strategy by arguing that these soldiers know the geography and the people of their own communities, which make it easier for them to recognise the presence of guerrilla fighters in the zone. 'It is like having a permanent intelligence network for dissuasion of terrorism' says a high military commander (ibid.: 30). By September 2003, the government had been able to organise 17,000 peasant soldiers in 500 municipalities (Ramírez, 2005).

The high personal risk that these soldiers *must* assume, since they have no option not to comply with the obligatory military service, includes getting themselves and their families killed. Private retaliation against the peasant soldiers, for example during the nights spent under their own roofs, and violence against their relatives seem to be the cost of the war, which the government thinks they have to assume. After leaving office as minister of defence, Marta Lucía Ramírez declared to the press that the risk that peasant soldiers must assume amounts to the same risk that any other soldier runs when participating in the war (*Semana*, 2002b). However, this is not entirely true. The military service for urban soldiers can be carried out performing other activities without participating in anti-guerrilla combat units. The fact that peasants are the soldiers who combat guerrillas is not a coincidence, for it is the poorest ones with only three months of training and no support that are sent to the front lines.

The systematic killings of peasant soldiers in the first years of the implementation of the DSP did not deter the state from this strategy. According to Marta Lucía Ramírez (2005), killings of peasant soldiers are not enough to question the DSP and this specific programme. 'On the contrary', argues Ramírez (ibid.), by their condition as locals, peasant soldiers produce a 'virtuous circle of population – armed forces – population' by knowing that the lives of their 'parents, brothers and friends, their most beloved ones' depends on them. Furthermore, argued Ramírez, 'in no way can we fall into the temptation of disqualifying the institutions, nor the tangible and objective results of the DSP, neither the goodness of the production of trust in the country and its institutions thanks to this figure of the peasant soldiers' (ibid.).

The questions raised in regards to the massacres committed against peasant soldiers are thus co-opted into the discursive limits of the DSP, which directs criticisms into a debate of how to improve military intelligence and leaves unquestioned the very grounds of in/security. Moreover, the militarisation of police functions is increased by this measure since the peasant soldiers are to report about suspicious persons. This task blurs the division between the military and the police, which, according to the constitutional framework, should be a civic force. To ascribe military functions to civilians leads to the arbitrary treatment of the population and erodes the political character of the police forces (Leal, 2004). Likewise, the involvement of peasants as warriors in the armed conflict exacerbates violence and turns the political involvement of civilians into pure military actions. The depoliticising effect of this measure is obvious. If peasants are turned into warriors and are directly involved in armed confrontation as part of anti-guerrilla units, the possibilities for rejecting or resisting the in/security discourse are reduced drastically, especially when the peasant soldiers fulfil their functions via obligatory military service.

This militarisation of society is heightened by an increase of other military units to combat terrorism. Special deadly new programmes have been created under the umbrella of the DSP, like the High-Mountain Battalions and anti-terrorist urban units, which, according to the government, help to combat terrorism by enhancing the extermination of terrorist and terrorist sympathisers:

throughout 2004, the strengthening of the Public Force will continue with: 2 additional high-mountain battalions, 3 mobile brigades, 9 mounted police squads, 146 additional municipalities under the 'Town Soldiers' program, 1,200 additional Infantry Marines, an increase of 10,000 members of the National Police plus 6,500 regular 'reserves'. This strengthening of the Public Force represented a 19% increase in Military Forces and Police members at the end of 2003, and by December 2004, will represent an increase of 75,000 men and women for an overall 27% increase of uniformed personnel since the beginning of the current administration in August 2002. (Presidency of the Republic of Colombia – Ministry of Defence, 2004: 9)

Military, police officers, and citizens all have to eliminate terrorists and terrorist sympathisers, who are depicted by the president as 'beasts who devour the hand of the one who feeds them' (Uribe, 2003b: 2). The 'other' is portrayed as an animal who cannot undergo any transformation and who does not even classify as human. This hostile image legitimises the use of violence against the 'other' and glorifies the violence deployed as a means of dealing with the armed conflict. It simultaneously naturalises both political categories of 'us' and the 'other' as opposite, unified, coherent and taken-for-granted entities, treating them as two absolutely different groups whose only relation is violent confrontation.

Arauca: regional paradigm of in/security

In the northeast of the country, the Province of Arauca, bordering Venezuela, has the biggest oil reserves in Colombia. The US government and multinational oil companies have organised a strong private armed force there. The case of Arauca is the paradigmatic example of the different strategies and programmes through which the DSP hails subjects into place. In Arauca, the DSP finds clear social, political and military expressions and produces the political violence it promises to arrest.

Arauca was declared one of the three zones of rehabilitation and consolidation within the framework of the state of exception (Decree 2002/2002). Immediately after the declaration, the executive branch and the military started to implement the different programmes announced in the DSP. Among the most well-known DSP actions carried out in the region was the conformation of anti-guerrilla units of peasant soldiers, networks of informants and cooperation. This led to massive captures, the strengthening of the military forces with special combat units, the implementation of a programme for children called 'Soldier for a day', innovative strategies obliging people to collaborate with the state and having the president govern *in situ* for three days.

The national government developed an aggressive military strategy based on a special armed and fast unit called Fudra (*Fuerza de Despliegue Rápido*) that has conducted ambitious attacks on rural areas (León, 2003a: 22). Exclusive urban-trained anti-terrorist units performed surveillance and interception activities in the cities (ibid.: 23). The government announced that there had to be a representative of the attorney general during military operations in order to provide the search and arrest warrants. Nevertheless, the government also stipulated that, if the need arose, it was no longer necessary for a member of the general attorney's office to participate in the operations. Similarly, if there was no possibility to make a phone call to obtain the judicial order orally, the military were allowed to conduct searches and arrests without previous legal permission (ibid.). This *ad-hoc* mechanism was called 'support structure', whose official aim was to 'reduce the risk of attacks by members of the guerrilla against judicial investigators operating in Arauca, but is often used to target human rights defenders and social activists' (AI, 2004a: 22).

On 11 November 2003, while the National Beauty Contest was being aired on television, a military airplane carrying representatives of the attorney general's office, 700 soldiers and policemen landed in Saravena, one of the top three priority in/security municipalities, according to the government. They searched dozens of houses, workplaces and shops. 'By the end of the night more than 2,000 people had been rounded up at gunpoint and taken to Saravena's stadium where they were photographed, videotaped, questioned, their background checked, and their arms marked with indelible ink' (ibid.: 1).

Out of the 2,000 detainees, the security forces arrested eighty-five people. Detention orders could be manufactured against half of them according to subsequent information provided by citizens' networks. Nevertheless, they were all detained for three days at an improvised investigation centre where they were interrogated. Afterwards, more than thirty detainees were released and the rest were sent to prison in the capital (León, 2003a: 22).

This case shows that to be detained, and to remain detained for three days, a person only needs to be *deemed dangerous*. There is no need for evidence, search warrants, arrest orders or any specific reason. Bureaucrats, soldiers and police officers can detain hundreds of persons and then unceasingly ask them questions for three days. For security reasons, the individual has to prove his/her own innocence. As Amnesty International's report highlighted, government measures exacerbated the crisis rather than shielding civilians from hostilities (AI, 2004a: 2).Consequently, the potentialities are marked in 'others' so that political violence can be *justified* against them (Dillon and Reid, 2001: 57). Paradoxically then, dangerousness acquires a concrete manifestation that aims at encapsulating the potentialities to become somebody else, challenging the fixed and 'secure' identities constructed by the DSP.

Since the underlying belief is that everyone is a suspect terrorist unless proven the contrary, not even children have escaped being recruited in the army of good people. In the rehabilitation zone, the army has formed the GEOS (*Grupo Especial de Operaciones Sicológicas* – PSYOPS (Psychological Operations) Special Group). Part of the activities of the GEOS was to *invite* local children to visit military camps every Thursday. 'Children from Saravena's public and private schools were encouraged to attend the battalion where they played with the soldiers dressed as clowns, used the swimming pool, participated in raffles and received cakes, fizzy drinks, played with the tanks, while soldiers showed them how to use weapons' (AI, 2004a: 16).

During the visits, children received war-talks from soldiers and high military officials in order to convince them of the 'terrorist character of the guerrillas' and involve them in the 'fight against terrorism' (León, 2003a: 23). According to reports by Amnesty International, 'children attending these events were used to garner information on alleged guerrilla activity by their parents and other family members' (AI, 2004a: 16). Children were given fake money to play with, which, on the front side, appeared to be legal currency and, on the back, had the slogan 'The government rewards you. You and your family deserve another chance. Demobilise now!' (ibid.; León, 2003a: 23). The idea behind this strategy, according to one of the soldiers, was that the children 'bring these bills to their homes and show them to their parents and older brothers in order to change the *mental-register* of the civilian population' (ibid.). The objective of this programme, Colonel Herrera told the press (ibid.: 24), was for the army to make such an impression on the child that 'the son of the *guerrillero* will question his dad'.

First, to assume that all the children of Arauca had parents among the guerrillas is an unfounded and dangerous belief. Second, to treat children as vehicles for the reproduction of the in/security discourse, disguising their visits to the camps as recreational in order to brainwash them and to use them to persuade their family members to collaborate with the security forces, is a perverse strategy. This is a questionable and violent way to turn children into soldiers of the army of good people.[7] This practice reinforced the DSP measures to close ranks against terrorists, where nobody can remain indifferent and 'we' all have to collaborate.

Since one of the 'security objectives' was to turn citizens into warriors, the military also created *psychological checkpoints*. Soldiers walked around the streets 'greeting the people and inviting them to work with the state' (ibid.: 25). A piece of paper was handed out and people were told to 'write whatever they want' especially 'information to combat terrorism' (ibid.). The situation in which persons are confronted face to face with a group of soldiers asking him/her about handing information to the security forces about suspicious persons is one clear expression of the solidarity strategy: those who cooperate with the security forces belong to the good ones, whereas those who do not collaborate are stigmatised as terrorists.

In Arauca, the psychological checkpoint strategy made thousands of people hand in information (ibid.). What alternative did they have? Confronting them with a military presence on the streets and giving them paper to collaborate or else be put on the list of suspects (possibly being arrested pre-emptively), was a strong and dissuasive way of collecting information based on fear. However, nobody knows how reliable their contributions to fight terrorism are.

Nevertheless, collecting information was not the only important effect of the psychological checkpoints. The most relevant aspect of this strategy was the effect it produced on the population. The fear of being labelled as a terrorist or terrorist-sympathiser, if one does not actively collaborate with the security forces, had already been installed and was being reproduced. Indifference to, not to mention rejection or criticism of, the security apparatus was not permitted. This biopolitical security strategy 'seeks to govern without government' (Dillon and Reid, 2001: 47) because once fear is installed as principle of behaviour, the government is no longer necessary to manage the population according to state in/security objectives.

Hand in hand with the army, paramilitary forces entered Arauca. 'As paramilitaries consolidated their presence in the municipality of Arauca they were able to carry out massacres and selective killings despite the heavy-militarisation of the region and the fact that the armed forces had been informed of their presence' (AI, 2004a: 30). The ministry of defence reported the presence of 950 paramilitaries who, during 2003–2004, selectively killed 300 people in Tame, one of the cities of the province (*Semana*, 2003a: 36).

The state has defended itself against criticism of the army and paramilitary joint anti-guerrilla strategy by saying that those criticisms are part of the guerrilla juridical dirty war. 'Each time that there is a house-search or a massive capture they [guerrillas ELN] react speedily to raise a complaint or an infamy against us', said General Lemus to the press (ibid.: 36). This way, 'criticism, which ought to be central to any democracy, becomes a fugitive and suspect activity' (Butler, 2004: xx).

The in/security logic expands all the way through the social tissue, justifying mechanisms like those mentioned above, which are unjustifiable under any other label which is not *security* (Wæver, 1995). The striving to homogenise the 'we', to erase differences among peoples concerning their political opinions and to regulate them as a mass of dangerous suspects, is an antidemocratic practice whose scrutiny is blocked by the label of 'security'.

To make sure that this 'we' is made homogeneous, that populations are regulated at the level of their possibilities to become (Dillon and Reid, 2001), and that the security label is unquestioned, President Uribe decided to exercise his executive power directly in the province. He first withdrew the management of the oil revenues that the provincial governor used to administer, since in the DSP (2003) this is considered money that feeds terrorism. The governor, even though he had been named by the president himself, was fired after being labelled as corrupt and incapable of administering the annual oil budget of ninety-five thousand million pesos (León, 2003a: 25).

Presidential advisor Christian Bleier has argued that the oil revenues would be administered in a much more efficient and transparent manner from Bogotá (ibid.). The government planned to sign contracts with the local population for infrastructure works in such a way that the 'citizens form a vigilance committee which will make sure that every terrorist attack against the oil pipelines or bridges affects their own interests. This way, civilians will help the state protect the pipelines from bombs', Bleier told the press (ibid.).

This investment plan for the oil revenues was based on the belief that the local population was potentially guilty of collaborating with terrorist-guerrillas. The executive power tried to recreate private security forces to take care of the pipelines. Unarmed, unlike the private security contractors that multinational companies had already hired for the job, these representatives obliged people actively to defend the state's infrastructure in the name of in/security and, this time, also in the name of transparency.

President Uribe went to Arauca for three days to 'exercise the sovereign power of the state' (*Semana*, 2003a: 38). This symbolic act of authority was received with great enthusiasm by the military, which provided him with housing (ibid.). On the military base, the president held meetings with the mayors of the cities in the province, constantly reminding them that the state was 'winning the war against terrorism and that the only option left for the guerrillas was to quit because their military defeat was imminent' (ibid.). He thereby generated material effects from symbolic speech.

Following the postulates of the DSP, the president promised to strengthen the military forces with 500 more peasant soldiers who would ride their horses into the countryside chasing guerrilleros (ibid.: 37). At the military base, President Uribe thanked the existing soldiers for their sacrifice: 'Thank you for your efforts for the homeland, we are going to defeat the terrorists, we are going to achieve victory, but we have to make sacrifices for it' (ibid.). In other words, their bodies were subject to the sovereign power of the state. They were to die in the name of recovering in/security.

During the president's stay, the guerrillas attacked the province three times, one for each day in which Uribe was there (ibid.: 36). On the second day of his visit to Arauca, President Uribe was informed of a guerrilla attack against the oil pipeline. He reacted by giving the order immediately to offer a twenty million peso reward to the peasants who handed in information. The media reported his words as: 'We have to create a dynamic in which people lose the fear of terrorism, in which they feel that the State is here to be trusted and that we are never going to abandon them again' (ibid.: 38).

On the last day of his visit, the president announced further measures to counter-attack terrorism (ibid.: 39). An important highway in the province was to be contracted directly by the military with the cooperation of the local civilian population. As presidential advisor Bleier explained, the people would be working on the construction site to make sure that they did not collaborate with terrorists in attacking the works. In the same tone, Uribe made public an increase in the fumigation of coca plantations and warned the candidates running for public posts that if they were holding conversations with the armed groups they would be sent to jail (ibid.).

During his three-day visit to Arauca, President Uribe made clear that the practices of the DSP were hailing subjects to kill and die for their homeland. Peasant soldiers could be sacrificed; poor rural male bodies were the means to search for the (impossible) end of achieving state's in/security.

This collection of orders, executive and military actions, as well as messages to potentially dangerous 'terrorists', sums up the core of the DSP. Everybody has to collaborate in the war against terrorism, whether sacrificing his or her biological or political life, or both. Peasants are recruited into the army of good people and local political leaders are banned from engaging in conversations with 'the enemy'. In case political leaders disobey the orders of the state, they can also be sent to jail and so inscribed in the category 'terrorists'.

As such, state and non-state actions, which focus on naturalising the idea of 'good nationals' as opposed to the 'other/terrorist' have, as one of its main consequences, the inability to first encounter the 'other' in any political space. These measures try to regulate the circulation of the population in a way that possibilities to connect with others are prevented. Second, such measures draw and oblige persons to construct a 'we' that does not allow any recognition nor acknowledgement of the value of differences, not on the inside of the same collective 'we', nor with 'them'.

The erasure of differences of thought, action, political projects, family values and social behaviour transforms citizens into warriors.

A secure peace

As examined in the previous section, Alvaro Uribe (2001) expressed his disregard for the democratic political regime from the inception of his campaign. For Uribe, democratic spaces have been black holes through which terrorists have infiltrated and corrupted the good society (ibid.). Therefore, to put an end to this threat those democratic spaces were closed. Part of this representation of democracy and democratic expressions as dangers has led the executive to engage in a persecution of NGOs which defend human rights. The president's public accusation of Amnesty International (AI) in June 2004 as being a 'terrorist-sympathiser' was a clear articulation of the way the state hails subjects to adopt the identity categories depicted in the DSP.

On 15 June 2004, thirty-four people were massacred in La Gabarra, in the Colombian province of Norte de Santander. The next day, during a police ceremony, the president asked 'why Amnesty International had kept silence in front of this massacre perpetrated by the narco-terrorist guerrillas FARC' (Uribe,

2004b: 1). In his words, NGOs could not be ideologically biased because they ought to be beyond any political appreciation. Human rights NGOs, like AI, could then not label state acts of authority against terrorists as human rights violations (ibid.: 1–2). President Uribe made clear that AI had to actively belong to 'us' or face the consequences of being inscribed in the category 'terrorists/other'.

> *Por guardar unas reglas de cortesía hipócritas y no tener el valor de denunciar a Amnistía Internacional, hemos permitido que legitimen al terrorismo internacionalmente. No. Con este Gobierno no es eso.* (Ibid.: 2)

The president gave Amnesty an ultimatum. It had to choose with whom it sided: 'with the ones who killed thirty-four peasants in La Gabarra, with the terrorists who have killed policemen and soldiers, causing mourning to their families, or with the Colombian institutions' (ibid.). The president framed AI as one of those NGOs which go around EU institutional corridors accusing the Colombian government of being 'terrorist', while at home (i.e. in Colombia), such NGOs side with the terrorists. According to Uribe (ibid.), such two-facedness made NGOs shut up in the face of violent acts committed by terrorists.

The president underscored how the quality of belonging to 'us' cannot remain implicit but rather must be an active role. It needs to be acted upon each and every one or face the consequences of being labelled a terrorist-sympathiser. Against this accusation, AI responded by saying that it sided with the victims.

> *Estos ataques contra Amnistía Internacional se dan coincidiendo con los esfuerzos del gobierno colombiano de conseguir el respaldo de la Unión Europea al proceso de diálogo con paramilitares … Amnistía Internacional espera que la comunidad internacional siga manteniéndose firme insistiendo en que tales procesos no terminen garantizando la impunidad de los responsables de violaciones de los derechos humanos o del derecho internacional humanitario.* (AI, 2004c: 1–2)

This last remark made by AI takes us to the core of the puzzle: the concept of a *secure peace*. Within the discursive limits of the DSP, peace appears as the demobilisation process of paramilitary groups. This process, in which the in/security policy plays a vital role, is intertwined with the construction of a large group of (former) combatants who are reinscribed in the category 'citizens'. The office of the high commissioner for peace advertises the Peace Policy as follows:

> *Para lograr que Colombia consiga la tan anhelada paz … la 'Política de Seguridad Democrática' … tiene como objetivo primordial garantizar el derecho de cualquier ciudadano a gozar de la seguridad como principio básico de desarrollo y bienestar. Sin seguridad no hay paz, sin seguridad no hay progreso, sin seguridad no hay confianza para la inversión, y por tanto no hay desarrollo.* (Oficina del Alto Comisionado para la Paz, 2004)[8]

In/security serves as grounds for development, progress, investment opportunities and peace. The Peace Policy dictates that *if there is no security, there is no peace*; only by achieving in/security can peace be achieved. Within these limits, on 23 December 2002, President Uribe sanctioned Law 782/2002 and issued its correspondent Executive Decree (128/2003). These enabled the state to initiate processes of demobilisation of armed groups with no political status and to grant amnesty for crimes already committed. Economic rewards for information were to be received as part of the demobilisation and reincorporation programme (Mininterior, 2004). The rewards were intended to prevent terrorism, and were included in the package like health and employment benefits.

This legal prerogative was designed for the paramilitary forces, which had been promising to enter a ceasefire since December 2002. However, 'despite the declared cease-fire, paramilitaries were still responsible for massacres, targeted killings, "disappearances", torture, kidnappings and threats. They were allegedly responsible for the killing or "disappearance" of at least 1,300 people in 2003, over 70 per cent of all attributable, non-combat, politically related killings and "disappearances"' (AI, 2003: 5–6).

In July 2003, government and paramilitary leaders signed the Santa Fé de Ralito Agreement, in which paramilitary groups promised a complete demobilisation by the end of 2005.[9] The agreement also included the commitment by the paramilitary to eradicate illegal crops and to provide compensation to the victims. President Uribe agreed that the crimes against humanity which the paramilitary leaders and low-rank combatants had carried out would be punished with a maximum prison sentence of eight years. Uribe promised not to sign any extradition order for the paramilitary leaders to the US, where they faced charges of drug trafficking and were on the list of foreign terrorist organisations.[10]

Part of this promise materialised through a law to be passed in Congress which the high peace commissioner had the task of pursuing. This law, initially called *Alternatividad Penal* (Penal Alternativity Law), was later renamed *Ley de Justicia y Paz* (Justice and Peace Law) and was finally approved as Law 975/2005.[11] The demobilisations were agreed to result in the reincorporation of former combatants into civilian life and contributed to the state in/security strategy by reducing the labour of illegal armed groups. Their confessions were used as a source of military information 'to stop illegal armed groups' assaults and formulate military counterattacks (Anaya, 2006: 2). In this way, it was made clear that the demobilisation process was a key element in fighting the war against terror.

From August 2002 until October 2008, the government's invitation for terrorists to lay down their arms, return to 'the nuclear family and abandon a clandestine life' (DSP, 2003: §116) had been heeded by some 49,000 demobilised persons, out of which roughly 31,000 were combatants who had demobilised in collective acts. The rest did so individually (Presidency of Colombia, 2008). The main common characteristic between collective and individual demobilisations is that both imply disarmament, provision of information to the security forces and reincorporation into civilian life. However, it is worth highlighting several important differences between collective and individual demobilisations to show how the DSP practices inform geopolitical and biopolitical security measures.

Collective demobilisations take place by order of the armed group's leader, which implies a hierarchical structure and obedience. These (unequal) power relations do not automatically disappear with the demobilisation act (Iniciativa de Mujeres por la Paz, 2006: 15). On the other hand, individual demobilisations take place based on combatants voluntarily abandoning the armed group. For many of them, this implies being labelled as traitors and thus living in constant fear of being killed by former comrades (Anaya, 2007: 16). Whereas most of the collective demobilisations take place in the locality where the armed groups operate, the characteristics of individual demobilisations imply the relocation from where the person was living with the armed group to a shelter in distant urban areas called *Casa de Paz* (House of Peace). At the same time, the isolation in the House of Peace is also an incentive for former combatants to hand information to the military forces since 'to give information that leads to capture former commanders or helps disband their former block or group is a way of protecting their own lives' (ibid.).

Since the project of state in/security overtly seeks to regulate the constitution of the nuclear family (DSP, 2003: §116), once the demobilised person has been assigned a shelter, his/her family is also relocated there. This has had significant effects on the circulation restrictions of the demobilised population and their relatives who have been summoned into the House of Peace. The stressful situation provoked by this 'secure family reunion', together with high levels of anxiety in the shelters, has resulted in an increased number of cases of domestic violence and abuse (Anaya, 2007: 15).[12]

Additionally, collapsing the ideas of nation and family in the name of in/security is further exposed as a practice that shapes who and where 'we' are by telling 'us' what a 'normal and secure family' ought to be by trying to contain communities in a seemingly coherent project of nation-state (Shapiro, 2001). The state demands from 'good citizens' to pay their in/security obligations to the nation by providing information to the security forces and to 'become one of us' by joining the nuclear family. However, whereas in demobilisations men are publicly recognised as former warriors and, once reinstituted into legality, as 'citizens' and sources of information in the war on terror, women are hailed to fulfil 'traditional' in/security duties for the biological and symbolic reproduction of the nation (Yuval-Davis, 1997). This practice of individual demobilisations called upon women to perform the desecuritisation of former male combatants, emphasising how women ought to signify the reincorporation of males into society (Yuval-Davis and Anthias, 1989: 7).

Nationalist women's duties are also present in collective processes of demobilisation where nation, state in/security and nuclear family turn into a complex (self-proclaimed coherent) unity that is presented as a security issue and, beyond the limits of public debate, scrutiny and accountability (Jabri, 2006). In the case of the city of Medellín, which in the period 2003–2006 received approximately thirteen per cent of all demobilisations in Colombia (i.e. 4,000 demobilised men and forty women, according to the Alcaldía de Medellín, 2006: 5), the reincorporation of former demobilised paramilitaries was geared toward 'turning warriors into citizens' (Iniciativa de Mujeres por la Paz, 2006: 15).

For this purpose, the local administration designed the institutional 'Peace and Reconciliation Programme: model of intervention for returning to legality' (PPR). The PPR assured that former combatants were successfully turned into citizens, defined by the local administration as a process in which the individual is prepared to fully enter society and acquire a formal job (Alcaldía de Medellín, 2007: 6). According to the PPR guidelines (ibid.), there were seven programmes of intervention to 'turn warriors into citizens', dealing with the precise reaccommodation of demobilised combatants' ways of living to fit legality.[13] The PPR supplied former combatants with two years of monthly stipends, training courses and job offers. These conditions sought to make demobilised persons 'economically productive and politically active citizens' (ibid.: 7) with clean records.

Despite suggestions to the contrary, according to testimonies by demobilised persons collected in the PPR itself (ibid.), their motives to join illegal armed groups were not financial reasons but external threats, the death of a loved one and conflicts with family members, friends and neighbours.[14] In the face of such reasons, less than twenty per cent argued that financial motivations led them to join paramilitary groups (ibid.). The picture that arises is in clear contradiction with the definition of violence espoused by the Colombian government (DSP, 2003). Listening to the testimonies of demobilised persons dissolves the frame for understanding violence according to the DSP postulates of the war against terror. These testimonies highlight the fact that there is much more to political violence than mere greed.

The state disregards the narratives of demobilised persons when these enter in contradiction to the official definition of violence. This is done in an attempt to normalise demobilised paramilitaries so that they can belong to the accepted political community. Demobilised paramilitaries are 'helped to verbalise and narrate what has happened to them; they receive counselling to help them accommodate once more to the social order and re-form relationships of trust' (Edkins, 2003: 9). Those who comply with the security programme are inscribed as belonging to the good citizenry. Those who dare to narrate unauthorised stories about the involvement of politicians, state officials and military forces in the organisation and financing of paramilitary groups, are excluded.[15]

This way, the state contours the limits of acceptable memories of the past, only allowing those whose speech and behaviour are set within the limits of the

DSP to belong to the 'nation'. These demobilised and obedient citizens contribute to construct the legitimate role of the state as conciliatory, as an entity detached from the traumatic past of violence and that now offers itself as the solution to war (Edkins, 2003). The demobilisation programme so reconciles state violence, both in the past and in the present, by adopting the narratives of violence of paramilitarism in Colombia as part of a linear history of events that legitimise the sovereign authority of the state as the tool for reconciliation, forgiveness and peace.

The demobilisation process so becomes a crucial part of the war strategy. Demobilisations are practices informed by the DSP that aim at constructing citizens fit to fight in the army of good people. At the same time, this process reinforces the state's legitimacy because it enables it to present itself as the solution to violence, as provider of security and as a conciliatory entity separated from the crimes of the past. As Jenny Edkins (2003) suggests, the state needs these traumas in order to reproduce itself as the mechanism for reconciliation. Just as the state needs insecurities to dynamically produce itself as the provider of security (Campbell, 1998; Dillon, 1996) and just like the state needs crisis to assert its identity (Weldes, 1999), so does the state require the trauma of violence (Edkins, 2003).

The notion of a 'secure peace', the promise made by the state in the DSP for those glorious future days in which 'security' will prevail, keeps postponing freedoms until the time when violence and authority give birth to peace. The trap in confusing processes of reconciliation and peace with demobilisation, as it is argued by the government when making peace synonymous with demobilisation, is rooted in the very way the state conceives of the armed conflict.

> *Cualquier política de paz tiene que ver con la interpretación del conflicto armado. ... Es necesario comenzar entonces por reconocer la guerra, entender su racionalidad y articular una política de paz ... que muestre de manera clara y confiable la disponibilidad del gobierno de dialogar sin que necesariamente se 'arrodille el enemigo'.* (Leal, 2004: 96)

We find ourselves again facing the problematic of representations. The Colombian situation is articulated as a democratic nation under the threat of narco-terrorism and, therefore, the only conceivable notion of peace is a demobilisation process. The self-evident consequence of this representation is that in/security keeps legitimating state violence and driving the victims' pain and grief to feed the war. The cycle of revenge and violence is not arrested and in/security co-opts any notion of peace by making both terms synonymous.

However, the provocations prompted by in/security discourses in the war on terror are manifold. Some identify alternative and less harmful ways of dealing with pain:

> To grieve, and to make grief itself into a resource for politics, is not to be resigned to inaction, but it may be understood as the slow process by which we develop a point of identification with suffering itself. The disorientation of grief – 'Who have I become?' or, indeed, 'What is left of me?' 'What is it in the Other that I have lost?' – posits the 'I' in the mode of unknowingness. (Butler, 2004: 30)

Consequently, the ways the problems are posed must be altered. And not just exchanging victims for victimisers, but actually rethinking the very way in which subjectivity is conceived. To accept and to assume grief and pain, as opposed to negating them, and to deactivate the cycle of violence and revenge, there has to be a different form of agency that enables reconfiguring power relations toward more respectful and peaceful horizons (Butler, 1995a: 46). This is where I would like to turn our attention now: what are the possibilities for reworking the very matrix of power of the DSP towards more peaceful alternatives?

Politics, peaces and identities

The question of peace is the main ethical concern of this book. There has been a heightened situation of violence in Colombia for decades to which the state has reacted by implementing measures such as those announced in the DSP. The effects of this discourse are diffused in society, making the achievement of in/security the precondition for politics, freedom and peace. Here the important question arises, how to arrest the cycle of violence? If every citizen, whether as an armed or unarmed soldier of the army of good people, fights actively in this war, recreating and reproducing direct, structural and cultural violence (Galtung, 1996), how can violence be stopped? How to stop this cycle of revenge fed by grief, anger and pain that feeds the war on terror?

Although I believe there is no single or simple answer to these puzzling questions, I suggest approaching the problem by acknowledging a collection of serious issues. The first one is the impossibility of in/security (Dillon, 1996). Politics and freedoms cannot be postponed until the day in which *democratic security is a reality for all Colombians* as the government has argued. In/security, as was explored in former chapters, is a trap. It is a worldview that feeds upon its own threats, which is indispensable for the discourse on state sovereignty and which cannot be achieved (ibid.; Martínez, 2001a; 2001b).

The sacrifices made in the name of in/security, the freedoms and rights renounced in order to pursue the higher promise of security, should not be erased from view. Forming an army of forty-four million Colombians cannot be the foundation of democratic politics. To train, to oblige and to induce people to live in a depoliticised and transparent way cannot be the solution to the problem of state authority.

I suggest looking for alternatives inspired by proposals which do not operate under the in/security logic, which do not naturalise and freeze individual and collective subjects, like the 'state', 'us' and 'them'. Proposals that, quite on the contrary, respect differences and value otherness. A good start might be to recognise that 'we' need the 'other' to exist, that it enriches 'us', that we can learn together and that our differences are not necessarily negative and deadly.

Peace studies has shed light on some important matters in this respect. The proposal made in 'A call for Many Peaces' (2006), the work of peace researchers Wolfgang Dietrich and Wolfgang Sützl, suggested the notion of peace as vernacular, as born out of specific contexts which should be respected in their different expressions. In this sense, peace starts losing its singular character and resembles a plural. It turns into the notion of peaces, which break away from the secure and violent illusion that defines peace as synonymous with security. Peaces are, then, open to resignification and plurality. The notion of peaces takes over the univocal notion of peace-as-security and highlights peaces as a possibility.

Along the same line of thought, Vicent Martínez has developed *Filosofía para hacer las paces* (2001b) in which he recreates forms-of-life based on the recognition of our connections with others and our own vulnerability and fragility. He has also proposed the comprehension of our performative identities in combination with a different notion of responsibility, underscoring the conception of a subject that is highly implicated with others (Martínez, 2002). This concept of the subject as constituted by otherness, and not just sameness, is paramount for reconciliation and political transformation of our deadly identities (Maalouf, 2000) into more peaceful understandings of 'us' and 'them' (Butler, 2004: 44). The instigation to recognise the other in 'me' as Butler has stated, is indispensable to comprehend 'that my own foreignness to myself is, paradoxically, the source of my ethical connection with others' (ibid.: 46).

Following this train of thought, there could be a radical change in the way we conceive of ourselves and of otherness, recognising the value of differences and allowing them to blossom in political encounters where transformation is possible. If this change does not take place, we will reproduce the in/security logic, only exchanging the labels under which 'us' and 'them' stand and without challenging the modes of exclusion and the legitimation of violence.

As Maria Stern (2004: 3) emphasises, 'the violent ramifications of the (im)possibility of security are often repeated in the very sites of marginality where people attempt to procure safety and resist the violence and exclusion inflicted by hegemonic practices of securing national (or other dominant identities)'. In this sense, Stern connects this (im)possible representation of in/security with the need to rethink identities as 'constantly being re-created; they shift and change, even instantaneously' (ibid.: 6).

If this type of subjectivity is assumed as always spilling over and exceeding representations (Edkins and Pin-Fat, 1999), and at the same time recognising our intimate relations to 'others' (Butler, 2004) and to 'ourselves' (Connolly, 1991), then we open up possibilities for transformation. The results cannot be known in advance because politics are insecure (Dillon, 1996); they are unpredictable and herein lays the importance of promoting political encounters where transformation can take place.

There have been various resistance discourses in Colombia in recent years, some of which deserve further investigation as they testify to the possibilities for resisting the DSP call for in/security in the identities made the centre of attention of the present book: state, nationals and others. Their different discourses of resistance allow comprehension of how the discursive formations of the DSP and the practices that produce identity categories necessitate the investment of the subject to articulate them, even if it is, as Stuart Hall (1996a) mentions, a temporary point of suture. I am interested in showing how the process of identification is not automatic, perfectly coherent and permanent. By looking at several discourses of resistance to the DSP, I want to underscore the always changing and dynamic tenet of the process of identification.

In the next chapter, I delineate a framework for analysing why the discourses of the FARC-EP guerrillas do not challenge the logic of in/security of the state discourse. Second, I investigate the design and implementation of a nonviolence state programme in the Province of Antioquia, which has proposed alternatives to the DSP. Likewise, different discourses of indigenous groups have confronted the DSP programmes with an energetic understanding of peace. It is quite relevant to know these responses against the mentioned background of the (im)possibility of in/security (Stern, M., 2004) and to analyse how their resistance is (or is not) articulated with a different logic that reworks the postulates of in/security. In this section, I evaluate the resistance discourse of the indigenous group Paeces del Cauca and highlight their main characteristics in relation to the examination of the DSP as seen throughout this chapter.

I believe that these multiple contributions have to be taken into account if the diverse expressions of violence and the feelings of pain and suffering are to be transformed into more peaceful ways of relating within and between 'us' and 'them'.

Conclusion

The objective of this chapter has been to distinguish the identity categories that the DSP *constructs* and *produces*. Taking identity as a process which is never complete, which is always in the process of *becoming*, the objectives of this chapter were first to recognise the subject categories produced by the in/security discourse in Colombia for the state, the sovereign people ('the nation) and 'us' and 'them'.

The construction of political identities produces a *nation*, which cannot mourn its deaths anymore, and needs a strong *state* erected on the principle of authority. Since *Colombia* appears to be *a democratic nation under the threat of terrorism*, peace and politics have to be sacrificed until security is achieved. The representations of dangers depicted in the DSP are reduced to a single threat: *terrorism*, which subsumes all other dangers and has to be fought by the whole society as an obligation. Everybody has to fight against terrorism by supporting state violence with *solidarity*. Solidarity can be expressed via participating directly in the armed confrontations as peasant soldiers, or via informing and reporting to the security forces any *suspect persons* and activities. The goal of the government is to create an army of forty-four million Colombians to defeat terrorism.

The idealisation of the category *Colombians* that the DSP creates, in a concomitant way to the representations of danger, has three intertwined levels, its common origins, its common present and a common destiny. In regards to the *common origins*, the DSP retakes elements of the construction of a virtuous armed republican citizen articulated since the times of Independence. This mythical birth of the nation is used by the state to highlight the republican violent virtues for contemporary political ends in the war on terror. The *common present* of the Colombians is represented through the lenses of the danger of terrorism as a nation who cannot mourn more dead. Pain and grief are thereby used in the DSP to feed the war of the good society against terrorism. *Good nationals* are willing to sacrifice their freedoms and lives in the name of in/security. They act in solidarity with the security forces and report any suspicious activities.

'Once security is achieved, people will enjoy their freedoms' and 'security will give birth to peace' promised the president (2002b: 20). This promise, in which the future is the time-space that takes precedence over the present, is of vital importance to consider. All the sacrifices are made in the name not just of security, but of achieving security in the future. The *common secure destiny* of Colombians is used to sacrifice politics in the present, channelling the hopes and aspirations of a *nation* that has lived in war for far too long. These feelings of hope invest the promise of in/security with the fantasy of representing a future destiny when *security will give birth to peace*.

The DSP also constructs the ideal of a Colombian *state* in which the threat of terrorism informs the state's interests and character as an authoritarian subject which is recovering from a historical moment of weakness. Therefore, the state needs to recover its authority and use force to eradicate the illegitimate violence in the country. As a *father taking care of his women-and-children* the state appears to redefine its subjectivity according to order and authority.

The political identity of the 'other' is subsumed under the label *terrorist*. The options that the state offers to the 'other' are either to convert to one of 'us', abandoning a criminal life and returning to the nuclear family (DSP, 2003: §116), or to be exterminated. As the concept of 'solidarity' serves to divide and separate 'good' from 'bad' people, 'we' have to fear and to exercise control and supervision not just against the 'other' or enemy, but 'we' are ever more looking for unveiling the otherness in ourselves in order to extirpate it. The notion of dangerousness, at the level of the potentialities of the individual, regulates the connection and circulation of the population, now seen as a mass of suspects in the war on terror.

In the second part of this chapter, I discussed the production of the political identities created by the DSP, and showed how state and non-state geopolitical and biopolitical actions hail subjects to adopt the positions depicted in the in/security discourse. The *information and cooperation networks* appear as one of the clearest manifestations of the politics of in/security of the DSP. Citizens are turned into warriors of the army of good people by being paid for information that leads to pre-emptively capture *suspect persons* without the need for judicial orders or evidence. In the rural areas, *peasant soldiers* complement the army of good people. The militarisation of police functions is increased by this measure in which the bodies of the rural and poor population are drawn into the war on terror as sacrifice for the security of the state.

A *secure peace* is one of the effects of the logic of in/security depicted in the DSP. The process of demobilisation of the paramilitary groups has been based on the notion that *peace will come after security is achieved*. The reintegration programmes of former demobilised paramilitaries overtly turned them into citizens/soldiers of the war against terror. Whenever narratives of former demobilised people challenge the official definition of Colombia as a democratic nation-state under the threat of narco-terrorism, they are excluded from the political community of *the good ones*. The state so seeks to guard its role as provider of security and attempts to present itself as a conciliatory entity, separated from the traumatic violence of its past. The problematic appropriation of the state to reinforce its role as conciliatory entity of the past and present history of paramilitarism in Colombia has impeded this process of promoting reconciliation. By making in/security a precondition for peace, the demobilisation process fuels grief and pain into the cycle of violence.

This chapter leaves a collection of enquiries regarding the construction and production of the identity categories that the DSP reproduces. These threads point to proposals that rethink the relationships between 'us' and 'them' and call for the recognition of the close connection to the 'other'. They also attempt to reconfigure a theoretical and political stand that does not work under the logic of in/security. The following chapter will attempt to draw an interpretative skeleton that allows analysing resistance discourses provoked by the DSP. Their analysis, reflection and exploration are necessary to comprehend some responses to the subject-positions created in the DSP and, as such, we might better recognise political identities as imperfect articulations.

NOTES

1   In the second section of this chapter, where some of the micro-practices of the DSP are analysed, I detail how such identification and accusation among neighbours for interpersonal and political conflicts predominate as the main motif for denouncing them as suspect citizens. This practice so shows the highly problematic of 'dangerousness' and

the reproduction of fear and mistrust among peoples it encourages. Furthermore, when accused persons are detained by the military, their legal rights to due process are suspended, expanding the arbitrary power of the state over the regulation of life. For an analysis of the problematic notion of 'dangerousness' in the global war on terror, see especially Vivienne Jabri (2006), who explicitly deals with how such measures target specific racial and cultural communities disclosing its racist tenet. In the Colombian case, discrimination as a form of direct, structural and cultural violence (Galtung, 1996) necessarily calls for also bringing to the front, next to racism, the entrenched identification and marginalisation based on socio-economic class.

2   After the prefaces by the president and the minister of defence, the DSP document is divided into sections for which the symbol '§' is used.

3   Luis Lobo-Guerrero (2007) argues that kidnap and ransom (K&R) insurance is part of the *security dispositif* that problematises kidnapping in terms of risk by rendering people as 'specific populations with the purpose of promoting and protecting their capacity to circulate' (ibid.: 320). Lobo-Guerrero analyses a large collection of micro-practices through which this insurance proceeds, pointing at the particular ways in which the securitisation of the concrete populations involved turn kidnapping prospects into 'the referent object of protection for which the instrument of K&R insurance is deployed' (ibid.: 320–3). In other words, K&R insurance 'is aimed at securing a potentiality rather than an actuality' (ibid.: 326), making this instrument both a form of reparational and preventive securities (ibid.: 328). The last reflections of Lobo-Guerrero (ibid.: 331–2) are extremely useful for analysing the in/security discourse, since they point at how biopolitical analyses of security may have no beginning or end and no levels of analysis that can be split into sectors and dimensions that add to a seemingly coherent whole. For him, biopolitics 'needs to be approached as a complex emerging ensemble with salient features' that demands that general forms of power, like sovereign and biopower, are understood 'while analysing the micro-practices through which they proceed' (ibid.). This call for analytical tools to understand how a particular reality is constantly being made, echoes the interrogations and puzzles that prompted this investigation of the DSP. Only by analysing detailed accounts of the micro-practices of geo- and biopolitics, I believe, can we start making sense of a configuration of in/security, identities and politics that legitimises political violence. At the same time, this book opens a future possibility for a more profound biopolitical engagement with the DSP, one that besides focusing on the geopolitics of this pervasive grammar of peace and war also looks at crucial political rationalities and security technologies, such as risk and insurance, with more depth (Dillon, 2008; Lobo-Guerrero, 2007).

4   The Peace Policy is further elaborated in this chapter under the subheading 'A secure peace'.

5   The testimony made of Slavenca Drakulic – compiled in *Theories of Nationalism* (Özkirimli, 2000) – has struck me profoundly because, I believe, nationalism is a prominent and violent feature of how the DSP portrays the common present of the Colombian nation. Drakulic recalls that the war fought in the name of the nation has reduced her to one dimension. 'The trouble with this nationhood, however, is that whereas before, I was defined by my education, my job, my ideas, my character – and, yes, my nationality too – now I feel stripped of all that. I am nobody because I am not a person any more' (Drakulic, quoted in Özkirimli, 2000: 167). Because I would not like to decontextualise both wars, the Croatian and the Colombian, I prefer to leave this testimony as a footnote, yet still call the attention to the violence that is forced upon subjectivities that, as Drakulic comments, are too fluid, contradictory and dynamic to be fully represented by fixed identity categories (Edkins and Pin-Fat, 1999; Stern, 2005).

6   For a constant update of the increasing number of registered private security companies in Colombia, visit the website of the Superintendence of Vigilance and Private Security (www. http://www.supervigilancia.gov.co).

7   Even though the 'Soldier for a day' strategy was supposedly disbanded in March 2003, human rights organisations report that 'children are still used by the military to incriminate their parents' (AI, 2004a: 16–17).

8   The Peace Policy of the High Commissioner for Peace, as it was announced in 2004, has been reworked in the past couple of years. Since May 2006, the High Commissioner for Peace announces the Peace Policy in direct relation to the demobilisation process of paramilitary forces (Oficina del Alto Comisionado para la Paz, 2006).

9   By December 2006, more than 31,000 members of self-defence groups had entered the collective demobilisation programme of the government (Presidencia de la República-Oficina del Alto Comisionado para la Paz, 2006: 100).

10 The process of demobilisation of paramilitary groups is – I believe – a historical episode in the political landscape. The nexus between military officials, congressmen, national and regional political figures – including President Uribe himself – and paramilitary leaders have been named in press-jargon 'the para-politics scandal'. 'Scandalous' is not so much about the coming to light of evidence on how the legal, armed and political apparatuses of the state have worked hand in hand with paramilitary forces, since such connections have been disclosed for a long time. Scandalous seems to be how institutional arrangements have been set into place in order to cover up these connections, like the extradition of paramilitary leaders to the US when they started confessing the financial and political involvement of Colombian politicians in paramilitary organisations (*El Espectador*, 2008).

11 The Law 975/2005 created the *Comisión Nacional de Reparación y Reconciliación* (National Commission for Reparation and Reconciliation), charged with the function of coordinating the demobilisation process. In sentence C-370/06, the Constitutional Court tried to delineate the institutional framework for state and non-state agencies to take over the demobilisation process to make effective the rights to truth, justice and compensation. The institutional apparatus is highly complex and involves a large number of institutions and procedures. A lack of transparency of what is being pursued with the demobilisation process (what) and the absence of a clear structure of accountability (how, who and when) is evident as far as the demobilisation process was thought of as part of the war on terror strategy and, as is my argument, not as a peace process. The legal procedures for demobilisation were signed before the reincorporation into civilian life had been thought out and before it was clear how the rights of the victims could be safeguarded and protected. This sequence in time reflects the priorities of the in/security agenda and discloses how the notion of a *secure peace* severely diminishes the possibilities of turning this war strategy into a peace process. The institutional make-up of the demobilisation process can be consulted directly on the website of the commission under www.cnrr.org.co.

12 Women suffer most of this domestic violence, since the state assumes that demobilised men (approximately eighty-five per cent of registered demobilised persons according to the Policía Nacional, 2007) are married in a heterosexual arrangement. Henceforth, the different institutions in charge of the demobilisation process reunite the family (composed of 'man, woman and children') as part of the state project of in/security. The state, however, has not yet considered increased domestic violence against women as direct result of the demobilisation process. For an excellent account of how Colombian processes of demobilisation since the late 1980s exhibit and produce sexual and gender discrimination, see Londoño and Nieto (2006).

13 Simultaneously, the support programmes are based on and target financial reasons for the continuation of political violence. As the national government assumes, the PPR is founded on the conviction that the problem of violence in the country is a consequence of a weak state authority in the past and keeps being nurtured by the desire of narco-terrorists to fill their pockets with money (DSP, 2003). Henceforth, the solutions to violence offered are to acquire a formal job and hand in information to win the war on terror, becoming 'one of us'.

14 As of July 2006, the official data reported that for more than twenty-five per cent the motives for joining paramilitary groups were avenging the death of a loved one (Alcaldía de Medellín, 2006). This topic of revenge has been widely researched by cultural scholars in Medellín (Blair, 1999, 2005; León, 2004; Salazar, 1993, 2001, 2002; Vélez, 2000) and what some of these findings suggest is that acts of violence perpetrated by young males have been justified and encouraged by the traditional female figure of motherhood (Vélez, 2000). The feminine figure of the mother in need of protection by a hyper-masculine warrior son keeps feeding the cycle of revenge in neighbourhoods of Medellín. Paradoxically, such relationships of a mother taking care of her children and in need of protection by a male figure which is strong, exhibits warrior features and acts as financial support of the family is precisely the representation of the family encouraged at the institutional level as part of the national in/security strategy.

15 Several paramilitary leaders, who started confessing the involvement of Colombian politicians and businesspersons with paramilitary groups, were extradited to the US in May 2008 where their unsettling narratives about the joint work between paramilitaries, politicians and militaries were silenced (Gómez, 2008).

5

Resistance and peaces

AS REPEATED THROUGHOUT THIS BOOK, the process of identification is a constant and unfinished negotiation (Stern, 2005). The working definition of identification which sustains this research is based on the notion that identity is an *articulation* (Hall, 1996a) for which the revealing of discursive formations is not enough to recognise processes of identification. Subjects need to invest in their positions to perform, albeit imperfectly, their subjectivities as specifically constituted in particular representations.

The ideal identity category that the DSP constructs for the 'state' was examined in the previous chapter. This ideal is pictured as an authoritarian entity that is recovering from a historical moment of weakness that resulted in the proliferation of terrorism in the country. The category 'us' is informed by the representation of the threat of terrorism as a mass of potential dangerous suspects who need to join the army of good people in a fight of all against terror. For 'them', the ideal identity category is portrayed in the DSP as fixed 'others', terrorists who have nothing in common with 'us'. Finally, the notion of active solidarity with the security forces in the fight against terrorism was highlighted in order to distinguish the markers that draw the boundaries of belonging between 'us' and 'them'.

We have explored different state and non-state measures that hail subjects to adopt the specific subject positions designed for them in the DSP. Among these practices of in/security, citizens' warning networks, peasant soldiers and the demobilisation process of paramilitary groups were analysed insofar as state and non-state violence create the notion of a *secure peace* that fuels the very violence the state promises to halt.

However, as was pointed out above, those idealisations are not enough to comprehend the process of identification. Therefore, we are now looking more deeply into different responses to those identity categories. How have some subjects resisted the DSP? This is the question that informs the present chapter and whose consideration is necessary to provide a more complete picture of the

177

effects that the DSP has on the constitution of political identities in Colombia. This picture must be conceived of as only an incomplete representation of what, in Hall's (ibid.) words, is a process of identification. It is not my intention to present these thoughts in a way that could be interpreted as *the true* depiction of the political subjectivities in question. My aim is to investigate one of many possible readings of the current political situation while paying close attention to the contingent character of identity.

In this vein, I want to underscore that the three discourses of resistance highlighted in the following section emanate from the very identities already studied in former chapters. The discourse of the FARC-EP shows the responses of 'others', the nonviolent programme of the Province of Antioquia discloses the very madeness of the identity of the state and, finally, the discourse of nonviolence of the indigenous group Paeces del Cauca demonstrates a possible provocation of the DSP by the 'nationals' themselves. This collection of discourses corroborates that identities are not coherent, unitary or unchangeable ways of being and becoming. On the contrary, by looking at these discourses, the identities of state, nationals and others as they are constructed in the DSP emerge as a permanent negotiation of contradictory discursive practices (Stern, 2005). In short, identities can never be fully represented (Edkins and Pin-Fat, 1999).

With these intentions in mind, the present chapter is arranged with an opening discussion of a brief theoretical outline, which is necessary to interpret the different resistance discourses to the DSP within the particular peace studies perspective espoused in this book. In the words of Maria Stern (2005), I am investigating resistance discourses against the background of the impossibility of in/security. More specifically, in the Colombian case, the resistance discourses I am looking into are those in which the logic of in/security is not reproduced.

Following this theoretical outline, I will present an analysis of resistance discourses to the DSP. I argue that the resistance discourses of armed groups reproduce the violent logic of in/security from the margins. Therefore, they do not constitute responses that arrest the cycle of violence and revenge but, on the contrary, continually reproduce it. I then consider two other types of discourses that aim to transform conflicts peacefully: the nonviolence programme of the Province of Antioquia 2001–2003 and the resistance discourse of the indigenous community Paeces del Cauca. These two discourses are analysed through lenses that examine how these subjects invest in or resist the logic of in/security constructed and reproduced by the DSP. We will then evaluate how those resistance discourses have reworked the very matrix of power relations of the DSP to counter-propose different understandings of peace and in/security.

This chapter finishes with open questions in further need of study, which I call the *politics of affinity*. This collection of proposals emanates from peace and security studies and illustrates the need to rethink in/security in direct relation to possibilities for democratic politics. From a critique of the different identity categories that the DSP creates and the ways subjects are hailed into place, I would like to conclude by underscoring the heterogeneity of available responses to the in/security logic. The seeming coherence and force of in/security should not deter us from posing questions and criticising its rationale and violence. On the contrary, I call for continuing to analyse, rethink and challenge in/security discourses guided by introducing ethical concerns that open up possibilities for lessening harm and suffering. This complements the fact that my final comments and reflections are presented without attempting to render my own conclusions as definitive, but are rather offered as a *route* that should be explored persistently.

Resistance to in/security discourses

Before examining different resistance discourses to the DSP, there is the need to outline a theoretical stance from which to investigate them. This preliminary section focuses on two aspects of analysis. First, I follow the conceptualisation of power and resistance as twin notions introducing ethical concerns in terms of peaceful alternatives for conflict transformation. Second, I reconstruct a particular peace studies perspective on resistance discourses that informs the analysis of the resistance discourses to the DSP. Once this grid is drawn, the second section of the chapter will focus on resistance discourses as such in light of the question of how responses to the DSP can (or cannot) break away from the cycle of violence perpetuated by the state in/security discourse. Let us then begin this task by reviewing the notions of power and resistance as well as their symbiotic relationship and expressions.

Power, resistance and responsibility

It is crucial to remember that resistance discourses are, by definition, discourses in themselves. Although they may not necessarily emanate from the so-called sovereign power of the state but rather generally from marginalised groups, they are still subject to the characterisations already noted in regards to in/security discourses. In the current analysis, some of the basic points made in relation to discourses will be reviewed.

First, discourses are representations of *us-in-the-world*. They cannot be equated to the true depiction of the world or 'us', 'them', 'who we are', or 'as we have always been'. In this sense, discourses do not resemble and present *the truth* but, as one of their effects, they produce contextual truths. In this vein, 'each discourse or "discursive formation" is simultaneously enabling and limiting. ... Discourses are local, heterogeneous, and often incommensurable' (Flax, 1992: 452). This is what is commonly known as *discursive limits*: at the same time discourses enable certain production of power/knowledge, they restrain themselves from considering alternative possibilities (Butler, 2000). Hence, for any discourse to exist coherently, alternative options have to be excluded from view (Jackson, 2005). These boundaries have to be constantly reproduced and guarded; they cannot be set once and for all, since discourses are living texts that change and are challenged constantly (Weldes et al., 1999).

Because of the productive character of discourses, the limits of what and who can be spoken are vitally important. Based on Hall's contributions, Jutta Weldes et al. (ibid.: 13–14) argue that discourses produce certain codes of intelligibility which 'constitute the world as we know it and function in it: they tell us "what the world is and how it works, for all practical purposes"'. According to this line of thought, it is crucial to retake the notion of discourse as constitutive of particular subjects. As Judith Butler (1995b: 138) argues, 'discourse not merely represents or reports on pregiven practices and relations, but it enters into their articulation and is, in that sense, productive'.

Many different authors argue that resistance discourses are embedded in the matrix of power relations they resignify. Jenny Edkins and Véronique Pin-Fat (2004) state that there is no resistance that can be said to emanate from a pure stand, because resistance is already constituted within representations. In their terms, resistance is located as an inseparable part of power relations (ibid.: 4). Hence, 'where there is power, there is resistance, and yet, or rather consequently, this resistance is never in a position of exteriority in relation to power' (Foucault, 1990: 96).

In this line of reasoning, following a Foucauldian interpretative line, power should not be made equivalent to domination or violence. Power is conceptualised as relational and productive. It is understood as relational in the sense that it is 'not an object: "power is neither given, nor exchanged, nor recovered, but rather exercised ... it only exists in action"' (Edkins and Pin-Fat, 2004: 4). Therefore, power is also productive of social relations and subjectivities and is not merely repressive. 'It is one of the prime effects of power that certain bodies, certain gestures, certain discourses, certain desires, come to be identified and constituted as individuals' (ibid.: 5). Thus, power and violence are not synonymous. Whereas 'a relationship of violence acts upon a body or upon things; it forces, it bends, it breaks, it destroys, or it closes off all possibilities', a power relationship is articulated on the basis of the 'other' being 'recognised and maintained to the very end as a subject who acts' and it opens up 'a whole field of responses, reactions, results, and possible inventions' (Foucault quoted in ibid.: 12).

Resistance discourses play an important role in the construction of dominant discourses. They are the *margin*, what is left outside, the co-constitutive outside that is required for drawing boundaries and giving a sense of coherence to the internal/self. Since competing discourses cannot just mirror the gaps of dominant ones, they can pose different questions. Herein lays the possibility of resistance discourses for raising unauthorised issues outside of a specific discourse community (Butler, 1999; Gusterson, 1999). They can pose unexpected interrogations and disrupt the seeming unanimity and coherence of dominant discourses (Dillon, 1996; Salih, 2004: 9).

> [I]f we view hegemony in historical and processual terms, then the attempt by dominant groups and classes to impose a 'discursive regime' on the whole society can be seen as subject to contestation and never fully achieved. Struggle becomes possible and spaces for counterdiscourses and for practices of resistance are opened up. (Alonso, 1992: 405)

Therefore, even though resistance discourses are already inherent to the matrix of power relationships they resignify, this does not mean that their discursive limits are the same as the ones of the contested discourse(s). There is no perfect match between the gaps of dominant discourses and their resistance since there is no single *reality* or *truth* that they articulate (Butler, 2000). Resistance has the possibility of articulating different logics than just the remnants of hegemony. Because of this, resistance discourses cannot be conceived of as *just* the complement or subsidy of hegemonic practices or discursive formations. There is interplay and there are common grounds, but all of it takes place within a multiplicity for which there cannot be enough account (Butler, 1999). Consequently, there is

> a plurality of resistances, each of them a special case: resistances that are possible, necessary, improbable; others that are spontaneous, savage, solitary, concerted, rampant, or violent; still others that are quick to compromise, interested, or sacrificial; by definition they can only exist in the strategic field of power relations. (Agamben quoted in Edkins and Pin-Fat, 2004: 5)

As Ana María Alonso (1992: 418) argues, counter-discourses cannot be studied either as purely autonomous or as expressions of total encapsulation. Alonso states that, in light of the notion of dynamic cultural articulations of realities, discourses and identities, it would be more appropriate and useful to analyse and interpret resistance discourses as the 'dialectic of reproduction and transformation, accommodation and resistance'.

Such a process would resemble permanent negotiations emerging from possible resignifications. Therefore, the question that arises is 'what possibilities of mobilisation are produced on the basis of existing configurations of discourse and power? Where are the possibilities of reworking that very matrix of power by which we are constituted, of reconstituting the legacy of that constitution, and of working against each other those processes of regulation that can destabilise existing power regimes?' (Butler, 1995a: 46) As such, within these negotiations resistance – just like agency – is always and only a political prerogative:

> For if the subject is constituted by power, that power does not cease at the moment the subject is constituted, for that subject is never fully constituted, but is subjected and produced time and again. That subject is neither a ground nor a product, but the permanent possibility of a certain resignifying process, one which gets detoured and

stalled through other mechanism of power, but which is power's own possibility of being reworked. (Ibid.: 47)

It becomes crucial to understand resistance as *a possibility*, in the sense that responses of different subjects to discursive formations produced by hegemonic discourses are not inevitable and predetermined bindings. In the very repetitions, reproductions of identity categories, lie options for resignification, which can take place through (un)expected subversion and/or contestation. This interpretation of resistance has a clear link to the notion of performative identity (Butler, 1999). If the successful chaining of the subject to specific positions is not an expression of a preconstituted univocal self, but if the articulation is the very constitution of subjectivity, then we are looking into resistance as the possibility of being constituted in a disobedient way.

Vicent Martínez (2001a; 2001b; 2002; 2005) formulates proposals that combine both of these grounds, performative identity and resistance, but he adds a crucial element for the arguments espoused in this book in relation to political violence: ethical responsibility. Martínez (2001b: 127) recognises the diverse competences by which we constitute ourselves as particular subjects with possibilities for constructing peaces and/or for inflicting violence upon others. For him, the social construction of human relationships makes us accountable to others for what we do, say and undo (Martínez, 2002: 1). In this sense, Martínez (ibid.: 9–10) argues in a similar vein to Chantal Mouffe (1992: 372) when recognising that the performative character of discourses opens up possibilities for transforming power relations. In *Philosophy for Peaces*, Martínez (2001b; 2002) argues that these possibilities can lead to political actions that lessen harm and suffering: 'due to the intersubjective character of performativity, we have the possibility for resisting reproducing the subjugation of "others'" knowledge and for opening up the possibilities for contesting hegemonic discourses' (ibid.: 10).

Martínez points to the following necessary reflections that concern us: alternatives. For him, understanding the performativity and the virtual character of representations, such as wars, does not exempt us from responsibility. On the contrary, such understanding challenges us towards creating new forms of responsibility and new answers that keep up with the ever-changing contexts. Consequently, performativity within this framework necessarily calls for performing a political future that puts forward alternatives to what we currently denounce (ibid.: 11).

Keeping the words of Martínez in mind for actually resisting dominant discourses by proposing more peaceful and less violent alternatives, we now turn our focus of attention to the possibilities of resignifying the very sites of power for resisting the discourse of in/security.

Resistance, identities and in/security

As is clear by now, resistance discourses can challenge violent discursive practices. However, as we have seen throughout the last section, resistance is only *a possibility*. When we are concerned with studying resistance discourses that contest the discourse of in/security by challenging its rationale and violence, then the type of alternatives or negotiations that contesting discourses articulate should be taken into account. Following Vicent Martínez (ibid.), what I am looking for is whether the provocations and rearticulations to the discourse of in/security represent peaceful alternatives to the violence prompted by the DSP. If the provocations repeat the very logic of violent exclusion and legitimisation of political violence of the DSP, then the cycle of violence would not be arrested but rather reproduced from the margins.

Johan Galtung (2004) has referred to these different options by naming them the 'security approach and the peace approach'. His contributions help to clarify what is meant by proposing alternatives to the logic of in/security that break away from violence and exclusion. According to Galtung, both peace and security approaches try to cope with violence, but in diametrically opposed ways. The security approach is based upon portraying an evil party with strong capability and evil intention. The security approach must offer strength to defeat or deter the evil party, producing security to bring eventual peace (ibid.: 1). On the other hand, the peace approach is based on a conflict which needs to be transformed through empathy, creativity and nonviolence, which would generate possibilities for peace (ibid.: 1–2).

Thus, following Galtung (2004), not all alternatives proposed by marginal discourses are necessarily peaceful. Neither do they automatically break away from the spiral of violence. The naming of dangers (Campbell, 1998), crucial for the construction of both identities of 'self' and 'other' (Weldes et al., 1999), can also be violently inscribed in resistance discourses (Stern, 2005). Several authors have pointed out this paradox when investigating resistance discourses to in/security. How do resistance discourses articulate their identities through the inscription of foreignness? Who and what is identified in resistance discourses as sources of danger or insecurity? What do these denominations of dangers tell us about the political identities of 'self' and 'other'?

Diana Saco (1999) has investigated resistance discourses in cyberspace where hegemonic discourses on official restrictions on communication technologies and devices are met by negotiating resistance discourses of civil liberty groups. Saco argues that 'both camps [computer civil-liberties groups and the government] frame their competing articulations of security and insecurity through a liberal discourse' (ibid.: 271). In other words, both dominant discourses and their resistance articulate insecurities on the same grounds of a dichotomy between private and public spheres. Saco points out how both hegemonic and marginal discourses refer to the greater good of democracy to sustain their claims. The discussion keeps being fuelled along the same discursive lines and resistance discourses thus become part of the incitement to discourse that hegemonic practices provoke without challenging its founding grounds (ibid.: 287–9).

Among other authors who deal with paradoxes of resistance is Karena Shaw. Her investigation of the Native Women's Association of Canada (NWCA) reveals a complex negotiation of identities (2004). Shaw's analysis highlights another important point in the discussion on resistance: discourses of sovereignty are not exclusive to states (ibid.: 165). They can be reproduced in marginal sites that replicate the logic and inner workings of legitimised violence on the same political grounds. 'Sovereignty has framed political possibility, enabling and legitimating resistances to hegemony and the emergence of new political agents and subjectivities. However …, sovereignty remains at best an ambivalent discourse for marginalized peoples, deeply embedded as it is in an ontology that assumes and reproduces their marginalization' (ibid.).

Shaw argues how, when marginal discourses adopt the violent construction of a 'sovereign coherent self' in opposition to an 'other' with the purpose of resisting dominant discourses of sovereignty, marginal groups incorporate the very practices of violence they try to contest. 'The multiple differences of situation, history, and ontology amongst Aboriginal peoples must be erased or homogenized in order to claim sovereignty on their colonizer's terms' (ibid.: 180). Shaw's argument in regards to the tension arising between and among aboriginal resistance claims is worth recapitulating because they point to non-closure as a crucial feature of resistance, politics and identities:

> This tension is a dangerous one, but also, crucially, a productive one. It is an expression of serious contradictions and challenges that are deeply embedded in modern political thought and practices. Thus, they need to be opened up and worked on rather than 'resolved' at a symbolic or formal level. The crucial thing that must be resisted is closure, which is the assumption that the struggles expressed by these tensions can and should be contained within existing structures and discourses. (Ibid.: 182)

This call for non-closure is also expressed by R. B. J. Walker (2004). Walker argues that in discussions about resisting the discourse of sovereignty what ultimately is in question is 'the place of violence in political life, the constitutive role of violence in constituting an order that might be free of violence, and the deployments of violence in the name of securing an order that is supposedly free of violence' (ibid.: 242). Alternatives posed by resistance discourses should not be forced to fit the current political arrangements of structures of insides and outsides (Walker, 1993). Their efforts to 'find something other than a structure of selves and others, to somehow transcend a structure of immanence and transcendence' should also be seen as endeavours to break away from the reproduction of violent inscriptions (Walker, 2004: 245).

At this point of the discussion, the works of Maria Stern (1998; 2004; 2005) are of paramount importance. She has investigated the resistance narratives of Mayan women in Guatemala and has indicated their problematic character when resignifying the workings of the security discourse they contest. Stern argues that 'the violent ramifications of the (im)possibility of security are often repeated in the very sites of marginality where people attempt to procure safety and resist the violence and exclusion inflicted by hegemonic practices of securing national (or other dominant) identities' (Stern, M., 2004: 3). Consequently, Stern (1998: 21) has been very careful in treating identities as always in the process of becoming, thereby avoiding the temptation to replicate the same in/security logic when dealing with resistance discourses. While investigating these resistance discourses she is careful not to reify Mayan women as a taken-for-granted, given once and for all, clear-cut, frozen and secured entity.

> The narratives [of Mayan women] therefore suggest that struggles for security do not necessarily avoid causing harm and re-constituting 'discourses of danger' in order to maintain internal homogeneity and sovereignty – discourses that re-produce injurious practices of exclusion and inclusion ... Their security sometimes demands prioritizing 'one struggle over another' ... these very negotiations shed light upon the need to look at in/security and identity as hybrid and contingent constructions in order to understand ... the complex and violent conflicts that arise within and between conflicting identity sites. (Ibid.: 23)

The impossibility of representing the subject of security, hand in hand with the (im)possible securing of the subject of security, led Stern (2005: 201) to assert that studying the ways in which resistance discourses conceal both these (im)possibilities might help us understand better the way in which 'violent mechanisms of inclusion/exclusion often seem to be part and parcel of the enactment of (identity) politics in the name of securing political subjects or communities in both hegemonic and resistant sites'. Acknowledging the gaps and excesses of resistance discourses as well as the violent ramifications of discourses of danger, Stern proposes that 'instead of reading seemingly contradictory claims as incommensurable, one can read these seeming contrasts as open, and, importantly, not yet decided "or technologized" political spaces' (ibid.: 205).

The concept of reading resistance discourses in a contingent way might already be the first entry point for constructing a theoretical frame to investigate discourses contesting the DSP. If discourses of danger are also present in contesting sites, the alternatives they propose and the very ways in which they deal with fear are crucial to disrupt the violence of the in/security discourse.

As has already been argued, fear of difference does not necessarily entail the condemnation of otherness. The relation between identity and difference might not automatically imply violence against the traces of the 'other' in oneself and against the otherness of the 'other'. In short, 'a simple contrast need not automatically result in the demonization of the other, and the differentiation of distantiation of one group from another does not require that their relationship be one of violence' (Campbell, 1998: 70). Danger can be experienced 'positively as well as negatively: it can be a creative force, "a call to being", that provides access to the world' (ibid.: 81). In a similar tone, Edward Said (2003a: xxix) calls attention to the 'slow working together of cultures that overlap, borrow from each other, and live together in far more interesting ways than any abridged or inauthentic mode of understanding can allow'.

Turning to the particular case of resistance discourses to the DSP in Colombia, Maria Teresa Uribe argues that there is a coexistence of multiple forms of resistance. For her, some fight state violence with more violence. They arm themselves and murder others to impose their ideas, to defend their privileges, to change the world or to maintain the status quo. Others, unarmed, risk their lives in different spheres. They believe in debate, dialogue and sisterhood. They try to promote justice and equality and remedy the effects of war and violence. Warriors and peace-weavers coexist side-by-side (Uribe de H., 1999: 9).

The ethical alternatives that resistance discourses propose should be analysed against the background of the (im)possibility of in/security. For this purpose, focusing on how resistance discourses put forward proposals that constitute *routes*, instead of roots for politics, breaks away from the promise of safety and certitude of in/security. As such, routes offer no prescription and anticipated framework, but are open-ended or, in Shaw's (2004) terms, point to non-closure.

Embracing fragility and vulnerability are two substantial challenges to the logic of in/security – grounded on certainty and (im)possible promises of safety – for consideration when drawing open-ended representations of political subjectivities. In Martínez' (2005: 36) view, vulnerability and fragility, how easily we break and are hurt (ibid.: 151), the fear of the 'other' and the fear of the traces of the 'other' in 'us', can also bring about the opening of political spaces for presenting interpersonal and institutional alternatives that deal peacefully with such free 'human condition'. Renouncing security seems so to be intimately linked to cherishing otherness as a constructive source for politics that can bring about unknown possibilities for transformation (ibid.: 153).

These last comments contour the limits of the following interpretations of resistance discourses to the DSP. On the one hand, the concept of identity that sustains this book recognises how the processes of identification are contingent, temporary, imperfect and, more often than not, different subject positions present paradoxes. Paying attention to the elaborations of resistance discourses mentioned, I proceed to study resistance discourses to the DSP careful not to reify the marginal collectives from which these discourses emerge as taken-for-granted political communities. In other words, I will try not to reduce discourses contesting the DSP to subsuming subjectivities into 'sovereign' labels, such as state, nationals and others, that suppose that who speaks is a pregiven and coherent entity. I would like to maintain an interpretative analysis of resistance respecting the heterogeneity of available responses to in/security and comprehending the overlapping representations that interplay between the DSP and the chosen resistance discourses. Consequently, I want to analyse them by asking the following questions: How do resistance discourses deal with fear? Which alternative means and ends do they elaborate to contest the logic of in/security? How far away are their means from the ends? Which concepts of peace and security do they name?

These ethical considerations guide my investigation of resistance discourses to the DSP through the interpretative grid recently elaborated which I would like to summarise as follows:

1 Resistance discourses are, in themselves, discursive formations that necessarily draw their own limits and have gaps and excesses.
2 Resistance discourses are a possibility born out of the matrix of power relations, but this does not necessarily mean that their formation can be reduced to remnants of hegemony.
3 Contesting discourses can pose unexpected questions and disrupt the discursive limits of dominant discourses.
4 The alternatives proposed by resistance discourses should be analysed against the background of the (im)possibility of in/security.
5 From the peace studies perspective adopted here, it is crucial to read resistance discourses in a contingent way, paying close attention not to reify the identities of marginalised groups under forced labels.
6 The alternatives that resistance discourses propose to the discourse of in/security have the possibility to challenge the logic of exclusion and violence and to deal with fear and otherness in a constructive way.

Any theoretical frame is limiting. By applying the one sketched above, several resistance discourses may not fit. They may not even be considered, as they might not even qualify as such. In this sense, this frame is quite limiting. It might make invisible other contestations, different provocations that might not even enter the discussion that follows. However, I hope that this interpretative structure serves the purposes of accessing resistance by questioning the political violence the DSP reproduces and by highlighting less 'secure', and therefore less harmful, alternatives to dealing with conflicts.

Resistance discourses to the DSP

As has been pointed out by several peace researchers (Alther et al., 2004; Caicedo, 2003; Muñoz, 2001: 41), there are plenty of resistance discourses in Colombia.

Some are violent and armed, while others try to resist violence and instead propose peaceful ways of dealing with conflicts.[1] A seemingly 'representative' analysis of resistance to in/security exceeds the scope and objectives of this book. I do not intend to provide a reading of multiple peaceful initiatives, but rather to underscore heterogeneous responses to the Colombian state's discourse on in/security.

Consequently, the analysis of resistance discourses in the following pages is a selection based on two criteria. First, these discourses emanate from the 'state', 'nationals' and 'others'. They corroborate how the process of identification is not one-sided and, thus, cannot be understood as automatically synonymous with the construction and production of identity categories as they are represented in the DSP. These discourses make clear that it is necessary for subjects to invest in the positions created for them in discourse in order to articulate their identities, even if they are temporary, contingent and imperfect.

The second motivation for selecting these particular discourses is that they offer three distinct possibilities to resist the DSP. First, there is the need to argue explicitly why armed resistance discourses cannot challenge the logic of violence and exclusion reproduced by the DSP. The discourse of the FARC-EP guerrillas will be taken as an example. In the line of nonviolent resistance discourses, the investigation focuses on two separate cases. The first one is the state programme Congruent Peace Plan (Plan Congruente de Paz, PCP) of the Province of Antioquia. I have chosen this political programme because it draws the limits of a conception of qualified nonviolent resistance when it emanates from a state institution. The second resistance discourse considered is from the Paeces del Cauca. This indigenous group proposes a peaceful way of resisting the logic of in/security by putting forward a trans-rational peace concept and embracing nonviolence as an orientative principle of action.

By choosing the three discourses named above, my aim is to provide a heterogeneous picture of the different and contradictory ways in which subjects respond and resist the logic of in/security. Acknowledging the varied and wide range of responses to the DSP, I hope to contribute to the academic discussion from the perspective of the construction of political identities as far as ethical concerns are raised.

The following analysis of resistance will be carried out by carefully reading the discourses as emanating from situated, particular and contextual circumstances. Bearing in mind the contextualisation of the national situation studied in the first chapter, each resistance discourse is introduced by a historical outline and then the exteriority of the texts is analysed. I look at the modes of representation of discourses, the objectives as stated, and the proposals as they are explicitly declared in the texts in order to make sense of the ways subjects are articulated through them. Again, my purpose is neither to discover nor to 'unveil the doer behind the deed'. Quite the contrary, my aim is to comprehend and unpack how the doers are being constituted by their deeds and how the alternatives presented contest the discourse of in/security of the DSP.

Violent discourses of resistance

I consider it necessary to clarify why the discourses of different armed groups do not constitute an alternative to the DSP or challenge its rationale of violence and exclusion. First, the ideal categories that the DSP constructs for different political identities were studied in previous chapters, as was the way subjects are hailed into place to articulate those subject positions. By examining geopolitical and material practices informed by the DSP, it was made clear how the DSP legitimises and reproduces violence in order to make 'us' renounce political freedoms, democratic rights and biological lives based on the illusory promise of achieving in/security in the future.

By prompting exclusion and violence against the 'other', the DSP erases potential times and places for encounters. It further denies the commonalities between purportedly fixed and autonomous identities of 'us' and 'them'. The DSP promotes the concept of a secure peace in which peace becomes part of the strategy to fight the war on terror. Hence, the DSP keeps feeding the very cycle of violence and revenge that it promises to halt.

Second, against this state in/security discourse, several armed groups *resist* the DSP while incorporating numerous historical, economical and socio-political conditions. The most well known of these armed groups is the guerrillas FARC-EP, mainly because of its long history, size and violence. A thorough analysis of the discourse of the FARC-EP is beyond the scope of the present book. What is useful is to highlight how this discourse does not halt the violence it promises to resist but rather reproduces and enhances it. Working along the same discursive lines of sovereign exclusion and violence recognised in the DSP, I argue that this armed resistance discourse does not, and, in the terms that is articulated, cannot, challenge the logic of in/security of the DSP.

According to the information provided by the FARC-EP (2002), their struggle is rooted in the years 1948–1950, during which

> the Colombian guerrilla movement was the principal and worthy stance of a people, its immediate response to a process of official violence that had profoundly degraded national life, the human devastation of which few regions escaped. Political violence, violence as a means to usurp land and expand the boundaries of large holdings, economic violence expressed as immeasurable lust for personal enrichment, religious violence against those not believing or practising the rituals of the official church. (Ibid.: 9)

In 1964, the attack of the state armed forces over the town Marquetalia marked the birth of the revolutionary army:

> 48 men, poorly armed and with insufficient resources, commanded and oriented by Comrade Manuel Marulanda Vélez, turned into an armed revolutionary nucleus infused by our people's tradition of struggle, by the resistance of the natives and the black slaves to the violent and bloody methods used by the Spanish when they came to these lands, by the 1780 Commoner insurrection lead by José Antonio Galán, by the valour, courage and dignity of those who liberated our nation from Spanish colonialism between 1810 and 1819 and raised the banners of anti-imperialism, social justice and Latin American unity, unfurled by the Liberator, Simón Bolívar but brought down and stained by the creole political class. (FARC-EP, 2000)

This image of a common origin based on the resistance of the *true people* against the *violent government* continually feeds the FARC-EP (2002: 10–64). The guerrillas continue to argue how the oligarchic state has excluded *el pueblo* from the centre of political power through different national administrations beginning in 1964. The FARC-EP claim to have 'a revolutionary programme calling together all the citizens who dream of a Colombia for Colombians, with equality of opportunities and equitable distribution of wealth and where among us all we can build peace with social equality and sovereignty' (ibid.: 2). They justify the violence of their struggle by claiming the behaviour and political treatment of the Colombian ruling class follows the orientation of the US government:

> We do not wage war for its own sake. Faithful to the marquetalian ideals, every time the possibility to pursue different paths than those of the confrontation has appeared, everything has been put in the service of a political solution that would open the course toward reconciliation and reconstruction and establish the basis of the New Colombia. But invariably we have come up against the stubbornness and intransigence of a ruling class that only thinks of making use of these spaces to get us to submit. (Ibid.: 9)

The FARC-EP (2004) portrays itself as the right option against direct and structural violence and, explicitly, as the alternative to the DSP:

> *Las FARC-EP como organización política-militar, indiscutiblemente popular, constituyen la más clara y avanzada opción del pueblo colombiano en contra de las injusticias, las masacres, los asesinatos selectivos, los desplazamientos y exilios forzados causados por el terrorismo de Estado a cargo de las bandas paramilitares, amparadas bajo el intervencionismo imperial de los Estados Unidos con el Plan Colombia y la fascista política de 'Seguridad Democrática' del paramilitar Álvaro Uribe Vélez.* (Ibid.: 1)

The arguments of exclusion and violence of the FARC-EP are similar to those of the Colombian state. There is a common origin based on the mythical figure of Simón Bolívar, along with other armed movements of resistance. This identity should bind the collectivity ('we') against the absolute 'other' (the ruling class) who has persistently failed to show a *real* desire for peace and reconciliation. This

Table 5.1   *Acts of violence committed by the FARC-EP, January 2003–November 2005*

	2003	2004	2005
Massacres	79	115	47
Kidnappings	672	279	179
Humanitarian Law denunciations	2.025	1.725	915

Source: Presidency of the Republic of Colombia, Ministry of Defence, 2005.

articulation aims to construct the real *pueblo*, a people whose true character is decided upon traces of violent revolutions and *noble* goals like social justice, real peace and *sovereignty*.

According to the FARC-EP, violence is not an option to justify choosing, but rather an imposition born out of the evil character of the 'other'. The fixed identity of the *pueblo* who wants social justice and peace for *all Colombians*, is constructed as a homogeneous and sovereign collective 'we' that stands in total opposition to its enemies. Using this construction of selected violent attributes to form a group of *true people* fighting against an evil 'other', the FARC-EP have organised an army which has systematically committed crimes for over five decades. According to official information provided by the Colombian government, by November 2005 the 'narco-terrorist organisation FARC-EP' had an army of 12,515 soldiers (Mindefensa, 2005: 34). Even though in this official document the state does not provide a specific number of crimes committed by the FARC-EP, I have added the data from the past few years in Table 5.1.

The story of the continuation of hatred, pain and revenge is inscribed in each number included in the table above. If the challenges posed by the DSP are contested in a violent way, the spiral of violence is not arrested; it is reproduced and its consequences are widened. The exclusion and violence prompted by the hegemonic discourse of in/security of the Colombian state is reinforced by the FARC-EP discourse from a marginal site. Based on their discourse and on the violent manifestations of their armed struggle, it is clear that the FARC-EP contestation of the DSP actually fuels and perpetuates more violence. The alternatives posed by this armed resistance group result in the annihilation of the 'other', whether trade unionist, journalist, soldier, peasant, foreigner or native (ibid.).

The economical, social and political conditions in Colombia testify to high levels of exclusion, poverty and marginalisation but, above all, they indicate a collective acceptance of the use of violence to deal with conflicts.[2] This spiral of violence cannot be ended with more war, whether it comes from the state or from the guerrillas. The means used to transform conflicts mark the process as well as its outcome. Just as there can be no suppression of democratic politics in the name of in/security, neither can there be a bloody revolution that brings peace to *all Colombians*, as the guerrillas argue. Means and ends should be harmonious. In other words, the violence reproduced by the state's in/security discourse and by the guerrillas' armed resistance discourse cannot give birth to peace. None of them offers alternatives to violence.

No war against the state will bring true peace, just as no war against terrorism will give birth to peace. Threats feed upon each other among these cynical representations of danger by both state and guerrillas. Both state and guerrillas claim to be the voice of the *true 'us'*. Both hold transcendental goods (in/security and sovereignty) for which we all must die and kill for. This extends a never-ending spiral of violence. The exclusion and violence of the promise of in/security is only enhanced by the discourse of this armed resistance group.

How then to arrest the cycle of violence? The number of conflicts in Colombia is vast and the seduction of the logic of violence draws many followers attempting to extirpate the insecurity of their own free lives (Dillon, 1996). With its metaphysical promises of a bright and uncertain future, the DSP appeals to many. However, several peace researchers have highlighted how the creative energy present in conflict situations can be used to break away from violence and even used to turn into a constructive source for peaceful alternatives. The key element lies in the way we transform conflicts, not in their resolution or containment. It is well worth investigating different individual proposals that call for transforming conflicts in a peaceful way.

Peaceful transformation of conflicts: a framework for analysis

Various currents of thought in peace studies deal with conflicts in diverse ways. Some theoretical and practical tendencies draw on conflicts as material in need of prevention, resolution or management. Contrary to those, based on a notion of conflicts as inherent to human relations, critical peace studies approaches draw on conflict *transformation*.

Vicent Martínez (2005: 109) argues that human relationships are intrinsically conflictual, yet from the clash between entities emerges the possibility for creative transformation. From Martínez' argument, a moral improvement through peaceful conflict transformation can be derived. '*Podemos crecer moralmente ante los conflictos. En este sentido los conflictos pueden ayudarnos a ver las cosas de otra manera y a "mejorar" moralmente, aunque no lleguemos a "ser amigos" de aquellos o aquellas con quienes estamos en conflicto*' (ibid.: 110).

However, in order to comprehend the discourses of resistance to the DSP examined in this book, a moral and rational viewpoint does not suffice. Especially relevant for understanding the resistance of the Paeces del Cauca is the notion of trans-rational and plural peaces that bring in creative aspects of conflict transcending moral codes. These contributions have been elaborated on by

Wolfgang Dietrich (2006, 2008), who has put forward the concept of 'trans-rational peaces' in conjunction with the method of elicitive conflict transformation (Lederach, 1995, 2005). For the purposes of analysing the Paeces discourse, I would like to draw out the most crucial points of Dietrich's thesis to evaluate how identities are articulated differently in the Colombian context. They put forward an alternative understanding of the world and of peace, security and conflict and are helpful in illuminating the Colombian case in particular.[3]

Wolfgang Dietrich (2008) argues that different variations of peace can be largely derived from moral and energetic worldviews. Dietrich (2006: 26) traces the moral concept of peace to a specific time and place in history: European culture. By looking at how Mediterranean cultures created and embraced the *unquestionable truth* as the highest principle of thinking (ibid.), Dietrich contends that this worldview entailed the formation of absolute norms underscoring the contractually arranged form of peace found in the *One Truth* of *Phobos* or the Great *Pax* (Dietrich, 2008: 111–78). Importantly for criticising the DSP and the resistance discourses provoked by it, Dietrich claims that moral peace

> inevitably produces a dangerous notion of security – *Phobos*, the phobic security of the institution – be it the empire, the nation state, the church or the capitalist world system. The institutional security overshadows the conviviality of individuals and communities. ... where *Phobos* reigns, it needs and constructs aggressors. It is fear that makes us perceive the mere existence of otherness as aggression, far more than a physically aggressive attitude of the other. (Dietrich, 2006: 29)

Morally based understandings of peace, says Dietrich (2008: 178), are characterised by their recourse to the norm as a comprehensive and inalterable explanation for grounding peace. In other words, the justification of a contractual peace arrangement, like *pax*, is driven by normative explanations of peace as the ultimate truth. This makes moral peaces self-referential and, more problematically, unresponsive to the situation at hand, while constantly referring to highest principles beyond the present moment. A case in point is the promise of a bright in/security future portrayed in the DSP. A parallel might be drawn between Dietrich's contributions to moral peace and the *secure peace* discursively constructed and produced by the DSP. Both point to the idea of sacrificing democratic freedoms in the name of a higher principle of truth, deferred to the future.

In contrast to monological understandings of peace, Dietrich (2008: 33–93) looks at manifold historic and contemporary examples of peace notions such as the Great Goddess, the Holy Wedding and the Big Triad. These allow Dietrich to analyse concrete and multiple expressions of peace, like the *damai* in Indonesia, the Mayan concept of *utzilaj k'aslen* and *kindoki* from the Congo Basin, in which peace is experienced in more than one prearranged modern and legitimate way (Dietrich, 2006; 2008). In Dietrich's view, energetic peaces demonstrate that peace acquires a different meaning in each particular context and – contrary to modern versions of peace – energetically based peaces are geared towards restoring a dynamic and contingent harmonic balance between man, the cosmos and nature.

A similar notion of energetic peace is also put forward in the discourses of resistance of the Paeces del Cauca, in which this indigenous group does not attend to the ultimate sovereign power of the state. Their notions of peace, world and conflict do not relate to universal norms, but rather to contextual and always changing dynamic circumstances. Plural peaces could be conceptualised, lived and experienced in multiple and often contradictory forms, because, by virtue of being created in particular times and spaces without obeying static principles of truth and in/security, they cannot be exported without turning into instruments of violence (Dietrich and Sützl, 2006).

Energetic understandings of peaces do not speak the ultimate truth. Unlike modern notions of peace based on a singular god, truth, justice or security, energetic understandings of peaces yield no metaphysical certainty (Dietrich, 2008: 10). In energetically based notions of peace, which run through times and places, no energy is lost. Nothing remains without consequences; nothing disappears without marking history. Everything is connected in one way or another (Dietrich, 2008: 93).

> The decisive factor is to no longer perceive conflict as an immoral opposite to negative peace [as the absence of war] but rather as a positive sign of social energy. This energy can then be extracted through nonviolent means in order to transform problematic situations. Under this proposition key terms of international politics such as conflict prevention, peace building, peace keeping or even peace enforcement no longer make sense but are shown to block the potentially positive energy of conflict. (Dietrich, 2006: 33)

Both Martínez (2005) and Dietrich (2006) arrive at the same conclusion: conflicts are inherent to societies. Furthermore, their energy, if challenged through nonviolent means, can lead to transformation and positive changes. As studied above, for Martínez this energy can help us to improve morally. For Dietrich, there is not just a moral improvement through conflict transformation, but also a spiritual and energetic enrichment.

Dietrich argues that both moral and energetic notions of peace coexist with each other in a trans-rational manner. In other words, Dietrich (2008: 320) does not present energetic notions of peace as outdated, historical incidents of archaic societies where magic, myth and alchemy ought to be regarded with romanticism after the advent of modernity.[4] Rather, he calls for conceiving of peaces as trans-rational and proposes 'integrating rationality and differentiating it from its divine status in the modern world, so that a higher spiritual-rational consciousness of peace and culture – which would always be then peaces and cultures – can be reached. Hence [...] [I call] for a courageous integration of morally based, normative concepts of peace and energetically based spiritual ones for a nonviolent and fruitful approach of the existing cultures' (2006: 26).

The notion of trans-rational peaces precisely aims for consciously *twisting*[5] the limits of reason via rethinking peace out of harmony, integrating the element of intentionality as well as the connectivity of all things (Dietrich, 2008: 401). As such, trans-rational peaces entail that the aesthetic connection between peace and truth to them is unconditional but not absolute, because the system world is understood as connectivity of the All-One, which implies that all values are relational and only intersubjectively communicable (ibid.).

This trans-rational peace perspective is far-reaching and can provide a much-needed perspective for the analyses of peaceful resistance discourses to the DSP. The call for trans-rational peaces made by Wolfgang Dietrich (2006, 2008) can complement the proposal made by Martínez (2005) in many ways. Synthesis of both insights provides us with a unique point of entry into comprehending nonviolent resistance discourses to the DSP. Conflict is recognised as inherent to human relations and as a source for enrichment and social energy when transformed peacefully. Peaceful transformation can take us to improve morally in the sense that dealing with conflicts, as an alternative to suppressing them, can help us to learn from and with 'others'. This moral improvement should be enhanced with trans-rational elements that also recognise and integrate the spiritual character of human kind (Dietrich, 2006: 42).

Consequently, the methods to deal with conflicts should also pay attention to more than rational and institutional improvements. This approach defies any prescriptive way of dealing with conflicts via the application of predetermined models of conflict resolution. It calls for elicitive forms of conflict transformation (Lederach, 1995, 2005), which include – among others – listening to how the persons involved constitute themselves and the conflicts that affect them by taking seriously their own narratives. As such, elicitive methods recognise people's authority to speak of and for themselves and their conflicts (Roof and Wiegman, 1995) and bear in mind the ways in which they (already) handle their problems. Elicitive conflict transformation renounces clear-cut conflict transformation methods and opens the door for acknowledging parties in conflict as legitimate knowers of their own situations.

For the purposes of analysing peaceful resistances discourses to the DSP, this particular framework allows us to comprehend different proposals that put forth diverse and often contradictory notions of peace and security. In the following pages, the focus of attention will be on two nonviolent discourses: the Congruent Peace Plan of the Province of Antioquia and the approach of the Paeces del Cauca. Each of these discourses presents a different understanding of peaceful conflict transformation. The state programme has put forward a notion of nonviolence as a method of struggle, while the discourse of the Paeces offers the notion of nonviolence as principle of action embedded in an energetic conception of being. Taking into account both the general framework for resistance discourses and the recently drawn insights for peaceful conflict transformation, let us now analyse these nonviolent visions in relation to the DSP.

The nonviolence programme of the Province of Antioquia

As analysis of the theoretical framework revealed, there is an intimate relationship between in/security and identity. The state is the product of statist discourses; it is not a homogeneous entity, a self-governed and prearranged actor. On the contrary, the state has fissures, its 'body' is not unitary and the institutions that compose it are not completely or perfectly aligned. This contradictory and imperfectly manufactured character of the state is one of the main reasons we are concerned with investigating what the nonviolent discourse of Antioquia is about and how it emerged. The state can, on the one hand, produce the DSP and, on the other, propose a nonviolent political programme. This conundrum points to the interlinked and contradictory character of political identities.

How does this particular nonviolence discourse challenge the logic of in/security? Following the interpretative framework outlined at the beginning of this chapter, a careful reading of this situation will next be pursued.

CONGRUENT PEACE PLAN (PLAN CONGRUENTE DE PAZ, PCP)

In 2000, Guillermo Gaviria Correa was elected governor of the Province of Antioquia. His political programme was called the Plan Congruente de Paz. The PCP was a political document that served as guideline for the different provincial projects and programmes. It was structured with the help of international peace advisors, among them Bernard Lafayette from the Nonviolence Centre Martin Luther King Jr. (United States) and Mario López from the *Instituto de Paz y Conflictos* (Peace and Conflict Institute, Spain).

The PCP is based on three pillars: day-to-day attention to the violent conflict, the implementation of the pedagogy of nonviolence, and a social plan for conviviality and the development of peace (Gobernación de Antioquia, 2001). The diagnosis of the situation of violence in Antioquia retakes several elements that draw on peaceful conflict transformation as the basic tool for dealing with it. It states that Antioquia faces the challenge of fostering a cultural transformation that delegitimises the use of violence as structuring element of society and the challenge of articulating a collective project that channels societal energies toward a common development and a new institutional order (ibid.: 1). In this vein, the objective of the PCP is to redefine the societal structures in terms of its norms, institutions and culture in order to create the necessary conditions for peaceful coexistence (ibid.). These goals and methods are based on a notion of nonviolence as philosophy and methodology for confronting societal tensions.

The naming of dangers made by the PCP coincides with the one made by the

DSP: terrorism (ibid.: 3). The PCP underscores how the combination of terrorism with the precarious character of the state, the fragility of the notion of citizenship and a non-existent public culture for conflict resolution, has perpetuated social problems and threatens the democratic security and peace in Antioquia. These dangers, hand in hand with a generalised acceptation of violence, threaten individual, collective, institutional and social security as well as democratic security (Ibid.: 4).

The characteristics of the provincial security discourse follow the structure studied in the preceding chapters. Dangers are recognised as threats to the political project of a unified, just, peaceful and educated Antioquia (ibid.). This articulation creates the subjectivity of the provincial government as a state office that defines the threats that put in danger the collectivity, designs characteristics and interests for the *Antioqueños* and presents itself as the provider of the solutions for the defined problems.

The crucial difference between this in/security discourse and the DSP is the proposal of embracing nonviolence as one of the solutions to insecurity. The provincial government (ibid.: 5) defines nonviolence based on the contributions of Mario López (2002) as the action, the duty and the conviction in justice with total respect for the individualities and lives of adversaries, renouncing all forms of violence. In this manner, nonviolence is portrayed as action because it is a method of intervention, a creative alternative as well as a duty, insofar as it creates a moral ideal that serves as a guiding principle of individual and collective behaviour. Lastly, nonviolence speaks to the conviction that there is the need to acknowledge self-responsibility for the actions and omissions of all (ibid.).

Nonviolence in the PCP appears intimately tied to a notion of peace that is not reduced to the absence of war or the presence of a negotiation process, but rather the existence of distributive justice that satisfies basic human needs and lessens, as much as possible, the harm and suffering for both 'us' and 'others' (Gobernación de Antioquia, 2001: 6). Following López (2002), the aim of nonviolence is not to win over the adversaries, but rather to convince them to abolish unjust structures and to preserve lives, respecting people and betting on their moral and material transformation. Regarding Antioquia, López (2002) elaborates on how nonviolence should be strengthened as a political method to deal with violent conflicts and calls for the recognition of many peaces (Dietrich and Sützl, 2006) in everyday life as a beginning for realising that the renouncement of violence is possible (López, 2002: 6–7).

López further discusses the paradox that institutional decision makers face whether to deal with conflicts through violent or nonviolent means. This conceptualisation differs from the one made above in the text of the PCP (Gobernación de Antioquia, 2001: 2). In the latter, nonviolence has a moral and spiritual connotation in the sense that it is not reduced to rational decisions as to how to deal with violence. Nonviolence also embraces spiritual components in order to channel social energy, which is present in the tension provoked by conflicts. However, if the question of nonviolence is reduced to the moral dilemma in which nonviolence is an option that *sometimes* works better than violence does, then in order to achieve certain goals, indeed when nonviolence fails, state violence can be deployed.

This understanding of nonviolence as a *method* of struggle is always and only a circumstantial tactic (López, 2001: 210–18). On the other hand, nonviolence as principle and not just as means, what Holmes (2000: 2) calls *unqualified nonviolence* referring to the harmonisation between means and ends, has a different connotation. In Gandhian terms, nonviolence would be an attitude (*ahimsa*), a principle for action and spirit indistinctively from the circumstances and goals in question. From this angle, violence is unjustifiable (Galtung, 1996: 114–126).

Once the PCP began to be implemented in Antioquia in 2001, it was clear that the form of nonviolence adopted referred to the first conception, that is, to a method that *sometimes* can lead to better results than violence. In this light, nonviolence is just one of the *weapons* of the state to exercise its power. This feature was officially acknowledged in the Constituent Assembly of Antioquia in 2003 when the regional agreements signalled that 'Antioquia' could not renounce its legitimate right to securing and protecting 'its' citizens by embracing nonviolence merely as a method (Gobernación de Antioquia, 2003: 1). Once again, the state was made the entity that enjoyed the legitimate monopoly on the use of force (ibid.).

Seen from this state perspective, the conundrum 'violence – nonviolence' flows into an easy way out. If the very essence of the state is being the so-called legitimate holder of violence, then proposing a nonviolent programme can only be reduced to a tactical and pedagogical project for the people. It cannot be equivalent to the renunciation of state violence as a whole. Renouncing violence would lead to the end of the state, as it is known in contemporary politics. In the case of Antioquia, the state would still reserve the deployment of violence in certain circumstances, turning the notion of nonviolence into *one* of many available responses for dealing with conflicts.[6]

NONVIOLENCE AND VIOLENCE

In 2001 and 2002, the provincial government followed the postulates of the PCP and put into practice an impressive nonviolence educational programme. The provincial administration organised municipal workshops where more than 2,000 people were trained in nonviolent methods for conflict transformation (Gobernación de Antioquia, 2002: 3). Likewise, the province sponsored the autonomous organisation of local leaders who wanted to hold regional peace dialogues with armed organisations. These meetings were later named Centros de Entrenamiento para la Democracia (Training Centres for Democracy) and were called and held without the initiative or even presence of local state authorities (ibid.: 5).

In the same vein, the province launched the campaign *Antioquia se toma la Palabra* (Antioquia takes up the word), which was grounded upon a fundamental respect for life, the belief that war was the worst option for dealing with conflicts and the need of the *Antioqueños* to achieve an agreement for reconciliation (ibid.: 9). The objective of the campaign was to collect different proposals and responses from civil society groups around the following issues: social conflict and direct violence (regional dialogues, humanitarian interventions, peace laboratories), social conflict and cultural violence (nonviolence, reconciliation and conciliation pedagogical tools), social conflict and structural violence (poverty, exclusion and inequality), and social conflict and several types of violence (institutional commitments).

In a document called *Nuestra Noviolencia* (Our Nonviolence) (Fajardo, 2002), the province further developed the different programmes and strategies previously assembled. *Nuestra Noviolencia* gathered the local version of what nonviolence meant within the institutional framework of the provincial office and throughout Antioquia. It called for adapting nonviolent theories to local realities in a way that nonviolence could turn into a real and concrete local alternative for dealing with specific vernacular conflicts (ibid.: 11).

Thought of in this way, the integral plan of nonviolence was part of a new way of transforming conflicts in the region: peacefully. An ideal image of a New Antioquia was presented as the result of development plans over the last decade. Antioquia Siglo XXI (Antioquia Twenty-First Century) is the projected collective identity of the *Antioqueños*. The nonviolence programme is geared towards creating this particular ideal identity construction.

Second, the image of the 'other' that the nonviolence plan constructs is based upon its recognition as a valid interlocutor. This is an important step towards dialogue and reconciliation since it decisively prevents focusing on the 'actors' of the conflict (as material in need of exclusion and normalisation) and moves towards collectively understanding the causes for violent conflicts (ibid.: 12). In clear contradiction to the construction of the 'other' made in the DSP, the PCP argues that we cannot treat the 'other' as exploiter, tyrant or terrorist. Above all, the 'other' is a necessary human component in the construction of new social and political realities (ibid.: 15). In this sense, the conflict parties should be brought into a dialogue in order to jointly transform structural problems. Finally and perhaps most importantly, the problematic notion of the role and functions of the state within the nonviolence project should be analysed. The province argues that the state should focus on recreating spaces for inclusive participation, leaving aside functions like order and security (ibid.: 14).

The difficulties and limits of adopting such a model of state nonviolence are explored in the following section. For the moment, it is important to underscore that the intention of the provincial government (ibid.: 12) was to expand the nonviolence programme from a governmental (temporary) to a state policy (permanent) and, hand in hand with a new concept for the state, to put forward a peace concept different from the secure peace of the central administration.

The province argues that peace should not be reduced to a negotiation between the state and the armed actors aiming for reaching consensus. On the contrary, the questions of peace should be based on respect for acknowledging the inability or inappropriateness of reaching consensus. This is a crucial matter, how to live without consensus? In the nonviolence programme, the office of the province outlined the necessity of recognising plurality and differences of opinions, of creating democratic spaces where disagreements could be discussed publicly and openly (ibid.: 14). The peace proposed by the province is referred to as *democratic peace*, which cannot be postponed for the future or until structural problems are solved, since this is a kind of procedural peace. This notion echoes the concept of *imperfect peace* coined by Francisco Muñoz (2001), for whom peace has an imperfect character in that it is not a stage to be achieved but an unfinished and conflictive process. Such peace is not a teleological objective, but rather a presupposition that is both recognised and built day by day. This understanding of the procedural nature of peace, in itself important for the advancement of the pacifistic praxis, is also upheld by theoretical and epistemological approaches regarding our understanding of the dynamics of nature and living beings. In this vein, imperfect would be equivalent to conflictive (ibid.: 43).

The path-breaking character of these nonviolent and participative initiatives launched by the provincial government can hardly be overstated. Antioquia had been the most violent region in Colombia for decades. The influence of the drug business on societal structures, combined with local adoration of warrior features such as the founding myth of the regional character, has long been the focus of analysis of sociologists, political scientists and economic researchers (Angarita, 2001; Echavarría, 2002; Monsalve and Domínguez, 1999; Nieto and Robledo, 2001; Sánchez et al., 2002).[7]

Governor Gaviria and his peace advisor Gilberto Echeverri, authors of the PCP who entered the provincial administration by popular election, turned into well-known political figures. They were responsible for sponsoring the pedagogical activities of the PCP and for calling on many others to participate. These two men became the faces of the state-sponsored nonviolent movement in Antioquia and came to symbolise the institutional effort to rethink conflict transformation in the region.

However, at the same time that the PCP was being implemented, the provincial government was keeping up with the postulates and programmes emanating from the DSP. According to the information provided by the Ministry of Defence (Mindefensa, 2005), from the beginning of the presidential period in August 2002 until the year 2004, the DSP was enforced in Antioquia through several practices. For instance, more than 2,500 peasant soldiers and 600 *Carabineros* squadrons were added to existing official armed forces. The information and cooperation networks were enhanced and the massive captures continued to occur (ibid.: 6).

THE LIMITS OF QUALIFIED STATE NONVIOLENCE

The discourse of the PCP draws on the notion of qualified nonviolence, meaning as a method of struggle. As was pointed out above, this particular concept serves to implement both violence and nonviolence according to the circumstances at hand. The difficulties and contradictions of a nonviolent state discourse were evident with the kidnappings and later assassinations of Governor Gaviria and his peace advisor Echeverri.

In April 2002, a delegation of the provincial government was conducting a long march through the region for nonviolence and reconciliation. The march took several days and participants travelled for almost one thousand kilometres. In the last section, nearly three kilometres away from the final town Caicedo, the FARC-EP interrupted the demonstration and kidnapped the governor, peace advisor, and five more representatives of the nonviolent movement and the church. The guerrillas argued that the group of officials should accompany them to dialogue with their leader, but the governor and his advisor were held for over a year.

On 5 May 2003, President Uribe ordered the military rescue of Gaviria and Echeverri, but the military operation was a failure. When the guerrilleros heard the army helicopters, they killed Governor Gaviria and his peace advisor, as well as eight others. That same night, President Uribe, the general commander of the army and the commander of the rescue force *Fudra* went on national television to explain what had happened. In their discourses, the limits of state nonviolence were clear: the state can deploy violence whenever state officials consider it necessary for *security reasons*.

In his televised speech, President Uribe (2003c: 9) argued that peace efforts were understood by the terrorists as weaknesses and that they were used to their tactical advantage in the war. For President Uribe, it was clear that nonviolence could not be an obstacle to the DSP. Whenever 'security' is at stake, state violence has to be deployed. According to the president (ibid.: 10), there are spaces for debating about economic policies and political reforms, but the defeat of terrorism by violent means is not a matter for public debate. It is a decision that has been made and cannot be negotiated. In this way, the limits of the public debate were contoured. The exercise of state violence is beyond criticism, these are the limits of what can be heard and said within the discursive articulation of the DSP (ibid.: 13).

In his speech, President Uribe touched upon one of the most discussed issues pertaining to nonviolence: war values, and especially courage in the battle on terror (ibid.). William James (2000) suggests that pacifist movements have failed to propose ethical and aesthetical arguments that are as attractive as martial values, like courage, pride and honour. For the author (ibid.: 69) there are ways in which pacifist discourses can reproduce these values in a nonviolent way, but he stresses the difficulties and how they fall short when confronted with the adoration of violence. It seems that James' concerns resonate in Uribe's discourse: peace efforts are the expression of weakness and war experiences are the expression of courageous peoples.

CHALLENGES AND LIMITATIONS OF THE PCP

In terms of the analysis of nonviolent resistance discourses to the DSP, we can sum up as follows. First, the PCP strives to counter-propose an alternative nonviolent discourse to the DSP. However, its scope is rather limited as far as it is still the executive power of the nation-state that presents this discourse not as an alternative to the DSP, but as a way of filling in its gaps.

The PCP calls for nonviolent methods to educate the population, but it cannot embrace it as a philosophy for its own state actions. In the terms in which the sovereignty of the state is articulated in (inter)national politics, state nonviolence is always qualified. It can be used as a pedagogical method for the people, but it can never be a norm of behaviour for state institutions in situations when *national security* is said to be at stake. At all times, the state reserves for itself the deployment of violence; it does not renounce violence as a whole since this would imply the negation of its very sovereign essence as it is known in contemporary politics.

> States are founded on violence, whether it takes the form of war, revolution or civil conflict. ... The right to use violence, in other words, is the prerogative of the state. And it makes use of this prerogative. ... The modern state, then, is a contradictory institution: a promise of safety, security and meaning alongside a reality of abuse, control and coercion. (Edkins, 2003: 6)

In this light, the type of qualified nonviolence proposed by the provincial state office attempts to challenge the discursive categories and material practices of the DSP that reproduce violence and exclusion. However, it suffers from important limitations in terms of its discursive coherence and execution. In clear contradiction to the DSP, the PCP proposes the concept of a *democratic peace,* which retakes elements of the notion of imperfect peace (Muñoz, 2001) separating its proposal from the secure peace of the central government. According to the PCP, peace is not born of authority, but rather from reconciliation. At the same time, the PCP constructs an image of the 'other' not as an enemy, but as valid interlocutor indispensable for conflict transformation. The PCP recognises the importance of bringing the 'other' into the public debate as necessary for reconciliation. In this sense, it does not ground politics on in/security, as the DSP does. Nonetheless, the provincial government has continued to follow and implement sovereign and biopolitical practices emanating from the DSP.

Certainly, the value of designing and carrying out nonviolence pedagogy in Antioquia is high. The notion that conflicts should be transformed peacefully and that their tensions can be understood as social energy to be channelled in a productive way, are two important steps for halting the spiral of collective violence. This subject matter might have been unthinkable in the past. The PCP is still an attempt to break the homogeneous and disciplined obedience of the very state structures to the DSP. For these reasons, it is crucial to recognise the symbolic, political and practical value of constructing a nonviolent state programme.

The limits of a state nonviolent discourse are clear, but there are other non-state and nonviolent resistance discourses to the DSP. In the following section, we will explore another example: the civil resistance movement of the indigenous group Paeces del Cauca. Their conditions of possibility, their structure, the very provocations they enact in response to the DSP are quite different from the ones we have studied in regards to the PCP of the Province of Antioquia. Let us look at their discourse of resistance and examine how it challenges the reproduction of political violence in the DSP.

Mingas, bastones *and nonviolence: the resistance discourse of the Paeces del Cauca*

I now turn my attention to a provocation to the DSP that has been articulated by a political entity that was not even officially recognised as such until the 1991 Political Constitution was issued: indigenous peoples in Colombia. Following the theoretical frame outlined at the beginning of this chapter, this discourse will be read paying close attention to the contingent character of identity. As done in regards to the PCP, it is crucial to situate this discourse in its particular historical and political conditions, which have shaped the ways in which the Paeces have articulated a competing notion of peace and security.

The nonviolence discourse of the Paeces is entangled with indigenous and civil resistance discourses. On the one hand, this community belongs to the indigenous population of the country. This plays an important role in the ways they articulate their collective identity. At the same time, the Paeces do not restrict their civil resistance activities to indigenous peoples, but open spaces for public debate within other institutional frameworks. This specific combination of proposals is also a result of the translation of their worldview, where an energetic understanding of being reigns, into rational elements of formal democracy. Therefore, especially in this context, the framework for analysis of trans-rational peaces is of great utility in understanding the Paeces discourse.

What type of nonviolence resistance do the Paeces propose and how do they contest the state discourse of in/security? These questions frame the following analysis that offers a different recount of resistance in Colombia.

CONSTRUCTING A MULTIETHNIC COLOMBIA

When investigating the resistance discourse of the Paeces del Cauca, its indigenous character must first be addressed. To perform a far-reaching account of the history of indigenous groups in Colombia exceeds the scope of the present section and deserves serious research on its own. For the purposes of this study, it is pertinent to broadly contextualise the latest happenings in regards to indigenous communities in the country as they offer a brief overview on the situational character of the Paeces discourses. It so becomes necessary to highlight aspects of their resistance in relation to the reading of the DSP conducted in the past chapter.

Hand in hand with constitutional reforms, the subjectivities of both national and indigenous identities have been deeply transformed in the last decade. In 1991, a new Political Constitution was adopted in Colombia. The former constitutional framework, drafted in 1886 and with countless reforms added since, was based upon a notion of citizenship that constructed the national population as a homogeneous group of *mestizos*, Catholics and Castilian speakers. This particular construction made that differences among ethnicities, beliefs, languages and competing conceptions of the world were violently assimilated into the dominant official culture, many of them annihilated. Entire communities, with their unique cosmovision, languages and traditions, have been literarily erased from view through systematic violence (ONIC, 2005f).

The 1991 constitution states that Colombia is a multiethnic nation and it recognises indigenous groups as autonomous communities.[8] This means that within their territories, indigenous authorities should be able to exercise autonomous powers over their peoples. At the same time, the constitutional norm is mainly based on individual human rights that are very often at odds with collective understandings of belonging.

This new discursive formation of national identity finds its conceptual grounds in the works of Will Kymlicka, whose notion of multicultural citizenship has shaped legal decisions of the Constitutional Court in the past decade. According to Kymlicka (1996: 18), both collective rights of minorities and individual human rights can coexist on the basis that the former have their limits in the principles of individual freedom, democracy and social justice. Kymlicka (ibid.: 47) recognises in national minorities, which are to be distinguished by their self-perception as differentiated nations, special rights and duties that separate them from other citizens. Group-differentiated rights play a doubly essential role. They both limit the actions of the state and the dominant culture regarding minority rights and furthermore they protect liberal freedoms and the fundamental rights of the members of minority groups.

In spite of this, the contradiction that emerges from the attempt to harmonise special protective rights for collectivities and, at the same time, to defend individual human rights causes tensions. Wolfgang Dietrich (2000) has elaborated on this conflict between universal human rights emanating from the modern nation-state and the different conceptions of human dignity, which are not reduced to laws. For Dietrich, there is 'a common nucleus of values on human dignity in all cultures' (ibid.: 1). However, 'the universality of the substantial meaning of dignity can be communicated in different forms such as rights, obligations, wisdoms, legends, dreams, etc. All of these diverse forms are as compulsory to their respective communities as laws and rights to citizens of the modern constitutional state' (ibid.: 2).

Accepting that 'others' express their concept of human dignity in diverse ways is complicated for the nation-state characterised by aggressive and expansionist actions. Likewise, respecting that 'others' deal with human dignity in a non-legal way is not that simple for a society which has negated the very existence of otherness in the past five centuries. This is especially the case when confronted with indigenous groups, who often have an energetic understanding of community, nature and cosmos.

The problem that Dietrich points to has been at the centre of attention in national politics since 1991. The challenge how to harmonise both the so-called universal individual and fundamental rights, born out of the modern concept of the nation-state, with the notion of human dignity as inherent to the energetic balance between humans, nature and cosmos is quite steep. The new model of the state requires articulation and respect for diverse worldviews that can be antagonistic. There are numerous examples of these contradictions, such as universal assumptions about human rights, the unitary character of the nation and the recognition of indigenous peoples as specific members of their communities and, simultaneously, as Colombian citizens (Gaviria, 2003).

The process initiated in the 1990s has resulted in a complex mixture of bittersweet experiences. In several decisions, the Constitutional Court has tried to refer to this core of human dignity but has still remained inside the legal framework of the nation-state. The court has solved concrete disputes by recognising a maximum of autonomy for indigenous communities while arguing for a minimum of core rights for individuals, irrespective of their membership in other collectivities.[9] In this sense, the court still requires observing a minimum of constitutional limitations considered as binding for *all* Colombians: the right to life, the prohibition of slavery and torture and the right to due process (ibid.).

This *solution* about where to draw the line between universal human rights and collective indigenous rights signals an agreement that does not necessarily fit all situations. Issues like environmental rights and biodiversity, free trade, the war against drugs, the punitive system, language and educational programmes and the exploitation of natural resources, among others, are constant subjects of tensions (Gaviria, 1997). For instance, the state and its armed forces claim the right to control the whole of the national territory militarily. The state and indigenous jurisdictions collide in their authority in concrete cases such as the implementation of Plan Colombia in several regions. Likewise, the exploitation of natural resources, such as oil, salt and gas, in indigenous territories remains a matter of dispute. For several indigenous communities, nature is an element and not a mere economic resource for companies to exploit. As is expected, the power and violence of state forces and multinational corporations constantly impose themselves over indigenous claims.

Finally, yet importantly, the armed conflict situation has drawn indigenous communities to a crossroads between illegal and legal violence. Even though this situation is not restricted to the last government or to the DSP, it is important to underscore how the current discourse on in/security has repressed the resistance of indigenous groups.

Consejo Comunal Indígena (Communitarian Indigenous Council)

In September 2005, the government held a National Communitarian Council and called upon all indigenous groups to participate. Although important indigenous groups like the Colombian Indigenous Organisation (Organización Indígena de Colombia, ONIC), refused to participate, the National Council was held between representatives of the government and indigenous leaders. During this meeting, the contradictions between the official discourse of democratic security and the position of the indigenous groups were made evident.

In a common letter to the president, the Indigenous Authorities (Autoridades Indígenas, 2005) expressed their petitions to the central government. They claimed that their requests had been systematically ignored by the government and that in the meantime social problems and human rights violations not only continued but deepened (ibid.: 1). They accused the state of having been deaf and blind to the problems of indigenous groups, especially to those in the Amazon region. Additionally, the letter drew upon matters from land ownership to bilingual education (ibid.: 1–5). Each of these subjects signalled crucial differences between the official discourse and the vernacular understanding of notions such as development, the war against drugs, indigenous autonomy and national borders.[10]

The multiplicity of discourses articulated in the letter paid allegiance to the contingent character of collective identity and to the fantasy of representation. However, for the sake of our discussion, we will concentrate on the issues that directly touch upon points of resistance to the violence produced by the DSP as it was previously examined. Given the violations of human rights in Colombia, the *Autoridades* declared themselves to be in a 'state of emergency'. Considering the situations of forced displacement, selective massacres, arbitrary detentions and armed confrontations in the indigenous territories, the *Autoridades* requested an integral humanitarian policy to safeguard their lives and territories (ibid.: 5).

Next, they put forward their will to participate in initiatives that construct *real peace*, which is presented by the *Autoridades* as a type of peace that is constructed hand in hand between the state and civil society and results from an inclusive political negotiation process (ibid.). This *real* peace is not a *secure peace* born out of authority, but rather is constructed through inclusive politics. Seen from the perspective of the DSP, the claims of respecting the lives and territories of indigenous peoples by not getting involved in 'the army of good people' are not even subject to negotiation. As the president had expressed in a past council in Cauca (Uribe, 2005b), everybody has to participate with solidarity in the fight against terrorism. This includes the appropriation of indigenous territories by the armed forces (ibid.: 9).

The attempts of the indigenous communities to rethink the DSP were not considered valid options by the government and the security forces. In his reply to the letter, President Uribe (2005c) made clear that ethnic diversity could not be an obstacle to a unified nation in search of a secure peace. According to Uribe, a unified nation should prevail over ethnic diversity and, above all, over competing political options to deal with violence (ibid.: 2–3).

These discursive limits were made clear in the concluding paper of the Communitarian Council. The official declaration made by the government press office (Servicio Nacional de Noticias del Estado, 2005) reads that, for every other theme not directly related to the DSP, there are lines of actions, responsible entities and further commitments. Nevertheless, in terms of the indigenous claims around their own position in regards to the control over the territory by the armed forces within the fight against terrorism, a timid conclusion is noted: 'the Office of the Vice-President should hold a new meeting with the indigenous organisations and their Congress Representatives around the issue of Human Rights' (ibid.: 3).

The 'issue of human rights', as it is called by the government, revolves around the indigenous stance regarding the war. It is of course not circumscribed to the application of international humanitarian law norms. Their discrepancies revolve around each axis of the DSP: massive captures, cooperation networks, fumigation of illicit crops, peasant soldiers, the militarisation of their territory and negotiations with the paramilitaries (León, 2005). It is a matter of politics, of ways of conceiving of society and conflicts, which differs from the official understanding of the government. The ONIC (2005a) reacted to the lack of governmental answers to indigenous claims and pointed out how the state did not treat them as valid political interlocutors and avoided addressing the issues of peace and security.

For the organisation, their rejection of participating in the council was a demonstration of their resistance and called for a national *minga* (nonviolent march) from 9 to 12 October 2005, a date that commemorates the 'discovery of the Americas' by Christopher Columbus in 1492. During these three days, indigenous people around the ONIC wanted to rise in pacific resistance, demanding solutions to the structural problems that oppressed ancestral peoples (ONIC, 2005b: 1). They argued that their resistance was to be expressed through a *minga* because they were peoples of life, peoples of the earth, and therefore would not take up armed resistance against the nation-state, even if it was the Colombian state that has ignored and despised them.

Though this *minga* was organised by the ONIC (ibid.), calling on 25,000 indigenous people to march for 'dignity, protection and autonomy of the indigenous peoples of Colombia', it also invited *Colombians* to regain their 'common sense' in order to understand that the commonalities that joined them were more than the differences that separated them (ibid.). Unfortunately, the *minga* did not testify to this call for nonviolent resistance. The national government forbade it, arguing that guerrillas had infiltrated the participants. According to the press release issued by the ONIC (2005c), during the *minga* the armed forces attacked them with toxic fumes, clubs and sticks, killing one protester and injuring more than ten others. The ONIC argued that this attack had been previously orchestrated by the national government and by the state forces, which at that time were also preventing 9,000 Embera people from joining the *minga* (ibid.).

As the national *minga* of October 2005 shows, the state and its security forces do not always respect the nonviolent character of indigenous demonstrations. The army, guerrillas and paramilitaries have frequently attacked peaceful indigenous protests. However, the success of *mingas* has been quite remarkable on other occasions. In the past, indigenous *mingas* have served as crucial mechanism for calling the attention of the government, other armed actors and the national and international community to hearing their claims. In former marches, indigenous communities have been respected in their decision not to participate as warriors. The Paeces and their resistance discourse occupy this particular niche, and it is to their specific situation we turn our attention in the next section.

The Nasa project

The resistance discourse of the Paeces exceeds provocations to the DSP. It is intertwined with multiple claims about how non-indigenous societies, government and the security forces have threatened their ways of life. We will recognise how this specific community has been able to resist the violence of in/security of the DSP by responding with an energetic understanding of peace and security which calls for the participation of other social groups in political spaces.

The Paeces constitute a population of approximately 120,000 indigenous peoples who live in the south of the country, mainly in the province of Cauca

(Mininterior, 2005: 2). They have had a long tradition of community organisation and have worked together with other indigenous groups on political empowerment over the past four decades.[11]

Since 1980, the Paeces have put forward a large-scale project called Nasa, which means *Plan Vida* (Life Plan) in their local language. Since its inception, the Nasa project was designed as an integral platform to fight poverty and the usurpation of indigenous' territories by landowners. During its beginnings, the project found multiple common interests with peasant movements and especially with the National Association of Peasant Smallholders (Asociación Nacional de Usuarios Campesinos, ANUC), which demanded agrarian reform.[12]

The *Nasa* project was envisioned as an integral and autochthonous plan of development according to their own standards. The Council Association of Cauca (Asociación de Cabildos del Norte del Cauca, ACIN) defines the main goal of the project as the recovery of the central unity of the community in order to strengthen organisational processes and social cohesion through education and training and productive programmes (ACIN, 2005). The project was designed according to the Nasa spirit and made use of three methodological tools: a) raising awareness through education and training; b) communitarian participation through community organisation; and c) integral development with programme and projects that include all human lives and mother earth (ibid.: 1–2). In terms of the Nasa spirit, a reactivation of their cosmovision was necessary to ground the project with loyalty to the local culture.

When he received the Ecuadorian Peace Prize from the UNDP in February 2004, the project's coordinator, Ezequiel Vitonás, explained that the objective and principles of the Nasa project were to recover their consciousness, identity and culture in order to turn them into a practical way of life in equilibrium and harmony with their territory. In this way, stated Vitonás, would their project articulate their conviction of being 'peoples of the earth' (Vitonás quoted in UNDP, 2004). The Ecuadorian Peace Prize was not the first recognition that the Nasa project had received. In 2000, it was awarded the Colombian National Peace Prize and the UNESCO *Maestros de Sabiduría* (Masters of Wisdom), which allowed them to create its correspondent UNESCO Chair for Communitarian Processes.

These national and international acknowledgments, as well as the nonviolent character of their resistance, have not freed the Nasa peoples from being persecuted by official as well as illegal armed groups. Nevertheless, their struggle for cultural and territorial autonomy continues against the systematic violence of both state and non-state forces.

MINGAS AND BASTONES

There are two distinctive elements in the resistance movement of the Paeces that have earned them substantial recognition. First, their popular and massive nonviolent marches, or *mingas*. Second, their unarmed and symbolic guard, to be distinguished by their sticks or *bastones*, to confront the attacks of armed groups. They have called on non-indigenous groups to participate in those strategies, thereby transcending ethnic claims and turning into an inclusive nonviolent movement. At the same time, these actions have made visible the violence embedded in the DSP. Thus, both *mingas* and *bastones* have made the discursive limitations and practices of the DSP subject to contestation within the political realm.

The Indigenous Guard of the Paeces was formally installed as such in March 2001, even though this nonviolent method has been part of their resistance since the seventeenth century. The guard consists of an organised group of indigenous people that stand together with vernacular sticks to defend the territory from usurpers.

> This special group of men, women, and youth are chosen and trained to defend against others who want to abuse their communities' lands and rights. They carry sticks ... [that] are carefully crafted, decorated, and consecrated wooden staffs of office. ... 'They're not weapons in the usual sense, but symbols of authority used to confront those who carry guns,' explains a *Nasa* leader. The *Nasa* know the warrior spirit flows in their blood, and the staffs represent a warrior's real weapons: the will, strength, and authority to defend life. This defense is nonviolent. 'At no time will we take up arms,' explains another *Nasa* leader. 'Arms are symbols of death.' (Alther et al., 2004: 21–2)

The Paeces mobilise large numbers of people to occupy ancestral lands that have been misappropriated by landholders. After the *minga* of October 2005, more than twenty-thousand Paeces occupied the ranch El Japio, breaking its fences to free the *pacha mama*, or mother earth, from laws imposed on her (Mendivelso, 2005). They argued that since 1999, when the state recognised the land titles for the Cauca communities, various central governments had failed to give them back what belonged to their collectivity, as seen from an ancestral as well as a legal point of view (ibid.: 3). The security forces tried to eject the guard from the ranch by using gas, killed one of its members, Belisario Camayo, and injured more than forty others. However, the indigenous people did not go away. On the contrary, they buried Belisario in the ranch and called upon his blood to spiritually strengthen their nonviolent resistance (ibid.: 4).

Even though the Indigenous Guard continue to be used for the recovery of territories today, the activities around the guard have also promoted other types of political participative processes. For instance, the guard calls on meetings, assemblies and cultural acts that define the organisation's lines of action; they promote *mingas*, rituals and public audiences where they denounce human rights violations. In short, the guard 'constitutes an exercise of alternative democracy grounded on their own knowledge that seeks to counterweight armed violence' (UNDP, 2005b). The armed actors include guerrillas and paramilitaries as well as the army. In this regard, Alther et al. (2004) have collected several testimonies of Nasa leaders. One of them explains,

> Now when an armed group comes into our territory, the community gathers and evaluates. Then we all approach the intruder, and say: 'Gentlemen, you're involving us in a conflict that is not ours. But you are in our territory, and here, we govern'. We've avoided many problems this way. We've saved many people — from killing and being killed. We'll let people go around our land, but they can't stay; because if the guerrilla is here, the army comes, or if the army is here, the guerrilla comes. Of course, if we have to kick out one group, then we have to kick out all the groups. We have to treat them all equally. (Nasa leader quoted in Alther et al., 2004: 23)

In this light, the guard both defends indigenous territories and approaches the armed actors who try to bring in a war that the Paeces consider 'foreign'. This means of nonviolent resistance has produced a range of positive results (León, 2004). For instance, in November 2001 the guard impeded a guerrilla takeover of the town Caldono. Four days later, the inhabitants of the town Bolívar followed their example. Peasants and indigenous peoples obliged the guerrillas to free four police officers who had been captured after more than twenty hours of combat. The voice spread fast and, on 15 December 2001, Jambaló indigenous groups rescued a Paéz boy who had been kidnapped by the FARC-EP and, a week later, elders and young people in Puracé stopped the crossfire between three-hundred guerrillas and eight policemen while shouting 'peace, we want peace' (ibid.: 13–14).

In July 2003, the FARC-EP kidnapped Florian Benedikt Arnold, a Swiss missionary who was visiting one of the Nasa reservations. More than one thousand Paeces put their guard into motion and confronted the kidnappers: 'if you don't set him free, you are going to have to kill us all', were the words of the indigenous governor according to the essayist Juanita León (ibid.: 21). The Paeces' guard was able to free the captive (Alther et al., 2004: 24). In August 2004, the FARC-EP kidnapped several community leaders, to which the guard reacted by entering the territory controlled by the guerrillas and demanding the liberation of the indigenous. In this case, the guard was also successful (ibid.: 25).

A month later, in September 2004, the Paeces called a national *minga* along the Pan-American Highway. This has been regarded as the most successful nonviolent march in Colombia. As a Nasa leader remarked,

> *Esta vez salimos a convocar pueblos, organizaciones y procesos populares. ... convocamos esta Minga con una propuesta para que entre todos, como pueblos, definamos un mandato indígena y popular que oriente el proceso para que podamos avanzar en pasos firmes y realistas desde esta realidad de confusión y muerte hasta un proyecto de vida tejido por nosotros desde los pueblos.* (Nasa leader quoted in Ferro, 2005: 4)

The march was guarded by more than five-thousand Nasa. Among the participants there were more than sixty-five thousand members of indigenous groups, Afro-Colombians, peasants and trade unionists (Alther et al., 2004: 26). It lasted for four days and participants traveled over one hundred kilometers.

The guard has also tried to resist the involvement of young people in the different armies. With this purpose, they have created the Youth Council of Tierradentro (*Consejo de Jóvenes de Tierradentro*), which includes young Paeces from more than twenty communities. The council emphasises resisting the military draft that, according to the constitutional framework, is not binding for indigenous peoples. However, during 2005 several boys joined the peasant soldiers and died in combat, making evident the need for the council to engage in preventive strategies to protect the young population in the face of governmental policies that constantly try to include them in the war (UNDP, 2005c). Thus, the resistance of the Paeces also touches upon one of the main components of the DSP: 'the army of good people'. By trying to implement programmes and leadership workshops, the Youth Council refuses to enlist in armies, whether legal or illegal. Their stance is a matter of principles: they do not want to participate as armed soldiers for any organisation.

Additionally, throughout their various resistance activities, the Paeces have tried to make guerrillas, paramilitary and army members accountable for their violence and have scrutinised the war practices they perform. In their call for accountability, when the Paeces were trying to liberate the captured police officers in Bolívar, Juanita León (2004) gathered the testimony of some of the indigenous people interrogating the guerrilleros. 'Why do you destroy Bolívar when priding yourselves of being the people's armies? Can't you see that they are as poor as you?' In Caldoso, after the fifth attempt by the guerrilla to take over the town, an Indigenous Council member appealed to the guerrilla leader to explain himself: 'How is it possible that he defended social justice and, at the same time, used gas cylinders to blow the school his children attended?' (Nasa quoted in León, 2004: 24).

The guerrillas did not answer any of these questions. However, these particular episodes revealed the fact that the Paeces had raised their voices and not their arms. They confronted with arguments and made palpable the lack of coherence between the promises of liberation of the guerrillas and their extreme and systematic violence against the people they claimed to defend. This is already an indispensable attitude. The confrontation of agonistic ideas and debates about how to harmonise peaceful means towards peaceful ends constitute a starting point for transformation. Engaging with the 'other', because it is subject to be made accountable for its actions and words, is part of the Paéz strategy for resistance. These indigenous groups do not condemn the 'other' to be the absolute evil, as the DSP proclaims. On the contrary, they still call on them as political subjects to be held accountable for the violence they perpetrate, whether they are guerrillas or army soldiers.

Unfortunately, as the events of April and July 2005 illustrate, the nonviolent Nasa resistance has not always been respected by armed actors, which does not necessarily mean that it has been a failure. It serves to call into question violence as a means to achieve peace and security. As the media reports (Sierra, 2005), during three weeks there was combat in Paéz territory between the FARC-EP and the army. On 14 April, the guerrillas attacked the municipality of Toribío using gas cylinders and destroying the town, killing both civilians and police officers. On 21 April, the guerrillas attacked the town of Jambaló and forced the inhabitants to flee in the midst of crossfire. On 27 April, the army entered the town of Tancueyó. All through those weeks, army and police forces were fighting with the guerrillas in several rural checkpoints.

When the indigenous people escaped the towns, they moved towards refugee camps, which had already been agreed upon, planned for and prepared more than three years before (ibid.). These were the *emergency plans* that the guard had set up as part of their resistance activities. The main idea was that the Nasa would not abandon their territories, no matter how difficult the war situation became (ibid.).

In July 2005, the FARC-EP attacked the town of Caldono again, for the seventh time in five years (Ideas para la Paz, 2005: 1). The inhabitants ran to refugee camps once again and the army again entered. The president announced the creation of a new High Mountain Battalion for the region. This battalion was intended to serve as a complement to the military operations which had been taking place in the region for months and which were part of the larger military action called Plan Patriota (ibid.: 2).

For Colombian conflict analysts, it seems evident that the FARC-EP and the security forces are fighting a war over the indigenous territories in order to control a land considered strategic in the war against narco-terrorism (ibid.: 3). The Paeces do not want guerrillas or army in their territories. As they claimed in a press release collected by the foundation Ideas para la Paz (ibid.), the public force should not attack them but protect them, which implies acknowledging that state sovereignty is relative, never absolute in indigenous territories where several sources of authority and legitimacy coincide (ibid.: 4).

The above entails that the state must come to terms with the notion of autonomy and resistance of the indigenous Paeces, which contradicts the notion of state sovereignty. Indigenous territories defy the geostrategic control by state security forces and, on the other hand, their stance concerning micro-practices of security is one of resistance. The Paeces will not join the army of good people that the state in/security discourse creates. They refuse to be ruled by the postulates of the war on terror that defies any spatial or temporal limit against a blurred enemy. The Paeces reject the notion of dangerousness as a principle of depoliticising behaviour. They talk to army and guerrilla representatives alike. They refuse not to engage with the 'other'. In short, neither their territories nor their bodies are accessible for this war.

Since the Paeces have maintained their nonviolent resistance, organised, planned and effectively defended themselves nonviolently from attacks, some have qualified the movement as a failure when the Paeces sought refuge (ibid.: 3).

213

Yet, what these critics fail to recognise is that the discourse of the Paeces is not based on nonviolence as a method of struggle. It is based on nonviolence as a principle for action, which is not circumstantial, but unqualified. The *mingas* and the Indigenous Guard are expressions of the Nasa people who 'strive to walk their talk, putting into practice a saying they live by: "Words without actions are empty, actions without words are blind, and words and actions outside of the spirit of community are death"' (Alther et al., 2004: 25). This coherence comes from the Paéz cosmovision for which there is no separation between means and ends and therefore no separation between humans, nature and cosmos. Herein lays its strength.

Nasa Peace and Security

The Nasa resistance movement and discourse are inspired in their cosmovision, meaning in the way they conceive being in/of the world, and which constitutes their approach to knowledge and spirituality. The two are perceived as twin notions, inseparable from their culture. For them, material and spiritual cultures are all in one, interconnected, involving internal and external worlds dictating their norms of behaviour, their rights, duties and daily activities (ONIC, 2005e: 3).

Therefore, the resistance movement of the Paeces cannot be measured according to specific situations seen from a win/lose perspective, as is the case with the PCP of the Province of Antioquia. Their nonviolence is unqualified; it is a philosophy, a way of life, and not just a means to achieve certain goals for their 'struggle'. This wholeness or coherence is embedded in their understanding of being. As Francesca Cerbini (2003) has documented about the Paeces' genesis, this group depicts their origins in *ks'a´w wala* (big spirit) who, because it was masculine and feminine at the same time, had the virtue of creating life. From *ks'a´w wala* ten spirits were born, *ekthe* (master of space), *t'we yase* (earth), *weet'ahn* (who leaves sickness to time), *kl'umn* (goblin), *daat'i* (social control), *tay* (sun), *a'te* (moon), *eeh'a* (wind) and *s'i'* (social transformation). After a long period of conflict amongst them, they found an agreement to create a special being called Nasa (Yule quoted in Cerbini, 2003: 4).

According to Paéz philosophy, the whole is composed out of three spheres in which all elements are to be found (Agencia Universitaria de Periodismo, 1998: 67). In the superior sphere (*êêka*) reign the sun, the moon, the stars, the thunder, the rainbow, the clouds and other spirits. In our land or middle sphere (*kwes kiwe*) live humans, animals, plants and *mohanos*, who transform into animals, sexually pursue men and women and take care of the fields. In the inferior sphere (*kiwe d'ihu*) live the spirits who engender positive energies towards our world and who are responsible for the growth of plants and water. As well, in the *kiwe d'ihu* live the spirits of negative energies, who cause erosions and landslides.

It is crucial to comprehend that all the elements in the Nasa cosmovision are essential for the whole. As negative spirits, negative cosmic energy (*pta'nz*) is indispensable for the proper functioning of the system since it expresses everything that negatively affects the relations of conviviality among humans and between humans and their surroundings (Cerbini, 2003: 5). The origins of imbalance are entirely human. Humans alone can cause disharmony when they do not attend to the order of things. The balance can be restored, until a certain limit, if the proper rituals of cleansing are performed. For the cleaning and healing rituals, indigenous authorities must go to the natural places where equilibrium should be re-established by *th'wala*, the medicine authority (Agencia Universitaria de Periodismo, 1998: 67).

The authority over the Nasa people also has its origins in its legends and territories. Gretchen Alther, John Lindsay-Poland, and Sarah Weintraub (2004) have gathered this oral history in their analysis of the Indigenous Guard. They recount how the Association of Indigenous Councils of Northern Cauca narrates the foundation of local authority:

> After the formation of Nasa territory, certain families and groups began arguing among themselves. Cosmic Wisdom, who was also Thunder, observed this, and chose two orphans to whom he gave power. One of the orphans received an axe, and the other, a slingshot. And the three of them defended Nasa Territory from those who tried to invade. But the problems continued. So Cosmic Wisdom chose a Nasa man, called him the Spiritual Authority, and gave him a wooden staff. There were now four authorities working together to protect Nasa territory. But difficult times awaited the People: the Spanish Invasion. It became necessary to defend Nasa territories and communities with written laws. So Cosmic Wisdom created visionary organizers and leaders. (Ibid.: 24)

Therefore, the notion of authority the Nasa live by is born out of their community. It is not a result of state sovereignty and/or armed control. Their *security* resembles a condition in which they feel *in harmony* within their territories and following their ancestral traditions in dynamic balance with changing circumstances. As seen in the different examples of *mingas* and public declarations, for the Paeces this balance and harmony between humans, nature and cosmos is not reduced to their ethnic group. Just as they have called guerrillas and the army to dialogue in a number of occasions, they have also set permanent spaces for political conversations with different groups, such as peasants and trade unionists. Their call for nonviolent resistance is then also tied to political participation with non-indigenous peoples and in formal institutional spaces beyond their territories and traditional settings.

Consequently, their discourse of resistance based on energetic concepts should not be adored in a romantic, conservative manner (Dietrich, 2006). However, can it be neither overcome nor read as prepolitical. Native resistance discourses 'contest the inscription of power in identities and bodies. ... What the rich bodily symbolism of peasant [and indigenous] discourses of resistance demonstrates is that the "social skin" [the body] is a site of political contest and transformation, that there is a somatics of rule and of resistance to rule' (Alonso, 1992: 418–19). Thus, the Paeces discourse of nonviolence can be 'recognized as common heritage of and for *all* human beings expressing the complete potential of our feelings, thoughts, words, actions and reactions' (Dietrich, 2006: 42). Consequently, the Paeces discourse cannot be inscribed upon conventional divisions between sovereign/non-sovereign, mestizo/indigenous, rational/ spiritual, modern/premodern, political/prepolitical and enlightened/barbaric. Most importantly, when we open the interpretation of their differences, their discourse of resistance defies the violent inscription of their 'otherness' as a threat to 'our' national and territorial unity and to 'our' war on terror.

Yet, articulated along the DSP lines of exclusion and violence against 'otherness', the Colombian government precepts cannot come to terms with the Paeces' particular understanding of resistance that merges nonviolence, spirituality and politics. The Nasa nonviolent discourse does not recognise state authority, but instead calls for peacefully transforming conflicts. Thus, when the security forces come down upon the Paeces' nonviolent resistance or when they abandon them to be massacred by guerrillas and paramilitaries – as was the case in Toribío – state violence is made visible. The state reveals the 'relations of violence on which it depends ... it can no longer conceal its violence under the pretence of politics' (Edkins and Pin-Fat, 2004: 17). In this sense, the Paeces' discourse of resistance uncovers the supporting and contradictory relations of the dominant state in/security discourse (Alonso, 1992: 421).

This evidence of violence also gives rise to rethinking the very basis of the political grounds of the DSP: can we achieve security by postponing freedoms and rising in arms against 'otherness'? Can peace be born out of state authority? The discourse of the Paeces puts under scrutiny the DSP and brings politics back into discussion.

THE PAECES CHALLENGE

The biggest challenge the Paeces pose to the DSP discourse is the unique way in which they merge spirituality with politics based on unqualified nonviolence. One of its effects is to bring back politics to the public debate, eroding the seeming consensus on the notion that politics should be postponed until in/security brings us peace. Let us recount how the Paeces contest the logic of in/security.

Facing the different types of violence that the DSP constructs and produces, the Paeces propose an understanding of peace that is vernacular and relational, neither subject to exportation nor importation. Their notion of peace is based upon respect for difference and for otherness, without turning these arguments into weapons for exclusion. As we have studied in the past section, the resistance discourses of the Paeces call for a concept of trans-rational peace. It is embedded in local conditions that do not need to be explored scientifically or apprehended morally, but must be respected as we value otherness and recognise the spiritual dimension of all human beings. Simultaneously, they participate in normative institutional arrangements to deal with conflicts, embracing the 'rationality' of modern politics.

This concept of relational peace clearly contradicts the secure peace of the DSP. The latter is based on the trap of founding politics in in/security. It is supposed to be born out of authority, a promise for a future that by definition cannot be achieved since it reproduces insecurities for its own dynamic. The army only generates more violence and suffering when insisting on its sovereign right to militarily control indigenous territory. In this way, it aims to hail subjects to fight terrorism as soldiers in the army of good people.

Nevertheless, for the Paeces, the security forces are not liberators, nor can they offer peace. For them, peace is only relational. Peace is not postponed, for it is here and on earth where it can be constructed in harmony. Their authority is not the state, but rather Cosmic Wisdom that forges balance between humans, nature and cosmos. The Nasa do not have an army, but a guard that is filled with symbolism for their own authority and does not resort to violence. On the contrary, it is always and only a nonviolent guard. Thus, the Paeces cannot be drafted into the army of good people.

The Paeces do not follow the construction of a homogeneous and unified 'us' fighting an evil 'other' with whom there are no possibilities for transformation. Quite the opposite, to 'others' – such as members of the army, guerrillas, paramilitaries and other non-armed groups – the Paeces extend invitations for conversational politics. The Nasa people make violent groups accountable for their actions. The Paeces resort to responsibility under which we can all be made accountable for what we say and do. They scrutinise the government and refuse to be ruled according to official practices of in/security.

One of the most valuable insights that the resistance discourse of the Paeces bring to light is the indispensable notion of disrupting the hegemonic understanding of in/security portrayed by the DSP. When the Paeces march through the country calling for a trans-rational understanding of peace and reconstituting their political identity, they unsettle the unanimity of that representation of *Colombia as a democratic nation under the threat of narco-terrorism*. They call attention to the heterogeneity of that absorbing concept of *a nation* named Colombia. At the same time, they bring back to the centre of discussion whether or not this is a democracy, because in a democratic system they should be politically valid subjects and the government's actions should be transparent.

In this sense, the resistance discourse of the Paeces, with all its imperfections and lacunae, challenges the monopoly of the state in defining what the Colombian reality is about, what security and peace (partially) mean, who is endangering who and at what price are we willing to postpone politics until in/security brings us freedom.

Those uncertainties should not be answered once and for all. Only by taking them for granted can the in/security discourse keep shaping political discussions around the instrumentality of security and deviating attention from its own foundations. But when homogeneity is unsettled and when unauthorised questions are posed, then we open up possibilities for resignifying the political, for unpacking the very notion of in/security as it is officially presented by the government and violently enforced upon 'us' and 'them'.

The politics of affinity

It is pertinent to sketch some of the academic routes that have been opened and that could and should be studied further. In the constant struggles between hegemonic and resistance discourses, as well as in the negotiations of identity/difference, what remains conclusive is the crucial feature to enjoy political spaces where to express, share and be transformed by encounters with 'others'.

In this sense, I do not propose a formula that will seem to be a full solution. I am afraid that this rationale of certain answers is precisely what draws us to embrace the promise of in/security. My impetus is to call attention to how conversations and discussions about peace and security can lead to politics that are more inclusive. It is an ethical call since it posits a higher value on peaceful ways of transforming conflicts and overtly seeks to participate in discursive practices that generate political inclusion. Nonetheless, it is not a prescriptive call, since the results of those conversational politics cannot be known in advance. I believe that the condition for their possibility is the openness of democratic spaces where connections, encounters and dialogue can take place. If we close down these spaces in the name of in/security, violence and exclusion to and from (de)authorised political subjects would only be fuelled.

Therefore, I would like to make an appeal for the reappropriation of politics within the concrete peace perspective put forward in the past chapters. This proposal is born out of a series of calls for democratic politics made by several authors whose thoughts and ideas have nourished this research.

Delineating the framework for analysis is Vicent Martínez (2001a; 2001b; 2005) and his approach of *Philosophy for Peaces*. This book has been based on many of these principles, especially on the proposal of embracing fragility and vulnerability to reconstruct a notion of insecure peace. This idea also promotes the notion of agonistic politics. It is grounded upon the concept that politics should serve as means for transforming conflicts, for encountering those with whom we disagree and engaging in conversations to face the fear of 'otherness' with respect. This particular insight has encouraged me to look forward to reconstructing a peace studies perspective that makes use of the notions of insecure peace, performative identity and conversational politics. This is what I have called the *politics of affinity*. Consequently, among the suggestions below, there is an underlying continuity: through agonistic politics based on respect, peaceful conflict transformation can take place.

Agonistic politics

Many scholars have made highly interesting suggestions and well-articulated proposals regarding agonistic politics. It would be impossible to provide a comprehensive literature review in this section. Rather, I would like to draw on several of the authors who have already nurtured the theses collected in this book and to highlight how they relate to agonistic politics. From my perspective, their calls suggest a common understanding of how to resist discourses of in/security towards more peaceful and less harmful horizons. Following this line of thought, I attempt to bring in their proposals and then use them to read the DSP.

Some understandings of the term 'women and agency' attempt to conceive of the subject as always in the process of becoming. Subjects open to resignification and focus of political debate, which emerge as a possibility for reworking the very matrix of power that constitutes them (Butler, 1999). I will analyse the conceptualisations of subjectivity, identity, exclusion and difference along ethical grounds that point to the violence invested in constructing identity categories and in occupying subject positions (Edkins and Pin-Fat, 1999, 2004; Jabri, 1999, 2006; Stern, 2005; Walker, 2004).

Judith Butler (1993, 1999), who is regarded as the founder of queer theory and pioneer of the notion of performative gender identity, has also made a powerful academic endeavour to recreate democratic politics. She appeals for more livable spaces of encounter and recognition of the 'other' (Butler, 2004). Her writings call into question the logic of security in the war on terror and make us rethink the definition of political inclusions and exclusions from the concept of who counts as human (ibid.).

In the Colombian case, Butler's calls might help us raise awareness of the racist and modernist epistemic violence that legitimises the violence deployed against indigenous peoples like the Paeces. As well, the portrayal of 'terrorists' as animals (Uribe, 2003b), bodies who do not belong to the human collectivity, facilitates their exclusion and extermination. By picturing 'others' as outside of humanity, the in/security discourse, emanating from the state but carried out by 'us', separates 'us' ever more politically and physically from those who are left outside the realm of reason. By being excluded from the authorised political community, 'we' negate to 'ourselves' the very possibility of encountering 'others' and hence, being transformed by the very act of petitioning their recognition (Butler, 2004). As the spaces and times for encounters, this holds true whether we are considering formal institutional democratic arrangements or informal politics when and where it occurs.

In the same line of feminist scholars, Chantal Mouffe's (1992) theorising of radical democratic politics strives to open opportunities for articulating various different struggles against oppression. In the Colombian case, such struggles evidence the frequent discriminations that intersect in/security practices. The fact that citizens in the city and of higher economic social status do not have to die on the battlefield, contrary to poor and rural populations who are drafted into the war (DSP, 2003: §128–30), is already a critical insight on how the politics of in/security target populations according to their particular (intersectional) identities (Jabri, 1999, 2006).

Those in the cities are predominantly regulated to live in aseptic spaces where there is an institutional explicit effort to avoid connection and circulation and to manage them as transparent citizens (Dillon, 2005; Echavarría, 2002; Lobo-Guerrero, 2007; Vattimo, 1992). Peasant soldiers, on the other hand, denote the sovereign power of the state over their deaths (Dillon, 2007). They are the sacrificial mass in the geopolitical war on terror.

Along this interpretive line, Chantal Mouffe's call for democratic radical politics, as it was put forward in her 1985 book co-authored with Ernesto Laclau (Laclau and Mouffe, 2001), brings up an important additional element for discussion: the impossible closure of the 'we'. For Laclau and Mouffe (ibid.), an impossible antagonism - evident in the shaping of political subjectivities - makes rational consensus a regulative anti-democratic ideal. Hence, for them the possibility of a final reconciliation, a fully inclusive 'we', is foreclosed when seen against the central role of antagonism in the articulation of the political. This impossibility embraces conflictive relationships, divisions and particularities as being the very political and, henceforth, calls attention to how any consensus is the result of a hegemonic articulation that – by definition – has an 'outside' that impedes its full realisation (ibid.: xviii).

For Laclau and Mouffe (ibid.: 188), a hegemonic articulation of the political that tries to 'pass beyond the constitutive character of antagonism and denies plurality in order to restore unity' is a danger that threatens democracy. This contribution appears to me as a key element to consider in the Colombian case. For instance, the hegemonic articulation of the end of peace after the breakdown of talks with the guerrillas on 20 February 2002 – that turned the call for in/security into the only plausible option left – though consensually embraced in the public sphere, could only be achieved by excluding alternative readings that still considered other possibilities for peace. In other words, the seeming consensus was already the result of an exclusive notion of in/security. Such a reading enables us to understand that the apparent unity of in/security necess-itates the production of an excluded 'we', not just concerning political comm-unities ('others') but also political options that had to be lost (Campbell, 1999).

Furthermore, Laclau and Mouffe's (2001) call for accepting conflictive relationships as the very nature of politics could be understood within the analysis of the DSP as the framework that allows attention to be paid to what remains 'outside' for the 'inside' to be apparently homogeneous. By being aware that the possibilities for politics are born out of conflictive relationships, these conflictive relationships stop being a threat to politics and become the very human condition that makes democratic politics possible. I believe that such an understanding of difference is especially urgent in the Colombian case. As such, calls like the ones espoused by nonviolent discourses of resistance to the DSP, democratic formal spaces as the Congress, unauthorised narratives of peace and war by demobilised peoples, and proposals for trans-rational peaces by the Paeces, among others, might be seen under the light of difference that do not automatically result in the condemnation of 'otherness' (Connolly, 1991).

Along the same line of thinking, contemporary academics who deal with issues of identity construction have also made several relevant proposals. Among them, William Connolly (1991) has put forward an ethical project called 'agonistic democracy', which is based on care for the diversity of human life and the interdependence of identity/difference. For Connolly, agonistic mutuality fosters an ethics in which alter-identities prompt agonistic respect for differences and care for life. In this group, we also find Stuart Hall (1996a) and his call for politics that engage with difference by recognising the situated character of identity instead of suppressing it. In this same vein, the proposal of Amin Maalouf (2000) argues to accept and cherish the different affiliations that make up our individual and collective identities. Maalouf encourages acceptance of a multiplicity of historical, political and religious allegiances as equally legitimate. For this project, democratic politics based on respect are needed (ibid.).

All this potentiality of encounters is precisely what is being repressed, excluded and carefully warred against in the in/security discourse of the DSP. It is a discourse that closes down possibilities; it excludes 'otherness' from formal political spaces and marginalises political communities that do not fit the securitised and fixed notions of *Colombians* as they are portrayed in the war against terror. The DSP aims to reduce the possibilities for becoming something different from the frozen and 'secure' identities constructed in its discourse. It does so by regulating life and death in such a powerful way that resisting its call for violence becomes a danger in itself. The systematic killings of 'terrorist-sympathisers', like the Paeces del Cauca and the leaders of the Peace Community of San José de Apartadó, as well as the incorporation of children into the army of 'good people', are obvious expressions of how the violent mechanisms of the in/security discourse work to lessen scrutiny of state policies and to diminish possibilities for dissent (Jabri, 2006).

Differences, uncertainty and politics

Many authors have explored the notion of politics as plural and uncertain. Politics are necessarily insecure, and attempting to extirpate such uncertainty involves a large extensive and intensive deployment of futile violence.

For instance, a great source of inspiration and debate has been Donna Haraway's (1991) myth of the cyborg, in which she reconstituted women's solidarity upon bridges of affinity built on political coalitions, challenging the taken-for-granted unity among essential conceptions of women and turned it into a call for consciously engaging in conversational politics. As such, political coalitions based on political affinities are not the expression of pre-existing political subjectivities, but rather are constituted in the encounter itself. Such political encounters could bring unexpected possibilities for transformation into existence. This is one of the most valuable insights of Hannah Arendt's extensive work. As Michael Dillon (1996) also points out, Arendt's notion of the unpredictability of politics was founded on how the 'other', in its difference, would be the condition *sine qua non* for politics and, thus, for freedom (Arendt, 1998).

In this realm, I also want to bring in the contributions of maybe one of the most influential intellectuals who call for opening debates and politically dealing with difference, Edward Said (2003a). Said made great efforts to unveil the violence of 'sameness' based on the 'homogeneous' and 'inferior' character of the 'other'. He challenged the notion that difference implied hostility. His ethical concerns voiced how to propose alternatives that forged libertarian, non-repressive and non-manipulative relations of power/knowledge (ibid.). Along with the insights of Michael Dillon (1996), these two academicians constantly underscore the importance of freedom. In Dillon's (ibid.) proposal of 'ethico-political responsibility', he has also explicitly conceived of politics as based on the impossibility of knowing its outcomes. This uncertain character of politics enables us to return to the idea of fragility that, in his view, revolves around care for the self and for the other.

These different calls for politics focus our attention on the importance of embracing politics as that unknown terrain that can bring into being unexpected possibilities for transformation. This notion of politics has two important foundations. The first one is the necessity for encountering the 'other' in places where to connect. This calls the attention to the richness of democratic spaces, both informal and formal ones. Hence, the first condition for the possibilities of politics is the existence of those spaces and times for encounters. If they did not exist as such, politics would not exist either.

Second, to *do* politics is to engage with the 'other'. In this sense and echoing Judith Butler (2004), to ask the 'other' for recognition is not a petition for the 'other' to see me as *I am* previous to the encounter itself, but rather to ask for a transformation in the process of recognition itself. This conversation with the 'other', in which I engage with the potentiality of being transformed through and because of the encounter, has already started by recognising that I need the 'other' to accept me as a politically valid interlocutor, and vice versa.

If the 'other' did not exist in its difference, politics would not be possible. Political conversations are constructed based upon and through difference. They are not based on a previously predetermined essential identification, but on the unknown terrain of encounter. Therefore, (dis)agreements, ties, solidarity and pacts can only be born from conversational politics, constituted as affinity (Haraway, 1991). This affinity is built on those political bridges. It cannot be equated to solidarity as a pre-given sense of belonging and sacrifice to a collective 'we'. On the contrary, affinity can only be born from the articulation of interests, needs, desires, projects and so forth. At the same time, building bridges of affinities with 'others' constitutes us as particular subjects with a high political meaning. The fact that our (dis)agreements are born within political encounters cannot but mean that we constitute ourselves in a constant and valid political conversation.

Both political foundations, the political space and the political recognition for encountering the 'other', seem to me paramount for calling for a space in which the negotiation of our political identities can take place in a nonviolent way. If we accept that democratic spaces, understood in this agonistic sense, are indispensable and valuable, the temptation to condemn difference and 'otherness' is twisted into the valorisation of those features. That the 'other' is different from me is not an obstacle, but rather the condition *sine qua non* for politics. Hence, when the DSP calls for an impossible search of 'security', when it closes down political spaces because they are threats to democracy, when it exterminates those who disagree and when 'we' participate actively in the army of good people, political violence is reproduced. It is not, as we have explored, a purely geopolitical enterprise. The DSP also discloses the power over life in multiple biopolitical practices.

Disrupting the biopolitics of the DSP

The managing of the population through several in/security measures, like warning networks of informants, necessitate opening the analysis of in/security from a purely geostrategic towards a combination of the latter with a biopolitical reading of this security *dispositif* (Lobo-Guerrero, 2007). When in more recent writings, Michael Dillon (2005, 2007, 2008; Dillon and Reid, 2001) calls attention to the combined workings of the geopolitics and biopolitics of in/security, his proposals for embracing uncertainty go beyond purely geopolitics and enter the realm of the biopolitics of security. I am aware that most of my reading of the DSP and the discourses of resistance to it rely heavily on geopolitical accounts. I want to acknowledge the vast richness of biopolitical disruptions to the DSP that can also contribute to more peaceful and less harmful horizons.

For instance, away from the notions of sedition, revolution or resistance, Dillon (2008: 329) calls for the possibility of contagion as the radical emergent and contingent of contemporary biopolitical governance, understood as life circulation, connectivity and complexity. In Dillon and Reid's (2001) reading of in/security, a geopolitical strategy cannot be devised for the global liberal governance that seeks power over life. For them, though a geopolitical strategy is honoured (ibid.: 65), the sciences over life seem to be at the core of biopolitical strategies of in/security.

Embracing uncertainty within the political realm that shapes subjectivities necessarily also calls for 'combining' them with biopolitical strategies that strive for life contagion, emergent and contingent connections and circulation of lives. Therefore, the life sciences that regulate in/security need to become also an integral part of the pool of possibilities for rethinking in/security discourses and practices towards articulations that challenge the production of violence. This implies that practices, such as insurance, appear as central to comprehend the biopolitical tenet of in/security.

By definition, biopolitical strategies of resistance cannot be known in advance (Lobo-Guerrero, 2007), since the very referent objects and subjects of security and the 'reality' of security are in constant change. Therefore, a concrete analysis of the biopolitical security strategies in place needs to be conducted (ibid.), paying attention not to circumscribe technological rationality under the same logic of biopolitical strategies of in/securities (Lobo-Guerrero, 2008: 233). In the words of Luis Lobo-Guerrero (ibid.), this call for biopolitical readings of in/security underlines how the study of technological practices ought to be immediately related to the promotion and protection of a liberal way of life (ibid.).

These last remarks on the analysis of possibilities for rethinking geopolitics and biopolitics of in/security towards the reconstruction of less harmful articulations of relationships is based on a previous conceptual yet crucial distinction between power and violence. As has been argued in the preceding section of this chapter regarding discourses of resistance to the DSP and following Vivienne Jabri (2006: 48), I understand power and violence, as well as power/resistance and violence, as differently constituted. 'Power and violence are hence separable analytical categories, separable practices; they are at the same time connected in ways that work on populations and on bodies – with violence often targeted against the latter so that the former are reigned in, governed' (ibid.). Precisely such separation within the framework of the geopolitics and biopolitics of in/security provides Jabri (ibid.) with a conceptual frame to recognise the 'matrix of war' of our present global il/liberal condition. The matrix of war can be succinctly described as 'a set of diffuse practices, violence, disciplinarity and control that at one and same time target the other typified in cultural and racial terms and instantiate a wider remit of operations that impact upon society as a whole' (ibid.: 52).

By utilising the matrix of war to highlight how in/security politics in 'police operations, in institutional discourse and in public arenas, comes to constitute the culturally marked other as the source of danger' (ibid.: 61), Jabri also points towards what I would call the politics of affinity. She claims that this matrix of war blurs the distinction between war and peace, peace and security and war and criminality, enabling liberal state practices to remain beyond scrutiny and accountability (ibid.: 48–9). The primacy of war evident in the politics of in/security, as they are lived and experienced by ever-shifting 'dangerous' subjectivities in a post 9/11 perpetual war setting, undermine political structures and political agency. They shrink possibilities for contestation and – ultimately – democratic government and politics.

I believe that these reflections might guide a different and more peaceful conceptualisation of in/secure identities, one that bears in mind the ethical commitment of lessening harm and suffering. Such a combination of possible ways of tackling and disrupting the politics of in/security points to horizons in which politics are valued as indispensable spaces for encountering the 'other' with the potentiality for transformation and as connections and open circulation as the necessary disrupting measures to the violence the DSP reproduces. In this sense, I also understand these reflections as grounded upon ethical concerns related to insecure peaces. The concrete shapes of these emerging proposals from different fields of study and viewpoints surely merit further analysis in the Colombian case, for which the present book might serve as a starting point.

Conclusion

To provide a more complete picture of the effects that the DSP has on the constitution of political identities in Colombia, the present chapter has been informed by one overarching question: How have some subjects resisted the DSP? In order to arrive at some answers, a couple of preliminary moves were necessary. First, I delineated a theoretical framework from where to investigate resistance discourses to the DSP. Such interpretive structure called on comprehending resistance discourses as discursive formations (Weldes et al., 1999), which necessarily draw their own limits and have gaps and excess (Flax, 1992). Moreover, resistance discourses emerge as a possibility from the matrix of power relations that constitute them (Edkins and Pin-Fat, 1999, 2004; Stern, 2005), though this does not necessarily mean that their formation can be reduced to remnants of hegemony (Butler, 1993, 1999).

On the contrary, contesting discourses can pose unexpected questions and disrupt the discursive limits of dominant discourses (Butler, 1999), they enjoy the possibility of challenging the logic of exclusion and violence of in/security and propose dealing with fear and 'otherness' in a constructive way (Campbell, 1998; Connolly, 1991; Stern, 2005). As such, the alternatives proposed by resistance discourses should be analysed against the background of the (im)possibility of in/security (Dillon, 1996; Stern, 2005). This interpretative structure served to access resistance discourses from a particular insecure peace studies perspective.

The first point of entry to these discourses was an evaluation of how violent responses to the DSP do not arrest the cycle of violence they claim to contest. The analysis of the discourse of resistance of the FARC-EP (2000, 2002, 2004) was used as a paradigmatic example to evidence that if the challenges posed by the DSP are contested in a violent way, the spiral of violence is not arrested. On the contrary, it is reproduced and reinforced from marginal sites.

To comprehend nonviolent resistance discourses to the DSP, insights from the *Philosophy for Peaces* (Martínez, 2001, 2001b, 2002, 2005) and trans-rational peaces (Dietrich, 2006, 2008; Dietrich and Sützl, 2006) were synthesised. On the one hand, the recognition of conflict as inherent to human relations and as a source for enrichment and social energy was made evident in terms of a possible moral improvement. Moreover, via embracing the critique of a univocal notion of peace and security, trans-rational elements were brought into the discussion as a way of twisting the One Peace into relational peaces.

With this prism, analysing the nonviolence programme of the Congruent Peace Plan of the Province of Antioquia revealed that qualified state nonviolence does not serve as an alternative to the DSP, but merely as a way of filling in its gaps. We then turned to the resistance of the indigenous group Paeces del Cauca as a non-state discourse of nonviolence. Since this discourse does not embrace sovereignty nor does it recognise the nation-state as a unique source of authority, the resistance discourse of the Paeces calls for a concept of trans-rational peace that contradicts the secure peace of the DSP. For them, peace is only relational, it is not postponed until in/security comes in the future – as the government claims – for it is here and now where peace can be constructed in harmony. Thus, the Paeces cannot be drafted into the army of good people. They disturb the hegemonic articulations of peace, security and politics of the DSP and open up possibilities for resignifying the political, for unpacking the very notion of in/security as it is officially presented by the government and violently enforced upon 'us' and 'them'.

These last reflections took us to structure possibilities for reconstituting politics on the bases for affinity. I collected what, in my view, are frequent and crucial calls for conversational politics, respect for difference and embracing of uncertainties that point to less harmful, more insecure and less violent ways of relating to each other. Therefore I would like to underscore this appeal for the reappropriation of politics in which peaces are insecure.

Originating in several academic fields, many authors call attention to the importance of embracing politics as that unknown terrain which can bring into being unexpected possibilities for transformation (Arendt, 1998; Butler, 1993, 1999, 2004; Connolly, 1991; Dillon, 1996, 2007, 2008; Dillon and Reid, 2001; Edkins and Pin-Fat, 1999, 2004; Hall, 1996a; Jabri, 1999, 2006; Maalouf, 2000; Martínez, 2001a, 2001b, 2002, 2005; Mouffe, 1992; Laclau and Mouffe, 2001; Lobo-Guerrero, 2008; Said, 2003a; Stern, 2005; Walker, 2004). This notion of agonistic politics of affinity has two important foundations. The first is the necessity for encountering the 'other' in places where it is possible to deal with differences in nonviolent ways. Hence, the first condition for the possibilities of politics is the existence in itself of those spaces and times for encounters. If they did not exist as such, politics would not exist either. Second, to *do* politics is to engage with the 'other' in a conversation in which I merge with at least the potentiality of being transformed through and only because of the encounter (Butler, 2004). This type of politics is not based upon a previous predetermined essential identification, but rather upon the unknown terrain of encounter. Both political foundations, the political space and the political recognition for encountering the 'other', seem to me to be paramount for calling for a time-space in which the negotiation of our political identities can take place in a nonviolent way.

In the Colombian case, reconstituting democratic spaces and refusing to follow the DSP geopolitical and biopolitical measures of separation, depoliticised lives and certain deaths, (I hope) would guide a different and more peaceful conceptualisation of political identities, one that bears in mind the ethical commitment of rethinking peaces as insecure.

NOTES

1 The United Nations Development Program (UNDP, 2005a) has created an online data bank of 'Good Practices', where actions, programmes and projects that 'dissuade the option of violence, mitigate its impact and generate conditions for a lasting and firm peace' are collected. In this data bank more than seventy different peaceful proposals can be found.

2 According to the data provided by the National Police (Policía Nacional, 2005: 33), every day in Colombia there is an average of fifty-five murders, eleven deaths due to traffic accidents, eighty-seven people wounded due to common delinquency, 146 robberies, fifty-three stolen cars, four kidnappings, six extortions, two terrorist acts, one subversive action and two attacks on the roads.

3 This section cannot provide a succinct yet nearly complete recapitulation of Wolfgang Dietrich's contributions to the five families of peace, which he categorises as: moral, energetic, modern, post-modern and trans-rational (2008). For the purposes of evaluating the resistance discourses to the DSP, I limit my analysis to Dietrich's proposal in relation to my own argument on how the DSP produces the political violence it promises to arrest and, furthermore, how resistance discourses to the DSP can be examined through the lenses of how they break away from the in/security discourses towards more peaceful horizons.

4 In postmodern contributions to peace research, Dietrich (2006) finds ground for putting forward his thesis of trans-rational peaces. Postmodernity's doubts in modern metaphysical truths underscored that the postmodern condition and wisdom is to know

and to act beyond the limits of one single criteria of truth; that individuals, issues and their relations change permanently; and that rationality is not enough for the categorisation of international relations (ibid.: 34–5). Postmodern contributions to peace research were able to *twist* moral and modern peaces towards liberation from the monological and violent notion of peace as derived from one God, one Truth, security or justice (Dietrich, 2008: 319). However, the postmodern 'critique of modernity was always characterized by the paradox that this critique of rational thinking had to be expressed in a rational manner and argued along the lines of rationality' (Dietrich, 2006: 36). Hence, such rational limits were an obstacle for rethinking peaces. They signaled the boundary that postmodern interpretations of peace did not dare cross and so postmodernity remained trapped in its own critique.

5 Throughout Dietrich's writings, the notion of *twisting*, as inspired in Gianni Vattimo's interpretation of Heidegger (Vattimo, 2006), is recurrent: '*Der Begriff der Verwindung sagt, dass das Verklungene erinnert und in das erweiterte Dasein jenseits seiner Grenzen integriert wird*' (Dietrich, 2008: 320) ('The notion of twisting says that the faded is remembered and integrated into the expanded being beyond its limits').

6 It is also worthwhile to call attention to the experience of the capital Bogotá. Mainly during the administration of Antanas Mockus as mayor, nonviolent programmes and civil resistance campaigns were designed and implemented within the frame of the city's development plan '*Bogotá: para vivir todos del mismo lado*', 2001–2004. Considering the particularities of each situation, nonetheless the civil resistance initiatives promoted by the office of the mayor also suffered from the limitations of qualified state nonviolence noted in regards to the PCP of the Province of Antioquia. For the philosophical and political bases of this programme, see Mockus and Corzo (2003) and for a pleasant chronicle see León (2004: 119–55).

7 Among the studies and investigations that show the impact on violence in the deep structures of society, Elsa Blair's (1999, 2005) can be counted as one of the most profound on the subject. Her research makes visible the symbolic meaning present in the local culture which has not gone through the necessary processes of mourning to deal with violence on a collective level. As a result, the spiral of violence has been fed by re-editions of old types of violence combined with new situations of direct and structural violence. For a politico-philosophical account on this topic in Medellín, see also 'El miedo en la ciudad' in Villa (2002).

8 Article 246 of the Colombian Political Constitution reads: 'The authorities of the indigenous peoples may exercise jurisdictional functions within their territorial area, in conformity with their own norms and procedures, but always insofar as they are not contrary to the constitution and laws of the Republic. The law will establish the forms of coordination of this special jurisdiction with the national justice system.'

9 There are several Constitutional Court decisions that deal with the development of the constitutional precepts that oblige the Colombian state to respect the jurisdiction of the indigenous communities in their territories (C-037/96; T-634/99; C-898/03; SU-383/03; T-955/03). Especially controversial has been the right of indigenous peoples to judge according to their own justice systems (C-370/02) and the exploitation of natural reserves in indigenous territories, like the U'was (T-188/93; C-139/96; SU-039/97). For a legal summary and insightful political analysis, see Gaviria, 1997.

10 Arturo Escobar has done extensive research on the governmentality of development in the making and unmaking of the third world (Escobar, 1995). Similar to the promise of in/security as argued in this book, Escobar states that precisely because the logic of development is never challenged in its core assumptions of universal progress, yet continues producing goods such as projects and reports, (under)development agonistically

reproduces its own existence. Escobar's call for imagining alternatives to development (1995), has been reinforced since the mid-1990s when arguing that vernacular ways of knowledge – such as those of Afro-Colombian peoples on the Pacific Coast and the indigenous peoples U'Was, by being tied to a specific place contrary to a 'space' (Sachs, 2006) – recreate alternative cosmovisions and, consequently, of development (Escobar, 2001, 2004; Escobar and Harcourt, 2002). I would suggest that Escobar's arguments could be extended to the discourses and practices of resistance to the state in/security discourse of the Paeces del Cauca.

11 In 1971, the Nasa and other indigenous groups formed the Regional Indigenous Council of Cauca, uniting more than 200,000 representatives for strengthening indigenous councils (*Cabildos*), fostering people-centered development and using their traditional nonviolent guard for recovering usurped lands (Alther et al., 2004: 22).

12 Over decades, differences among the peasant and the indigenous movements became more pronounced. Yet even today, they still find several points of agreement concerning struggles for land-ownership and stigmatisation and victimisation from several armed actors, including state forces (ONIC, 2005d: 5).

6

Final remarks:
in/security, peaces, identities and politics

IBEGAN THIS RESEARCH WITH THE THESIS that the state in/security discourse contributes to shaping political identities in such a way that the writing of war is intermingled with the writing of peace, ultimately moulding political imaginaries in Colombia. Such imaginaries are written according to security concerns, legitimising state and non-state violent actions that propel the very political violence the state promises to end. The state in/security discourse produces – it does not prevent – more violence. This thesis has been partly confirmed in examining the relationship between in/security and identity throughout this book. At the same time, it has also become increasingly obvious that the conclusion of this analysis resembles a route far more than a known destination.

I would like to use these last remarks to highlight precisely how the writing of in/security discloses several notions of peaces that are constituted and constitutive of political identities and imaginaries in the Colombian context.

After closely reading the end of the peace talks between the Colombian government and the FARC-EP guerrillas in February 2002, it became evident that the option to engage in a war against terrorism could only be consensually constructed after the possibility for peace negotiations was confirmed as a 'lost option'. This hegemonic articulation of the Colombian situation asserted that the call for in/security was the road to peace. Hence, paradoxically, peace was absorbed within the discursive framework of security. Security defined any understanding of peace and filled it with specific warrior content.

The Colombian presidential elections that took place after the breakdown of the peace talks turned the promise of in/security into a democratically chosen programme. Candidate Alvaro Uribe (2002b) promised that peace would be born out of state authority, which he conceptualised as a new strategy to stop criminal activity in Colombia. This programme made security the founding ground for

230

politics (ibid.: 27) and the precondition for enjoying freedoms and peace (ibid.). Peace was rewritten as the result of erecting a strong state that would defeat the terrorists with the collaboration of the whole (good) citizenry. The promise of in/security drafted 'us' to 'a war of all against terror'. The electoral results were read as the erasure of the peace option and as the success of the political project of in/security and, this way, pursuing war became the path to achieve peace in the future.

By democratically electing Alvaro Uribe and his programme of Democratic Security in May 2002, the institutional DSP was embraced as the 'solution' to war in Colombia. Additionally, this electoral success was by then embedded in the post-9/11 discursive limits of the global war on terror. This permitted the state an extraordinary source of legitimacy for incorporating non-democratic practices to deal with the terrorist threat. In order to fight this war, the state issued the DSP in June 2003.

After analysing the construction of identity categories in the DSP, I concluded that by recognising the danger of narco-terrorism as posing a vital threat to the Colombian state and its people, the state has been able to reshape its own subjectivity and those of 'nationals' and 'others'. In this war on terror, the state calls on the citizenry to join an army of 'good people' so that everybody's obligation is to contribute to the war enterprise. This produces the subjectivities of 'nationals' as divided between 'good' and 'bad' people, counting on the marker of 'solidarity' with the security forces as the mechanism to distinguish between one of 'us' and one of 'them'. The 'other' is constructed as a terrorist facing the choice to convert to one of 'us', 'abandoning a criminal life and returning to the nuclear family' (DSP, 2003: §116), or to be exterminated (Uribe, 2003b). In this relationship between 'us' and 'them' there is nothing 'we' can have, think or do which resembles connections to the 'other'.

The idealised constructions of identity categories in the DSP for state, nationals and others, disclosed an understanding of peace, politics and freedoms as postponed. In the present, the state calls to close ranks against terror and justifies shutting down democratic spaces and renouncing the exercise of political freedoms to fight the war. 'Once security is achieved, people will enjoy their freedoms' and 'security will give birth to peace' promised President Uribe (2002b: 20). This way, peace and politics are sacrificed in the name of in/security. The state so summons the population to refrain from expressing political dissent and restrict their physical circulation until security brings peace in the future.

The material practices informed by the absorption of peace and politics within in/security take the forms of geopolitical strategies to control the territory and biopolitical measures to regulate the population (Dillon, 2007). With the aim of conforming an army of '44-million Colombians' (Uribe, 2002b; DSP, 2003) to defeat terrorism, warning citizens' networks have been organised in cooperation with the official security forces and private security companies. The information passed on to the military and police force led to massive pre-emptive captures of suspects, installing the notion of dangerousness as a principle of behaviour (Jabri, 2006). In the rural areas, peasant soldiers have complemented the army of good people, making clear that the sovereign power over death has as much actuality as the biopower over the life of urban citizens.

Warning networks and battalions of peasant soldiers reveal how the DSP works to regulate the circulation and connection of the population. It additionally illuminates how the state governs with sovereignty to send 'its' people to die in war. The combination of these in/security measures reinforces the in/security promise through diffuse mechanisms of power that reduce political spaces for encounters between 'us' and 'them' and prevent the possibilities for becoming something/somebody else other than the fixed identity categories that the DSP designs for subjects at war.

Furthermore, the investigation of the demobilisation process of paramilitary groups, as both a geopolitical and a biopolitical strategy of in/security in Colombia, discloses the notion of *a secure peace*. The process of demobilisation of paramilitary groups has been based on the notion that peace will come after security is achieved, guarding off unauthorised narratives (Edkins, 2003) of demobilised persons who challenge the official definition of collective and individual violence in Colombia as the result of a weak state authority. The reincorporation of former paramilitaries into society through the figure of warrior citizens, who collaborate with information in the war on terror, in addition to the lack of transparency to guarantee the victims' rights to truth, have prevented this process from becoming a reconciliatory mechanism. *A secure peace* is put forward by the state in such a way that grief and pain fuel the cycle of revenge and violence. The logic of in/security of the DSP inscribes itself in the notion of peace as, once more, the pursuit of 'the war of all against terrorism'.

By reading some resistance discourses to the DSP, I have drawn on alternative concepts of peace and security that emanate from the very subjects governed and regulated by the DSP. These alternatives include various options to contrast with the widely acknowledged and too easily accepted notion of a *secure peace*. First, the violent discourse of the FARC-EP guerrillas (2000, 2002, 2004) was examined, as was their counter-proposal of a *true peace*. The *true peace* is grounded on the same mechanisms of fear, violence, exclusion and extermination of 'otherness' as the *secure peace* of the state, so this type of peace understanding does not challenge the foundations of the DSP. On the contrary, by evaluating the FARC-EP discourse, the *true peace* of this organisation reinforces a sovereign discourse of harm and violence from the margins.

The enhancement of harmful practices from the margins became a clear indication that an analysis of resistance discourses to the DSP had to consider how these conceive of dealing with fear of 'otherness' and the deployment of violence to construct peace (Stern, 2005). If the violence of the DSP is to be challenged, then such conditions appeared necessary to open up possibilities for rethinking peaces towards more peaceful horizons. I constructed a brief framework for analysis that integrated the conceptions of peaces as plural (Dietrich, 2006, 2008) and always insecure (Martínez, 2001, 2001b). These conditions testify to my belief that, once peace is filled with a prearranged meaning – like security or truth – it necessarily turns into a weapon of violence that imposes itself over dissenting opinions and politico-philosophical differences (Dietrich and Sützl, 2006). Second, insecure peaces depend, by their very essence, on not knowing in advance what their results will be. Hence, reading peaces as insecure also denotes the very uncertainty of those results since the concrete shapes of peaces can only come to life in a real encounter with 'otherness'. This is the very moment of transformation that can bring into being possibilities for becoming otherwise (Dillon, 1996; Butler, 2004).

Against this background, I realised that the discourse of the Province of Antioquia (2001, 2002), though based on the philosophy of nonviolence and an acceptation of conflict as a positive sign of conflictual energy (Dietrich, 2006), had severe limitations. The *congruent peace* proposed by this state office put forward the limits of qualified state nonviolence. In other words, although it is based on the principles of nonviolence as a method of struggle, when faced with situations when 'national security' is said to be at stake, the state deploys its apparatus of violence to 'secure' whatever and whomever is said to be endangering the state.

Although limited in scope, the PCP put forward a challenging alternative notion of peace different from the *secure peace* of the national government. The Province of Antioquia (ibid.) called for peace as being born out of reconciliation, in direct opposition to the national peace born out of state authority. Such *democratic peace* attempted to challenge the logic, inner workings and mechanisms of exclusions of the DSP. At the same time, the PCP constructed an image of the 'other' not as enemy, but as valid political interlocutor indispensable for conflict transformation. The PCP recognised the importance of bringing 'others' into the public debate as necessary for reconciliation. In this sense, it never grounded politics on in/security, as the DSP has done traditionally and still does today.

Precisely by challenging sovereign discourses, the nonviolent movement of the indigenous groups, Paeces del Cauca, has called into question the largely unquestioned notions of peace/security of the DSP. The main element with which the Paeces contest the DSP is the unique way in which they merge spirituality with politics based on unqualified nonviolence. One of its effects is to bring back politics to the public debate, eroding the apparent consensus that politics should be postponed until in/security brings us peace.

In direct contravention to the DSP precepts, the Paeces face the grief and pain of violence with an open invitation to join political spaces for conversations, both within and outside institutional frameworks. They openly and unapologetically defy the regulation of their circulation through securitised rules. This notion of insecure politics is based on their concept of *trans-rational peace*. This type of peace is vernacular, relational and, consequently, neither subject to export nor import. The Paeces merge rational arguments about democratic governance with spiritual components that, importantly for our discussion, do not recognise the sovereign power of the state over their lives and deaths.

Moreover, by refusing to reconstruct their resistance as competing sovereign claims, the Paeces reject enrolment in the 'army of good people' to be ruled according to the in/security concerns of the DSP. They demand both politics and peaces that cannot be postponed but are past due and ought to be delivered more immediately. It is here and now among 'us' – indigenous and non-indigenous peoples – and with the 'others' – army, paramilitaries and guerrillas – that they propose to recreate spaces and times for peaceful conflict transformation. In this sense, the resistance discourse of the Paeces challenges the monopoly of the state in defining what security and peace (partially) mean, who is endangering whom and at what price we are willing to postpone politics until in/security supposedly brings us the long-awaited freedom promised so easily but as yet undelivered.

By embracing this call for non-closure, I have attempted to bring forth several calls for insecure politics and insecure peaces (as I read them) that originate in a wide field of studies. What these proposals have in common, from the perspective of insecure peaces put forward in this book, is their call for attention to the violence that is constantly being reproduced in the war against terror and its promise of in/security to ground politics. I have sought to read these contributions in light of the many notions of peace proposed in this research.

I have named these last reflections *the politics of affinity* since they call for engaging in conversations and discussions about peace and security that *could* lead to more inclusive ways of politics. I want to underscore how possibilities are ingrained in the very idea of transformation, because the results of those conversational politics cannot be known in advance. I believe that the condition for their possibility is the openness of democratic spaces where encounters and dialogue take place. If we close down these spaces in the name of in/security, violence and exclusion to and from (de)authorised political subjects would only be fuelled. Additionally, since the DSP is also an instance of the biopolitics of security, this call for insecure peaces also calls for disrupting the regulated connection and circulation of life species, striving for life contagion, emergent and contingent connections and circulation of lives (Dillon, 2008).

This notion of a politics of affinity resembles two important insecure foundations. The first one is the necessity for encountering the 'other', for asking for its recognition and thus being transformed in the immediate moment (Butler, 2004). This conversation with the 'other', in which I merge with at least the potentiality of being transformed through and only because of the encounter, has already started by recognising that I need the 'other' to accept me as a politically valid interlocutor, and vice versa. Second, only by resisting the fear of 'otherness' and venturing into times and places for encounter can we construct possibilities for devising alternative types of peaces, insecure politics and, hopefully, less harmful ways of dealing with conflicts.

Such bridges of affinity are built on political routes. They cannot be equated with 'solidarity' as inscribed in the DSP by presupposing a pregiven sense of belonging and sacrifice to a collective 'we'. On the contrary, affinity can only be born from the articulation of interests, needs, desires, projects and so forth. Via such articulation, 'we' constitute 'ourselves'. Building bridges of affinities with 'others' constitutes 'us' as particular subjects, with a high political meaning. The fact that our (dis)agreements are born within political encounters cannot but mean that we constitute ourselves in a constant and valid political conversation. Therefore, this appeal is not an encounter among predetermined and prediscursive subjects that *do* politics as they are, but rather who are created as subjects in the very act of performance of their subjectivities.

These last thoughts bring us back to the previously mentioned proposals that are sketched as routes. I can propose neither roots nor destinations for peace, politics and identities, but only routes that underscore how 'we' merge, change almost constantly and can break away from the unfree illusion of security. Although I can imagine other ways of conceiving of politics by disrupting the seeming coherence and certainty of the promise of in/security as it is written in the DSP, I cannot, by definition, trace the results of what such encounters might produce. What type of politics, political imaginaries and peaces would they bring to light? Away from the *secure peace* inscribed in the DSP, this is precisely the question that I hope to have raised not only as a general principle, but also as a time-sensitive and crucial question in the pressing case of Colombia.

References

Books and articles

Ackerly, B., M. Stern and J. True, 2006, 'Feminist methodologies for International Relations', in B. Ackerly, M. Stern and J. True (eds), *Feminist Methodologies for International Relations*, Cambridge, Cambridge University Press.

Agamben, G., 1995, *Homo Sacer: Sovereign Power and Bare Life*, trans. Daniel Heller-Roazen, Stanford, Stanford University Press.

Agamben, G., 2005, *State of Exception*, trans. Kevin Attell, Chicago, University of Chicago Press.

Agencia Universitaria de Periodismo, 1998, 'Kwes kiwe: Nuestra Tierra', *Cespedesia*, 21, 67.

Alape, A., 1996, 'La reinserción del EPL: ¿Esperanza o frustración?', *Colombia Internacional*, 36.

Alcaldía de Medellín, 2006, 'Programa Paz y Reconciliación: Modelo de intervención regreso a la legalidad', paper presented at the Conference Democracia, Narcotráfico y Paramilitarismo en Colombia, Medellín, 20 September 2006.

Alonso, A., 1992, 'Gender, power, and historical memory: discourses of *Serrano* resistance', in J. Butler and J. W. Scott (eds), *Feminists Theorize the Political*, London and New York, Routledge.

Anaya, L., 2006, *Individual Demobilization and Reintegration Process in Colombia: A Nation Building Policy from a National Security Perspective*, Washington, School of International Service, American University.

Anaya, L., 2007, 'Individual demobilization and reintegration process in Colombia: A nation building policy from a national security perspective', paper presented at the Conference Bridging Peacebuilding and Trauma Recovery, Denver, University of Denver, February 2007.

Anderson, B., 1991, *Imagined Communities: Reflections on the Origins and Spread of Nationalism*, London, Verso.

Angarita, E. (ed.), 2001, *Balance de los Estudios sobre Violencia en Antioquia*, Medellín, Universidad de Antioquia.

Aranguren, M., 2001, *Mi confesión: Carlos Castaño revela sus secretos*, Bogotá, Oveja Negra.

References

Arendt, H., 1998, *The Human Condition*, Chicago, University of Chicago Press.

Ashley, R., 1989, 'Living on borderlines: man, poststructuralism and war', in J. Der Derian and M. Shapiro (eds), *International/Intertextual Relations: Postmodern Readings of World Politics*, Lexington, Lexington Books.

Bagley, B. and J. Tokatlian, 1992, 'Dope and dogma: Explaining the failure of U.S. Latin American drug policies', in J. Hartlyn, L. Schoultz and A. Varas (eds), *The United States and Latin America in the 1990s: Beyond the Cold War*, Chapel Hill, University of North Carolina Press.

Beck, U., 1992, *Risk Society: Towards a New Modernity*, London, Sage.

Beck, U., 2005, 'War is peace: on post-national war', *Security Dialogue*, 36, 1.

Bejarano, J. A., 1995, *Una Agenda para la Paz: Aproximaciones desde la teoría de resolución de conflictos*, Bogotá, Tercer Mundo.

Bejarano, J. A., C. Echandía, R. Escobedo and E. León, 1997, *Colombia: Inseguridad, violencia y desempeño económico en las áreas rurales*, Bogotá, Universidad Externado de Colombia – FONADE.

Blair, E., 1999, *Conflicto Armado y Militares en Colombia: Cultos, símbolos e imaginarios*, Medellín, Universidad de Antioquia.

Blair, E., 2005, *Muertes Violentas: La Teatralización del Exceso*, Medellín, Universidad de Antioquia.

Blanchard, E. M., 2003, 'Gender, international relations, and the development of feminist security theory', *Signs: Journal of Women in Culture and Society*, 28, 4.

Bushnell, D., 1994, *Colombia, Una Nación a pesar de sí misma: De los tiempos Precolombinos a nuestros días*, trans. C. Montilla, Bogotá, Planeta.

Butler, J., 1990, 'Gender trouble, feminist theory, and psychoanalytic discourse', in A. L. Martin and E. Mendieta (eds), 2003, *Identities: Race, Class, Gender and Nationality*, Padstow, Blackwell.

Butler, J., 1993, *Bodies that Matter: On the Discursive Limits of 'Sex'*, New York and London, Routledge.

Butler, J., 1995a, 'Contingent foundations: feminism and the question of 'postmodernism'', in S. Benhabib, J. Butler, D. Cornell and N. Fraser, *Feminist Contentions: A Philosophical Exchange*, New York, Routledge.

Butler, J., 1995b, 'For a careful reading', in S. Benhabib, J. Butler, D. Cornell and N. Fraser, *Feminist Contentions: A Philosophical Exchange*, New York, Routledge.

Butler, J., 1999, *Gender Trouble: Feminism and the Subversion of Identity*, Tenth Anniversary Edition, New York and London, Routledge.

Butler, J., 2000, 'What is critique? An essay on Foucault's virtue', in S. Salih and J. Butler (eds), *The Judith Butler Reader*, Oxford, Blackwell.

Butler, J., 2004, *Precarious Life: The Powers of Mourning and Violence*, London and New York, Verso.

Buzan, B., 1991, *People, States and Fear: An Agenda for International Security Studies in the Post-Cold War Era*, Harlow, Pearson Education Limited.

Buzan, B. and O. Wæver, 2003, *Regions and Powers: The Structure of International Security*, Cambridge, Cambridge University Press.

Buzan, B., O. Wæver and J. Wilde, 1998, *Security: A New Framework for Analysis*, Boulder, Lynne Rienner.

Caicedo, C., 2003, 'Aproximaciones a la Noviolencia como alternativa política: Algunos casos Colombianos', Interpeacenet: International Network of Peace Research, www.interpeacenet.org/rr/caicedo-noviolencia.htm, accessed 14 August 2008.

Camacho, A., 2002, 'Credo, necesidad y codicia: Los alimentos de la guerra', *Análisis Político*, 46.

Campbell, D., 1998, *Writing Security: United States Foreign Policy and the Politics of Identity*, Minneapolis, University of Minnesota Press.

Campbell, D., 1999, 'Violence, justice, and identity in the Bosnian conflict', in J. Edkins, N. Persham and V. Pin-Fat (eds), *Sovereignty and Subjectivity*, London, Lynne Rienner.

Cerbini, F., 2003, 'Aproximación a la cultura Paéz del Departamento del Cauca, Colombia', *Territorio Social*, 1, April 2003.

Chilton, P. A., 1996, *Security Metaphors: Cold War Discourse from Containment to Common House*, New York, Peter Lang.

Collier, P., 2000, 'Doing well out of war: an economic perspective', in M. Berdal and D. Malone (eds), *Greed and Grievance: Economic Agendas in Civil Wars*, Boulder, Lynne Rienner.

Collier, P., 2001, 'Causas económicas de las guerras civiles y sus implicaciones para el diseño de políticas', *El Malpensante*, 30.

Collier, P. and A. Hoeffler, 2001, 'Greed and grievance in civil war', Washington, World Bank Research Policy Paper WPS 2355.

Comisión de Estudios sobre la Violencia, 1995, *Colombia: Violencia y Democracia*, Bogotá, COLCIENCIAS – Instituto de Estudios Políticos y Relaciones Internacionales (IEPRI).

Connolly, W., 1991, *Identity/Difference: Democratic Negotiations of Political Paradox*, Minneapolis, University of Minnesota Press.

Crocker, C. A., 2003, 'Engaging failed states', *Foreign Affairs*, 82, 5.

Croucher, S., 2004, *Globalization and Belonging: The Politics of Identity in a Changing World*, Lanham, Rowman and Littlefield.

De Soysa, I., 2000, 'The resource curse: are civil wars driven by rapacity or paucity?', in M. Berdal and D. Malone (eds), *Greed and Grievance: Economic Agendas in Civil Wars*, Boulder, Lynne Rienner.

Deas, M. and F. Gaitán, 1995, *Dos Ensayos Especulativos sobre la violencia en Colombia*, Bogotá, Tercer Mundo.

Delumeau, J., 2001, 'Miedos de ayer y de hoy', trans. M. Bernaud and R. Moncada, in M. I. Villa (ed.), *El Miedo: Reflexiones sobre su dimensión social y cultural*, Medellín, Corporación Región.

Dietrich, W., 2000, 'A structural-cyclic model of developments in Human Rights: an alternative chronosophy as base for the formal reconstruction of Human Rights', *Human Rights Working Papers*, 6, University of Denver, 27 April 2000.

Dietrich, W., 2006, 'Peaces: an aesthetic concept, a moral need or a transrational virtue?', *Asteriskos Journal of International and Peace Studies*, 1, 2.

Dietrich, W., 2008, *Variationen über die vielen Frieden, Band 1: Deutungen*, Schriften des UNESCO Chair for Peace Studies der Universität Innsbruck, Wiesbaden, VS Verlag für Sozialwissenschaften.

Dietrich, W. and W. Sützl, 2006, 'A call for Many Peaces', in W. Dietrich, J. Echavarría and N. Koppensteiner (eds), *Schlüsseltexte der Friendensforschung*, Wien, Lit.

Dillon, M., 1996, *Politics of Security: Towards a Political Philosophy of Continental Thought*, London, Routledge.

Dillon, M., 1999, 'The sovereign and the stranger', in J. Edkins, N. Persham and V. Pin-Fat (eds), *Sovereignty and Subjectivity*, London, Lynne Rienner.

Dillon, M., 2005, 'Global security in the 21st century: circulation, complexity and contingency', *World Today*, ISP/NSC Briefing Paper, 05/02.

Dillon, M., 2007, 'Governing terror: the state of emergency of biopolitical emergence', *International Political Sociology*, 1.

Dillon, M., 2008, 'Underwriting security', *Security Dialogue*, 39, 2–3.

Dillon, M. and J. Reid, 2001, 'Global liberal governance: biopolitics, security and war', *Millennium: Journal of International Studies*, 30, 1.

Dudziak, M. L. (ed.), 2003, *September 11 in History: A Watershed Moment?*, Durham and London, Duke University Press.

Duffield, M., 2001, *Global Governance and the New Wars: The Merging of Development and Security*, London, Zed.

Duncan, G., 2005, 'Del Campo a la ciudad en Colombia: La infiltración urbana de los señores de la guerra', Bogotá, Documento CEDE, Universidad de los Andes.

Echandía, C., 2003, 'El conflicto interno colombiano: Cambios recientes y sus implicaciones en el proceso de violencia', *Obstacles to robust negotiated settlements of civil conflicts*, Santa Fe Institute and the Javeriana University, Bogotá, May 2003.

Echavarría, J., 2002, 'La vivienda: Los miedos de la ciudad', in M. I. Villa (ed.), *El Miedo: Reflexiones sobre su dimensión social y cultural*, Medellín, Corporación Región.

Edkins, J., 2003, *Trauma and the Memory of Politics*, Cambridge, Cambridge University Press.

Edkins, J. and V. Pin-Fat, 1999, 'The subject of the political', in J. Edkins, N. Persham and V. Pin-Fat (eds), *Sovereignty and Subjectivity*, London, Lynne Rienner.

Edkins, J. and V. Pin-Fat, 2004, 'Life, power, resistance', in J. Edkins, V. Pin-Fat and M. Shapiro (eds), *Sovereign Lives: Power in Global Politics*, London, Routledge.

Edkins, J., N. Persham and V. Pin-Fat (eds), 1999, *Sovereignty and Subjectivity*, London, Lynne Rienner.

Eriksen, T., 1993, *Ethnicity and Nationalism: Anthropological Perspectives*, London, Pluto Press.

Escobar, A., 1995, *Encountering Development: The Making and Unmaking of the Third World*, Princeton Studies in Culture/Power/History, Princeton, Princeton University Press.

Escobar, A., 2001, 'Culture sits in places: reflections on globalism and subaltern strategies of localization', *Political Geography*, 20, 2.

Escobar, A., 2004, 'Imagining a post-development era', in M. Edelman and A. Haugerud (eds), *The Anthropology of Development and Globalization: From Classical Political Economy to Contemporary Neoliberalism*, Malden, Blackwell.

Escobar, A. and W. Harcourt, 2002, 'Women and the politics of place', *Development*, 45, 1.

FARC-EP (Fuerzas Armadas Revolucionarias – Ejército del Pueblo), 2002, *Historical Outline FARC-EP*, International Commission, Canada.

Flax, J., 1992, 'The end of innocence', in J. Butler and J. W. Scott (eds), *Feminists Theorize the Political*, London and New York, Routledge.

Foucault, M., 1990, *The History of Sexuality, Volume 1: An Introduction*, trans. R. Hurley, New York, Vintage Books.

Franco, L., 2002, 'El Mercenarismo corporativo y la sociedad contrainsurgente', *Estudios Políticos*, 21.

Fukuyama, F., 2004, *State Building, Governance and World Order in the Twenty First Century*, London, Profile Books.

Galtung, J., 1996, *Peace by Peaceful Means: Peace and Conflict Development and Civilization*, London, Sage – International Peace Research Institute (PRIO).

Galtung, J., 2004, 'The security approach and the peace approach', paper presented at the UN Conference Building Peace through Harmonious Diversity, New York, 10 September 2004.

Garay, L. J., 2002, *Colombia: Entre la exclusión y el desarrollo. Propuestas para la transición al Estado Social de Derecho*, Bogotá, Contraloría General de la República.

Gaviria, C., 1997, 'Alcances, contenidos y limitaciones de la Jurisdicción Especial Indígena', in *Del olvido surgimos para traer nuevas esperanzas*, Bogotá, Ministerio de Justicia.

Gaviria, J. O., 2005, *Sofismas del Terrorismo en Colombia*, Bogotá, Planeta.

Giddens, A. and W. Hutton (eds), 1990, *En el Límite: Vida en el Capitalismo Global*, trans. M. L. Rodríguez, Barcelona, Tusquets.

Gronemeyer, M., 1992, 'Helping', in W. Sachs (ed), *The Development Dictionary: A Guide to Knowledge as Power*, London, Zed.

Gusterson, H., 1999, 'Missing the end of the Cold War in international security', in J. Weldes et al. (eds), *Cultures of Insecurity: States, Communities and the Production of Danger*, Minneapolis, University of Minnesota Press.

Gutiérrez, F., 2003, 'Criminal rebels? A discussion of war and criminality from the Colombian experience', Working Paper 27, Bogotá, Crisis States Programme - Instituto de Estudios Políticos y Relaciones Internacionales (IEPRI).

Hagen, J., 2003, 'Uribe's people: civilians and the Colombian conflict', *Conflict and Security: Georgetown Journal of International Affairs*, 4, 1.

Hall, S., 1996a, 'Who needs identity?' in S. Hall and P. du Gay (eds), *Questions of Cultural Identity*, London, Sage.

Hall, S., 1996b, 'New ethnicities', in A. L. Martin and E. Mendieta (eds), 2003, *Identities: Race, Class, Gender and Nationality*, Padstow, Blackwell.

Haraway, D. J., 1991, 'A cyborg manifesto: Science, technology, and socialist-feminism in the late twentieth century', in *Simians, Cyborgs, and Women: The Reinvention of Nature*, London, Free Association Books.

Herz, J. H., 2003, 'The security dilemma in International Relations: background and present problems', *International Relations*, 17, 4.

Hobbes, T., 1651, *Leviathan, or The Matter, Forme and Power of a Common Wealth Ecclesiasticall and Civill*, www.earlymoderntexts.com/f_hobbes.html, accessed 14 August 2008.

Holmes, R., 2000, *Nonviolence: Theory and Practice*, Belmont, Wadsworth.

Hoogensen, G. and S. V. Rottem, 2004, 'Gender identity and the subject of security', *Security Dialogue*, 35, 2.

IEPRI (Instituto de Estudios Políticos y Relaciones Internacionales), 2006, *Nuestra Guerra sin nombre*, Bogotá, Universidad Nacional – Norma.

Illich, I., 1988, *Alternativas II: Obras de Iván Illich*, México, Joaquín Mortiz and Planeta.

Iniciativa de Mujeres por la Paz, 2006, 'Tregua Incierta: Mesa Nacional de Incidencia "Por el derecho a al verdad, la justicia y la reparación con perspectiva de género"', Bogotá, Medios Gráficos.

Jabri, V., 1999, 'Explorations of difference in normative international relations', in V. Jabri and E. O'Gorman (eds), *Women, Culture, and International Relations*, Boulder, Lynne Rienner.

Jabri, V., 2006, 'War, security and the liberal state', *Security Dialogue*, 37, 1.

Jabri, V. and E. O'Gorman, 1999, 'Locating difference in feminist international relations', in V. Jabri and E. O'Gorman (eds), *Women, Culture, and International Relations*, Boulder, Lynne Rienner.

Jackson, R., 2005, *Writing the War on Terrorism: Language, Politics and Counter-terrorism*, New Approaches to Conflict Analysis, Manchester, Manchester University Press.

James, W., 2000, 'The moral equivalent of war', in D. Barash (ed.), *Approaches to Peace*, New York, Oxford University Press.

Kaldor, M., 1999, *New and Old Wars: Organized Violence in a Global Era*, Cambridge, Polity Press.

Kearney, R. and M. Dooley (eds), 1999, *Questioning Ethics*, London, Routledge.

Kymlicka, W., 1996, *Ciudadanía Multicultural*, trans. C. Castells Auleda, Barcelona, Paidós.

Laclau, E. and C. Mouffe, 2001, *Hegemony and Socialist Strategy: Towards a Radical Democratic Politics*, second edition, London, Verso.

Lair, E., 2003, 'Reflexiones acerca del terror en los escenarios de guerra interna', *Revista de Estudios Sociales*, 15.

Lair, E., 2005, 'Características y tendencias recientes del conflicto armado Colombiano', paper presented at Empresas Públicas de Medellín (EEPPM), Medellín, September 2005.

Leal, F. (ed.), 1999, *Los Laberintos de la Guerra: Utopías e Incertidumbres sobre la Paz*, Bogotá, Tercer Mundo – Universidad de los Andes.

Leal, F., 2002a, *La Seguridad Nacional a la Deriva: Del Frente Nacional a la Posguerra Fría*, Bogotá, Alfaomega – CESO Uniandes – FLACSO Ecuador.

Leal, F., 2002b, 'La seguridad: Difícil de abordar con democracia', *Análisis Político*, 46.

Leal, F., 2004, 'La seguridad durante el primer año del gobierno de Alvaro Uribe Vélez', *Análisis Político*, 50.

Lederach, J. P., 1995, *Preparing for Peace: Conflict Transformation Across Cultures*, New York, Syracuse University Press.

Lederach, J. P., 2005, *The Moral Imagination: The Art and Soul of Building Peace*, New York, Oxford University Press.

León, J., 2004, *No somos machos pero somos muchos: Cinco crónicas de resistencia civil en Colombia*, Bogotá, Norma.

Litzinger, R., 1999, 'Reimagining the state in Post-Mao China', in J. Weldes et al. (eds), *Cultures of Insecurity: States, Communities and the Production of Danger*, Minneapolis, University of Minnesota Press.

Lobo-Guerrero, L., 2007, 'Biopolitics of specialized risk: an analysis of kidnap and ransom insurance', *Security Dialogue*, 38, 3.

Lobo-Guerrero, L., 2008, '"Pirates," stewards, and the securitisation of global circulation', *International Political Sociology*, 2, 3.

Londoño, L. M. and Nieto Y. F., 2006, *Mujeres no contadas: Procesos de desmovilización y retorno a la vida civil de mujeres excombatientes en Colombia 1990 – 2003*, Medellín, La Carreta Social.

López, M., 2001, 'La Noviolencia como alternativa política', in F. Muñoz (ed.), *La Paz Imperfecta*, Granada, Universidad de Granada.

López, M., 2002, 'Noviolencia y cambio(s) social(es)', *Actas del I Congreso Hispanoamericano de Educación y Cultura de Paz y Noviolencia*, Granada, Universidad de Granada.

Maalouf, A., 2000, *In the Name of Identity: Violence and the Need to Belong*, New York, Penguin Books.

Malešević, S., 2008, 'The sociology of new wars? Assessing the causes and objectives of contemporary conflicts', *International Political Sociology*, 2, 2.

Marshal, R. and C. Messiant, 2004, 'Las guerras civiles en la era de la globalización: Nuevos conflictos y nuevos paradigmas', *Análisis Político*, 50.

Martínez, V., 2001a, 'Hacia una Paz Insegura', *Noticias Obreras*, 1.301, 17.

Martínez, V., 2001b, *Filosofía para Hacer las Paces*, Barcelona, Icaria.

Martínez, V., 2002, 'Virtualidad, performatividad y responsabilidad', paper presented at VI Congreso Internacional de Fenomenología: Filosofía y Realidad Virtual, Albarracín, September 2002.

Martínez, V., 2005, *Podemos Hacer las Paces: Reflexiones éticas tras el 11-S y el 11-M*, Bilbao, Desclée De Brouwer.

Mockus, A. and J. Corzo, 2003, 'Dos caras de la convivencia: Cumplir acuerdos y normas y no usar ni sufrir violencia', *Análisis Político*, 48.

Monsalve, A. and E. Domínguez (eds), 1999, *Democracia y Paz en Colombia*, Medellín, Universidad Pontificia Bolivariana.

Mouffe, C., 1992, 'Feminism, citizenship and radical democratic politics', in J. Butler and J. W. Scott (eds), *Feminists Theorize the Political*, London and New York, Routledge.

Mowitt, J., 1999, 'In/security and the politics of disciplinarity', in J. Weldes et al. (eds), *Cultures of Insecurity: States, Communities and the Production of Danger*, Minneapolis, University of Minnesota Press.

Münkler, H., 2002, *Die neuen Kriegen*, Reinbek b. Hamburg, Rowohlt.

Muñoz, F., 2001, 'La paz imperfecta en un mundo en conflicto', in F. Muñoz (ed.), *La Paz Imperfecta*, Granada, Universidad de Granada.

Nasi, C. and A. Rettberg, 2005, 'The interlink between resources, development and conflict: Conflict over coffee and bananas in Colombia', paper presented at the annual meeting of the International Studies Association, Hawaii, 4 March 2005.

Nasi, C. and A. Rettberg, 2006, 'Los estudios sobre conflicto armado y paz: un campo en evolución permanente', *Colombia Internacional*, 62.

Nasi, C., W. Ramírez and E. Lair, 2003a, 'La guerra civil', *Revista de Estudios Sociales*, 14.

Nasi, C., W. Ramírez and E. Lair, 2003b, 'Respuesta al debate 14: Guerra civil', *Revista de Estudios Sociales*, 15.

Nieto, J. R. and L. J. Robledo, 2001, *Guerra y Paz en Colombia 1998–2001*, Medellín, Universidad Autónoma Latinoamericana.

Norval, A. J., 1999, 'Hybridization: the im/purity of the political', in J. Edkins, N. Persham and V. Pin-Fat (eds), *Sovereignty and Subjectivity*, London, Lynne Rienner.

Norval, A. J., 2004a, 'Hegemony after deconstruction: the consequences of undecidability,' *Political Ideologies*, 9, 2.

Norval, A. J., 2004b, 'Democratic identification: a Wittgenstenian approach', *Centre for Theoretical Studies in the Humanities and Social Sciences*, Online Papers, University of Essex, www.essex.ac.uk/centres/TheoStud/onlinepapers.asp, accessed 14 August 2008.

Orozco, I., 2002, 'La posguerra colombiana: divagaciones sobre la venganza, la justicia y la reconciliación', *Análisis Político*, 46.

Özkirimli, U., 2000, *Theories of Nationalism: A Critical Introduction*, New York, Palgrave.

Palacios, M., 1995, *Entre la Legitimidad y la Violencia en Colombia 1875–1994*, Bogotá, Norma.

Pastrana, A., 2005, *La Palabra bajo Fuego*, Bogotá, Planeta.

Pécaut, D., 2001, *Guerra contra la sociedad*, Bogotá, Espasa.

Peñaranda, R., 1999, 'De rebeldes a ciudadanos: el caso del Movimiento Armado Quintín Lame', in R. Peñaranda and J. Guerrero (eds), *De las Armas a la Política*, Bogotá, Instituto de Estudios Políticos y Relaciones Internacionales (IEPRI).

Piazza, J. A., 2008, 'Incubators of terror: Do failed and failing states promote transnational terrorism?', *International Studies Quarterly*, 52, 3.

Pin-Fat, V. and M. Stern, 2005, 'The scripting of Private Jessica Lynch: biopolitics, gender, and the "feminization" of the U.S. military', *Alternatives: Global, Local, Political*, 30, 1.

Pizarro, E., 1990, 'La insurgencia armada: Raíces y perspectivas', in F. Leal and L. Zamosc (eds), *Al Filo del Caos: Crisis Política en la Colombia de los Años 80*, Bogotá, Tercer Mundo – Instituto de Estudios Políticos y Relaciones Internacionales (IEPRI).

Pizarro, E., 1991, *Las FARC 1949–1966: De la autodefensa a la combinación de todas las formas de lucha*, Bogotá, Tercer Mundo.

Pizarro, E., 1996, *Insurgencia sin Revolución: La guerrilla en Colombia en una perspectiva comparada*, Bogotá, Tercer Mundo – Instituto de Estudios Políticos y Relaciones Internacionales (IEPRI).

Pörksen, U., 1995, *Plastic Words: The Tyranny of a Modular Language*, Pennsylvania, Pennsylvania State University Press.

Ramírez, W., 2002, '¿Guerra civil en Colombia?', *Análisis Político*, 46.

Rangel, A. (ed.), 2005, 'El Poder Paramilitar: Narcotráfico, Poder Local, Balance Estratégico y Perspectiva Internacional', *Ensayos de Seguridad y Democracia*, Bogotá, Fundación Seguridad y Democracia.

Reid, J., 2006, *The Biopolitics of the War on Terror: Life Struggles, Liberal Modernity, and the Defence of Logistical Societies*, Reappraising the Political, Manchester, Manchester University Press.

Reyes, A., 1991, 'Paramilitares en Colombia: Contexto, aliados y consecuencias', *Análisis Político*, 12.

Richani, N., 2002, *Systems of Violence: The Political Economy of War and Peace in Colombia*, Albany, State University of New York Press.

Roe, P., 1999, 'The intrastate security dilemma: Ethnic conflict as a "tragedy"?', *Journal of Peace Research*, 36, 2.

Romero, M., 2003, *Paramilitares y Autodefensas: 1982–2003*, Bogotá, Instituto de Estudios Políticos y Relaciones Internacionales (IEPRI).

Roof, J. and Wiegman, R. (eds), 1995, *Who can Speak? Authority and Critical Identity*, Urbana and Chicago, University of Illinois Press.

Rotberg, R., 2003, 'Failed states, collapsed, weak states: causes and indicators', in R.

Rotberg (ed.), *State Failure and State Weakness in a Time of Terror*, Washington D.C., Brookings Institution Press.

Rubio, M., 1999, *Crimen e Impunidad: Precisiones sobre la Violencia*, Bogotá, Tercer Mundo – CEDE.

Sachs, W. (ed.), 1992, *The Development Dictionary: A Guide to Knowledge as Power*, London, Zed.

Sachs, W., 2006, 'One world', in W. Dietrich, J. Echavarría and N. Koppensteiner (eds), *Schlüsseltexte der Friedensforschung*, Wien, Lit.

Saco, D., 1999, '"National security" and the internet', in J. Weldes et al. (eds), *Cultures of Insecurity: States, Communities and the Production of Danger*, Minneapolis, University of Minnesota Press.

Said, E. W., 2003a, *Orientalism*, New York, Vintage Books.

Said, E. W., 2003b, 'The clash of definitions', in A. L. Martin and E. Mendieta (eds), *Identities: Race, Class, Gender and Nationality*, Padstow, Blackwell.

Salazar, A., 1993, *Mujeres de Fuego*, Medellín, Corporación Región.

Salazar, A., 2001, *La Parábola de Pablo: Auge y Caída de un gran capo del narcotráfico*, Bogotá, Planeta.

Salazar, A., 2002, *No Nacimos pa' Semilla: La cultura de las bandas juveniles en Medellín*, Bogotá, Planeta.

Salazar, B. and M. P. Castillo, 2001, *La Hora de los Dinosaurios: Conflicto y Depredación en Colombia*, Cali and Bogotá, CIDSE – CEREC.

Salih, S., 2004, 'Introduction', in S. Salih and J. Butler (eds), *The Judith Butler Reader*, Oxford, Blackwell.

Sánchez, L. A., Villa, M. I. and A. M. Jaramillo, 2002, 'Caras y contracaras del miedo en Medellín', in M. I. Villa (ed.), *El Miedo: Reflexiones sobre su dimensión social y cultural*, Medellín, Corporación Región.

Security Dialogue, 2004, 35, 3.

Shapiro, M., 2001, *For Moral Ambiguity: National Culture and the Politics of the Family*, Minneapolis, University of Minnesota Press.

Shaw, K., 2004, 'Creating/negotiating interstices: indigenous sovereignties', in J. Edkins, V. Pin-Fat and M. Shapiro (eds), *Sovereign Lives: Power in Global Politics*, London, Routledge.

Stern, D., 2004, *The Present Moment in Psychotherapy and Everyday Life*, New York, W. W. Norton & Company.

Stern, M., 1998, 'Reading Mayan's women insecurity', *The International Journal of Peace Studies*, 3, 2.

Stern, M., 2004, 'Perhaps they don't have a name for that which makes me who I am ... The promise of security and the fantasy of representation as enactments of violence', unpublished manuscript, Universitat Jaumé I, Castelló, November 2004.

Stern, M., 2005, *Naming Security-Constructing Identity: 'Mayan-Women' in Guatemala on the Eve of 'Peace'*, New Approaches to Conflict Analysis, Manchester, Manchester University Press.

Sylvester, C., 1994, *Feminist Theory and International Relations in a Postmodern Era*, Cambridge Studies in International Relations, Cambridge, Cambridge University Press.

Tickner, A., 1988, 'Hans Morgenthau's principles of political realism: a feminist reformulation', *Millennium Journal of International Studies*, 17, 3.

Tickner, A., 1992, *Gender in International Relations: Feminist Perspectives on Achieving Global Security*, New York, Columbia University Press.

Tickner, A., 2006, 'On the frontlines or sidelines of knowledge and power? Feminist practices of responsible scholarship: reflection, evaluation, integration', *International Studies Review*, 8, 3.

Uribe de H., M. T. and L. M. López, 2006, *Las Palabras de la Guerra: Metáforas, Narraciones y Lenguajes Políticos. Un estudio sobre las memorias de las Guerras Civiles en Colombia*, Medellín, La Carreta Histórica.

Uribe de H., M. T., 1999, 'Réquiem para un amigo', *Estudios Políticos*, 14.

Uribe de H., M. T., 2001, 'Esfera pública, acción política y ciudadanía: Una mirada desde Hanna Arendt', *Estudios Políticos*, 19.

Uribe de H., M. T., 2004, 'El Republicanismo patriótico y el ciudadano armado', *Estudios Políticos*, 24.

Vattimo, G., 1992, *The Transparent Society*, trans. D. Webb, Baltimore, John Hopkins University Press.

Vattimo, G., 2006, 'Dialectics, difference and weak thinking', in W. Dietrich, J. Echavarría and N. Koppensteiner (eds), *Schlüsseltexte der Friendensforschung*, Wien, Lit.

Vélez, M. C., 2000, *Los hijos de la Gran Diosa: Psicología Analítica, Mito y Violencia*, Medellín, Universidad de Antioquia.

Villa, M. I. (ed.), 2002, *El Miedo: Reflexiones sobre su dimensión social y cultural*, Medellín, Corporación Región.

Villarraga, A. and N. Plazas, 1994, *Para reconstruir los sueños: Una historia del EPL*, Bogotá, Progresar – Fundación Cultura Democrática.

Vranckx, A., 2004, 'Colombia and Europe: relations and perceptions', *International Peace Information Service (IPIS)*, Antwerp, January 2004.

Wæver, O., 1995, 'Securitization and desecuritization', in R. D. Lipschutz (ed.), *On Security, New Directions on World Politics*, New York, Columbia University Press.

Wæver, O., 2004, 'Aberystwyth, Paris, Copenhagen: New "schools" in security theory and their origins between core and periphery', paper presented at the annual meeting of the International Studies Association, Montreal, 17–20 March 2004.

Waldmann, P., 2007, *Guerra Civil, Terrorismo y Anomia Social: El caso Colombiano en un contexto globalizado*, trans. M. Delacre, Bogotá, Norma.

Waldmann, P. and F. Reinares (eds), 1999, *Sociedades en Guerra Civil: Conflictos violentos de Europa y América Latina*, Barcelona, Paidós.

Walker, R. B. J., 1993, *Inside/Outside: International Relations as Political Theory*, Cambridge Studies in International Relations, Cambridge, Cambridge University Press.

Walker, R. B. J., 1999, 'Foreword', in J. Edkins, N. Persham and V. Pin-Fat (eds), *Sovereignty and Subjectivity*, London, Lynne Rienner.

Walker, R. B. J., 2004, 'Conclusion: sovereignties, exceptions, worlds', in J. Edkins, V. Pin-Fat and M. Shapiro (eds), *Sovereign Lives: Power in Global Politics*, London, Routledge.

Waltz, K., 2001, *Man, the State and War: A Theoretical Analysis*, New York, Columbia University Press.

Weber, C., 2005, *International Relations Theory: A Critical Introduction*, London, Routledge.

Weber, M., 1994, *Weber: Political Writings*, trans. Ronald Spiers, in P. Lassman and R. Spiers (eds), Cambridge, Cambridge University Press.

Weldes, J., 1999, 'The cultural production of crises: U.S. identity and missiles in Cuba', in J. Weldes et al. (eds), *Cultures of Insecurity: States, Communities, and the Production of Danger*, Minneapolis, University of Minnesota Press.

Weldes, J., M. Laffrey, H. Gusterson and R. Duvall, 1999, 'Introduction: Constructing insecurity', in J. Weldes et al. (eds), *Cultures of Insecurity: States, Communities, and the Production of Danger*, Minneapolis, University of Minnesota Press.

Wibben, A., 2004, 'Feminist international relations: old debates and new directions', *Brown Journal of World Affairs*, 10, 2.

Williams, P. and L. Chrisman, 1994, 'Colonial discourse and post-colonial theory: An introduction', in P. Williams and L. Chrisman (eds), *Colonial Discourse and Post-Colonial Theory: A Reader*, New York, Columbia University Press.

Yuval-Davis, N. and F. Anthias, 1989, *Women-Nation-State*, New York, Palgrave.

Yuval-Davis, N., 1997, *Gender and Nation*, London, Sage.

Zamora, M., 2005, 'Temas clave del derecho penal latinoamericano: "Política criminal y seguridad ciudadana" bases para un control social de nuevo cuño', *Revista de la Judicatura*, 1, 2.

Zinecker, H., 2007, *Kolumbien und El Salvador im longitudinalen Vergleich: Ein kritischer Beitrag zur Transitionsforschung*, Leipzig, Nomos.

Zuluaga, J., 1999, 'De guerrillas a movimientos políticos. Análisis de la experiencia Colombiana: El caso del M-19', in R. Peñaranda and J. Guerrero (eds), *De las Armas a la Política*, Bogotá, Instituto de Estudios Políticos y Relaciones Internacionales (IEPRI).

Speeches, documents and reports

Note: All Colombian administration speeches, press releases, documents and news are available online at http://web.presidencia.gov.co

'Call zur Langen Nacht der Forschung 2005', 2005, BMVIT - Bundesministerium für Verkehr, Innovation und Technologie, BMWA - Bundesministerium für Wirtschaft und Arbeit, BMWF - Bundesministerium für Wissenschaft und Forschung, Innsbruck.

ACIN (Asociación de Cabildos del Norte del Cauca), 2005, 'Proyecto Nasa: resguardos de Toribío, San Francisco y Tacuelo', Santander de Quilichao.

AI (Amnesty International), 2002a, 'Colombia: Human Rights and US military aid to Colombia IV', AI Index: AMR 23/122/2002, Amnesty International Publications, 1 October 2002.

AI (Amnesty International), 2002b, 'Colombia, San Vicente del Caguán after the breakdown of the peace talks: A community abandoned', AI Index: AMR 23/098/2002, Amnesty International Publications, 16 October 2002.

AI (Amnesty International), 2003, 'AI report 2003: Colombia', AI Index: POL 10/003/2003, Amnesty International Publications, 28 May 2003.

AI (Amnesty International), 2004a, 'Colombia. A laboratory of war: repression and violence in Arauca', AI Index: AMR 23/004/2004, Amnesty International Publications, 20 April 2004.

AI (Amnesty International), 2004b, 'Informe anual 2004: la guerra contra los valores mundiales. Los ataques de grupos armados y gobiernos alimentan la desconfianza, el temor y la división', AI Index: POL 10/016/2004, Press Release, 26 May 2004.

AI (Amnesty International), 2004c, 'Colombia: Amnistía Internacional está siempre con las víctimas de los abusos y violaciones de los derechos humanos, sea quien sea el autor', AI Index: AMR 23/029/2004, Press Release, 17 June 2004.

AI (Amnesty International), 2005, '2005 UN Commission on Human Rights: the UN's chief guardian of human rights?', AI Index: IOR 41/008/2005, Amnesty International Publications, 10 March 2005.

Alcaldía de Medellín, 2007, 'Propuesta para una Política Nacional de Reinserción: El modelo Medellín', Temas de Ciudad: Modelo de regreso a la legalidad, Medellín.

Alther, G., J. Lindsay-Poland and S. Weintraub (eds), 2004, *Building from the Inside Out: Peace Initiatives in War-Torn Colombia*, American Friends Service Committee and Fellowship of Reconciliation: Task Force on Latin America and the Caribbean, San Francisco.

Annan, K., 2002, Secretary General of the United Nations, 'Declaración Emitida por el secretario General de la ONU, con respecto a la ruptura del proceso de paz entre el gobierno Colombiano y las FARC', 21 February 2002.

Autoridades Indígenas, 2005, 'Peticiones de los Indígenas al Gobierno Nacional', Letter sent to the President of the Republic of Colombia, 25 September 2005.

Betancourt, I., 2002, 'Programa de Gobierno: Por una Colombia Nueva', Verde Oxígeno, Bogotá.

Boucher, R., 2002, US Department of State Speaker, 'Rompimiento de los diálogos de paz entre el Gobierno de Colombia y las Farc', Washington, 21 February 2002.

Bush, G. W., 2002, 'President Bush, President Pastrana discuss trade, terrorism', Remarks with President of Colombia at the White House, Office of the Press Secretary of the White House, Washington D.C., 18 April 2002.

Castaño, C. and S. Mancuso, 2002, 'Comunicado de las Autodefensas Unidas de Colombia (AUC), sobre el rompimiento del proceso de paz con las FARC', 20 February 2002.

Consejo Gremial, 2002, 'Comunicado emitido por el Consejo Gremial, tras la ruptura del proceso de paz con las FARC', Bogotá, 21 February 2002.

DSP (Democratic Security and Defence Policy), 2003, Presidency of the Republic – Ministry of Defence, Republic of Colombia, Bogotá, June 2003.

Ejército Nacional de Colombia, 2005, 'Red de Cooperantes', www.ejercito.mil.co/ index.php?idcategoria=435, accessed 14 August 2008.

ELN (Ejército de Liberación Nacional), 2002, 'Declaraciones del Ejército de Liberación Nacional (ELN) sobre la ruptura del proceso de paz con las FARC', 21 February 2002.

EU (European Union), 2002, 'Colombia: Country Strategy Paper 2002-2006', European Commission, http://ec.europa.eu/external_relations/colombia/csp/02_06_en.pdf, accessed 14 August 2008.

EU (European Union), 2003, 'A secure Europe in a better world: European security strategy', Brussels, 12 December 2003, http://ue.eu.int/uedocs/cmsUpload/ 78367.pdf, accessed 14 August 2008.

EU (European Union), 2007, 'Colombia: Country Strategy Paper 2007–2013', European Commission, E/2007/484, 28 March 2007.

Fajardo, J., 2002, Secretary for Citizen Participation and Social Development, 'Primeros pasos para definir nuestra Noviolencia', Secretaría General de la Gobernación de Antioquia, Medellín, September 2002.

FARC-EP (Fuerzas Armadas Revolucionarias – Ejército del Pueblo), 2000, '36 years for peace and national sovereignty', Mountains of Colombia, May 2000, www.farcep.org/pagina_ingles/, accessed 18 December 2005.

FARC-EP (Fuerzas Armadas Revolucionarias – Ejército del Pueblo), 2004, 'Ponencia para la presentación del N° 32 de la revista Resistencia Internacional', November 2004, www.farcep.org/nuestrahistoria/07_noviembre_2004.php, accessed 18 December 2005.

Ferrero-Waldner, B., 2004, Commissioner for External Relations and European Neighbourhood Policy, 'Situation in Colombia', Plenary Session of the European Parliament, Brussels, 2 December 2004.

Garzón, L., 2002, 'Programa de Gobierno', Polo Democrático, Bogotá.

Gaviria, C., 2002, General Secretary of the Organization of American States (OAS), 'Comunicado emitido hoy por el secretario General de la OEA, César Gaviria, con motivo del rompimiento del proceso de paz en Colombia', 21 February 2002.

Gaviria, C., 2003, Senator (PDI), 'Ponencia para primer debate al proyecto de ley 035 de 2003 Senado por medio de la cual se desarrolla el artículo 246 de la Constitución Política de Colombia y se dictan otras disposiciones', *Gaceta del Congreso*, 633/2003, Bogotá, 27 November 2003.

Giraldo, A., 2002, Archbishop of Medellín and President of the Episcopal Conference, 'Comunicado de la Iglesia sobre el rompimiento del proceso de paz con las FARC', Bogotá, 21 February 2002.

Gobernación de Antioquia, 2001, 'Plan Congruente de Paz: una Antioquia nueva', Medellín, Impresos Ltda.

Gobernación de Antioquia, 2002, 'Plan Congruente de Paz: compromiso comunal', Secretaría de Participación Ciudadana y Desarrollo Social, Medellín, December 2002.

Gobernación de Antioquia, 2003, 'Acuerdos de la Asamblea Constituyente de Antioquia', 13 November 2003.

Gómez, C., 2002, High Commissioner for Peace, 'Declaración del Alto Comisionado para la Paz sobre el proceso de paz', San Vicente del Caguán, 10 January 2002.

Grupo de Río, 2002, 'Comunicado del Grupo de Río sobre la ruptura del proceso de paz con las FARC', San José, 21 February 2002.

Ideas para la Paz, 2005, 'La soberanía del Macizo', Siguiendo el conflicto, hechos y análisis de la semana, 20, 8 July 2005.

International Crisis Group, 2003, *Colombia: Negociar con los paramilitares*, Informe sobre América Latina, 5, 16 September 2003.

Lambach, D., A. Daun and B. Maas, 2003, 'State Failure and Regional Security', Ph.D. project of empirical analysis of the regional effects of fragile statehood in the third world and resource site for the study of failed and collapsed states, Lehrstuhl für Internationale Politik und Außenpolitik, Köln, University of Cologne.

Lemoyne, J., 2002, Special Advisor of the UN Secretary General for the Peace Process in Colombia, 'Declaración del asesor de la ONU sobre el proceso de paz', Bogotá, 10 January 2002.

Mesa de Negociaciones, 2002, 'Texto completo de la propuesta de las FARC para reactivar el proceso de paz', San Vicente del Caguán, 20 January 2002.

Mindefensa (Ministerio de Defensa Nacional), 2001, 'Resultados Operacionales de la Fuerza Pública', Boletín, 8, Bogotá, 10 December 2001.

Mindefensa (Ministerio de Defensa Nacional), 2005, 'Logros y Retos de la Política de Seguridad Democrática', Centro de Información y Estadística, Bogotá, 7 December 2005.

Mininterior (Ministerio del Interior y de Justicia), 2004, 'Programa de Reincorporación: Programa para la reincorporación a la vida civil de personas y grupos alzados en armas', SIGOB (Gestión y Seguimiento a las Metas del Gobierno), Bogotá.

Mininterior (Ministerio del Interior y de Justicia), 2005, 'Acciones del Gobierno Nacional ante la Comunidad Indígena del País: Informe del Ministerio del Interior y de Justicia', Dirección de Etnias, Bogotá, 25 September 2005.

Oficina del Alto Comisionado para la Paz, 2004, 'Política de Paz', www.altocomisionadoparalapaz.gov.co/poli_paz/poli_paz.htm, accessed 6 December 2004.

ONIC (Organización Nacional Indígena de Colombia), 2005a, 'Consejo comunal de Uribe: un irrespeto con los pueblos indígenas de Colombia', Press Release, 7 October 2005.

ONIC (Organización Nacional Indígena de Colombia), 2005b, '¡25 mil indígenas listos a marchar! Gran minga nacional por la dignidad, protección y la autonomía de los pueblos indígenas de Colombia ', Press Release, 7 October 2005.

ONIC (Organización Nacional Indígena de Colombia), 2005c, 'El gobierno de Uribe Vélez responde con muerte a la minga pacífica de los pueblos indígenas de Colombia', Press Release, 11 October 2005.

ONIC (Organización Nacional Indígena de Colombia), 2005d, 'Luchas de ayer y hoy', www.onic.org.co/quienes.shtml, accessed 14 August 2008.

ONIC (Organización Nacional Indígena de Colombia), 2005e, 'Programas. Cultura: Lo que yo aprendí no puede quedar sólo para mí, yo le voy a enseñar a mis hermanos también', www.onic.org.co/a_cultura.shtml, accessed 14 August 2008.

ONIC (Organización Nacional Indígena de Colombia), 2005f, 'Pueblos Indígenas', www.onic.org.co/nuevo/pueblos.shtml, accessed 14 August 2008.

Pastrana, A., 2001, 'Discurso del Presidente Andrés Pastrana Arango, con motivo del quincuagésimo aniversario del Comando General de las Fuerzas Militares celebrado en la Escuela Militar de Cadetes "José María Córdoba"', Bogotá, 16 April 2001.

Pastrana, A., 2002a, 'Alocución radiotelevisada del Presidente Andrés Pastrana sobre el proceso de paz con las FARC', Bogotá, 9 January 2002.

Pastrana, A., 2002b, 'Alocución radiotelevisada del presidente Andrés Pastrana sobre el proceso de paz con las FARC-EP', Los Pozos, 10 January 2002.

Pastrana, A., 2002c, 'Discurso pronunciado por el presidente Andrés Pastrana durante la XI Sesión del Consejo Nacional de Paz que se celebró en el Palacio de Nariño', Bogotá, 19 February 2002.

Pastrana, A., 2002d, 'Alocución radiotelevisada del Presidente de la República, Andrés Pastrana Arango, dirigida al país el 20 de Febrero de 2002 y en la que pone fin al proceso de paz con la guerrilla de las FARC y a la zona de distensión', Bogotá, 20 February 2002.

Piqué, J., 2002, European Union Representative, 'Declaración emitida por el representante de la Unión Europea, Joseph Piqué, sobre la ruptura del proceso de paz con las FARC', 21 February 2002.

Policía Nacional, 2005, 'Balance Operativo, Criminal y Contravencional 2004', Directores y Comandantes de Policía, Bogotá, 26 January 2005.

Policía Nacional, 2007, 'Primer Informe Control y Monitoreo de Grupos Desmovilizados', Bogotá, January 2007.

Presidencia de la República de Colombia – Oficina del Alto Comisionado para la Paz, 2006, 'Proceso de Paz con las autodefensas: Informe ejecutivo', Bogotá, December 2006.

Presidency of Colombia, 2008, 'Individual and collective demobilisations', Office of Communications, Bogotá, 6 October 2008.

Presidency of the Republic of Colombia – Ministry of Defence, 2004, 'The effectiveness of the Colombian Democratic Security and Defense Policy: August 2002 – December 2003', Bogotá, January 2004.

Presidency of the Republic of Colombia – Ministry of Defence, 2005, 'Avances en Metas de Gobierno: Enero 2003 – Noviembre de 2005', Oficina de Comunicaciones, Bogotá, December 2005.

Registraduría Nacional del Estado Civil, 2002, 'Informe de Votación: Corporación Presidente', Resultados Elecciones 2002, Bogotá, 7 June 2002.

Rice, C., 2005, US Secretary of State, 'United States Remains Committed to Aiding Colombia, Rice says', US Department of State – Office of the Spokesman, Bogotá, 27 April 2005.

Sanín, N., 2002, 'Programa de Gobierno', Sí Colombia, Bogotá

Serpa, H., 2002, 'Programa de Gobierno', Partido Liberal, Bogotá

Servicio Nacional de Noticias del Estado, 2005, 'Conclusiones Consejo Comunal de Gobierno No. 113 realizado con las Comunidades Indígenas', Bogotá, 25 September 2005.

Superintendencia de Vigilancia y Seguridad Privada, 2003, 'Personal de Seguridad', base de datos a Septiembre de 2003, www.supervigilancia.gov.co, accessed 25 September 2003.

UNDP (United Nations Development Program), 1994, 'Human Development Report', New York and Oxford, Oxford University Press.

UNDP (United Nations Development Program), 2003, 'Resumen del Informe Nacional de Desarrollo Humano de PNUD: Entender para cambiar las raíces locales del conflicto', 11 September 2003.

UNDP (United Nations Development Program), 2004, 'Un Plan de Vida que mueve Montañas: Entre los mejores del Premio Ecuatorial 2004', Kuala Lumpur, 24 February 2004.

UNDP (United Nations Development Program), 2005a, 'Banco de Buenas Prácticas para Superar el Conflicto', www.saliendodelcallejon.pnud.org.co/buenas_practicas.shtml, accessed 14 August 2008.

UNDP (United Nations Development Program), 2005b, 'Guardia Indígena', Buenas Prácticas para Superar el Conflicto, 5 December 2005, www.saliendodelcallejon.pnud.org.co/buenas_practicas.shtml?x=729, accessed 14 August 2008.

UNDP (United Nations Development Program), 2005c, 'Consejo de Jóvenes de Tierradentro: Semillas de Identidad y Autonomía', Buenas Prácticas para Superar el Conflicto, 7 December 2005, www.saliendodelcallejon.pnud.org.co/buenas_practicas.shtml?x=432, accessed 14 August 2008.

Uribe, A., 2001, Presidential Candidate, 'Evaluación de la Constitución de 1991 a sus diez años de vigencia', Asociación Primero Colombia, Bogotá, 26 July 2001.

Uribe, A., 2002a, Presidential Candidate, 'Discurso de lanzamiento de candidatura', Asociación Primero Colombia, Bogotá, 21 March 2002.

Uribe, A., 2002b, 'Programa de Gobierno: Manifiesto Democrático', Primero Colombia, Bogotá.

Uribe, A., 2002c, 'Palabras del Presidente electo Alvaro Uribe Vélez', Asociación Primero Colombia, Medellín, 27 May 2002.

Uribe, A., 2002d, 'Let us again seek our common bond of unity, the law; democratic authority, freedom and social justice', discourse of possession as President of the Republic of Colombia, Bogotá, 7 August 2002.

Uribe, A., 2003a, 'Para que la economía crezca necesitamos orden público', speech of the President during the inauguration of the High Mountain Battalion 'General Benjamín Herrera', Popayán, 15 December 2005.

Uribe, A., 2003b, 'Opositores políticos tienen garantías reales y no retóricas', speech by President Uribe during the inauguration of the eco-tourist train in 'Las Flores', Barranquilla, 21 December 2003.

Uribe, A., 2003c, 'Relato de los Hechos que condujeron a la muerte del Gobernador de Antioquia, su ex Consejero de Paz y ocho miembros de la Fuerza Pública secuestrados por la guerrilla de las Farc', televised address by President Uribe to the Nation, Medellín, 5 May 2003.

Uribe, A., 2004a, Speech by President Uribe during the Forum 'Democracia y Desarrollo en Iberoamérica', Cartagena de Indias, 21 February 2004.

Uribe, A., 2004b, Speech by President Uribe during the ceremony of promotion of Police Officers at the Police School 'General Santander', Bogotá, 16 June 2004.

Uribe, A., 2005a, Remarks by President Uribe at the Forum '¿Amenaza Terrorista o Conflicto Interno?', Chía, 26 April 2005.

Uribe, A., 2005b, Remarks by the President during the inauguration of the Communal Government Council No. 93, Santander de Quilichao, 30 April 2005.

Uribe, A., 2005c, '¡Qué bello unir la nación en la contradicción permanente y creadora como reconocimiento de la diversidad!', remarks by the President during the inauguration of the Communal Government Council No. 113, Bogotá, 25 September 2005.

US Department of State, 2004, Fact Sheet, 'US Identifies 39 Groups as Foreign Terrorist Organizations', Office of Counterterrorism, Washington, 19 October 2004.

US Department of State, 2005, Office of the Coordinator for Counterterrorism, 'Country Reports on Terrorism 2004', Department of State Publication 11248, April 2005.

References

Legal sources

Presidential resolutions

Res. 85/98, 'Por la cual se declara la iniciación de un proceso de paz, se reconoce el carácter político de una organización armada y se señala una zona de distensión', Bogotá, 14 October 1998.

Res. 31/02, 'Por la cual se termina el proceso de diálogo, negociación y firma de acuerdos con las Farc y se deja sin efecto el reconocimiento de carácter político a la organización mencionada', Bogotá, 20 February 2002.

Res. 32/02, 'Por la cual se da por terminada la Zona de Distensión', Bogotá, 20 February 2002.

Res. 33/02, 'Por la cual se deja sin efecto el reconocimiento de los miembros representantes de la Fuerzas Armadas Revolucionarias de Colombia, Farc', Bogotá, 20 February 2002.

Decrees

Decree 1837/2002, 'Por el cual se declara el Estado de Conmoción Interior', Presidency of the Republic, Bogotá, 11 August 2002.

Decree 1838/2002, 'Por medio del cual se crea un impuesto especial destinado a atender los gastos del Presupuesto General de la Nación necesarios para preservar la Seguridad Democrática', Presidency of the Republic, Bogotá, 11 August 2002.

Decree 2002/2002, 'Por el cual se adoptan medidas para el control del orden público y se definen las zonas de rehabilitación y consolidación', Ministry of Interior, Bogotá, 9 September 2002.

Decree 128/2003, 'Por el cual se reglamenta la Ley 418 de 1997, prorrogada y modificada por la Ley 548 de 1999 y la Ley 782 de 2002 en materia de reincorporación a la sociedad civil', Ministry of Defence, Bogotá, 22 January 2003.

Laws

Law 684/2001, 'Por la cual se expiden normas sobre la organización y funcionamiento de la Seguridad y Defensa Nacional y se dictan otras disposiciones', Gaceta del Congreso 44.522, Bogotá, 13 August 2001.

Law 782/2002, 'Por medio de la cual se prorroga la vigencia de la Ley 418 de 1997, prorrogada y modificada por la Ley 548 de 1999 y se modifican algunas de sus disposiciones', Gaceta del Congreso 45.043, Bogotá, 23 December 2002.

Law 975/2005, 'Por la cual se dictan disposiciones para la reincorporación de miembros de grupos armados organizados al margen de la ley, que contribuyan de manera efectiva a la consecución de la paz nacional y se dictan otras disposiciones para acuerdos humanitarios', Gaceta del Congreso 45.980, Bogotá, 25 July 2005.

Jurisprudence Colombian Constitutional Court

T-188/93, Judge-Rapporteur Eduardo Cifuentes Muñoz [T-7281] 12 May 1993.
C-037/96, Judge-Rapporteur Vladimiro Naranjo Mesa [PE-008] 5 February 1996.
C-139/96, Judge-Rapporteur Carlos Gaviria Díaz [D-1080] 9 April 1996.

References

SU-039/97, Judge-Rapporteur Antonio Barrera Carbonell [T-84771] 3 February 1997.

T-634/99, Judge-Rapporteur Alejandro Martínez Caballero [T-180391] 30 August 1999.

C-370/02, Judge-Rapporteur Eduardo Montealegre Lynett [D-3751] 15 May 2002.

C-898/03, Judge-Rapporteur Marco Gerardo Monroy Cabra [D-4558] 7 October 2003.

SU-383/03, Judge-Rapporteur Alvaro Tafur Galvis [T-517583] 13 May 2003.

T-955/03, Judge-Rapporteur Alvaro Tafur Galvis [T-562887] 17 October 2003.

C-370/06, Judge-Rapporteur Manuel José Cepeda Espinosa, Jaime Córdoba Triviño, Rodrigo Escobar Gil, Marco Gerardo Monroy Cabra, Alvaro Tafur Galvis, Clara Inés Vargas Hernández [D-6032] 18 May 2006.

Newspaper articles

Arboleda, J., 2005, 'Una visión política no define el conflicto', *El Colombiano*, 8 May 2005, 12A.

El Colombiano, 2002a, 'Así informó el mundo', 21 February 2002, 11A.

El Colombiano, 2002b, 'Las Farc responsabilizan a Pastrana por ruptura del plan de paz', 21 February 2002, 4A.

El Espectador, 2008, 'H. H. se confiesa', 2 August 2008, 3.

El Tiempo, 2002, 'Gran Encuesta de intención de voto para Presidente', Napoleón Franco & Cía., 19 May 2002, 12A–13A.

Ferro, G., 2005, 'La Guerra contra la Esperanza', *Semana.com*, 24 April 2005, www.semana.com/noticias-on-line/guerra-contra-esperanza/86125.aspx, accessed 14 August 2008.

Gómez, G. L. and C. I. Vélez, 2005, 'Uribe ordenó a la Policía entrar rápido a San José', *El Colombiano*, 21 March 2005, 2D.

Gómez, S., 2008, '"Paras" extraditados seguían delinquiendo e incumplían compromisos de ley de Justicia y Paz: Uribe', *El Tiempo.com*, 13 May 2008, www.eltiempo.com/archivo/documento/CMS-4162180, accessed 14 August 2008.

León, J., 2003a, 'La reconquista de Arauca', *Semana*, 1.083, 1 March 2003, 20–5.

León, J., 2003b, 'Una Colombia más segura', *Semana*, 1.129, 21 December 2003, 56.

León, J., 2005, 'La Seguridad Democrática y los Indígenas', *Semana.com*, 3 December 2005, www.semana.com/noticias-on-line/seguridad-democratica-indigenas/90909.aspx, accessed 14 August 2008.

Mendivelso, N., 2005, 'Rompiendo el cerco: "liberar a la pacha mama"', Periódico de la Universidad Nacional, 27 November 2005, 84.

Mogollón, G., 2005, 'Censo de San José no pasa de diez familias', *El Colombiano*, 27 March 2005, 6A.

Ospina, C., 2004, 'Las FARC ya no se tomarán el poder', *Semana*, 1.140, 8 March 2004, 36–7.

Pérez, P. and others, 2002, 'Pastrana no tenía otra salida', *El Colombiano*, 21 February 2002, 11A.

Pizarro, E., 2005, 'Sí hay Guerra, señor Presidente', *Semana*, 1.188, 2 June 2005, 24–8.

Ramírez, M., 2005, 'Debemos apoyarlos aún más', *Semana.com*, 6 February 2005, www.semana.com/noticias-opinion-on-line/debemos-apoyarlos/84559.aspx, accessed 14 August 2008.

Rodríguez, C., 2005, '¿Por qué acudir a la justicia internacional?', *Semana.com*, 21 March 2005, http://www.semana.com/noticias-on-line/acudir-justicia-internacional/85382.aspx, accessed 14 August 2008.

Semana, 2002a, 'Un hombre enigmático', 1.047, 27 May 2002, 36–48.

Semana, 2002b, 'Vientos de Guerra', 1.060, 19 August 2002, 38–42.

Semana, 2002c, 'Campesinos Armados', 1.060, 19 August 2002, 26–32.

Semana, 2003a, 'La toma de Arauca', 1.107, 21 July 2003, 36–9.

Semana, 2003b, '¿Culpables o Inocentes?', 1.124, 17 November 2003, 50.

Sierra, A., 2005, 'La guerra en el norte del Cauca tiene a los indígenas Paeces en medio de todos los fuegos', *El Tiempo*, 10 May 2005, 4A.

Velásquez, C., 2004, '¿Conflicto armado o amenaza terrorista?'; *Semana*, 1.192, 7 March 2004, 36–7.

Vélez, I. M., 2002, '"FARC cerraron las puertas del diálogo": Pastrana', *El Colombiano*, 21 February 2002, 3A.

Yarce, E., 2005a, 'San José de Apartadó: la historia de 162 entierros', El Colombiano, 6 March 2005, 8A.

Yarce, E., 2005b, 'Si llega la Policía habrá un desplazamiento en San José', *El Colombiano*, 9 March 2005, 10A.

Yarce, E., 2005c, 'La presencia del Estado en San José debe ser integral', *El Colombiano*, 23 March 2005, 10A.

Index